THE
FOOL'S
PARDON

THE
FOOL'S
PARDON

The Autobiography of
KENNETH GRIFFITH

WARNER BOOKS

A *Warner* Book

First published in Great Britain in 1994 by Little, Brown and Company
This edition published by Warner Books in 1995

A CIP catalogue record for this book is
available from the British Library.

ISBN 0 7515 1504 3

Typeset by M Rules
Printed and bound in Great Britain by
Clays Ltd, St Ives plc

Warner Books
A Division of
Little, Brown and Company (UK)
Brettenham House
Lancaster Place
London WC2E 7EN

To my grandparents
Emily and Ernest Griffiths

And to my children
David, Eva, Jonathan, Polly and Huw

And to Chiara Peretti

The Documentary Films of Kenneth Griffith

SOLDIERS OF THE WIDOW
On the siege and relief of Ladysmith

A TOUCH OF CHURCHILL, A TOUCH OF HITLER
A life of Cecil Rhodes

SONS OF THE BLOOD
Four films on the story of the Anglo-Boer War, told by its
survivors

KEEP PRETORIA CLEAN!
In praise of Black South African rubbish collectors

THE MAN ON THE ROCK
On Napoleon's final years spent on St Helena

CURIOUS JOURNEY
Interviews with survivors of the 1916 Easter Rebellion and the
Anglo-Irish War

BUS TO BOSWORTH
On Henry Tudor's march from Mill Bay to Bosworth Field

SUDDENLY AN EAGLE
(retitled GIVE ME LIBERTY OR GIVE ME DEATH for the BBC)
On the causes of the American War of Independence

HANG OUT YOUR BRIGHTEST COLOURS
The life and death of the Irish patriot, Michael Collins

THE PUBLIC'S RIGHT TO KNOW
On the prevention of a film about Baden Powell and the
suppression of the Michael Collins film

BLACK AS HELL; THICK AS GRASS
On the South Wales Borderers in the British–Zulu War of 1879

THE SUN'S BRIGHT CHILD
A life of Edmund Kean

A FAMOUS JOURNEY
The journey of the Magi

THE MOST VALUABLE ENGLISHMAN EVER
A life of Thomas Paine

CLIVE OF INDIA
A life of Robert Clive

BUT I HAVE PROMISES TO KEEP
A life of Jawarharlal Nehru

THE LIGHT
A life of David Ben-Gurion

ZOLA BUDD: THE GIRL WHO DIDN'T RUN
On the persecution of an athlete

THE HEART OF DARKNESS
The life and death of Roger Casement

PREFACE

I *was* going to call this book *Out of Step*, because if one has a strong impulse not to join anything – club, political party, *anything* – and to try and puzzle things out for oneself, according to one's even poor conscience, as I try to do, then one is rarely in agreement with the consensus. But some American nicked my title.

My friend Michel Pearce and I once travelled to the northern extremity of Ireland, to the astonishing Giant's Causeway. We were searching for locations at which we might film sequences of our film *Roger Casement: The Heart of Darkness*. It was a magnificent, wild day, and apparently deserted. Suddenly, two people appeared: a tall Englishman and a younger German woman; he had done thirteen years' social work – as I understood it – in the Six Counties, she three. The man recognized me and we got talking. I plied him with an urgent question: 'I am an Irish Republican in spirit and action and therefore I am not surprised that members of Sinn Fein greet me warmly. But I have also had separate meetings with two senior members of the Protestant Royal Irish Constabulary and, as always, I have made precisely the same statement to them as I might have made to Mr Gerry Adams or to Mr Martin McGuinness: I urged the two Protestant policemen to welcome a United Ireland, and I gave my detailed reasons. They both listened intently and with kindness shook my hand and thanked me for being so open with them. Why was this?'

The Englishman replied: 'But you know what they say *you've* been given up here? They say that you've been given

"The Fool's Pardon". Like the court jester who can say what he likes to the King. You are being pardoned for saying unspeakable truths.'

Of course, with the arrival in the post of a death threat from my fellow Protestants in Belfast, I must now presume that my Fool's Pardon has been somewhat brutally withdrawn.

ONE

Tyrone Guthrie suspected that I had prenatal memories. Tyrone Guthrie was, in my opinion, the greatest creative force in drama during my long experience. I loved him deeply. He personified my highest hopes: human perception, honesty, wit, and above all, kindness. I am fairly sure that other Guthrie virtues will emerge as I remember on . . . If he could read these words he would give me a penetrating humorous glance which would challenge my spirit, but the look would also underline that I was truly alive. He was and is my hero. Of course without his mild failings he might have been unbearable.

I told no one of my earliest dreams till I told Guthrie. He would listen to any sincerity with great care. I told him that when I was a baby – I could just stand upright – I dreamed of a stone cave with a natural stone basin filled with limpid water and I, naked, was in it. Nearby was an old man with a long white beard who was also naked. I told Guthrie how early this memory was and that there were two other dreams which were fading away and how over the years I had felt a compulsion to nurture them. Guthrie said: 'I think you have prenatal memories.'

Where did the naked old man come from and the stone and the limpid water? I remember the room where it began; I shared it with Lily Phillips who looked after me. I left Lily's room at Rhos Cottage, Church Park, Tenby, when I was two years old. I was born in that house on the 12th of October 1921. My mother was Margaret (Peggy) Griffiths (maiden name Davies) and my father was Harold Griffiths. Rhos Cottage was the home of my father's parents, Emily and Ernest Griffiths.

You may note that all of the above were 'Griffiths' with an 's' and you may also note that I have no 's'. Some fifteen and a half years after my birth I was fumblingly preparing to leave the Greenhill Grammar School, Tenby, because of a combination of academic failure on my part and financial poverty caused by the Depression, when the Headmaster, Mr J. T. Griffith, ordered me to his study. Now he had spoken to me about twice during the preceding three years, so the interview was an event to remember.

J. T. Griffith leaned back in his chair, handsome face, wavy silver hair and said: 'I hear that you plan to be an actor.'

'Yes, sir.'

'Do me one favour, will you?'

'Yes, sir; if I can.'

'Knock that "s" off your name; it's an Anglicization.'

'Yes, sir, I will.'

'Good luck.'

And from that day on I have never regretted it.

They have told me that it was about six months after my birth that my mother and father both left Tenby, going their separate ways and leaving me with my paternal grandparents, Emily and Ernest, who immediately became virtually my mother and father.

Wisps of information have come my way about the circumstances of Peggy and Harold. Harold became a ticket clerk on the Great Western Railway and while still a teenager was posted to Newcastle Emlyn in the county of Cardigan. And as I understand it, my mother was a very young nurse there. While on his death-bed, I asked my father if he and Peggy *had* to get married because I was expected. 'No, no,' said Harold, perhaps too hastily and looking a little shocked. I don't know the truth and it is no more than an academic point.

However, what I do know is that Harold was extremely unhappy on his marriage morning. My Auntie Ivy (Harold's youngest sister) was the one member of our family who fought and succeeded her way to scholastic honours. She got her way to University College, Cardiff and won a Bachelor of Arts degree. She was also a good, hardworking, responsible soul and she kept a feeling, interested eye on me to the end of her days. Ivy also murmured to me, over the years, about some of the astonishing skeletons in our family cupboard. We were a Wesleyan Methodist family and Ivy was the one who rose intellectually above the traditional taboos. She told me that on the morning of my mother and father's wedding, Harold disappeared. Ivy, fearing a disaster, began searching Newcastle Emlyn and eventually found him, unshaven, sitting on a doorstep. He was very miserable and told Ivy that he didn't want to get married. Did he *have* to? Perhaps I *was* expected and perhaps only Peggy and he knew . . . Surmise, surmise. Ivy firmly told Harold (and Ivy was still a young schoolgirl) that he shouldn't go through with the ceremony. But my dear old Dad was not a strong character (more unadulterated charm than should be possible, but definitely not strong) and spliced he was.

I am glad that they got married, come to think of it for the first time, because if they hadn't Peggy might have plonked me with her parents and they were a very different kettle of fish from Emily and Ernest. Ernest was as near to being a walking working saint as possible. A beloved man.

Peggy's mother and father lived in Swansea. She, so I have been told, sold fish in Swansea Market; a classic, traditional Swansea occupation which I am proud of. She had a lot of hair and looked to me like a formidable Welsh witch. Her husband rose to be a train guard on the Great Western Railway. He was always immaculate; he cultivated a fine waxed moustache. Always a fresh flower in his lapel – at least when in uniform. My grandfather could properly personify the tragic decline of the Great Western Railway to British Rail; when one considers the grubbiness and irresponsibility of Britain's contemporary railway scene today.

Ernest, my paternal grandfather, was a stonemason by trade and, let it be understood, a very fine one. He was the son of Edmund Griffiths who was also a stonemason and the family home was at 'The Square', Stepaside, Pembrokeshire. Why the little house was called 'The Square' I don't know and at this moment I am sitting in a small town named Knysna on the

south-eastern tip of Africa and very far from my old friend
Roscoe Howells who is an historian living in Pembrokeshire,
and who probably knows. The name 'Stepaside' is said to have
been created by Oliver Cromwell, who, during his punitive
march through Wales, reached the little valley cleft and
announced: 'We will step aside here for the night.'

Edmund Griffiths and his wife, Susanna, had one daughter,
my 'auntie' Polly, and three surviving sons: my 'uncles' Dick
and Tom and my grandfather, Ernest. They were all in the
house-building trade. The three sons were shortish in height,
compact in build and all carried with them a quiet, bright
integrity. A memorable feature of them all, though it was
strongest in my grandfather (as I remember them), was a twinkle in the eyes, presaging a blessed sense of humour. Polly
had astonishingly light blue eyes and was, over the years, a
colourful, reassuring comfort to me.

I believe that there was a fourth son, but I have heard that he
was killed when a tree rolled onto him. I have also heard, from
my grandfather, that there was some dangerous violence perpetrated by Edmund against one of his sons, but that is now
lost, perhaps for the best, in the receding years.

Edmund was, undoubtedly, a formidable, enigmatic man.
He seems – I have no clear evidence – to have been larger in
physical size than his sons: handsome and full bearded. I understand, from long ago, that people feared him; he glowered
silently, which was the safer part, because he could suddenly
explode with rage. The dark hint of violence aimed at a son.
He was a consummate stonemason and for his own satisfaction
of an evening would carve flowers out of hard stone. But look
at his photograph with me on his lap. Surely that is the humour
in his eyes which I remember in my dear grandfather's?

My Aunt Ivy, who felt that I should know more about the
family than the others thought safe or wise or proper, once confided to me that Edmund received a small pension all of his life
from 'a lord' because he was that lord's illegitimate son. Not a
matter of pride in our Nonconformist Protestant environment.
A matter of glittering possibility probing a lusting blackness;
excitement, but not vanity or public pride!

For me, the bar sinister is a welcome enigma because I am a romantic. And these days I view history, the intrigues of human survival, with consuming interest. What would my life have been if we – my great-grandfather, my grandfather, my father and me – had emanated from the legitimate side of the blanket?

I remember the Marquis of Anglesey, while reviewing a book I had written about aspects of the Second Anglo-Boer War (it was called *Thank God We Kept the Flag Flying*), stating something to the effect that he regretted my class consciousness. The Marquis was inferring that I showed bias for the common soldier as against the officer class. I thought to myself at the time: 'Ha!'

Not that I regret the Lords or the Kings and Queens. In fact, at my present age of sixty-eight years (1989), I tend to regret their passing. A firm social structure is vitally important for any definition of civilization and the grey, dulling changes towards legislated equality that have slopped over Britain during the past thirty years have proven to be a foretaste of hell's potential. But being dubbed a commoner, with only a whisper of reproach, I embrace my commoness. It is ingrained in me. Yesterday I walked with my beloved friend, Chiara Peretti, through the tropical garden which is much of Knysna and, viewing the material privilege which has invaded this natural paradise and with that material privilege the human foolishness of expressed superiority, I murmured one of my worries: 'I always feel ill at ease amongst middle and upper class environments.' I added: 'Of course it is a weakness on my part.'

Who was my great-great paternal grandfather? Hints were dropped and I thought that I knew. By a coincidence of such monumental unlikelihood (these impossibilities happen to me frequently) I was befriended by the present Lord of our region of Wales. He made me a guest in his castle. I stood contemplating the portraits of his ancestors and the implications, if the rumours were true. Into the grand room quietly came his present Lordship – though I was not aware of his presence. Later the nobleman said to a mutual friend, the distinguished Welsh poet and prose writer, Emyr Humphries: 'Kenneth is very strange; I found him in a room of the castle and there was such an atmosphere that I withdrew.' Of course, I am capable of manufacturing that atmosphere plus others in anybody's living-room, so the event may not be significant. I believe that Emyr Humphries then told my friend, his Lordship, about the rumour. But neither of us have ever mentioned it to each other and I mention it now only because autobiographies should be, essentially, the channels of indiscretion.

However, since then my second wife, Doria, (née Noar) and mother of our daughter, the actress Eva Griffith, has investigated this family mystery with some astonishing thoroughness and her findings are, if possible, even more exotic; they are inconclusive but potentially hair-raising. The only established fact remains that Edmund, my great-grandfather, received a small pension all of his life because he was the son of a 'nobleman' . . .

Rhos Cottage, Church Park Road, Tenby, was a good safe home during my very early years. I think that my grandfather Ernest had built it. The front was a small affair but with the elaboration then fashionable: a bay window from which the bay was well hidden, a little front garden which contained a wonderfully aromatic verbena bush, elaborate iron railings and gate (on which I can remember swinging) and two gateposts surmounted by two large concrete balls.

The inside of the house was unusual. One entered into a hall passage; on the right was the sitting-room which was only used on Sundays, at Christmas and at Easter. From the street doorway looking down the hall were the stairs to some of the bedrooms – three I think and one of them was known as the white room, with good cause because it was all white – the walls and even the furniture. Occasionally I slept there for unexpected reasons and that room always made me feel uneasy. Later I was told that Emily and Ernest had one child, before my time, who was in some way retarded and the white room was hers. She died while still a child; maybe twelve years old. Their other children were Harold, my father, who was the eldest, Elsie, Reginald and Ivy.

The downstairs hall passage continued past the stairway and the unusual aspect of the house began; there was a door and two or three steps descended into the kitchen which was the true living-room and then on to a further room where cooking was done and, unbelievably, from which another staircase ascended to further bedrooms; again I guess three. And also from that cooking room another passage led up steps around a corner to a long scullery in which was kept a great metal cauldron for washing clothes, and from the scullery beams hung hams and Christmas puddings in basins and other things. A mysterious, threatening room. Oh! And close to that scullery was a door which led into an entertaining back alley.

I can remember sitting in a child's high chair in that cooking room and confronting, for the first time, a brown sausage. I was horrified and the horror still lingers. In that high-chair, in that place, began my instinctive revulsion against meat.

For a time Reg lived there; he was a carpenter who worked for his father, Ernest, and had risen in life to become a builder of very fine houses. Harold was there for a short time working as a ticket clerk at Tenby railway station; Ivy was away at university in Cardiff and Elsie was in London, married to William Godden, a sanitary inspector and a decent interesting man in his own right. All of us – I mean the grown-up children and me, the grandchild – suffered a compulsion to strike away into the big world east of Tenby.

Tenby is a beautiful place, an ancient walled town on a peninsula between two impressive beaches: the North Beach – cosy; and the South Beach – relatively exposed. I still have friends in Tenby from my schooldays who wonder why I strayed away and to what . . . I slowly began to realize during the course of my life – too slowly – that people can be very different from each other; even neighbours in the same environment. It is one of the most difficult and yet one of the most important lessons for humanity to learn and digest – that what *I* want is not what my neighbour wants. Or not to state: 'If I can do it why can't you do it?' We are all as different as fingerprints. The Griffiths clan had to wander: Tenby was not big enough for us – even if the world outside was darkly lurking and likely to swallow us up without trace. Yes, what a frightful, enormous beast the world outside was! It is still giving me a difficult time, though I am managing to have my say and my place in it.

A few years ago I inveigled my way into Rhos Cottage once again. I believe that it is now a council house owned by the local authority. The occupants were kind enough to welcome me in. They were all in the sitting-room and it was neither a Sunday nor Christmas. They stared at me, uncomprehendingly, as I tried to explain the significance to me of my return. The verbena bush had gone; my grandmother's treasures of course were dispersed; the set of encyclopaedias which had been bought for my benefit were no more. The room had become very small. My hosts were sitting; it seemed that they were almost crouching as they looked up at me: an alien interloper. As I moved along the hall towards the steps that led down into the kitchen-cum-true living room, Rhos Cottage ended. There was a wall. On the 12th October 1941 a German aircraft, hoping to bomb Pembroke Dock, dropped its lethal load across the North Beach; one bomb hit Tenby itself and killed a local lady, 'Mrs Thomas the Pop' (she owned the local lemonade factory), and demolished only one building: the back half of Rhos Cottage. Gone was the little lino-floored room where as a baby I slept with Lily Phillips and where I had experienced my prenatal dreams. The 12th of October 1941 was my birthday. On that day I was far away . . . working unsteadily in the Royal Air Force.

I can remember that we had a pony and trap to journey in and afterwards my grandfather was successful enough as a builder to own a little Citroën motor car with outside back seating called a 'dicky'. But he constructed inside the car a high seat immediately behind him especially for me. Off we would go on picnics through magical Pembrokeshire: to Bosherston lily pools; the spectacular Stack Rocks; to Amroth to see Auntie Annie and Uncle Dick; sometimes to Newcastle Emlyn to visit friends of my father's time there, I presume. And there at Newcastle Emlyn the women would put on the old Welsh tall hats. Oh yes, I remember it! And when we passed under a railway bridge at Moreton, Grampy would warn me, 'Duck your head, Ken!' And when I go under this bridge in latter days, my head always lowers slightly.

In Newcastle Emlyn as a very small child I saw decaying ruins from an antique past. I remember the sun on the old stone and the flowers. The continuity of my Welsh blood was meaningful to me even then.

But above every other expedition, and fortunately, the most regular, we would visit Auntie Polly and Uncle Wilfred, her husband, at 'The Square', where they then resided – my great-grandmother and Edmund having died. 'The Square' was a perfect fairyland for me. On the way we would pass Kingsmoor Common with its large gypsy community, through Kilgetty, down into the intimate valley at Wiseman's Bridge and then sharply hairpin to the left and up the hill past the little hard coalmine, past the stone school which my grandfather and his brothers and sister had gone to and where Ernest must have learnt his fine use of English, always inscribed in copper-plate handwriting. He left school before he had reached fourteen years. What has happened, I appeal, to the quality of our British education since then? Many dissatisfied students at universities who can barely spell the words of the English language. What went wrong with the Socialist dream? Literal liberalism, I suspect. Discipline was dismissed from our land.

Up the hill to Deer Park with its ruined classical summer-house, perhaps a shadow of my noble forefather, but suddenly to the left down the flower- and fern-laden lane, past the spring well where a trout swam in its grotto, past the hay haggard, to the ivy covered, thick-walled cottage: 'The Square'.

How can I convey its quality? The immaculate little dairy through which a cool air ever moved over the polished slate. The living-room which was packed with human time. The fireplace, polished and glowing from a fuel made of coal dust bound with water (I think it was called loam). And around the fire were Auntie Polly's cooking ovens in which she baked (with all due respect to the other skilful kind ladies of my life) the best rice puddings that I have ever tasted – and other unforgettable treats. Thank you again, Auntie Polly.

The little windows, ivy fringed, set in the thick stone walls. The cottage was completely enveloped in ivy and to hell with the fear of damage to the fabric of the dwelling place, though it was ever watched by house builders of quality. The flower beds and the vegetable gardens were immaculate. The lawns, the redcurrant, the blackcurrant and the gooseberry bushes. And in this garden was the little lavatory, creaking with wood through which the precious ivy wound and entered. There will never be another lavatory like that for me. And in that consummation of human happiness, Uncle Wilfred died. Of a heart attack, I think. What a good way to pass over.

Uncle Wilfred was a schoolteacher at the seaside village of Saundersfoot, a few miles away. When I eventually found myself a pupil at the Green Hill Grammar School, Tenby, I came into contact with some of Wilfred's former pupils. They told me that he was called 'Biff' and that he was a very hard disciplinarian. And also that there was a scandal about Uncle Wilfred and one of his girl pupils. The details I am unsure of and even if I were I wouldn't relate them here, but I gather that it was a Saundersfoot-shaking event . . . I cannot recall Auntie Polly ever looking disturbed though. Just those very blue eyes and the rice puddings and the many wonders that surrounded her.

Uncle Wilfred was a little lame. I believe that he was a veteran of France in the First World War. I feel that he had known the worst that that indescribable hell could offer. So I would deny him nothing: not 'The Square' or his death amongst the wood and ivy or the pretty schoolgirl for that matter.

Uncle Wilfred gravitated from owning a motorbike to owning some simple motorcar. He became famous for exaggerating the prowess of his machine. Even I, so young, can distinctly remember him saying to my grandfather: 'Ernie, I approached Wooden Hill (en route from Tenby to Stepaside) and as I was going up Wooden Hill, passing other cars, I glanced down and she (his motorcar) was doing forty-five!' Even I, at five years old, took that statement with a pinch of salt.

But Wilfred was a real historian. He may have been the first to talk to me about the significance of the past. I could point to you the bit of road, close to Wiseman's Bridge, where sitting beside Uncle Wilfred in his miraculous car he said to me, the little boy: 'This county of Pembrokeshire *reeks* with history!'

I'm buggered if I'll ever happily call my homeland Dyfed! And that is pure cussedness on my part, I confess.

At the top of the lane leading to 'The Square' was a little cottage and in it lived a boy a year or two older than myself; his name was Arthur Llewellyn. He was a very decent young man and he understood the countryside around perceptively well. Close to his house was a dangerous deep airshaft to old coal workings. If you threw a stone into its darkness the stone would echo and echo as it descended, culminating in a splash into the sinister water with a sound like a bell. Arthur showed me the revealing wonders of bird nests and I, always a collector, was hooked. But Arthur would never allow me to take more than one egg from a nest and never a robin's. I remember the nests and the colour of the eggs of the thrush, the blackbird, the skylark and the tiny wren and the indiscriminate spread of the pheasant.

Once, up by that old neo-classical ruin known as the summerhouse I saw my first snake, moving quickly and lustily away from me in the summer sun. I was shocked and a primeval tension gripped me. What a mystery the snake is to humankind. I didn't have to be told about death in a snake; I knew about it from centuries past. I am still horrified yet deeply fascinated by the creatures; I have encountered them here in Africa, in India and in the Middle East. Once even in Canada! And now, the revealing bit about snakes and me: I have kept them in my various homes! And over the years I have sweated in the company of my wilfully chosen companions. I am ever expecting to be bitten with their needle-sharp fangs channelling their sophisticated lethal fluid. A few hours ago, here on the edge of the great rain forest around Knysna in Southern Africa, a 'boomslang' whipped a few feet in front of me. If I had been bitten, I would have died within minutes.

Close to 'The Square' is a sloping meadow at the bottom of which is a small river, unexpectedly called Ford's Lake. And in this water, Arthur Llewellyn would try to teach me to tickle trout. Gently his hand would touch the belly of the fish and suddenly it was out on the tumble-treed bank. In this meadow I remember a cow getting bitten by an adder; I remember our

Griffiths family assembling for the hay-making. What hard work for the grown-ups! What joy for us all as everyone celebrated with lemonade and cider (which inexplicably got past the total abstinence rule which normally was sacrosanct) and the bountiful endless treats from Auntie Polly's treasured ovens.

But of all of these memories in that particular meadow it was the oak tree that grips me firmest. Under and around that particular oak tree I sat and stood and wondered. To me it was like the excitement of Father Christmas, but unlike Father Christmas that oak tree was searingly real. That oak tree addressed a message to me which is now part of my nature. No one had then told me of distant Druids invisible to the physical eye. But far beyond prenatal memories, race memories linger, firmly and watching.

Sometimes we would visit Stepaside by railway train. Waiting outside of Kilgetty's little station would be an elongated covered wagon drawn by one horse, I think. Inside the wagon were benches and on these we sat and were driven to Wiseman's Bridge. Where the wagon went to then I don't know. It seems today that I once touched the world of Dickens and Hardy.

On one occasion I was walking that route when I met a woman who was carrying two small milk cans. Come to think of it I have usually been a polite social person unless I recognized 'The Enemy' – and then I have always opened fire. Anyway the woman was no recognized enemy and I, as small as I was, offered to help her with her load and she accepted. When we reached Wiseman's Bridge she told me that she lived in one of the cottages below the bridge and she asked me if I would like a cup of tea and a piece of cake. I think she told me that she had a son. I remember feeling a little uneasy as she unpadlocked the front door. In we went and there in front of a fire, was a large inarticulate man, sitting in the gloom. He was not what we humans are pleased to call 'normal'. He was not like 'the rest of us'. Perhaps he lolled. The woman behaved as if there was nothing untoward and gave me my tea and cake. I don't think that I told anyone about this experience. I remember the woman with admiration and distant affection.

Around Rhos Cottage I played with a few friends; and the survivors (the Second World War intervened) remain my friends to this day. Next door to Rhos Cottage, across the alleyway, was a terrace of 'coastguard' houses; they were all of the same unusual design – *very* minor gothic as I recollect. The first one, next to us, was not occupied by a coastguard's family, but by Police Constable Griffiths (no relation), his wife and their son Dennis. A house or two further up was a coastguard's family: the Smales, who came from across the Bristol Channel in the West of England, with their son, Jackie. Around the corner was Harris Street and on one side was the Nichols family with three sons: the older boys, Mervyn and Jackie and my contemporary and therefore peer, Hughie (known as 'Mandy'). And then – arriving from India! – came the Booker family. Mr Booker had been an engineer on the Indian Railways and he, having married a Miss Rouse, whose father I believe was a Brixham (West of England) fisherman who had settled in Tenby, had himself retired there. There were two sons of my approximate age: Arthur, the eldest, and David. I can remember their exotic arrival when I was about five years old. When they attended the Tenby Council School, poor lads, they were stricken with appalling tummy trouble, to all of our discomfort and embarrassment. It is interesting to note that tummy trouble between the old Imperial Country and the great subcontinent is not a one-way traffic as we arrogantly presume. Arthur and David also owned magnificent Indian costumes, which as far as I can recall they only wore once in Wales and never again.

These boys were our particular gang. Arthur Booker was an outstanding all-round athlete; David not quite so good. 'Mandy' Nichols, a spectacular goalkeeper; this ability, I believe, came from his great sense of drama. Everything that Mandy did had to be dramatic, even at the risk of life or limb. Therefore he never hesitated to throw himself around the goalmouth, particularly through the air, or even at a carelessly kicking football boot. Sometimes we boys would play on the Burrows, the sand dunes, to the south of Tenby and one of our games was to 'die' violently from the top of one of the great sand holes – no one could touch Mandy as he hurtled downwards arse over head to a regular spectacular death.

Jackie Smale was a friendly inoffensive little boy whom I always liked very much. Dennis Griffiths disappeared from our immediate close scrutiny when his father was transferred to the police station at Saundersfoot. Though, since we were close friends, I visited him there occasionally.

Oh, and me? Well, if anyone of us was the odd-man-out it was me. I was the one who fitted into the gang least easily. Of course I was an 'only child'. And then and then . . . As I have said, I could have called this autobiography *Out of Step*. But I definitely belonged to the gang – to a point.

The old stone alleyways with their little plants and mosses behind Church Park and Harris Street were exciting places particularly when it was night-time. 'Jack, Jack, show a light' was the most sophisticated game because it involved flashing torches when the call was given. And Harris Street, which slopes regularly downward, was an excellent race-track for our tricycles. Mine, unhappily, was more infantile than the others, but Mandy was the worst off, he didn't have a tricycle at all; only a bear on four small wheels which, of course, gave him little speed and precious little direction. It was, as now, always an important matter of prestige. I was not so much at the bottom of the hierarchy as slightly to the side of it. Do one's fundamental predicaments in this life ever change?

At the southern end of Church Park was a grassy, small open space and on it was a large locked, unused wooden building and outside, on the grass, were two rusting field guns. Well, this was obviously the gateway towards big adventure. And the area was called the Silent Battery. We just used that name and never gave those strange words any more thought than, say, Church Park. Only in latter years has it dawned on me what a simple, moving title it was. A battery of war guns that no longer fired. Who named the place thus? I feel sure it was a hardened warrior who had learnt, probably painfully, to be a poet. Of course I became very familiar with every inch of those rusting souvenirs of, I presume, the then recent First World War. And the big, very secret, wooden building? I never asked anyone. We probed slowly. Eventually we squeezed entry and incredible to behold, inside in the gloom, was an enormous rocking horse! Receiving a bunk-up from one of the gang the giant thing moved. Yes, we played on it, but sparingly and a little uneasily.

Adventuring beyond the Silent Battery there was a steep rough path down towards the Burrows and at the bottom was the Old Mill: an ancient stone building, several stories high, with large old wooden doors – locked. I never penetrated this mystery. When I was very small I believe that part of it was occupied by the Boy Scouts and Cubs. But I never had the wherewithal, even in later years, to get into that degree of sophistication.

Down the road which passed the Old Mill was the Quarry: a vertical cliff of stone which was no longer worked and at whose summit was the Silent Battery. Here I toddled; it was one of my first distant expeditions alone and there at the base of the Quarry I suffered one of the major traumas of my life. It inexplicably became dark – suddenly – and then there was a great flash quickly followed by an explosion and heavy rain beat down. I was very frightened. I think I made my own drenched way home through the awful mystery of a thunderstorm.

Beyond the Quarry was the Burrows and these wild acres were our magnificent playground, stretching away for a mile or so to Giltar Point. The aroma of the herbs and the delicacy of the shaking grass and most miraculous of all: the sweet-scented Burrow roses clinging to the sand earth. And in the spring, skylarks would suddenly soar upwards from my feet and, with experience, there were the carefully hidden skylark nests.

Two

I can remember my first day at school, aged five years. Was the pretty girl who took me Eluned Williams? Certainly I remember being very upset with the smallness of my 'lunch' (the mid-morning break). Was it only a banana? Two oldish gentle ladies were in charge of us infants and I vaguely remember a reasonable moustached headmaster. How early we make human-character judgements!

We infants had our own playground and it was there that I first exercised my sense of storytelling and drama. During those early years of my life, fortunately, I was allowed to go to the cinema – quite regularly. To begin with there was the Royal Gate House Cinema with its classic facade proving that it had once been a living theatre before the invention of cinematography. And I saw the original *Ben Hur*. What an impression it made on me! The handsome hero who was so hard pressed by magnificent terrifying Rome! And the villain whom I designated the Ratty Man. Where did 'Ratty' come from? And above all; the great chariot race, featuring the Hero and the Ratty Man and how the latter did such dreadful acts with his whip in the Hero's face and cutting the wheels of his chariot.

Anyway, in that infant's playground of the Tenby Council School, I organized re-enactments of the Ben Hur chariot race. I was the Hero, holding onto the shirts or pullovers of two boys in front of me. And one of these boys was Arthur Booker because he could run faster than anyone else.

I cast the Ratty Man and also supervised the other parts. Girls were allowed to be nurses. And round and round that playground we thundered. I, the Hero, surviving the prearranged misdemeanours of the Ratty Man. There were cut knees and the girls gave token first-aid.

Yes, I was then truly in the ascendant but I was never able to hold onto it. My mind was never with the mainstream. I was losing myself somewhere on my own and was distracting myself away from all conventional structured activities. Would I have been more 'normal' if I had had brothers or sisters? Or younger parents? I had Emily and Ernest, whom I called Gran and Gramp, and I had Lily Phillips from Pembroke Dock, who was employed to look after me. I had my very own dreams and they disallowed me from moving in the same direction as the rest. Therefore I could not compete easily; not in the classroom; not on the sportsfield; not even socially unless a few friends thought it worthwhile – and fortunately for me a few friends did.

As a rule I attended chapel three times every Sunday; in the morning wedged between Gran and Gramp, in the afternoon on my own to Sunday School and again in the evening and again wedged. During the morning and evening I learnt what claustrophobia is. It was not nice. I wanted to take my clothes off; I did take my shoes and socks off surreptitiously.

In those days the services were very long, ending with the spectacular part: the sermon. And in those days there was no messing about; no namby-pamby ecumenical semi-apologizing. We were Methodists and the visiting minister would get up there and fire every gun he possessed. Some of these professional Men-of-God were famous around Wales. And they were masters of their mission. They could terrify us into appalled attention. Their varied methods in histrionics were audacious in the extreme. They came after Edmund Kean but were forerunners of Donald Wolfit, Laurence Olivier, Peter O'Toole and indeed, more relevantly, myself. There was no difference whatsoever between those preachers and the (now dying) breed of great Thespians. Both had major written works to use; the former the Bible, the latter Shakespeare.

I have seen a preacher in that pulpit in Tenby build vocally and emotionally to a terrifying climax and slowly turn his back on us – we the shattered congregation. Would we take our eyes off that imperceptibly pulsating back? Would we dare!? And then round he came again, like a great feline, striking and striking directly at our apathetic failure to come to a direct understanding with Gentle Jesus during the course of the preceding week.

Of course, if there are any readers of this book who happen to be unperceptive viewers of the style of historical films which I am responsible for, I should point out that all of my films are sermons. Somehow, in me, *Ben Hur* had got synthesized to the Old Welsh Preachers and I am, these days, dishing out the word of history intermingled (Oh! I trust) with the Word of God. If the study of history does not consider the Great Spirit – I mean what is Right and what is Wrong – then please forget it as far as I am concerned. I only hope that my sermons on film and thence on television are as skilful and as entertaining as my teachers were in the old stone chapel. And, let us be fair, at the Royal Gate House Cinema as well.

And one last astounding fact about the phenomenon that could happen in that pulpit: occasionally a minister would deliver his sermon in the Welsh language – which none of us in South Pembrokeshire understood! For historical reasons – though we are as deep into Wales as is possible – the Welsh language is not spoken. South Pembrokeshire has been called: 'Little England Beyond Wales'. I think most of us resented the title but you can comprehend how it came about. More about this geographical/historical anomaly later in my tale; for now I want you simply to dwell briefly on the fact that in those Welsh language services, the Spirit alone had to suffice: the Welsh cadences, the choreography of the body and the blazing eyes.

I still acknowledge my style of communication towards those old preachers, towards Edmund Kean's 'flashes of lightning', towards Donald Wolfit and, palm-leaf in hand, towards Laurence Olivier and I am happy to walk hand in hand with my terrible beloved friend Peter O'Toole. We are *all* out of step, though still fighting. Some of us still in the sweaty arena, the others, Up There.

Some years ago I was invited by the British Broadcasting

Corporation, Wales, to make a humble little film (the original idea was a magazine piece) about me going home to Tenby. Well, with the near non-existent budget I pushed the project as near to a saga as possible and we had our sequence in the Wesleyan Methodist Chapel; I took with me on location my daughter Eva and for the purpose of the film I had to try to guess in which pew I had always sat between my grand-parents.

I said: 'I think it was that one.'

Eva wriggled along the pew and suddenly called: 'Daddy, look!'

I joined her and there, cut in the beautiful woodwork deeply with a knife, were the initials 'K.G.' I was very taken aback; was I really that sort of a boy? I recall myself as being rather good. So we deceive ourselves.

Sunday School could be fun. After the solemn propaganda about Jesus – which, incidentally, was inculcating some very proper and valuable rules for a decent society, so I do not wish to knock it – there was much fun and games. The high-lights were the Christmas Party, the Sunday School Treat (on a summer's day) and the Sunday School Concert.

I believe my grandfather used to donate the big Christmas tree, and afterwards I think it was removed to not-so-big Rhos Cottage. I also suspect that Grampy was hidden behind the white beard and the red suit – or sometimes Mr Rees the stationmaster. I became a Doubting Thomas at a very early age. All of the Sunday School activities were held in the base-ment area of the chapel, but it was all warm and tea and cakes and at Christmas: presents and glitter. Yes, pagan magic in chapel.

The Sunday School Treat was the great Ecumenical Day. But not completely. Certainly the Roman Catholics did not join in; whether they were barred or declined I don't know. And I don't think that the Church of England people paraded either; but I'm hazy about that. The miracle was that we Methodists were joined by the Congregationalists, by the Baptists and by the Presbyterians. Most sadly I don't think that the Salvation Army people were there either. But the solid middle ranks of the Nonconformists marched together on that one day – or at least we children did.

We would march towards Wiseman's Bridge and Auntie Polly. But long before that, indeed on the very perimeter of Kilgetty, we would right-turn through a five-barred gate into a huge meadow. And what a summer sight that was.

First of all there were enormous cylindrical metal urns placed strategically around the grand field. These urns were surmounted by tall chimneys with mushroom-like cowls on top. And they were all steaming. Around these dramatic contraptions for refreshment were busy groups of bosomy mothers anxious to hand out happiness. Where have all the bosomy mothers gone? Certainly not to Greenham Common!

Then there were huge trestle tables piled high with sandwiches and cake. There were good competitions: sack races, three-legged races, straightforward races. And there were prizes; I wasn't a big prizewinner. Don't weep for me but I never have been. These days I don't think that I want to win cups and things. I want to win something else. Certainly I never agree to my films being entered for any sort of competition.

The day would begin to end; the School Treat was one of the major highlights of the year. I think in Amroth, where Uncle Dick and Auntie Annie lived, they actually had such a holiday which was simply called 'Big Day'.

I can recall odd impressions at the end of the Sunday School Treat: the evening desolation of the now emptyish meadow and the happy debris. I stood and stared at a tall reddish foxglove flower in the hedge. I will never experience such joy from a foxglove again, I sadly suspect. Joy, but not that unique discovery. And at the gate which led to the road I joined a small group of my contemporaries who stared in awe at a lean tall boy, nonchalantly leaning and beaming a smile. He had rosy cheeks. He had recently fathered a baby – so it was said (and I have never doubted it) – but I think I remember a shyness in his beaming smile. Not too far away, a few miles east, was Laugharne where Dylan Thomas was to live and occasionally write. That boy, whom I saw only once, as far as

I know, could have been the prototype of my favourite character in *Under Milk Wood*: No good Boyo – 'I don't know who's up there, and I don't care.'

Of course the bonny father was not from Tenby, but from somewhere around Kilgetty, which we all knew was Indian Country.

Then we returned to Tenby and separated into our different denominations all serving Jesus. I feel that Jesus' message is clear enough to disallow any differences of opinion about anything he stood for. The Roman Catholics are a bit fancy for us Welsh, but I am prepared – indeed I do – to pay close attention to anything that His Holiness Pope John Paul has to say. He is so clearly a good intelligent brave man who has given the words and deeds of Jesus a lot of deep thought. Which is more than I can say of my fellow Protestant, Ian Paisley. Anyway back we went to our respective chapels.

I am soon to return to Britain to help make a film about the seriously underrated Welsh poet, Idris Davies, and I am reminded here in Africa of a short verse he wrote about Capel (Chapel) Calvin:

> They don't like beer or bishops
> Or pictures without texts
> They don't like any other
> Of the Nonconformist sects.

Not entirely true but well worth writing; not only for the laugh, but for Jesus' sake too.

And lastly the Sunday School Concert. It was put on in that basement area under the chapel. There was a stage. The only interesting fact about those concerts, for this book, is that I was the only child, as far as I can recollect, who was too frightened to appear in such an enterprise. I actually was coerced to begin rehearsal one year but ran away from the ordeal screaming. Mark you, it is not such a mystery to me even at this very time, sixty-odd years later. The last time I appeared on the London stage was in Terence Rattigan's final play, *Cause Célèbre*, and I dreaded every single performance.

I do not expect to go on the stage ever again and there will be no tears from me.

As I grew up in the Tenby Council School my fate for better or for worse was inexorably forming. I lagged behind in everything: lessons, music, athletics. The headmaster was now Mr Ossie Morgan; a good passionate Welshman who quivered along the critical path of that singularly complex responsibility. There were several very decent teachers but towering above all of the personalities in my scarred memory was Mr Ensor Morgan, a hard-working, neurotic tyrant who perhaps should never have been allowed amongst children. But I am now too old to be categorical about such a judgement. It was Ensor Morgan's job to flog us into the possibility of achieving a scholarship to the Tenby Greenhill Grammar School – and flog us he did!

Ensor Morgan was a mysterious man. He was handsome in a traditional villain's way: well-built, good strong head and a thin trimmed moustache. He had a fanatical drive at his job. We poor creatures were his success or failure and he lusted for success; I wasn't up to academic prowess and I suffered for it.

Ensor had a very cutting, incredibly posh English accent. I haven't the whisper of an idea where it came from. He struck real daily terror into my heart. Any learning failure – and they were daily in my case – and we were out in front of the class to have the open palms of our hands thrashed with a cane. It was agony. I have seen tough Arthur Booker stand there with tears running down his cheeks. No one got more than me. That agony ended when I was about eight years old and while my grandmother, Emily, was confined to the Tenby Cottage Hospital, suffering from an ulcerated stomach caused by the trauma of the Depression. Visiting her one evening she and my grandfather questioned me closely about my nervous manner and I confessed my fear of Ensor. The next morning my grandfather called on the headmaster, Ossie Morgan, and the beatings on me ceased.

Mr George Webb who was Tenby's meteorologist, and a very quiet man, simply walked into the classroom and gave

Ensor a real bouncer on the chin and walked out. Jack, his
gentle son, never got beaten again either!

After my grandfather's visit, Ensor turned on me and pointing at my long trousers, given to me by my mother (who had
reappeared in my life), said to the class: 'I presume that those
trousers are your grandfather's, cut down to size' – or words
very similar. I have no recollection that the class laughed but
I was stung.

Yet the man worked so hard. He coached us with terrible
energetic passion at rugby football and I can clearly remember
the occasion when he was demonstrating the side step and,
having challenged us relatively little ones to bring him down,
David Booker casually reached out a hand and 'tapped'
Ensor's ankle causing the teacher to go crashing to the
Heywood Lane turf.

Well, before I was eight years old I was having some remarkable conversations with my grandfather. Ernest had a
vegetable garden perched on a bank above his builder's sheds
in Lower Park Road and often I would keep him company
there. One summer's evening I was sitting on a mound of the
very sandy soil watching him working.

I said: 'Grampy, yours is a very good garden.'

Ernest stopped and sat down: 'Ah, you should have seen
my father's – your great-grandfather's – garden; that was perfect. And then after your great-grandfather had finished his
work in the garden he would sometimes collect his tools and
he would walk up into the meadow above 'The Square' and
there he would carve flowers out of hard stone.' I remember
my grandfather emphasizing to me the significance of hard
stone.

'Now, my son,' Ernest continued, 'I was very frightened of
my father, but one evening I followed him up into that
meadow. From a distance I watched him cut away at the stone
and after a while I edged closer and closer till I could see what
he was carving. Finally, Ken, I found the courage to speak to
him and I said: "Father, that must be very difficult, to carve
flowers out of hard stone." Now, Ken, my father didn't tell me

to go away, but he didn't look at me. He put his hammer and chisel down carefully and *then* looked at me and said: "No, Ernie, it's very simple, all you have to do is to knock off what you don't want and leave on what you do!" Then my father picked up his tools and continued his labour of love.'

Well, that is how I remember the conversation and I must have been between six years and seven when it took place. The story left a profound mark on my knowledge of the potential of this life. It is the very essence of all of humankind's creative work. Of course each and every artist makes his own creative decision what precisely to knock off and what precisely to leave on.

When I was in my early thirties I went off to Italy with a young American lady named Alexandra MacCallum and we arrived in Florence. Most of all we both wanted to see Michelangelo's *David*. An Italian friend walked us down a corridor, avenued on either side by human figures, cut by Michelangelo, struggling to escape from the raw stone. At the end of the corridor was a circular room and in the centre was the famous masterpiece. I remember the Italian telling us that Michelangelo had carved *David* from a piece of marble that had been rejected by another Florentine sculptor when Michelangelo was twenty-three years old. I was very moved by the information and detached myself from Alexandra and the Italian.

Around the wall of the circular chamber (though my memory may be playing me false) were legends in many different languages. I am the worst linguist in the world, so I moved till I saw it in English. It read: 'Michelangelo said: "It is very simple; all you do is knock off what you don't want and leave on what you do."'

I was now deeply disturbed as I remembered my grandfather's story and I retreated even further away from Alexandra and the Italian. Particularly, I didn't want my ladyfriend to see me weep. Today I wouldn't mind anyone seeing me weep.

And one more example of the conversations I had with Ernest. I had noticed that he showed great respect for one of his labourers, a man named Tom Phillips.

I asked Grampy: 'Why do you love Mr Phillips so much?'

My grandfather replied: 'One morning I came onto a building site very early. As I approached I could see Tom removing objects from the lime pit and washing those objects under a tap and then placing them in the grass. When I got close I saw that the objects were worms. That is why I love Tom Phillips.' To this day (thank God) I am in the habit of removing vulnerable worms from pavements, etc., and placing them in the safety of grass or earth.

One day, years ago, I was traversing Green Park, in London, and I removed a worm from the footpath. As I did so I was overtaken by an elegant man heading toward Whitehall. The man stopped, turned, and touching his bowler hat, addressed me. He was a Tory minister of the ruling government.

'Excuse me; why, may I ask, did you do that?'

I told the minister the story of Grampy and Tom Phillips. The minister of our government again touched his hat and, saying 'Good-day', proceeded south-eastward. I like to believe that when he next came to make a momentous decision, my grandfather and Tom persuaded him to plump for the kindly decision. In this way I know that we are all immortal. And the good is not always 'interred with their bones'.

I suspect that the unusual division of Rhos Cottage into two upstairs, with their separate staircases, was deliberately designed to accommodate paying guests during the summer season. Gran, like many people in Tenby, catered for these very strange people who arrived, invariably, from England.

Tenby's only industry is professionally looking after visitors. It was a strange environment; for nine months of each year we four and a half thousand natives were isolated in our ancient beautiful town. And then, around June, the visitors would begin to arrive; in those days mainly on the Great Western Railway. Tenby's population would be steadily multiplied till they all seeped away by the beginning of October.

It was an élite time. Class structure was firm and clear in our own South Pembrokeshire society and I think that almost everyone was happy about it and sensed that it was an essential part of our ever evolving national structure. Looking back I think people knew that they had an essential place in society and yet they were free to work themselves out of that social place if they so wished. We knew that the grandson of a Welsh cobbler (Lloyd George) could become Prime Minister. Of course it was more difficult for him than it was for Winston Churchill, but there were good British historical reasons for that. In those days there was very little of the cult of envy which has so sickened Britain over the past thirty years or so. And I write this as someone who has claims on both 'upstairs' and 'below stairs' but whose fate placed him – more or less – in the latter. Though I have worked myself somewhere else by these days.

In Tenby, on a summer's evening, before the Second World War, English men and women plus, presumably, Pembrokeshire 'County' folk, could be seen strolling in very strange costumes: dinner jackets and long gowns. We local children watched impressed and amazed. And the children of these visiting Martians were equally astonishing: they wore, usually, grey short trousers (the boys), grey jackets with a badge on their breast pockets and very often a sort of soft grey, wide-brimmed bowler hat. And they all talked with that detached posh manner which we knew to be English. Of course, at that time, we did not know that there were millions of other English people who were more like us – with different accents of course. But not with the same Celtic passions, I hasten to claim.

The incomparable sands of Tenby were arenas for much of our pleasure. We Griffithses would often picnic on the North Beach with visiting relatives or friends. A great feature was the Italian ice-cream barrows, painted yellow, which were wheeled across the sands. Tenby was blessed with three Italian families: the Feccis, the Sterlinis and the Rapaciolis and they all were in the café business which included their own superb home-made ice-cream. Tragically, when the war came, some of them were packed off into internment and one of them – I think it was Mr Rapacioli – was put aboard the awful *Arandora Star* and the valuable gentleman went down with her into the Atlantic Ocean en route for Canada.

And also on Tenby sands would appear, regularly, our splendid Salvation Army Band. Now I have always been drawn to this Church; pretty well as soon as I could stand I would join their circle and sing with them. I took a particular liking to Mr Greenstock who looked like my grandfather.

Also, during the summer season, alien Christians would arrive and play a harmonium on the beach. These evangelical visitors I can't pin down definitely. They were robust young men in black cassocks – I think. Somehow I got the impression that they came from Oxford. Could they have been forerunners of the Oxford Group? I am pretty sure that they were Anglicans. And they only catered, so it seemed, for the posh young English visitors – people like themselves. I remember they organized Japanese-lantern processions through the early darkness of a summer's night. I can remember watching this strange phenomenon wending its way along the South Beach Promenade. I observed the excited chatter and the pretty lights and I remember feeling a little inferior because for some reason we locals were not encouraged to join in.

Every summer I got stung several times by wasps while playing on the North Beach. I knew the details of almost every rock-pool. There again were places of excitement and pleasure. But I never learnt to swim; I was, and still am, extremely nervous of being immersed in water. Once, long ago, I was told that I was fished out from beneath the surface of the sea, on the North Beach. I think that they said that my mother pulled me out; if that is true, I must have been a small baby. Or are these dreams?

And then secretly and imperceptibly crept the Depression. The first evidence for me (though I didn't understand the cause) was my grandmother becoming very ill with those stomach ulcers. I could hear her, at night, scream with pain. And then she almost went blind; she wore a black shade over her eyes during the daytime. What had happened was that my grandfather (such an honest and skilful stonemason who was now building very fine houses) was going bankrupt in the national calamity. What it must have meant to them – the very essence of integrity – not to be able to pay bills can best be communicated by Gran going temporarily blind.

Of course they did their utmost to shield me from any knowledge of the bitter experience. For me it was a gradual realization. I can't remember the car going. But I do remember Lily Phillips going. Lily Phillips was my surrogate mother; she must have appeared on the Griffiths scene as my mother left, when I was six months old. I went everywhere with Lily, pushed in a little pram. I can remember it vividly: often into her friend's house – Mrs Warlow – and that was very Tenby, the heart of it.

Lily and I walked out with soldiers. In particular I remember Private Small and Private Ball, of the Royal Welch Fusiliers, I think; with their little black cravats – a famous battle honour – worn from the backs of their necks. Ball and Small were a bit naughty, I felt, but always jolly and nice to me. Many years later, Huw Wheldon, the man who led BBC Television to its zenith, told me that during the First World War a request was made in Parliament for that little black cravat at the back of the neck to be removed. German Intelligence, seeing it, could identify the Regiment. King George the Fifth intervened, pointing out that no enemy would ever see the back of a Welch Fusilier. The cravat was retained.

But the very big time for me – through Lily – was when the Fleet was off Tenby. (Lily did not confine her favours to the British Army; indeed I feel that her greatest weakness was towards the sailors.) What a time that was! The great grey warships at anchor out to the south and beyond Caldey Island, off Tenby. Lily and I would go in a picket boat and up the great grey walls of steel we would clamber. I can remember the Jolly Jack Tars giving me great slabs of 'ship's chocolate', not simply to keep me quiet while they flirted with Lily but because they were good kind lads – at least, that is the impression they left with me. But they were hardly innocent; I can still remember the shrieks of laughter from Lily when I heard them say: 'Have a banana'. And even then, during my pushchair years, I knew there was something more to the excitement than the mere image of fruit.

Lily came from Pennar on the outskirts of Pembroke Dock and she would take me there to visit her parents. They lived in an ancient little cottage on the very edge of the mud flats of that arm of Milford Haven. Her mother was a small dynamic woman with a mass of hair which seemed to stand out from her head like a great rounded frizz. She was a busy loving angel to me; the little woman would refuse me nothing. She made me endless rice-puddings, baked solid in black bread tins. She allowed me to mix salt and mustard and flour and anything in a hole on the window-sill from which I could look out across the mysterious mud-flats and the lapping water.

It was there that I saw my first shooting star on a clear winter's night.

Lily's father was a big round powerful man who worked in the naval dockyard. He was silent but kind to me.

Oh, those visits to Pembroke Dock with Lily! What very frequent adventures they were. That town has the granite starkness of an old naval war-base but its indefinable human warmth pervaded the place. Warm ghosts. Little fancy iced cakes; anything I wanted was provided by those materially poor people.

Lily took me to the cinema: Tom Mix, Douglas Fairbanks Senior, Charlie Chaplin, Harold Lloyd. Many, many great silent performers from Hollywood.

One evening, with Lily, I was peering up at the magic screen, when suddenly it was filled – remember the size – by a negro's face. He rolled the whites of his eyes and I began to scream and to scramble over Lily to get out. (Any Black reader of this book, please be patient with me. In those days there were barely any people in Britain who were not Whites; certainly I had seen no other and no one had told me . . .)

It was Lily who escorted me to my first political encounter. The Welsh Wizard himself, Lloyd George, was going to address the citizens of Tenby from the little balcony of the Liberal Club in Tudor Square. Before leaving Rhos Cottage,

Uncle Reggie whispered some words of political advice into my innocent ear. Lily carted me off and hoisted me behind the railings of St Mary's Church – a shrewd vantage point for any heckling debate; of course Lily had no idea of my plans. The hollow hero of Wales appeared and I waited for the great cheers to stop so that I could be heard. Lloyd George was a master of effective timing, but so was I, though no one knew it. The famous leader held on to his pregnant silence and into it I went like a flash: 'Give Labour a chance!' I shrieked. What happened immediately afterwards I don't know because, understandably horrified, Lily bundled me away before the local constabulary could intervene. I do recall howling vociferously in deep frustration; I hadn't completed my demonstration.

Well, the Depression had arrived and my 'mother', Lily, finally had to go. I was then about eight years old. She assured me that we would see each other often, but I knew that it was the end. I went, alone, to see her off from Tenby station. I was choking with grief.

The impending poverty couldn't be hidden from me. Once I found a ten shilling note in a drawer and I was reassured that we were all right for that week. At this time my grandfather got cross with me for the very first time. He had told me not to read a certain comic paper which was about ghosts and such-like. He found me reading an edition and completely out of character he snatched it from my hands and threw it on the fire. He then made the only remark critical of my mother I ever heard him say. It was very simple: 'You are exactly like your mother!'

Previously nothing was ever said about her, either for or against. But those words still sear my spirit. It is a horrifying admission for me to make, but Grampy had said the worst possible thing; that is what I felt. And then the poor, hard-pressed man, embraced me and told me that he loved me. Well, I have always loved him. At that time he was being crucified, if you can understand what I mean.

Gran had known days, and I have witnessed them, when she would recite long epic poems to entertain us and guests. It was before radio had entered our lives and we lived in comparative blessed innocence. The recitations would often be of a moral Christian nature. I can recall, 'How Sam's Pipe became a Pig'. How Sam stopped smoking and was thereby able to buy a pig with the money saved. Was Gran getting at Gramp who smoked pipes like chimneys? I never thought of that possibility till now. I cannot recall Gran nagging him directly on the subject, or any other for that matter. Another epic was 'Buy your Own Cherries'. But now she had finished with her histrionics. The Depression almost broke her, except that she was really indestructible – until God's chosen time.

You see, I really was brought up by good Victorians. When I was ill a big folding screen would be put around me which was covered with Victorian coloured 'scraps'; cut-outs as it were – flowers, fruit, soldiers, sailors, Father Christmases. And a message would be sent to Dr Charles Mathias known to everyone as Dr Charlie. Now the Mathiases were 'County' class and Dr Charlie was also very well-off. He owned one of Tenby's very first motorcars. But as rich and as relatively privileged as he was, one murmur that anyone was ill and up he would come, roaring into the house and saying words that no one else would dare to utter in our Nonconformist Protestant home: 'Where is the little bugger!? Where are you, you little sod!?'

And he would begin his thorough caring examination of the poorly child. In these days of socialized medicine it is a lucky British citizen who can persuade a doctor to attend a home even if there is a heart attack in progress. What the hell has gone wrong with our society in so short a time? I have grown nervous of uncaring Socialist do-gooder clap-trap. An irony!

During those eight years of my life my mother appeared briefly one summer's afternoon. I was on the South Beach and someone told me that she was close by waiting to see me. I must have been very young; I can barely recall meeting her on the zigzag walk up towards the promenade. There was a bit of hasty weeping on her part; to me she seemed a totally unsafe pretty woman. I was numb with shock. That meeting confirmed one phenomenon of my unorthodox life: in Tenby, during the preceeding five years or so, I used to observe an unknown woman whom I secretly told myself looked like my mother. As Peggy jerkily embraced me I learnt that my baby-hood memory was correct. The anonymous woman in Tenby *was* like my mother in appearance. That was a memory from the first six months of my life.

My attitude towards my missing parents is interesting to consider; particularly in relation to some of the perverted pro-paganda which is put out by a section of the feminist movement. Though both mother and father had departed, the deep dangerous injury was done by my mother's absence. The relationship of a child to his or her mother is completely dif-ferent from the relationship to the father. It is extremely harmful for the child when adults try to practice rigid sexual equality and, God forbid, to legislate for that impossible state.

I have never been able to totally forgive my mother for leaving me; therefore I have never been able to love her. No one ever knew how much I loved and missed my father. I wept myself to sleep for love of him on many many nights. From a feminist theorist's point of view this may be argued as one of their stream of much publicized injustices. But, fortu-nately, the majority of women in this world (as I have observed them) happily embrace the unique relationship between mother and child. The strong lesbian influence on the feminist movement has often thrown a spanner into the very nature of things.

However, there were qualities in my mother's behaviour towards me which were very moving. Every birthday, every Christmas, every Easter, without the slightest chance of non-appearance, a huge parcel would arrive for me, with a message of love, from my mother. Inside these parcels would be a wild miscellany of gifts. Years later I learnt that my mother after leaving me had become, once again, a poorly paid nurse in Bedfordshire in England. Eventually I became friends with the matron of mother's hospital, a Miss Winter, and she told me how Peggy would save from her thin earnings and despatch these parcels to me three times a year.

And to add to the element of instinctive injustice towards

my respective parents, I received nothing from Dad; just an agonizing silence. For very long periods he might just as well be dead. But of course this question of a child's attitude towards mother and father is not a matter of justice but the reality of human needs.

An often tragic by-product of my mother's absence long ago is that I have a deeply ingrained aggressive wariness towards women which has left a trail of domestic disaster behind me during most of my grown-up life. And who is to blame? Well, that raises the ancient human problem of justice; which, perhaps is best answered by the cliché: 'To know all is to forgive all'. My poor mother inherited her problems and I submit that I inherited some of mine from her. But then the human fabric of virtues and vices becomes too mixed and cross-fertilized for my brain to comprehend.

The effects of the Depression then pressed us very hard. Gran went into the Tenby Cottage Hospital and most of the contents of Rhos Cottage were quietly sold. Grampy and I moved to a smaller house in Tenby.

It was an ambivalent time for me: I possessed a vague dread of changing circumstances. Grampy was given some work and I was fed during the school lunch hour by a Mrs Kingdom, the wife of one of Tenby's old-time fishermen. I began to note that in those days of adversity only a few friends held to my grandparents. Their great virtues, I began to realize, were not appreciated by most of their acquaintances any more. Mr and Mrs Kingdom held out their hands and I remember a few other kindnesses as well. My grandfather, ever gentle and smiling through the trauma said to me: 'Ken, we'll manage well, the two of us, won't we?' Or words to that effect. But again I was learning about the reality of human quality, and my character, for better or worse, was forming. In retrospect I do not recall the élite, the Freemasons, giving my grandfather (who had been one of them) much comfort.

Then Tenby decided to extend its sewerage arrangements further out into Caldey Bay and Grampy's life and mine changed for the better. Tenby's sewage pipes ran out under the sand from the North Beach and emptied themselves into the sea; but not far enough, as any walker along those sands could see for themselves! An engineering firm was engaged to enlarge the pipes, I think, and then to extend them. First land work and finally work under the sea. And my grandfather was appointed by the Tenby Town Council to be Clerk of Works for the project; he was to be Tenby's supervisor of the project.

Well, what excitement and interest was generated; particularly for me. There were boats and a floating platform and a previously unheard-of object called a pile-driver, which was used to thud supports into the sea-bed to hold the underwater pipe. And there were divers in diving suits with their great round metal head-pieces. In charge of the project was a young engineer who quickly became a romantic figure to me. I suspect he replaced the disappearing image of my father. The man was friendly towards me. I can see him, in my mind's eye, diving into the sea, without the diving suit, to supervise what was going on down there.

My grandfather now wore a neat grey tweed suit and a collar and tie and his watch-chain across his waistcoat. That period must have been a blessed interval for that fine man.

When (after eighteen months) the work was completed, Tenby Town Council asked Grampy to sign his name to state that the engineering contract had been carried out satisfactorily and he disconcerted them by replying that he could not do that!

'Why not?'

'Because I have not been able to view the section under the sea.'

'But that is impossible for you to do. If the land section is acceptable then you must take the underwater part for granted.'

'I can't do that.'

'Then what do you propose? We have to receive your signature.'

'I will go under the sea and examine the work.'

The above is the gist of the conversation that took place as related to me years ago – but not by my grandfather. What is absolutely certain is that Ernest Griffiths, who must have been about sixty years old at the time and who was a country man who could not swim a stroke, was taken out in the diving boat, had the diving suit placed on him and the helmet screwed around his head and was lowered beneath the surface of the sea. I know that that is what happened because I was allowed to be in the boat and saw it.

I also recall a big knife being fastened around his waist because, as it was emphasized, there were some very big conger eels 'down there around the pipe' that could bite a piece out of a man, diving suit or no diving suit.

I waited a long time in that boat and finally the signal came to pull him up and he emerged from his heroic inspections. The helmet was unscrewed and there was my grandfather, smiling. He announced that the work under the sea was satisfactory and that he could now sign.

Any virtues that I may have as a maker of things come from him: 'It is very simple; all you do is knock off what you don't want and leave on what you do.' And if I am opposed by the Establishment – either of the political Right or Left – in doing what I think should be done, I hope that my grandfather's quiet example will always prod me into finishing the job properly whatever the threatened consequences.

After the Clerk of Works job was over, Grampy was back to casual labour. There was no sort of medal coming out of Tenby's flint-like character. But let me make one thing clear, this stricture is mine, not my grandfather's; I never heard him complain – ever. He was glad to get any respite from unemployment.

Gran came out of hospital and the three of us moved our home to the outskirts of the village of Penally, just a mile and a half across the Burrows from Tenby. There we lived in an unusual, small community of five or six houses built and owned by Major Julian Allen. The houses were unusual because Julian was blessedly unique. He was a member of a distinguished Pembrokeshire 'County' family and like so many of them he had served the British Empire in India. The houses were inspired by his Indian experience; they were bungalows – and they had water-tanks on their roofs. Julian, for me, was a very happy meeting. He was a tall, dear, kindly man with a non-stop inventive spirit. And his inventions were always of an entertaining nature. He built and floated a catamaran – and this before Britain's shores had seen such a thing afloat. He built a land-yacht; down we two took it to the South Beach, he invited me aboard and suddenly, alarmingly, I had covered a mile in precious little time. Then one day he said that he had something special to show me and he produced a box and out of it he gently removed a very large strange seed, with wings. Then, inside a room, he carefully held it up and let go. The seed, quite slowly and steadily, glided away. Julian had brought this remarkable object back with him from India. We talked of building a big one and indeed he started it, but that was never completed; perhaps fortunately, though hang-gliding could have been pre-empted by thirty years. I contented myself by copying the seed with silver paper; they were very successful. Soon I will try to do it again.

When we first moved to Penally I would sometimes go to school in Tenby by bus, but sometimes I would walk and often I would walk at night. Now, one of my many problems had been fear of the dark and the journey home to Penally gave me two choices of route. One over the Marsh Road, which was exactly what it stated: a road over an ancient inlet of the sea which had become an eerie water-land with a myriad bullrushes and then up the hill skirting Trefloyne Forest with its cave, the sometime home of prehistoric humans. Or, I could return over the Burrows, the sand dunes. The choice was not easy to begin with but it was at that time that I conquered my particular fear of the dark. Conquered? Well, I felt easier travelling the Burrows path. I talked to myself a lot. One night I came across a great scattering of glow-worms, the first that I had ever seen. And on that path, in the daylight, I would meet Mary Thomas, as she then was; a beautiful, shy, intelligent young woman. Yes, I was smitten, but I was only a young boy . . .

Now that we were in the country Grampy acquired a greyhound named Daisy. She was a beautiful animal in every respect: affectionate, loyal – all of those qualities so rare in human beings – and Daisy could move very fast.

Near to us lived one of my grandfather's old team from the days when he was an active master-builder: Charlie Phillips (brother of Tom who washed the worms). Charlie had also been a labourer for my grandfather; that is, he dug the holes in the earth and carried the hods full of bricks. Charlie Phillips was a labourer because he felt, probably quite rightly, that labouring was what suited him best. There was, naturally, a hierarchy in a building team and the reality is that the labourer was at the bottom of the ladder of technical skill. Above him would come the bricklayers, the plumbers, the carpenters (who had their order of precedence right up to the cabinet maker, where one might rightly be considered to be an artist) and the stonemasons who might be master-builders.

Then there was a class barrier across to the architects. But if one had sufficient skill and drive and wished to, the son of a labourer could cross. But he would have to prove that he had the academic intelligence to go to a university. School friends of mine did precisely this.

Now, Charlie Phillips, as a labourer, was certainly paid less than the others. But he did his job superbly; Charlie dug the best and, if necessary, the straightest holes that Britain could ever see. And no one could carry bricks better than him. And no one on the building site looked down their noses at Charlie because he had chosen not to be a carpenter. And the point is, for our ruthless, lazy, greedy times to consider: Charlie Phillips (like the millions of others in those distant days) worked very hard, very efficiently and suffered no jot of envy. Very rare qualities today! And Charlie, when I knew him, was, perhaps the happiest and most contented man I have ever met. The question is (and I am putting some of my best friendships in jeopardy by asking it) has Socialism and above all the appalling British Trade Union Movement (possibly the biggest misuse of a good idea in the history of Britain) largely destroyed our national capacity for hard work, efficiency and contentment? Charlie Phillips personifies for me what we once were, as against what we are now.

Charlie Phillips was also a master poacher, which is not what I would call a thief, more of a Robin Hood. He kept ferrets and, I am sorry to relate, snares and traps. And he took me under his entertaining wing. Of course I took Daisy with me. What fantastic excitement it was out hunting with Charlie. And the great redeeming fact was that everything we caught was for straightforward, direct eating.

But I think my greatest pride was when I went off with Daisy alone. Along the Ridgeway we would go: a long ancient road on the crest of hills above Penally pointing all the way to Pembroke Town. On the northern side of the Ridgeway the land swept roughly down into the mysterious valley which became Tenby Marshes. To the south were softer fields overlooking the Bristol Channel and far out Lundy Island and out to the west, the Atlantic Ocean itself. And it was in those fields that Daisy and I hunted, but, truthfully, Daisy did it on her own. Off she would head for the patches of bracken, ideally in the centre of the fields. Out would shoot the rabbits and Daisy would be on a white blob of tail. Sudden turns and Daisy would lose ground. But then alongside and she would pick the rabbit up, leaving it often unmarked. Back to me Daisy would trot, her tail whipping with pleasure and offer me her prize and I would catch hold of the rabbit by its hind legs and give it a quick chop on the back of its neck. Dead. With what breathless elation I would return home to Gran with, say, two rabbits. Sometimes Gramp and I would return home with many more, strung from their hind legs from a long stick carried between the two of us. I seem to remember that a rabbit was worth about sixpence, but what we couldn't eat were given to friends – friends like Julian and Mrs Allen.

During this period I experienced my first personal political impulse, which many years later was to cause a ripple right across Britain and even reaching the shores of America.

I was about nine years old and I was in a darkened kitchen (I don't think it was ours). In the warm gloom was my grandfather and two other men. I was lost in a big chair. My grandfather lowered his voice and in a secretive tone said to the two men: 'Flynn had to leave Ireland because he had the roof of his house burnt over his head.' The words were not meant for my ears, but they entered my being far deeper than the simple tablets of my memory.

I presumed that 'Flynn' was Mr Flynn who lived in a grandish house close by. He was a husky man with red hair and I recall that he was always decently friendly to me; not so his wife and daughters who struck me as snobbish.

Where exactly was Ireland? I have never learnt anything till I have recognized a reason for learning it. Who would burn Mr Flynn's roof and why?

Later in life I was able to pursue these child questions and I now have reason to suspect that Mr Flynn was a sometime officer of the Royal Irish Constabulary (Britain's quisling police force which once operated in today's Republic of Ireland and similar to today's Royal Ulster Constabulary, still policing the remaining Six Counties of Ireland, which are under the questionable Union Flag). And strangest of all, I eventually, many, many years later became a good friend of the man who, possibly, gave the orders to destroy Mr Flynn's house: Commandant General Thomas Barry of 'Barry's Flying Column', an impressive part of the Irish Republican Army during the Anglo-Irish War of 1916–1921. This is a tenuous anecdote but more I cannot say.

Probably there will be readers of this book who will surge against me as they read the above and because I here acknowledge my support today of the Irish Republican cause for a United Ireland. But that statement by my grandfather in that candlelit kitchen fifty-eight years ago started my interest in what we British have done on that small island and I don't like what we have done; indeed I am ashamed of my British root responsibility in that ancient tragedy.

One afternoon I had returned home from school in Tenby and was sitting in my little oblong room. (Again I am reminded of our South Wales spokesman, Idris Davies:

> And I woke on many mornings
> In a little oblong room
> And saw the frown of Spurgeon
> Beware, my boy, of doom.)

When unexpectedly Gran was standing in the doorway, I knew something startling had happened because if she had needed me in the normal way she would have called out – and then there was the expression on her face.

'Ken, your mother has come to see you.'

It has only just occurred to me, for the first time, that it was typical of my mother to arrive, after years of absence, without any warning.

Both Gran and I were deeply disturbed; she for my sake, I believe. Gran took me to the front room and there was my mother: pretty, plumpish and enveloped in a fur coat (to us an astonishing symbol of wealth). Gran left us when she thought best. I don't remember what was said; just being enveloped in the thick fur and my mother weeping. I think the visit ended with a discussion between Peggy and Gran about my visiting my mother at her new home in a place called Sandy in Bedfordshire. There she lived with a baker named Bob Everett; a man that I remember with great affection. And then my mother was gone and we three resumed our lives – but my mother was now certainly a new element in my life.

Eventually the time came for me to sit for the examination which decided who went to the Greenhill Grammar School and who did not. I held out little hope for myself; nor did anyone else. I had no idea what would become of me except in the wildest general terms. I was an adventurous romantic without any qualifications to do anything. I knew that I would not go into the building trade. I had read adventure books about District Commissioners in Africa (where I am now) and about tea planters in India (where I worked last year) but I knew that such exciting jobs were beyond my reach. I had a vague panicky idea of getting into the army – as a private soldier because then I could get to foreign parts, possibly India. But again I informed myself that I would make a poor soldier and the Second World War proved this to be true.

I had met a number of real soldiers. I hope you still remember Privates Ball and Small who were both walking out with Lily Phillips. Then there was Sergeant-Major Keloe of the Shropshire Light Infantry, who with his family was a friend of my grandparents from the days of the First World War. And then there was some sort of relative, on my grandmother's side I think, who was also a Sergeant-Major. I can remember meeting him when he came home on leave from India. Very tall and very upright and justifiably impressive in his uniform. The businesslike khaki and the white webbing. And did he have a red insignia across his chest? And then there was dear Julian, the unassuming good Major. All of these soldiers had been kind to me and I had looked up to them all. Yes, including Ball and Small with their little regimental canes. Also, I was extremely keen on playing with lead soldiers.

And then the results of that examination were announced. I think I came ninth! It was unbelievable. I can remember Ensor Morgan peeping at the list on the notice board in the corridor of the Council School.

'Good Lord! Kenneth Griffiths ninth – there must be a clerical error!'

He chortled and barked but I think that he was pleased and I am nearly sure he said: 'Well done!' He was not without virtues which probably wrestled with his terrible personal demons. He had certainly put a lot of his energy into me. But clerical error or no clerical error I had gone up in the world.

THREE

The Greenhill Grammar School was a most excellent school, not only because it had a fine teaching staff and because the whole place had character – which of course came largely from those teachers – but also it was contained in a big old rambling house and I think that there were only about two hundred and forty pupils. Also the school had a delightful domestic history which has been recorded in a detailed loving book by my history master at that time and later my particular friend: Wilfred Harrison.

I do believe that the best arrangement for such human activities as education and which job to go after is to get there on personal merit and not by State right. And I write the above acknowledging that my entry into the Greenhill Grammar School might have been a clerical error, but that having got there the experience did help me in my life no end. However, there may have been some liberal area amongst the examining body that judged: 'Griffiths is not good at mathematics, spelling, and so on, but there is a special unorthodox spark in his history and English literature, so we will place him ninth.' I doubt whether this reasoning went on, but if it in any way did, I now publicly thank the anonymous Shade.

Apart from the headmaster, J. T. Griffith, and Wilfred Harrison, whom I have already mentioned, I remember particularly, from amongst the teachers, Miss Bowen, who worked very hard to teach me the French language; she was (and is) petite and firm of spirit (yet under no circumstances ever harsh). And Miss Ellis, who taught Latin and drawing and who helped us with the energy and unpretentiousness of a hard-working, enthusiastic senior schoolgirl prefect. Also

Mr Bennet, who taught us geography and who pronounced 'Himalayas' with the correct emphasis, which is rare. He was tall and rather stiff and we daringly called him 'Feet'; I think because he had large ones. He moved with long strides and once I ran through the school trying to catch him to deliver a message. I got within striking distance and called (respectfully): 'Mr Bennet.' He stopped and rebuked me for not calling him 'Sir'. To this day I do not comprehend why 'Mr Bennet' was ethically incorrect. After all, there were a number of 'sirs' in the vicinity. But generally he was a friendly man and not without good humour. 'John Willie' (Williams) taught us science in the school laboratory (what sophistication!) and he was, so I think, the most vulnerable of the entire teaching staff. He was assistant headmaster and I suspect that he suffered a comparatively colourful domestic life. Now I am an expert on this subject and in retrospect my heart goes out to him. I believe he received bombardments at base and, battle-scarred, he then had to marshal us pupils into a semblance of progress. He did it well and again with kindness and humour; though sometimes a perceptive observer might perceive his scratched nerves.

I am particularly interested in who we happen to live with. I have stopped remarking to a husband or wife who has, say, an attractive, serene, caring, loving partner: 'Oh, how lucky you are!' because there is little luck about it. People go off searching for partners or stumble on them and they usually *choose* what *they* want. Yes, I could have a long heart-to-heart with John Willie. Not that I want any reader to think that I have, personally, had a bad time. Well, we all have bits of bad times, but generally I have been fortunate with my best chums. But we do light on qualities, characteristics, and some of us have a compulsion never to play safe – if you sense what I mean.

And then there was my English literature mistress, Evelyn Ward. Well, she turned out to be my particular godsend. She was an extremely good-looking young woman and with her liberal wisdom, very impressive. If fate had led her to run the Royal Shakespeare Company or the British National Theatre,

I believe that they would both be better and happier institutions than they are now.

How can I believe this? After many years of careful consideration of such institutional theatres and of the character and talents of Evelyn Ward! I have now returned from Africa and have been able to visit Evelyn, my teacher and friend, once again. She was and is one of those rare humans who seem incapable of even a whiff of cant. To visit her now when I am over sixty years old is still like a refresher course. And her knowledge and appreciation of dramatic literature, amongst many other things, and its creative potential is a revelation to me.

While filming in Israel this last summer (on one of my own subjective responsibilities, a life of David Ben-Gurion) I could not get Evelyn out of my mind; not for one day. Was she ill? I telephoned her at Cardiff where she lives and after a long pause (she was in her garden) she spoke to me. She didn't confess to being ill, though I now know that she was. I gave her my usual list of problems and she commented shrewdly and I felt reassurance.

When, in Evelyn's English literature class, we came to study Shakespeare, she gave us characters to read. And it was there that I (and she) quickly learnt that I had a talent – indeed a ravenous hunger – to become other people. With what elated relief I escaped from the uneasy wandering of Kenneth Griffiths to the certainty of Shakespeare's strictly delineated creations. And I already had an understanding of the nuances of Shakespeare's mind which are embedded in the text. Above anyone else Evelyn Ward and Tyrone Guthrie knew I possessed this talent. But those two are creatures of a kind. And, of course, I not only understood the text intellectually but I had that strange ability to become an imagined character in drama more authoritatively than I could handle whatever 'myself' was. My whirling skill in reading characters and becoming them, again gave my middle teen years another prestigious boost. Perhaps I was better at drawing than anyone else in school but I was definitely the best at acting.

One of the curious experiences of being an actor – so I

have learnt – is that while becoming someone else, particularly if the character has been invented by a great writer, I understood areas of human experience that no academic instruction could impart. Because I have *experienced* the thought, the reflexes, and so on that go to make up the part.

Sex, I suppose fortunately, became a stark reality. Quite early in my life I became adept – to a point. And after that point I was ever floundering in serious trouble. My skill was in the search and in getting to meet the young women, and the problems began out of the uncontrolled depth of my emotions which obviously left some of my female friends disconcerted and some alarmed. I wouldn't wish my nature upon myself.

Of course these sexual/romantic episodes were divided into two distinct parts, like everything else in strange Tenby; the nine months when we were all isolated and the three months when we were inundated with visitors. I never had a regular Tenby girlfriend; regular spasms and that was all. But the visiting girls had a different effect. I suppose it was my ever-present instinct to explore the unusual and the unexpected. Join with the outsiders.

The overture to seduction was, initially, disgracefully clinical. I still feel uncomfortable when contemplating the facts. I would even hang about Tenby's station-yard to watch the new visitors arrive and would mark, in my mind, the girls that attracted me. Isn't that shocking? Or is it essential enterprise? But once a relationship was formed I was pulled into an intensity which was, generally, unbearable.

However, the uncertainty of where my hopes of emotional fulfilment lay were arrested for a prolonged period when I met Florence Mary Jefferies who lived in Carmarthen. At 'Sunnybank', Parcyrafon Road, to be precise. It is a measure of my preoccupation with Florence that I remember such details as her address when I have forgotten so much else. I can forget the names of even close friends – never what they are like, but their names, often. Once, for a period of about six months, I could not remember either my mother's first name or her surname. Of course the latter was not 'Griffiths'. At that time it was Siskova (she had married a Czechoslovakian flyer during the war). But I could not remember 'Peggy' either. Ponder that one! But forget Florence Mary Jefferies – never!

Florence was slim and fair and very pretty. She was also quietly intelligent and a gentle person. I suppose to a point I was also searching for 'mother', as I suspect I always have. Three divorces later I haven't positively found Her, which is – to a point – my fault.

Oh, how I loved Florence! With such an innocent intensity that I still remember it as a unique experience. It could never happen again. Just like the *first* recognition of a flower. Other flowers can still be recognized as beautiful but the miracle is unlikely to recur. We walked through the cliff lanes to Waterwynch and, should I take that path tomorrow, Florence will certainly be close by. For years I clasped a photograph of her standing on the steps of the Seamen's Chapel at the harbour in Tenby. I loved her and was so proud of her. She was the dream of completion that I presume many human beings hope for.

Florence even came to stay with me and my grandparents when we finally moved to a house high on the Ridgeway, perched above the Bristol Channel. But my hopes were outrunning my ability to handle them. My prospects were perhaps nought. Florence lived with her widowed father whom I never met.

My best friend while at the Tenby Grammar School was Dennis Griffiths (not to be confused with Constable Griffiths' son). Now Dennis was a first-class student. Very intelligent, a hard worker, an honest Christian, a skilful sturdy footballer and not lacking a sense of humour. It is surprising to me that he accepted me as his friend. His open standards were far higher than mine, but now, in these distanced years, I must believe that he recognized some special flicker in me.

I remember us visiting Carew Castle together. I believe we cycled there. It was a summer's afternoon and we were standing by the great Celtic cross. Dennis quietly told me about his Christian faith and he told me that if another war came to our country he would not fight. Already Adolf Hitler was frightening me with his enraged hysteria – over the radio. When war came Dennis kept his faith and suffered to be a conscientious objector. And the day also came when he and I walked through the streets of Tenby; I in the uniform of a Royal Air Force cadet – a pilot under training – and Dennis in civilian clothes, when young local men attacked him physically. I escorted Dennis away. I have never been on the side of my British people when they have been in the wrong. And that stubbornness still gives me aches and pains.

Another illustration of Dennis Griffiths' character was on the occasion when I asked him if he would lend me his immaculately kept bicycle.

'Yes,' he said.

'I will look after it as if it were my own.'

'Please look after it better than that!' replied my school-friend as he handed his precious machine into my keeping.

My mother's unexpected intervention in my life took me to the little town in Bedfordshire, Sandy, where she now lived with Bob Everett, the local master-baker. Bob was a singularly warm-hearted man. He was big with a full unhandsome face but his good spirit shone out of it. He worked extremely hard – even for those days, when Britishers felt more self-respect in hard work than they do today. The business was very successful in its small-town way. I think that there were two vans which were used to deliver the bread and cakes around Sandy and to the surrounding villages.

I believe Bob had got married to a Frenchwoman during the course of the First World War; he had served in Europe during that holocaust. This wife I understood had died but Bob was left with a daughter, Margot, a gentle girl.

I went to Sandy only during the school holidays and these breaks in my Tenby existence added a big new dimension to my experience. It was a soft rural English place. And like our Pembrokeshire it had a class structure. But the emphasis was very different. In Pembrokeshire the privileged had some claims to blue blood; in Bedfordshire the upper class tended to be successful farmers and millers and Anglicans. And that experience was an entertaining, exciting adventure for me.

My best friends in this milieu were the Jordans (seed merchants and millers) and the Strongs (the family of Sandy's Anglican rector).

The centre of my life at the Jordans' was John, the son. He was a shade older than myself and a quiet formidable young man. He was tall and all of my life I have never known anyone so packed with dynamic energy and yet so quietly parcelled, as it were. He was capable of unbelievable daredevil acts; rumour had it that he had lain down between the railway lines and had allowed a fast moving train to pass over him. This is probably apocryphal but there are certain legends in my life that I prefer not to disturb so I have never asked him.

John Jordan had access to sufficient money – from his good solid old Dad – to own a motorbike and a red sports car. Before we were old enough to hold driving licences we drove on private roads and round and round a field. Again I was surprised to be allowed 'in'; I have always suffered this emotion. I suppose I *know* that I don't easily fit in anywhere. But big heroic John made me feel welcome enough.

I met him again a little while ago. His sister Joan wrote to me out of the blue and when I expressed a desire to see John again after so many years she explained that he was very elusive and difficult to pin down. But Joan wrote to her brother and by return he agreed to meet me in London. He arrived early and there he was: the same tall man, pulsating with inventiveness which chuckled through his facade of contained reserve. Again I felt, as I did when I was a boy, surprised that such a man as John Jordan liked me. I admire very much his qualities and I must presume that he admires mine. Perhaps the common factor is that we both insist on being true to ourselves, without much camouflage.

The other significant family for me in Sandy, the Strongs, were very different, and if the English can be exotic, this family was. Mr Strong was the Rector of Sandy and he was a handsome, even darkly enigmatic man. Certainly he conveyed to me little human warmth as Mr Jordan the miller did. But in no way did he prohibit his two youngest sons, Peter and Michael – both about my age – from making me feel at ease in the rectory.

Sandy's church is a good-looking Anglican building and close by it was (it has now been demolished) the classic English Rectory: an enormous early nineteenth-century (maybe earlier) building made of well-worn red bricks. Away from the road, at the back of the place, was a bushy English garden planted around the perimeter of an immaculate croquet lawn. I rarely saw anything of the interior of the house except the big kitchen which was where the boys seemed to spend most of their indoor time. The Reverend Strong gave me the impression of being, and I hope that I am not unjust, an aloof, even arrogant person. Not that he was noisy; indeed I rarely heard him communicate in my presence. And all of the children had something of their father's quality in varying ways. Michael, the youngest, was the noisiest, the most extrovert. I believe he died in a military tank fighting in Northern Italy. Peter, the next in age, and who was to change the direction of my life in later years, was most like his father; aloof, even a superior bearing and conservative with his words, he nevertheless encouraged me to spend some time with him – mainly fishing.

You must have noticed how I have regularly suffered the pleasant surprise of being valued by others during my early years. Indeed, and this will come as a doubt to many, I am still *surprised* when it happens to this day. Mark you, I am also deeply hurt when people whom I have thought *should* be my friends have rejected me or even betrayed me. As I get older I feel more and more confusion about human behaviour. Perhaps I no longer take anything for granted. I now stop and think; and that can lead to real confusion – and some happiness and some despair.

Then there was the Strongs' one daughter Mary. Very pretty – no, beautiful. Perhaps *her* aloofness was simply, for me, the unattainable. I remember once standing in their kitchen and I said something. Mary was ironing clothes to my right and her eyes flicked over towards Michael who was grinning in the doorway to my left. Was Mary laughing at me?

No, I don't think so; I now suspect that I was, as I still am, a very 'odd' person and elder sister and younger brother were signalling that fact. The trouble for me was that she was so beautiful and I could not know what she meant by that look across the room. Many years later Mary wrote a letter to me: 'I don't know whether you will remember me . . .'

Then there was Tommy who was already, or so it seemed to me, on the fringe of the professional side of the Anglican church – where his father was firmly ensconced.

Well, it was all a staggering but exciting change for me; from the isolation of the lonely house on the Ridgeway with my grandparents, from the candles and oil-lamps and the carrying of water from the well, to a red sports car and a fine croquet lawn – and much else besides.

And now my mother. I come to her last – I think – because of a reluctance to meet her again. The short truth is she was often hysterically cruel to me. She frightened me far more than ever Ensor Morgan had, at Tenby's Council School. All could be sunshine and spoiling and then hell would break loose. What touched it off? Very small mistakes I made. Once I became so terrorized that I sought refuge with Bob Everett's good mother, who also lived in Sandy. My mother easily traced me there and weeping copiously begged me to return. Peace for a day and then the terrorizing would begin again.

Poor Margot Everett was spiritually bludgeoned by my mother. But, somehow, Bob, her father, was too weak to defend even her. My mother had a hold over him. Bob also cared very much for me. Once he told me that he had had a son but that the boy had died – perhaps at the same time as his French mother – and that he now wanted me to be his son, and the big baker wept. He did stand up for me on occasions, but I think he dreaded losing Peggy. I suspect.

At about this time I also met my father again. Harold was struggling through life in London. He was a gambler; particularly fond of cards. He was associated with the promotion of professional boxing and all-in wrestling. He had been known to fight in the ring; once, so I have been told, as a Nazi and giving the salute. As ever, he was lovable and charming; very popular with cockneys and street-traders, which I recognize as a credit to him. He lived very simply; usually as a lodger with cockney friends.

During one of my mother's explosions against me she suddenly ordered me to go to my father in London: 'Let him look after you!'

I was bundled onto a train and eventually I found my father's dwelling place somewhere in South London. The place was empty, he and the other occupants were away. I remember sitting on the concrete steps. I remember feeling very frightened. In a way it was the worst day of my life. I don't think that I have ever fully recovered from that experience. Certain fears that I experience even to this very day – fears of irrational insecurity – I believe were nailed down at that time. Since then I have suffered hunger and great physical dangers, but that day outside of the locked door where my father lived was the most dangerous watershed of my entire experience. So traumatic was it that I can't remember what was the outcome. I can't remember my father returning. Maybe neighbours took me in. I have no idea where I eventually went to and have amnesia on the subject. I am incapable of loving my poor mother. And that, as I have already mentioned, has created certain difficulties in my relationships with women. Needing them in various ways very badly, but generally – and no doubt irrationally – distrusting them. The world is full of Frankensteins creating dangerous minor monsters to be let loose on a largely unprepared world. I believe this to be so.

Back at home with Gran and Gramp I was hanging on to a meaningful existence by a thread. I felt very isolated. But that feeling is a substantial portion of my existence; every day, including this one, I wrestle with that subtle demon. For what it is worth, on several occasions, I walked along the levels of Tenby's old pier and looking at the cold grey waters contemplated ending the misery. I don't know whether many children fantasize about suicide. But I never came close to trying it; always there seemed to be a bright small dream far far away that gave me hope. Today I have realized the dream, indeed it has become – in my own social historical film making – an achieved reality. I can preach the sermons that I believe in, to many millions of people. What a turn-up for the book! Of course now there are new weighty burdens – primarily the heavy responsibility of speaking one's mind to people here in Britain, and in many other countries throughout the world, including the United States, Canada, Australia, New Zealand and South Africa. I find both the praise and the blame dangerous thrusts. Of course when people support me I thank them deeply and usually add that their support off-sets the attacks. Let my enemies know that their whacks do hurt me. But speak your truth and that pain must be part of the game.

It was clear to me that I must leave school and look after myself in life. I was not capable of reaping the academic crops that Greenhill School was offering. And every penny was hard-won by my beloved grandparents. Now I must take that cold plunge and strike out for the city of London where many things, I deduced, were happening that were relevant to my little organism.

Evelyn Ward, my English literature mistress, intervened. She broke the school protocol in several ways. She decided not to put on the annual school play in the school hall but to take over an unused cinema in Tenby, the Super Cinema, and do the annual play there. She chose a play written by 'Gordon Daviot', the pseudonym of a Scottish woman schoolteacher, which was about King Richard the Second; it was called *Richard of Bordeaux*. And without any quibbling over demo-cratic auditions chose me to play the King. I believe the intention was to show me off to the utmost of her ability before I disappeared into the probable oblivion of England.

Of course it was a tremendous boost to my tremulous predicament. My seniors, my academic superiors and the best athletes were now supporting me. I remember nothing from them except goodwill. They recognized that I was special at the game of acting and they were all pleased.

Now I had *spoken* drama sitting down in the classroom but I had never before attempted it while mobile. I found that Shakespeare's dictum via Hamlet to 'suit the action to the

word, the word to the action' came, immediately, to me as
nature itself. And my sense of timing was nearly as sure as it
is today. A mystique has clouded around theatrical timing.
People speak of good timing and bad timing. All timing is
simply the *truthful* response of a particular character to a specific happening. Every human being has a unique reaction to,
say, the question: 'How old are you?' Every human being is
unique and therefore his or her response, even to a simple
question, will be unique. That is theatrical timing – with this
one proviso: in theatrical work, if not in ordinary life itself, it
is wise to make that truthful statement as *effective* as one can
intellectually devise it. I remember during the rehearsals of the
school play that Robert de Vere had to ask his friend King
Richard: 'Don't you trust me?'

And Richard was written to reply: 'My dear Robert, the
only persons I trust are twenty thousand archers paid regularly
every Friday morning!'

And then Richard had to exit. Well, I knew that the King
was quite clear what the answer to Robert's question was
with no prevarication. But no one had to tell me that it would
be *less* effective to reply immediately and *then* walk for the
exit. So Robert asked the question, Richard heard it, digested
it, smiled – which made Robert very uncomfortable – and
then the King turned away and walked to the door (knowing
the effect he was having on poor Robert – and *I* on the audience), and when the King was about to exit, stopped, turned
and *then* gave the chilling reply before finally disappearing.

All of that was obvious to me. Did I get it from Douglas
Fairbanks Senior or Charles Chaplin? Or my grandmother
and her recited sagas? Or the great Nonconformist preachers,
who dared to turn their backs on their congregations; their
audiences? Or did it come from a Celtic element far more
ancient. Perhaps an admixture of them all.

Also I was obsessed with looking as real as possible. I
remember rejecting any suggestion of a beard; school beards
frightened me as much as the thought of working in a
chemist's shop or a bank. I went to see Mr Rouse, the barber.
I explained to him as well as I could that my hair must look as

true to the period as possible. This was summed up between myself and Mr Rouse as erasing the parting of my hair.

And learning and living that character of King Richard as inscribed by Gordon Daviot was the beginning of my *intensive* education. About fifteen years ago I got pleasantly inveigled into helping my friend Peter O'Toole while he was acting in the film of *A Lion in Winter*. We were in a castle close to the town of Arles in Southern France. I fell in the castle and broke the bones of my left wrist. When I got back to England O'Toole had arranged for me to be operated on by his friend (he became mine also) the late distinguished orthopaedic surgeon, Lipman-Kessel. I was given a general anaesthetic related to the truth drug. After the operation I sat in a little rest-room with Lipman-Kessel, his nursing sister (who became his wife) and my last wife, Carole. We were drinking tea and Lippy, as he was popularly known, suddenly asked me: 'Do you remember what you said while you were under the anaesthetic?'

'Yes; I kept saying: "I love Benjamin Franklin" (which is true). And I couldn't stop saying it.'

'You don't remember saying anything else?'

'No.'

'What did you mean, Kenneth, when you kept saying: "Oh Anne we could make this England so rich and so beautiful"?'

I sat with my cup of tea, greatly disturbed; the last time I had said those words was, then, thirty-five years before in that school play. Richard says to his Queen, Anne of Bohemia: 'Oh, Anne, we *could* make this England so rich and so beautiful!'

Saying those very words in that play and *living* the experience of Richard was, I think, the first time I became truly conscious that human beings all carry the power to *change* things. It began to dawn on me with those words, invented by someone else, that even *I* might bring some influence to bear on issues that I disapproved of and therefore do something to change them. In deeply experienced acting, ideas can be etched very deeply. Much of my impetus in the films which I am nowadays responsible for could be explained by that longing: 'Oh – we could make this Britain – this world – so rich and so beautiful.'

I stood in the wings of the Super Cinema, Tenby, waiting to make my first entrance, with terror. Evelyn Ward stood at my side and whispered: 'Breathe deeply, Kenneth.'

I did, and as always, felt better. Those whispered words were one of the three pieces of advice about acting that have been of fundamental use to me over all of these years. The others were from Tyrone Guthrie about not being afraid of big size – during this present theatrical era when everything (in histrionics) is being urged to get smaller. And from Roy Boulting the distinguished film maker, who repeated the very difficult formula to me: 'Relax and concentrate.'

Oh the discovery and exhilaration of that school performance! When the local newspaper came out, Mr Fred Coles, the local critic wrote: 'If this boy chooses to make the stage a career . . .' And the idea was born in my head. Could I escape from my meaningless maze by acting for a living? Mr Coles was, I think, Lord Merthyr's private secretary and a skilful performer himself who had often visited the London theatres. I think that he also wrote to the young Emlyn Williams about me.

My mother secured (if that is the word) a job for me as assistant in an ironmonger's shop in Cambridge. The shop was part of the business enterprise of a Swiss friend of hers, a Monsieur Dubois. For me it was unadulterated dread; but I was out of Tenby. During my first week of employment amongst the nails and screws I reconnoitred the beautiful city and found its Festival Theatre in the Newmarket Road.

FOUR

O f course I did not know then that the Festival Theatre had achieved provincial fame through the presence of the young Tyrone Guthrie and such players as Miss Flora Robson. I found enough money to get into the little gallery to see for myself. It was the first time that I had ever been in a theatre building to watch live professional acting. The company was performing *The Merchant of Venice* and I am sure that my judgement today would have been what it was then: 'wonderful'. What magic I experienced! The colour and the warmth of skilful sophisticated Thespians interpreting one of Shakespeare's great plays.

Was it the day after that I escaped from the ironmonger's shop and presented myself at the stage-door of the Festival Theatre? I was asked what I wanted: 'Please may I see the producer?'

To his astonishing credit, Mr Peter Hoare appeared.

'What do you want?'

'Sir, I want to be an actor.'

'What have you done?'

I produced my enthusiastic notice from the *Tenby Observer*.

'Can you do an audition?'

'Yes, sir.'

'Come on then,' and he led me down onto the stage.

For the first time I smelt the unique mixtures and caught sight of the essential realities of the professional side of the curtain.

Peter Hoare sat in the darkened stalls; that ritualistic relationship between director and player. The latter in glaring light and the former in darkness: 'Take your own time, Mr Griffith.'

I gave a piece of my *Richard of Bordeaux*. Then I acted Henry the Fifth's Crispin's Day speech. At the end of my passion Mr Hoare climbed onto the stage and asked me if I could return on the following day: 'At, say, 3 pm and do it again?'

'Yes, sir.'

I did it. What I didn't know was that the director had asked his players to assemble in the gallery, very quietly, and to watch me carrying on. Amongst those present were the late Richard Wattis and the much alive Judy Campbell. Mr Hoare then offered me the part of Cinna the Poet in Shakespeare's *Julius Caesar* which was about to go into rehearsal. He also offered to pay me three pounds per week, which was riches, because food and lodgings need only cost twenty-five shillings.

I was sixteen years old, spotty-faced and yet I was now a professional actor in the very first professional theatre I had ever entered. What a new eruption of experience it was! The handsome, the beautiful and the unbelievably sophisticated were now my fellow professionals. And we were all working in that great centre of learning: ancient Cambridge.

The talk I heard was an avalanche of revelation. I remember the wind-up portable gramophones in the dressing-rooms and a finely modulated man's voice singing: 'All through the night-time a little brown bird singing . . .' I saw a beautiful woman sitting naked on a man's lap in a dressing-room happily chatting to others.

Came the dress rehearsal and I learnt what the theatre must be unless it is to be turned into a factory, as wretched people have attempted to do recently at the British National Theatre – I mean wretched trade unionists. Late into the night everyone anxiously worked and I had reason to be worried. I lodged in a little house kept by two miserable, elderly people who had threatened: 'If you're not in by ten o'clock, we'll lock the door!'

I hadn't considered the practical problems of running a theatre company. At eleven o'clock or so players noticed my unease, including the leading man who had played Shylock and who was now rehearsing Mark Antony. I rightly admired this actor very much; he was a considerable talent. So imagine my feelings when *he* asked me what was the trouble. I explained my dilemma and he said: 'Oh, don't worry, you can come back to my apartment; you can stay there.'

Well, I couldn't believe the honour that was being bestowed on me.

At an early hour of the morning I went with 'Mark Antony', the leading man. I was a little disconcerted to realize that there was only one bed and even more uneasy when my new distinguished friend got into that bed naked. Now I had slept with a man before: with my 'Uncle' Cyril at 'The Square' in Stepaside. That was during hay-making time when all friends and relatives rallied to help. Anyway into bed I got; I think I instinctively kept my underwear on. The actor touched me. I sat up and I said: 'Sir, I don't know what this is about, but I am quite sure it is not for me.'

And my bed-fellow replied: 'I am very sorry, Kenneth, I misunderstood. I promise you that it won't happen again.'

And it didn't.

The curious fact is that until that moment I didn't know that such a condition as homosexuality existed. At school we boys – if not the girls – were, generally, preoccupied with sex. Jokes were what were known as 'filthy'. And actual sexual activity was surprisingly advanced; but nothing, either sympathetic or cruel was even said about homosexuality. Remembering back I can now strongly suspect that two boys at school were homosexuals; one of them, belonging to that lonely brave type, who move forward with apparently unstoppable humour. We saw them as uncomplicated eccentrics.

From the time that the actor made a sexual advance at me I have been on the side of the homosexuals. Not only did he not attempt to seduce me again, but he did what he could to help me. When I finally arrived in the horrendous loneliness of London, it was he who took me to see the best theatre that Britain had to offer – twice. Afterwards he would escort me to my bus stop and say: 'Good night, Kenneth.'

I remember him with great respect.

The production was very advanced; it was interpreted by Peter Hoare as an anti-fascist piece. We did it in modern dress.

As Cinna the Poet I wore grey flannel trousers, a powder-blue sports jacket and a yellow tie. Cinna's predicament is that one of the murderers of Caesar is also named 'Cinna' and the populace of Rome are rampaging to kill all of the conspirators and he is mistaken for Cinna the assassin. Onto an empty stage I had to wander into a spotlight. Under an arm I held a pile of books and Cinna the Poet spoke:

> I dreamt tonight that I did feast with Caesar
> And things unluckily charge my fantasy:

Well that is what I was *supposed* to say on that first night, but what I *did* say was:

> I dreamt tonight that I did *sleep* with Caesar
> And things unluckily charge my fantasy:

From all around the dark perimeter beyond my spotlight, where the players representing the citizens of Rome were waiting to attack poor Cinna, came smothered hilarity. Was my slip of the tongue born out of my night with the actor? Of course he was playing Mark Antony and not Julius Caesar, but I believe it did come from that inoffensive but traumatic experience. No one blamed me, and indeed I was assured that I was a success.

From Cambridge the production moved to the Theatre Royal, Brighton. I explored the attics and dark corners of the impressive old place. I imagined Henry Irving inhabiting these same rooms; already I was beginning to receive an education about the history of the strange profession that I had squeezed into – largely from the talk I heard from my well-educated colleagues. One day I was on Brighton's beach with some of the actors. I made a remark and an astonishing player named Bethel Datch turned to another actor and said of me: 'Native woodnotes wild.'

Such experiences were so interesting and revealing to me in my totally unsophisticated state. I pondered those words and divined that I really had a talent for the cadences of spoken

English. So my self-awareness was slowly and painfully constructed.

Bethel Datch was as fantastic as his name. I think he played the Soothsayer. He was small, indeed delicately formed. He was undoubtedly a homosexual. He wore make-up not only while on the stage, but outside the theatre as well. He seemed to me, all those years ago, very cultured. And he was certainly kind and considerate towards me. I have always remembered him with affection. About ten years ago I saw him in the Salisbury Public House in St Martin's Lane. He sat there with rouge lightly on his cheeks. I was so pleased to see him again; I am not sure whether he remembered me. I don't think he did.

After Brighton the fate of our theatre company seemed to me a little vague. Fortunately the director of the West Pier Repertory Company saw *Julius Caesar* and offered me the part of a cheeky cockney office boy in a play called *London Wall*, at four pounds per week. And what is more he offered me accommodation in his flat.

Miss Judy Campbell of the *Julius Caesar* company, amongst others, watched me with sympathetic care. Before I removed myself to my new job she had a brief quiet talk with me about the perils of theatrical life and I think that she also introduced me to her mother. Then she took me and my luggage in her small car to my new address. She gave me her visiting card and urged me to telephone her or her mother if I ever found myself in trouble. For several years I kept that card close to me. Trouble did come my way aplenty, but I have always been reluctant to ask for help. However, Judy Campbell's concern for me was a help in itself; she was a tall, very beautiful young woman. I was then about sixteen years old and was remaining spotty-faced.

My life had begun to become so unpredictable and irregular that it was certainly not conducive to letter writing. Indeed it remains unpredictable to this day: out in the open market place, hoping that someone will give access to one's talent. The only respite from this non-stop insecurity was to happen through the incipient Second World War, when I joined the Royal Air Force. Of course that entailed insecurity of another sort. However, I was in some communication with my grand-parents, Emily and Ernest, because I received from them a copy of the *Tenby Observer* and in it was an announcement that a theatrical repertory company was forming there for a Summer Season and that it was to happen in that same Super Theatre where I had made my debut in the school play.

I made some effort to remain with the West Pier Company – incidentally you could hear the sea lapping during perfor-mances – but roles for such as my young self were rarish and I refused to do anything except act (no stage management) and so I made my way back to Tenby wearing clothes that were influenced by my Bohemian experience plus, I think, eight pounds in cash.

My refusal to do any job except acting has always been tenacious; indeed every alternative remained outside any con-scious possibility. I still suffer this singleness of purpose; though today it is exemplified by my refusal to shift – particularly in my own film-making work – from what I believe is the right creative thing for me to do. All of this behaviour has something to do with my time and place of death. I have a preoccupation with wanting a minimum of regrets as I pass over. 'The readi-ness is all.' It isn't fear of God. It has something to do with having as much self-respect as a miserable human being can manage to acquire. And it isn't a worry about what the neigh-bours will think. 'I could accuse me of such things . . .' but I am still surprised, indeed deeply hurt, by basic lack of self-respect in many people; particularly when they are tempted by money. I am quite often asked if I don't see that I am naive, Yes, but often I am afraid – or reluctant – to face the wretched truth about aspects of human nature.

Anyway, I was back in Tenby, or more correctly with my grandparents above Penally. It was summer and the local peo-ple, as against the visitors, knew that I had plunged myself into unexpected adventures in England.

I made my way to the Super Theatre one morning and the producer talked to me after their rehearsal had ended. He gave me an audition and asked me if I would perform again for the leading lady, Miss Gwenda Sayre. I was then told that they would put on a famous play by Emlyn Williams called *Night Must Fall* so that I could play the psychopathic leading character, Danny. Now Danny, like so many characters that Emlyn Williams invented in his numerous plays, is – from an actor's point of view – foolproof. His characters are so well understood theatrically and so well written in terms of *drama*, that even an untalented actor must succeed to a point. I have often felt that Emlyn Williams is the *cleverest* craftsman of drama that I have ever read. There it is, the chill along the spine, inscribed on paper.

Danny in *Night Must Fall* was perfect for me. Quickly I discovered that I could comprehend extreme evil in a human being and metamorphose into that particular consistent mental shape. My fellow townspeople and summer visitors banged the seats and cheered their enthusiasm. The Super Theatre was sold out. I had reason to feel that I was going to be an earth-shaker; little did I comprehend what difficulties I was sailing into.

I once again saw my beloved Florence Mary Jefferies. And the manager of the Tenby Repertory Company had a meeting with me and my grandfather about my being contracted to him and moving on to somewhere like Cheltenham. But I was determined to delve into the brightest lights of London. What lunatic compulsion born out of ignorance! Bidding astonished Gran and Gramp farewell, off I went.

My grandparents' eldest daughter, Elsie, lived with her husband, William Godden and their son, Brian, at Ruislip and they gave me shelter for some time. But this was a difficult twilight period. I was being given a little security while I began to closely explore the alarming arena of professional theatre activity centred in the West End of London.

I learnt about players' agents. Those omniscient business people of entertainment who were the magic suppliers of work – or so it was said . . . That was the Faith. There were strata of agents as there were strata of theatre companies. In those pre-Second World War days the British Theatre was firmly and clearly structured, like everything else in Britain, and everybody had a place in it. And that was now my prime problem: to find *any* place as an actor.

The task for me was monumental. I was, what, seventeen years old? Thin, spotty and grasping for some knowledge. And the conventional doors of employment were guarded by the agents who, generally, were not the most perceptive people when it came to assessing creative ability – leave alone unorthodox creative ability and unorthodox appearance!

The great repertory agent was Mrs Nelson-King, whose office and physical presence was at the very top of floors of narrow wooden stairs in St Martin's Lane. I learnt of such beings from other actors. I would breathe in deeply to give myself courage and ascend to the customary summary rejection. *Day after day, five days a week*. I recall Mrs Nelson-King being a big heavy woman. At that time I was a whiff, barely nine stone. She was not vulgar but silently practical and she never forbade me to enter.

Of course Mrs Nelson-King was not the only repertory agent; there were many and I desperately plodded around them all. Some *were* very vulgar and careless of human feelings indeed. It was a life of constant, daily rejection. Yes, it leaves a mark.

Eventually I left my good friends Auntie Elsie and Uncle Will and I survived here and there from day to day. My full-time occupation was looking for work. I strove so hard at it. Often penniless; often hungry. The truth is I have looked back at myself in those days, only able to perceive myself as a stranger; nothing to do with my well-fed body of these latter times. I have been able to view that strange Welsh teenager plodding around the then foreign West End of London with some awe and admiration. I find it difficult to believe that *I* did it. Often I had no money for telephone calls and no pennies for buses. My predominant memories are of hunger and wet feet. Perpetual holes in my shoes. It was a very prolonged nightmare. That is the truth. Finally the ridiculous dilemma of my continuous struggle to avoid defeat has crystallized in one representative memory. Charing Cross Road, eastern side. I possessed one shilling. I would buy, at a Lyons Tea Shop, a fine bun and a glorious cup of coffee. Northward I walked. Stopped. No, toothpaste! Southward I walked. Stopped. No, bun and coffee! Northward. And so it went on. All alone. If someone had observed me they could have presumed that I was deranged. Of course, the road to madness was there, directly in front of me. But it didn't happen. Frightened I was. Weary I was. But the poor little bastard wouldn't give up. It is difficult for me to believe that he was me. Whatever *you* think, I have a regard for that stranger.

I had two places of refuge: St James's Park and the National Gallery. Having been defeated by the agents or waiting to make yet another assault, I would rest on one of those seats in that beautiful park and marshal the energy and control the fear. Failure! Failure! Of course in the National Gallery I gained a new education and observed and digested an unknown creative dimension. One day I watched a dishevelled tramp gaze at a great Italian Renaissance painting. He peered forward; leaned backward like a connoisseur. Then very close, I presumed, to examine the very texture of art. But no! He was examining his own beard; he was not examining the work of the Master, but his own reflection.

One day I was ascending Mrs Nelson-King's wooden stair-case when I heard a massed clatter from above. Suddenly an avalanche of young actors descended on me. I remember being thrown to one side. I grabbed one of the lads and asked: 'What's happening?'

Decently he replied: 'Nancy Price wants a young actor at the Playhouse!'

And he was gone. Down the stairs I sped and then south-ward, running past St Martin-in-the-Fields towards the Playhouse, close to the River Thames Embankment.

Nancy Price is the great enigmatic unsung heroine of the British Theatre. This woman, before the Second World War, started the People's National Theatre. At the time, while I was running, I knew very little about her; as I knew little about any-thing. In actual fact, in those days, when almost everything in our British society was won or lost on its own unaided initia-tive, she had built a theatre company with the sole purpose of presenting the best quality in writing and acting that she could visualize. She was, as far as I know, completely on her own.

And she called her invention: The People's National Theatre. When I reached the stage door of the Playhouse there was a concourse of young actors and the stage door man was marshalling them into some order.

'What exactly is Miss Price looking for?' I enquired.

'She's putting on Thomas Dekker's *The Shoemaker's Holiday*.'

'Thomas Dekker?'

'An Elizabethan playwright. And Miss Price needs a young actor.'

As far as I remember, the auditions for this small part – a few words – went on for many hours. But backstage, inside the Playhouse, it was exciting. It was a big place and certainly there was that now-dead-for-me atmosphere of theatrical human warmth. Eventually my name was called and I demonstrated my ability to that black anonymity of stalls; my usual audition repertoire was now supplemented by a piece from *Julius Caesar*. A woman's voice: 'Very good, dear; please wait.'

What awful tension! After all, it was a matter of food basically. And that vital battle against defeat. Finally the crowd of young men had been thinned down to two of us. I don't remember the name of my rival but he was a little older than me, lean and more experienced; but everyone was! And then the special lady herself, Nancy Price, emerged and announced: 'Very good, young men; I think we must have *both* of you.'

How I worked on my next-to-nothing part! Came the first night and for the scene when the apprentice boys of the City of London (I was one of them) riot and fight, I secreted in the palm of my hand some blood-coloured make-up and during the episode I contrived to be wounded. Some of my colleagues were understandably put out by this piece of unexpected histrionics. But after the performance when friends and always the producer parade their congratulations and reassurances to the exhausted cast, Miss Price detached herself from the grander people and came up to me and touched my hand and said: 'Well done.'

Nancy Price is a candidate for being the finest actress that I have ever seen. While we were rehearsing *The Shoemaker's*

Holiday she was appearing as the stricken mother in Emile Zola's *Thérèse Raquin*. I will never forget her still, terrifying, silent power. Why is she not very famous like Sarah Bernhardt or Sarah Siddons? I have never probed her life. Was there a reason? Had she offended those who should not have been offended?

Emlyn Williams, through a letter of introduction from Mr Coles, the theatre critic of the *Tenby Observer*, invited me to meet him. Afterwards he put me forward for the part of a young master at a girl's school in a play called *Little Ladyship*. It had been written by a distinguished soldier and writer named Ian Hay. The two principal parts were to be played by Cecil Parker and Lilli Palmer. The part proposed for me was excellent; very funny. After an audition I was told that it was mine. However, shortly after this happy news and after I had met Ian Hay, I was informed that the latter was disconcerted by my extreme youth and he said that I couldn't possibly pass for even a *very* young teacher with an academic degree. It was an impossible point for anyone to seriously argue over; I looked more like fifteen years rather than the seventeen which I actually was. Emlyn Williams again intervened saying: 'Give him the understudy.'

And this I accepted. My part was then given to David Tree, the grandson of the famous actor–manager, Sir Beerbohm Tree. David, older than myself, had just gained success in young Terence Rattigan's *French Without Tears*. Anyway, a fortune was offered to me: six pounds per week. And off we went on our pre-London tour.

I shared a dressing-room with Cecil Parker's understudy, an eccentric and lovable man: Stringer Davies. Stringer was a bit of luck for me; a big bit of luck. He must have been forty years old. Nevertheless he retained an enthusiastic innocence about all good things. He was clearly well educated. And he accepted me as a friend. It was a valuable friendship for me during those critical early years. He had an enormous romantic love of the theatre. And yet asked and expected little for himself. I cannot judge Stringer as an actor, but that sort of humility is well-nigh fatal in a Thespian. Stringer Davies had one other

great romantic love: he doted on the distinguished actress Miss
Margaret Rutherford. And I soon learnt that she perceptively
admired Stringer. The famous lady visited our dressing-room.
Before the event I was given ample warning and assisted
Stringer in the tidying-up and indeed the decoration of the
room. In years to come, after devoted courting, they married.
One of the best romances that has crossed my life.

Now I had edged myself into a higher league of the British
Theatre. In those days the structure of companies was ranged
from twice-nightly repertory in tough industrial towns in the
north of England up to high-class repertory companies such as
Sir Barry Jackson's company at Birmingham and the Playhouse
at Liverpool. Everyone in the theatre was acutely aware of this
variable status. Then there were the many touring companies.
After a play had achieved a West End of London success there
would be a Number One Tour (very grand) and then a Number
Two touring company and even a Number Three (playing the
less auspicious towns of Britain). Of course to appear in a play
in the West End was well-nigh, seemingly impossible for most.
But I had nearly made it at a very early age and, anyway, I was
understudying in one and was earning six pounds per week.

There were two other exotic possibilities somewhere in the
beyond: the classical companies such as Stratford-upon-Avon
and the Old Vic; and unattainable glamour on glamour – films!

I had no experience of where to stay while on tour but
Stringer Davies had me under his wing and he understood the
intricacies of theatrical landladies and their establishments.
Our first place of call was Glasgow and Stringer assured me of
the quality of the lodgings that he had booked us both into and
he put particular emphasis on the landlady's fish pie. I remember entering this granite tenement and then the heavily dressed
Victorian decor. I recall Stringer's beatific expression as our
Scottish hostess carried in the famous pie. The truth is I was
not all that impressed with it; indeed disappointed, but I
wouldn't have told Stringer.

And then a traumatic event occurred that is part of the very
stuff of Theatre. I was informed that David Tree, my principal,
had to return unexpectedly to London to redo, or something,

a scene from the film of *French Without Tears* which he had been engaged for and that therefore I would have to go on for a few days while he was away.

Understudies in a well-run company – and ours was very well run – have rehearsals with each other; in those days conducted by the stage-manager. So I had rehearsed, but not with the principal players. As I recall the sequence of events I had developed a bad cold and I was feeling very low physically. So I told the landlady that I would have a rest before journeying to the theatre in the afternoon where I was to suffer the accolade of rehearsing with the stars as a preliminary to appearing with them that night. And the nightmare began. To this day I am shuddering. I awoke on my bed and knew that I was late. I had received no promised call. I tore across the city. Can you imagine the stony famous faces as I shuffled onto the stage? I apologized; no one said anything.

Well that night an announcement was made that Mr David Tree was not playing and that I, his understudy, was. I knew that my performance went well. Very funny. But I was astonished at the demonstration that the Scottish audience made for me that night. I still am a little mystified; they cheered and rattled seats as I recall. Of course there was sympathy for a young actor coming on at short notice. But it was astonishing; I presumed that my mishap in being late for the rehearsal would be overlooked and forgiven in view of my unexpected triumph, but it was not to be!

Amongst the 'schoolgirls' of the cast was a very young Joan Greenwood and I was smitten with infatuation. She looked something like Florence. We went to Loch Lomond for a whole day but my hopes were opposed by her romantic inclination towards David Tree, whom I realistically recognized as telling competition. He *was* my principal; he was the grandson of Beerbom Tree; he was a film actor! And he was six feet tall!

David Tree was an interesting man. In his dressing-room, along his mirror were photographs of his illustrious grandfather, who had built Her Majesty's Theatre in the Haymarket, London, I believe. David was a sensitive young man and he was marked to be, indeed he already was, a very successful comedian. And then, during the war, I was informed that one of his hands had been blown off. To me that has always been a particularly terrible story. He so loved the theatre and after that wound he withdrew to farming, so I have been told.

When we opened in London at the Strand Theatre I hastened to pay my respects to my benefactor, Emlyn Williams, who was just beginning his famous success in his autobiographical play *The Corn is Green*. I was told to go to his dressing-room. It looked to me like a ship's cabin; it seemed to have port-holes. Emlyn Williams did not prevaricate. Very coldly he asked: 'Why were you late for rehearsal in Scotland?'

I was totally thrown that my one important ally was cross with me. The impresario, Stephen Mitchell, who had put on *Little Ladyship* had informed Mr Williams of my late arrival. Mr Mitchell had thanked me profusely for my successful performance; all had seemed forgiven. And so I made a stupid mistake; I denied the fact of my late arrival. I felt that there was so much more to be said: that I had been ill; hadn't been woken. And on top of it all, hadn't I known my part backwards with little rehearsal and hadn't I achieved a triumph? Only my lateness was mentioned. But I should have made an honest declaration. I don't think that Emlyn Williams ever forgot or completely forgave. He did continue to help whenever he could, though I was never to be his favourite Welshman. During my last appearance on the stage in London I saw Emlyn Williams after a performance. Having called him 'Emlyn' I remarked that I had at last caught up with him in years and that this was the first time that I had presumed to use his first name . He replied: 'And you've caught up with me as an actor.'

I was moved by those words. Anyone who lifted an eyebrow to help me during those dangerous early years has my thanks engraved in my memory. Long ago I thanked Emlyn Williams for having helped me.

'I haven't done anything to help you!' he replied, in his off-hand, whimsically cutting manner.

'I thought to myself: 'You may not have done *much* but you have certainly helped me more than anyone else!' – up to that juncture.

Just up the road from the Strand Theatre was fabulous
Drury Lane Theatre where so much of Britain's theatrical history had taken place. Playing there at that very time was the
astounding Ivor Novello. I recalled my mother's mother telling
me that I was related to the famous phenomenon; that his real
name was Ivor Novello Davies (Davies was my mother's
maiden name) and that young Ivor and his mother 'Madame'
Clara Novello Davies used to visit her – or vice versa.

Now, even then, every fibre in my being informed me that I
had absolutely nothing to do with this élite romantic side of the
British theatre. I'm sure that it would have equally applied to,
say, the fashionable side of the Chinese theatre. Good or bad,
I am an ingrained, nonconformist puritan. Nevertheless, with
my desperate shortage of sympathetic friends, I decided to
write to the glamorous man. I simply stated what my maternal
grandmother had told me, that I was related and that I was
gainfully employed as an understudy a block of buildings away
at the Strand Theatre. Would it be possible for me to meet
him? No reply ever came; that silence has always stung me a
bit. My first instinct to keep away from such a milieu was
correct – for me.

Years later (it must have been 1951 or 1952) Emlyn
Williams was helping to organize a memorial concert for Ivor
Novello (at Drury Lane?) and he asked me if I would appear in
a sketch about Mr Novello's early life. The young Richard
Burton was to play Ivor. Incidentally Richard Burton *was*
Emlyn Williams' favourite Welsh actor. I agreed and did it,
but I never mentioned that I had reason to believe that I was
related to the hero. I was beginning to learn that if I wanted to
get on as an actor it was often best to keep my mouth shut. Of
course these days I don't want to get on in the British theatre
particularly and so it is a blessed relief to say exactly what I
think.

With my six pounds per week from *Little Ladyship*, I was
able to take a big breather. I was able to look around and *pay*
to see creative work. I went to the theatre. I could cross
Waterloo Bridge and fork out fourpence to see a matinee at the
Old Vic (we sat in the gallery on wooden benches). I would

even venture, after the evening performance of *Little Ladyship*, to the old forerunner of the Player's Theatre, then called Ridgeway's Late Joys, somewhere in Covent Garden. I recall that entertainment as being, then, a totally natural evolution for actors. In no way pseudo. It was then, simply, an enterprise in which actors and actresses entertained other Thespians after their work was over for the day. I loved it; I think it is fair to state that I instinctively feel happy or at ease with events that have naturally evolved. I suffer extreme discomfort if I sense that they are not *true*. One of the many advantages of writing an autobiography is the continual self-clarification that the writer experiences. Of course, at Ridgeway's Late Joys there was much high talent to amuse; people like the very young Peter Ustinov and the ubiquitous Emlyn Williams.

In those days of my new well-being I went to Burton's the tailors and ordered a made-to-measure dinner-jacket suit; carefully made, it cost six pounds. Of course if anyone sat in either the stalls or the dress circle before the war they were expected to dress traditionally for the occasion. I also had visiting cards printed which, again, were obligatory.

While with *Little Ladyship* I got to know a woman named Katie Pilkington who became one of the best friends that I have ever had. Katie was a dresser in the company; that is she looked after one or several of the actresses. Katie, learning that I was without a permanent home, told me that I could stay with her and her husband and young son at Myatt's Park, close to Camberwell Green in South London. I lived in Katie's home till the war swallowed me up.

Katie was a dear soul. She was tiny but with all the resilience of a Londoner. She loved working in the theatre; her mother was a wardrobe mistress. Katie would talk to me about actresses that she had looked after; some of them then famous and in Hollywood. She spoke of them with such affection, enthusiasm and loyalty. Her husband, Len, was a mechanic or engineer; he was quiet, kind and patient. These two gave me a home.

When *Little Ladyship* ended I renewed my difficult time. I got odd jobs in provincial repertory companies which were low in the scale of status and with them I often behaved badly. The plays could be rubbish and therefore so could my roles be rubbish. But that was no excuse for my unprofessional relatively uncaring performances.

Hard-pressed and back in London looking for work I became alarmed at the prospect of not simply being unemployed but at the likelihood of being driven into further inferior work which would be a far distant call from, say *Richard of Bordeaux* or *Julius Caesar*, so I began to think of getting into a drama school. That would give me a respite and perhaps I could learn how to get onto a better quality course. The most famous drama school was the Royal Academy of Dramatic Art. And so I applied, personally. It has always been a compulsion of mine to approach a problem in person. Even if I write a letter, on an important issue, I like to deliver it myself inscribing the envelope by hand. It is a belief that only a personal appeal can really be heard. When I was researching the life of Cecil Rhodes, before writing the script which I afterwards filmed, I noted with great interest Cecil's continuous dictum: 'Do it on the personal'. If the Colossus of Africa really *wanted* something he requested it personally.

The principal of the Royal Academy of Dramatic Art was Sir Kenneth Barnes. His office, on the ground floor, on the left as you entered the building was like a little posh sitting-room. I believe he wore a bow tie and cuddled a little dog. He was friendly and helpful. I explained that I had no money. Sir Kenneth told me that there was *one* scholarship which not only gave the winner free instruction but also paid the winner enough money to live on. It was called the Leverhulme Scholarship. Well, came the day and I competed for it. I was told that John Gielgud was one of the judges. After my audition I was singled out to be a finalist, but I didn't get the Leverhume.

I then applied for help at the Webber Douglas drama school and here they were very sympathetic. I received the impression that it was run by well-meaning southern English gentry. And as an unpolished Welshman I have learnt that though such people may be very alien to me they can also be a great help. I did my audition and they told me that they would very much like me to attend the school. There would be no charge for tuition and they would supply me with all books needed free of charge. Unfortunately they had no funds to feed and keep me. So, with my built-in reluctance to do anything except creative work I sadly declined the Webber Douglas offer.

I became disturbingly aware of Adolf Hitler and read about the formation of a Royal Air Force 'City of London' Air Squadron. The volunteers for this fighting outfit trained at weekends and the flyers were known as Weekend Pilots. This squadron was similar to the University Air Squadrons at Oxford and Cambridge. I volunteered for the 'City of London' but when it was learnt that I had no regular job and was likely to depart for a provincial repertory company at short notice I was a non-starter. Incidentally these 'Weekend Pilots' were to the fore in the Battle of Britain and not many of them survived.

What I did succeed with was being accepted as a student at the St Martin's School of Art. I had often seen the building in the Charing Cross Road and felt that studying to paint pictures was not breaking my rule of not doing other work away from acting. I persuaded myself that knowledge of another branch of the arts could be deemed complementary. Again I talked my way into the principal's office and he asked me what I wanted.

'To learn to paint, sir.'

'Show me your drawings.'

'Haven't got any, sir. But I was good at school.'

'Bring me some drawings and I'll decide.'

'Sir, may I draw for you now?'

And I went into the Gentleman's Washroom of the St Martin's School and drew myself from my reflection in a mirror. Back I went to the principal and looking at my work, he said: 'We'll teach you to *paint after* you've learnt to draw!' But I was in and attended classes there.

Why didn't I accept the similar arrangement which the Webber Douglas was offering me? It was because drawing and painting was casual for me; I could walk away from it at the smallest hint of an acting opportunity. But I wouldn't want to do that in a drama school – *that* would be a very serious commitment.

In life classes at St Martin's I found myself confronted by a naked woman *while in the company of other people* and this was a unique experience for me. We all stood at easels with large pieces of white paper pinned onto them and we had to draw the naked creature as we each saw her – creatively. And I immediately began to betray an unusual inhibition. Every other student, male or female, stood there with an apparent terrible confidence and thereby filled the whole whiteness of paper with arms and legs and tits and what-else while I got very close to the paper and perhaps furtively drew a miniature naked woman in one small corner of my vast drawing area. No one could prevail upon me to spread myself. I think that I was afraid of losing control of the whole pulsating enterprise. I do not wish to analyse it any further.

Amongst the miscellaneous acting jobs that came my way at that time was an engagement at the Gravesend Repertory Company which was run by Mr Arthur Lane. I never quite fathomed Arthur; he was the leading man of the company, specializing in the more romantic roles. I received the impression that he had a special attachment for the leading lady who quickly – and I am sure with justification – took a particular dislike to me. Arthur genuinely longed to run a theatre in a first-class manner. And he did his utmost at Gravesend but the cards were poorly stacked for him. The theatre building was little more than a small impermanent hall. Nevertheless, Arthur Lane installed an orchestra in the pit; I think it was a piano, a violin and a drum. The violin I will never forget. And to make some money (for the management) we did one play per week, twice nightly and for one unbelievable spell: *TWO* plays per week, twice nightly! Well it stands to reason we couldn't *learn* the parts; the Memory Man himself couldn't have coped with that burden. I suppose we got the gist and winged it.

The tendency was to melodramas, but Arthur demanded that we did them well. The alternative leading man to our manager was George Crocker. George was a big impressive looking chap who was undoubtedly a fine actor. And a likeable man. I vividly recall one evening when George had to make a heart-breaking exit clutching a romantic bunch of flowers. I was on the stage and our violinist was giving his sentimental all. George was gentle tragedy personified. He took the door-knob and turned it. Nothing happened. George took more positive action. Nothing. Now I have already mentioned that he was a hefty man and when at the third go he demonstrated real determination, the entire door came away in his hand. And like the pro he lovably was, he exited still in character, with the entire object under his arm. I believe I succeeded in completing the scene which suggests something complimentary about me also.

George Crocker died violently. And I have never been able to think of his death without suffering a degree of hysteria; even now. Approaching Charing Cross Station he put his head out of the window and was killed.

Our hard-pressed stage-manager at Gravesend was an old hand at the theatrical game. I remember him as tall, lean and a shade neurotic. His wife was small in size and very mild. How she needed protection (which her husband gave her) I thought. Her name was Margot Bryant and when Mr Bryant died I silently dreaded sweet Margot's fate. As millions were to learn, she survived well enough as one of the famous names in *Coronation Street*. We Thespians may be the most vulnerable people in the world but such fates as Margot's splendidly happen.

Gravesend must represent a number of repertory theatre experiences, all equally bizarre. Perhaps I should also mention for the historical record that my personal romantic escapades at this time were catholic and fairly indiscriminate, though I had a particular admiration for a young Gravesend lady who acted as an usherette in our theatre. I remain very grateful to her.

Out of this jumble of bits and pieces, Emlyn Williams gave me a small job in *The Corn is Green* which had now transferred to the Piccadilly Theatre. I played a coachman, I think, and I did a bit of minor understudying. I shared a dressing-room with four other Welshmen. Mr Williams was ever ready to promote our fellow countrypeople and we were a well assorted quintet. One prided himself on his tenor voice which he would exercise without warning; another, so I was told, had an exceptionally large penis and I was also advised that he would show me the phenomenon if I requested. This I did not do; more out of dread than lack of curiosity. And then there was an imperceptibly sad ex coal miner. And finally, a young man named William John Davies whom Emlyn had 'discovered' in Wales and had brought to London to play the small part of Idwal Morris. William Davies was a bright, enthusiastic young man with all of that keen intellectual potential that bubbled out of our hard-pressed Welsh industrial areas. He and I became friends and he was something of a comfort to me. Of course I was now more sophisticated about the theatre than he was, but his status in the company was higher. I was simply there to earn a few pounds per week to pay my way in life. Already the extreme fluctuations of my fortune had begun.

Emlyn Williams' attitude towards me was very curious. He seemed to pretend that I didn't exist. At almost every performance I would unobtrusively stand in the wings and watch most of that fine play. Emlyn, as Morgan Evans, the hero of the play and based upon his own early life, would walk past me without looking at me or speaking. If I said: 'Good evening, sir,' he would reply: 'Good evening' without looking. It was an ordeal but I was being strengthened through ordeals. His cold relationship persisted for months; then one evening while he was standing in the wings waiting to make his entrance and I was behind him in my customary corner, he addressed me in that detached North Welsh tone of his. He didn't look at me.

'Do you know Norman Marshall who runs the Gate Theatre?'

'Yes, sir,' I lied. Perhaps it was my fear of Emlyn Williams that made me lie to him, then for the second time.

'He's doing a play by Cocteau called *Les Enfants Terribles* and I've recommended you for the boy. He's expecting you at 11 am tomorrow morning.'

'Thank you, sir.'

And Emlyn Williams made his entrance onto the stage of the Duchess Theatre.

On another occasion my young friend William Davies was

ill and I had to go on for him. This entailed my learning the Welsh words he spoke in the play, phonetically. During the afternoon a rehearsal was called, with the principal players, to prepare me for the evening. They were all there including the great Dame Sybil Thorndike who was playing Miss Moffat, a part inspired by Emlyn Williams' schoolteacher, Miss Cooke. Emlyn Williams told me to do something and I replied: 'Yes, sir.'

He stopped, looked around the assembled cast and in very mock astonishment said: 'What, *me*, "sir"! *Me*, "sir"!?'

It went on longer than that. There must have been something about myself which he disliked very much. It probably dated from the report of my being late for rehearsal and then my denying it. Also many Welsh people have found me suspect; a pseudo Welshman because I do not speak the language and indeed, normally, have almost no Welsh accent. This is a geographical problem. My blood and nature is as pure Welsh as Owen Glendower's. But on the other hand, Emlyn Williams was privately still persuading Norman Marshall to help me.

I was *very* early for my appointment with Mr Marshall who was the ruler of that sometime important little theatre, The Gate in Villiers Street. Norman Marshall appeared to me to be a tortured soul, always suffering a stern emotional pressure. And therefore he carried a dangerous temperament. During my interview he explained to me that he had already offered this important leading part in *Les Enfants Terribles* to another (distinguished) young actor but that the young man might not be available to do it and if this was to be the case he would offer it to me.

'If Mr Williams thinks so highly of you, that's good enough.'

Unfortunately for me the actor *was* available and so I never did *Les Enfants Terribles*.

'However,' Mr Marshall said, as he eventually gave me the bad news, 'my next production is a play about Borstal and though the leading parts are already cast there is one minor role which you can have if you want it.'

He gave me the play to read; it was the part of Gormy Evans, a mentally deficient lad who is part of an intake into the

famous corrective institution. With Emlyn Williams' ready
blessing I left *The Corn is Green* to rehearse *Boys in Brown*.

Of course, Gormy Evans was so retarded that he could not
truly comprehend what Borstal was or why he was there.
Again he had great difficulty in expressing himself so he spoke
very little. And there is a tendency to judge a part by how big
it is. I knew that in playing Gormy I could communicate something worthwhile; but I wasn't prepared, and neither was
anyone else, for the outcome after the first night.

In those days there were two very famous critics: Brown of
the *Sunday Observer* and Agate of the *Sunday Times*. Again I
am reminded of the substantial structure of our society in those
days. Those two men were established like twin rocks of
Gibraltar. Two very different but definable substances. And I
opened my Sunday papers, not nervously, because in that large
cast of bigger parts I was apparently an 'also-ran', and to my
delighted astonishment both of the great critics singled me out
for praise.

I don't know how many young men there were in *Boys in
Brown*; about twenty. The competition for work and survival
as actors, leave alone fame and fortune, was pretty strong.
Again status amongst one's peers was acutely important. Those
notices lifted me up again. No career can have had more
extreme undulations than mine. Mind you, very little if anything was *said* to me by the other young actors, but there must
now have followed an unspoken readjustment of attitude
towards me and that was a blessed relief. It is one of the sad
facts of the acting business that it is not so much a matter of
how talented you are as how famous you are. In my not
unknowledgeable opinion one of the greatest acting talents in
Britain over the past thirty years was Mr Noel Willman, who
unfortunately is now dead. But sadly he is not as famous as Sir
John Gielgud. Therefore I have one unshakeable rule (I have a
few others too) and that is that I do not wish to compete for
official accolades.

I shared a dressing-room at the Gate Theatre with a number
of other actors and my success became underlined by the influential people who came backstage afterwards to visit me.

About a week after the first night there was a curious, embarrassing and then exciting event for me after the performance. Suddenly Norman Marshall burst into the room in a towering rage, all of it directed at me.

'What the hell do you think you're doing? Do you realize that you almost ruined the play tonight?!'

Our producer's face was mottled with emotion. I was nonplussed. I had woven my way carefully through the performance. I remember thinking: 'Maybe I have developed a note of hysteria into the repeated statement "Not much like home"', which was poor Gormy's summing-up of Borstal. I couldn't guess at any other possibility. And at that awful moment, while Norman Marshall was breathing very heavily, there was a knock on the dressing-room door and in came the film director, Anthony Asquith and the American film director, soon to become Britain's most famous film agent, Al Parker. And behind him was the author of *Love on the Dole*, Walter Greenwood.

Mr Asquith was a highly sensitive quiet man. He said to me that he had been deeply moved by my performance and that he hoped that we could work together. Norman Marshall left the room without another word and he never again renewed his attack on me. Then Al Parker, who was the American film man personified, told me that he was setting up an actors' agency in Britain; that he wanted to limit it to 'about fifteen or twenty outstanding clients' and that he wanted me to be one of them. Then Mr Greenwood said that a film was to be made of his book, *Love on the Dole*, and that he would push for me to play the leading part, that of a young man.

I didn't join forces with Al Parker, which was probably one of the many mistakes that I have made in my professional life. I joined a substantial agency which had an oak-panelled office and that was conservative. However, the head of the agency was remarkably responsible in a generally irresponsible business and he sent me to the old Associated British Studios, which were then located at Welwyn Garden City, to be interviewed for the part of George Smerdon in a film adaptation of Eden Philpotts' play *The Farmer's Wife*. And so I arrived at a film studio for the first time in my life; but it was not a bit like the image of a film studio that I had been conditioned to expect from propaganda emitting from Hollywood. The entrance hall and reception area looked to me like a large dark shed and contained a couple of wooden benches for visitors. In the gloom I could see two figures and one of them got up and approached me.

'How are you, son?'

It was Al Parker.

'Good luck; I'm sorry I'm not looking after you.'

The handsome sulky looking young man with Al was James Mason who had wisely joined the dynamic American.

At that moment a Mr Ingles appeared and asked if I was Kenneth Griffith. Mr Ingles had a speech disability which used to be described as 'not having a roof to one's mouth'. He had come to collect me to introduce me to the head of the studio, Walter Mycroft. Into Mr Mycroft's office I went and discovered that the boss was virtually a dwarf. No one had warned me about anything. And the shocks were not over. Mr Mycroft received me in a friendly manner and as I was about to sit there was a sharp knock on the door.

'Come in.'

It was Al Parker.

'Mr Mycroft, this young man, Kenneth Griffith, has nothing to do with me, but I've seen him act and I want you to know that in my opinion he's outstanding.' And Mr Parker was gone. I got the film part, my first, and I think of Al with gratitude and affection.

Al Parker quickly became a legend in the British film industry. Britain had seen nothing like him before. He had great faith in young James Mason and he would brook no denial of his protégé. Rumour had it that on one occasion Al had resorted to fisticuffs at Denham Film Studios on behalf of Mr Mason, physically attacking a film producer who did not share his enthusiasm for his client. I wish I had agreed to let Al hustle for me. This book might have been a less painful tale. Or, of course, a more painful one.

Before I started work on *The Farmer's Wife* I went home to

Penally to see my grandparents. Paddington Station is the great gateway to South Wales. During the preceding time since I had travelled to London aged sixteen years I had mentally rejected Paddington Station's very existence. It is the truth that I prohibited myself to consider the significance of the place. At the other end of that railway line was the world which I had fought to leave. And anyway, I had no money to return. I missed my grandparents but there was no acceptable alternative. Well, the alternative would mean the end of me. I would disintegrate at the western end of that railway line. Better to fail in London.

But now circumstances had changed. I had prospects of some financial security. And on top of that was the seemingly inevitable revolution of a coming Second World War. My pattern of survival was taking a change for the better and at the same time universal disruption was rumbling very close by.

It was a beautiful summer in south Pembrokeshire. And other members of our family were there: Auntie Ivy, now a schoolteacher, and Uncle Reg who then seemed to be involved in the business side of the building trade. I remember the afternoon on the North Sands at Tenby when I heard that war had come. I went home to Penally and a family tea was in progress. I was suffering a strong emotional turmoil. No one said anything about the catastrophe. Finally I blurted out that I would return to London and join the army.

Everyone continued eating except Uncle Reg who said: 'Shut up!'

'What do you mean?' I felt outraged.

'You're upsetting your grandmother and grandfather. Shut up!'

'Don't you realize what's happening and *what* we'll have to fight!?'

'I'm telling you to shut up!'

'I won't.'

And Reg got up and hit me from one end of the room to the other. I don't remember what happened immediately after that.

Uncle Reg only hit me that once, ever. I have puzzled why he felt so strongly. He was just too young to be in the First World

War and would probably be just too old for the impending one. Perhaps it was something to do with that.

I left the sunny beaches and returned to Katie Pilkington at Myatt's Park in London and soon I was travelling to the ABC Studios at Welwyn to act in *The Farmer's Wife*.

There were four juvenile leading parts in the film. There were two sisters, played by 'Bunty' Payne (who was distinguished both for being one of 'Mr Cochran's Young Ladies' – Charles Cochran, the king of sophisticated revues – and for being the sometime wife of 'Kid' Berg the world boxing champion) and a very young Patricia Roc, later to be a star of the Rank Organization. And then there were the two young suitors to the ladies: myself and young Michael Wilding.

Again I found myself in a different league. The three of them were 'people about town' in varying degrees; but they were all friendly towards odd-ball me. Usually I travelled on public transport and then walked to Bunty's little house in Mayfair. There, Michael would also be and we would motor, in Bunty's car, to the studio. It was an exhilarating time for me; I wasn't broke and I was making haphazard progress. I remember, particularly, the excellent bacon sandwiches which were available early in the morning at the studio.

I attended my first 'rushes': that is sitting in a small theatre and watching the uncut film from the previous day's work. I remember walking out into the sunshine and saying to myself: 'I don't know how good I am, but I'm sure I'll go a lot further than the others!' It is one of the many curious realities of show business that there was a time, in the 1950s, that when I told this story, even kind friends would fall about laughing. And I meant it to be funny! Patricia Roc was then a famous film star and so was Michael Wilding, busy travelling between Anna Neagle and Hollywood. Where was I at that time? I'm not sure. But today the story is no longer funny.

FIVE

One day we were out in the country filming. Above us was the beginning of the Battle of Britain. The scattering aircraft could be seen. Several small objects hit the earth around us; astonishingly they were spent bullets. That afternoon began to reshake me into some determination to join the armed forces. On another day we worked late at the studio and I therefore had to spend the night in a hotel at Welwyn with other members of the film unit, and while we were having supper we were called out into the garden and there, over distant London, was a red glow. The great blitz had begun; London was burning.

The next day, as soon as I was free, I hurried back to Katie and family at Myatt's Park. To get there was like solving the puzzle of a maze: so many streets were barred by debris and unexploded bombs. But Katie and company were all right. All the occupants of her house crowded around me. On one floor was a maiden lady whose brother had died serving on a British destroyer during the first weeks of the war. Then there was a great cockney husband and wife; indomitable. He was a young stevedore in London's dockland. Katie's husband, Len, was away doing engineering war work. Katie brought me my supper from the oven. As I began to eat they all laughingly bombarded me with tales of the terrible excitement of the night before.

'Oh!' I said to them, 'it can't be *that* dangerous; London is a huge city. What a small proportion of it has been hit.'

At that moment the air-raid siren went.

'You wait!' someone said.

I went on eating my supper. And then it began. In the distance we could hear soft, distant thumps. Barely perceptible but undoubtedly sinister.

'Here they come,' someone warned.

I continued eating. Then, 'Boom, boom; bang, bang!' The noise was appalling. Glass was shattering and then the noise stopped.

I was found standing in the doorway to the hall with my plate of supper held in my hands. I don't remember moving there.

'There you are; what did we tell you?'

I remember the laughter and the good humour. What people those Londoners were! What people the British once were! I don't accept that we are finished; I believe that we have grown dormant through over-protection from the State. Self-respect and character have been interfered with. Either we submit to bureaucratic state control or we return more to the personal responsibility that we once had when I was young. Not that those days were faultless. Oh no!

My young stevedore friend took command of the situation. Everyone would squeeze into the cupboard under the stairs, he ordered. It had been widely advertised that this specific location was generally the safest in a house. That is, everyone under the stairs, except him and me; no room for us. He and I would occupy Katie's bed on the ground floor. The explosions were again in full swing. It was terrifying and it is strange for me to recall that I was there.

During the night I broke. My cockney friend appeared to be impervious. The glass was disintegrating in the house.

I nudged him: 'Here, I can't stand this any more; I'm getting *under* the bed.'

'All right.'

I wedged my way onto the lino when suddenly his upside-down face was grinning at me: 'Heard about concussion; they found blokes in Fleet Street this morning, *standing up* dead. Perhaps you shouldn't lie on the hard floor.'

I was out from under very fast. A year or so later I was told that my friend and bedfellow was badly injured rescuing people from a direct hit. I haven't seen him since those days; I've even lost his name.

It was during that night that I made up my mind to take positive action once again and I volunteered for air-crew duties in the Royal Air Force. Eventually I was called to take examinations to qualify and this I succeeded in doing and finally I was ordered to go before an Air-Crew Selection Board. Mine was held at Cardington aerodrome where the enormous R101 airship hangars are located.

I was shown into a room where perhaps four Royal Air Force officers presided. 'Sit down, Mr Griffith,' and they jointly perused my papers. 'So you're keen to fly?'

Now I've nearly always been a stickler for Nonconformist Methodist truth. It is both my strength and vulnerability in this world. I pondered the officer's question. A bad start; perhaps no one had pondered that question before.

'Well, sir, it might be more accurate to say that I am *prepared* to fly rather than *keen* to fly.'

The effect of this simple declaration on the four officers was remarkable. There was a profound silence; I don't exaggerate. They again conferred but now rapidly. The presiding officer, a Wing-Commander, I think, gazed at me very steadily: 'Mr Griffith, we are looking for young men who would rather fly than have their breakfast.'

And that terrible compulsion to say what I felt gripped me irrevocably.

'Oh! I'm quite clear about *that* sir; I'd much rather have my breakfast than fly.'

The top table was in mild disarray. They put their heads together and then the wing-commander turned to me like a father: 'Mr Griffith, we must tell you that we have never been confronted with this problem before. Your papers are in good order; everything about you is most acceptable – but . . .'

There was a pause.

'You see, we *must* have young men who would rather fly than have their breakfast. We are all very sorry, but we have to turn you down.'

And I made my chastened way back to London.

So, again my instinct to help save Britain (not to mention Czechoslovakia and Poland) from Hitler was frustrated. But, fortunately, another temporary service was offered to me. An organization called the Council for the Encouragement of Music and the Arts (CEMA) had been formed and they had approached the Old Vic to perform for them. The revolutionary idea was to take the Old Vic Company to the 'ordinary' people of Britain. And they meant by this concept to take the Vic Company to small places that had no theatres; well away from the beaten track to Birmingham, Manchester, Glasgow, and so on. The Old Vic at that time was run by the incomparable Tyrone Guthrie and it was he who wanted me to be recruited. The leading players were Dame Sybil Thorndike and her husband Sir Lewis Casson. The chosen play was *Macbeth*.

The Old Vic in the Waterloo Road had copped a bomb from the Luftwaffe and so we were removed to Burnley in Lancashire and there we rehearsed. Apart from Dame Sybil and Sir Lewis and of course Tyrone Guthrie, I remember, particularly, Abraham Sofaer who was playing Macduff. He was a memorable man. He looked like an Afghan. He was extremely colourful in his very varied opinions. I remember him breaking up, theoretically, the various race strains that inhabited Britain and Ireland. Where they originated from and what their respective characteristics were. All the time I was being injected with 'further education'. Also Abraham, to me, was an impressive actor. He delved into the depths of his exotic emotions. There was no Anglo-Saxon blank-faced understatement. I am still impressed by the memory of his Macduff's: '*All* my pretty ones? Did you say *all*? Oh, hell-kite!' Perhaps Abraham was the first Jew that I consciously considered and began to reap a deep harvest from.

As soon as I was away from London I volunteered for the Royal Air Force again. I presumed that since there was so much going on no one would trace my previous rejection. I was right. When I reached a second Air Crew Selection Board I volunteered the untruth that I was *very* keen to fly and, indeed, that I would rather fly than eat my breakfast. And I was accepted; I was placed on 'deferred service'. That is, I had to take my place in the queue.

The CEMA tour of Wales was a happy event. We all travelled in a bus and the very portable set in a large furniture van.
It was a bit like an ancient royal progress. We were given prearranged hospitality wherever we played; that is, we stayed in
the homes of the grander local people. Again I was receiving
an intensive crash-course on the very variable nature of British
society. On the way to Wales we played in two Lancashire
towns and at one of them I was the guest for a couple of days,
of a formidable middle-class husband and wife. They were
very kind to me and as I was leaving I presumed to cut out the
review of our production from the previous day's local paper.
Later on in the tour I received a North of England rebuke by
post for having removed the piece without asking permission.
It was an unforgettable lesson.

It had been decided that since such a production had never
penetrated rural fastnesses before, a 'chorus' of plot explanation should be composed. It was written by Lionel Hale and
my job was to share the responsibility of speaking it with an
actress. We both sat on the stage throughout the performance;
she on the prompt side, I on the other and then, in turn, we
stood up and addressed the audience, separately, where
indicated, in this novel adaptation of *Macbeth*.

One of the larger places we played was Colwyn Bay and the
mayor and corporation gave the Vic company a luncheon.
The mayor, without meaning to be either amusing or provocative, referred to Dame Sybil Thorndike as 'a member of the
oldest profession in the world'. Also at Colwyn Bay I met a
daughter of the leading lady at the local repertory company
and I made tentative arrangements with the producer to join
his company when I was free of the Vic and to play for him till
my country needed me. Of course it was the young lady I was
pursuing, not my career. Progress in drama at that lethal time
didn't seem important.

I was now very uneasy about my ambiguous predicament.
I had been told that I might have to wait nine months before
I actually got into uniform. But I had also been told that one
could get into the Fleet Air Arm much quicker, so I volunteered for that service. I was given an appointment to gauge

my suitability for flying for the navy in a building on the southern perimeter of Trafalgar Square. I rang the bell at the appointed time and the door was opened by an immaculately uniformed officer, but he had little recognizable face left. The stylish man (his bearing was perfectly normal) was apparently beyond the aid of cosmetic surgery. I don't remember much else about my visit. The reality of war personified by that wounded man overwhelmed me; I presume that he had been consciously posted to the job of receiving young volunteers for that very testing purpose.

I think that I was discouraged to pursue the Fleet Air Arm when the officials discovered that I was already on deferred service for the Royal Air Force and so I left the Old Vic and hastened to the Colwyn Bay repertory company to be near the pretty lady. However, she was much put out because I hadn't written to her and our relationship failed to develop.

The most memorable experience that I had in Colwyn Bay occurred in my lodgings. The daughter of the house did most of the housework, and she and I became friends. Also staying there was a young man who told us that he was on sick leave from one of the military services. He was very friendly and remarkably generous. In those days I heaved a portable gramophone around with me and a case full of miscellaneous records and my new chum was offering to buy me more records if I wanted them. One day the young lady of the house, who had been cleaning the rooms, visited me in a state of excitement.

'Come with me; I want to show you something!'

I remonstrated that I didn't want to go into the young officer's room uninvited, but she persisted and pulling a suitcase out from under his bed she opened it. What a staggering sight! There were thousands of new ten shilling notes all wrapped up, presumably by the hundred. Neither of us reported it to the police or mentioned it again.

Having lost the affection of the leading lady's daughter, I found solace with the local ballroom instructress. And since she was often expected to attend dances held on the pier, I would call for her there after our plays had been performed.

Well, she rather insisted that I learn to dance properly; the fox-trot, the slowstep, the waltz, and I would even have a go at the tango. I became quite proficient; even performing the intricacies of the 'fish-tail'. However, when I was called upon to dance with any other party it was unadulterated disaster. I could never improvise because of the formal drill that had been dinned into me.

And she, innocently, became one of the reasons for my eventual downfall in the repertory company. I was still guilty of giving my all when I thought that the play and my role in it was interesting and less than full value when I thought otherwise. Also the producer had certainly been friendly with the red-headed dancing instructress. Whatever the whole truth was, I was eventually sacked.

Back in London and still hanging on in that limbo world, I acted in a little theatre which was located towards Notting Hill Gate, in a production of Clifford Odets' anti-Nazi play *Till the Day I Die*. And during the course of that run I befriended an apparently 'cultivated' husband and wife who urged upon me the virtues of fascist if not Nazi policies. They were both very well read and very gentle. Their whole tone on the subject was quiet reasonableness. I don't recall arguing back; only listening and being mildly astonished.

My military service was now very near, I surmised, and so I again returned to Tenby to visit my grandparents. I resolved my waiting predicament by organizing and producing and playing the principal character in that same *Till the Day I Die*. I recruited a miscellaneous group of friends to help; an astoundingly miscellaneous group when I come to recall them.

At Saundersfoot (just North of Tenby) was the headquarters for training Marine-Commando officers and I had surprisingly become friends with several of them. One of them was William Hambling, after the war to become a Socialist Member of Parliament for Woolwich West. He was a stalwart of our production team. Then, in contrast, on the other side of Tenby, was a camp for male refugees from Hitler's occupied Europe. I visited these men and what a strange image they presented – I remember a long line of them digging a

ditch. I was introduced; they looking up from the ditch, me on
the grass above. I remember the quizzical smiles on their faces.
I was looking at a line of remarkably intelligent men: doctors,
lawyers, artists and academics. They were mostly Jews: when
they learnt that I needed help to put on such a play there was
no shortage of volunteers.

Evelyn Ward, my sometime English literature mistress also
appeared in the play and we performed it at the De Valence
Gardens, Tenby, for some wartime charity. It was a success,
playing to full houses. One other important thing I remember
about that production was writing to Charles Fox Ltd to hire
the costumes; they sent everything in high order but refused to
submit a bill. I've never thanked them properly till now.

Before leaving my grandparents, to go to war, they said
that they wanted to give me a present to remember them by. I
considered this very carefully and asked them for a copy of
Adolf Hitler's *Mein Kampf*. At that time you could buy it in an
English translation and all of the proceeds went to the Red
Cross. I wanted the book so that I could try to understand
fully what the war was about. I submit that very few soldiers
understood anything except that a neurotic leader had easily
persuaded the German people to threaten us. It was generally
believed by the British people to be a simple matter of self-
defence. Of course, that was the simplistic truth. But I suffered
that unconventional hunger to know the deep historical *cause*.
I still suffer this hungry subjective hunger today; about many
issues. I was given *Mein Kampf* by Gran and Gramp. I had a
special leather jacket made for it and I carried that book everywhere with me. As a British soldier was I unique in this
respect?

I collected my uniform and air-crew kit, with thousands of
other young men, from a motor garage fifty yards south of
Lord's cricket ground. We were called cadets – air-crew under
training. We were billeted in those rather posh blocks of flats
to the west of Lords; I was in one of them in Hall Road. By
coincidence I joined the Royal Air Force on the same day as
the actor David Tomlinson and we were shoved into the same
'flight' together. David was entertainingly superior to everyone

else and perfectly tailored; he must have whipped his issued uniform down to Saville Row like lightning. On parade our terrifying bully of a Flight-Sergeant peered at young Tomlinson's shining boots: 'Been painting 'em?'

'No, Flight, but if you want to know how it's done, come to my room at about seven this evening.'

I heard him say it; these are the words in life that you never forget. I think I derived a reflected glory from David Tomlinson because we were both actors and he appeared to be fearless.

Close by, just off Baker Street, I had found a distant relative – Peggy Jeremy. She is a sensitive painter; I remember the flowers and greenery of her compositions. She is also a sensitive human being. I recall walking with her on misty evenings in the lamplight. It was a time that seemed unreal. Very little to hold on to. I also remember parading in a street in St John's Wood, early in the morning, and dozing off while at 'attention'. It was the preamble to a not distinguished military career.

We cadets were then sent to fields alongside the river just outside Ludlow in Shropshire. It was called a toughening-up course. We were packed tight in bell tents and there were cement-mixers to be handled and roads to be built, presumably to bring us romantic young warriors down to reality. But I immediately succumbed to cheating the system. I managed to escape from the physical labour and I would lie in the reeds of the river bank, reading. It was the same questionable characteristic that allowed me to work very hard at a good play but not to pay my dues on a bad one. Many years later I would play Shylock in Ludlow Castle for the Ludlow Festival and I promise you that no one under this sky could have worked harder than I did then.

One day while lying in our tent with the other innocents I pulled out my wallet and peered at the photographs of Florence Jefferies which I had always carried with me. Then, on impulse, I handed them round.

'For you. For you.'

Suddenly one of the young airmen said: 'That is the lowest bloody act I have ever witnessed.'

For me it was a reflection of those nihilistic times.

Before leaving Ludlow I gallantly offered to carry a large tin of boiling water for a NAAFI (military catering) lady and some of it slopped over my left hand and scalded me; badly enough for it to be bandaged and my arm placed in a sling. And thus wounded I was posted to an Initial Training Wing at Stratford-upon-Avon. That was a pleasant bit of luck.

I was now billeted in the Shakespeare Hotel and my room was named 'The Merry Wives of Windsor'. Of course the Shakespeare industry on which that town mainly subsists was in abeyance because of the war and so instead of culture seekers there were many of us cadets studying the rudiments of air warfare.

I think that it was on Friday evenings that a Cadets' Ball was held in the Conference Hall, attached to the theatre. I went reluctantly, still with my arm in a sling, and it was there that I met the young woman who was to become my first wife and the mother of my eldest son, David. Her name was Joan Stock and she was visiting her home in Stratford during her summer vacation. She was a student reading mathematics at London University which for wartime reasons was located at Oxford. Joan was sitting on some stairs and I introduced myself. Soon I had met her mother, father, sister and her sister's husband, George Mills, who was already a distinguished airgunner in the Royal Air Force. George was the genuine article. He was the famous 'Pickard's' rear gunner in the Wellington bomber 'F for Freddie'. The Royal Air Force film unit made a documentary about that aircraft. The memory of George Mills has always moved me very much. He was a singularly quiet man. Handsome. Self-effacing. He came from Staffordshire, I think. From a working-class background like myself. He was a good husband. He must have been invaluable when the going was rough high over Europe. One day I was sitting with him in front of a coal fire and minute sparks were shooting up the soot into the chimney. George said, more to himself than to me: 'That looks exactly like flak.'

I don't think he ever mentioned to me his time in the air except with that one remark. And I never asked him anything.

Those young men weathered such terror night after night that one sensed that it would be a dangerous intrusion to say or ask anything. I remember many years later rebuking Dudley Moore for a *Beyond the Fringe* satirical sketch about a British war-time air crew. Of course films, not the young men themselves, had made a cliché of the subject. Dudley Moore very carefully discussed with me the ethics of my argument. George Mills was, I think, the only member of F for Freddie to survive the war and shortly after peace came he died of cancer. His wife never recovered completely from her outrageous loss.

While at Stratford-upon-Avon we were given a half day for sports and it was discovered that I had developed a talent for running abnormally fast. And because I was Welsh and had played a bit I was allocated to rugby football; scrum-half. Well, that game was all very fine until I got physically caught. This happened so many times that I was being steadily annihilated, and so I talked to our rugby captain, who was also a friend of mine, and I immediately put in for golf as my athletic speciality.

Now the truth is I was already marked in our flight at Stratford as a troublemaker. My misdemeanours were of a very minor nature. One example was that when, as part of our training, I had to command the entire squadron in the forecourt of the Shakespeare Theatre, and I impersonated our famous commanding officer, the renowned cricketer and golfer, Leonard Crawley. I was duly placed on a charge. Indeed I held the record for charges at that time. With the curious jargon of those days I was called 'Kitty the Janker King' and as I used to leave the Shakespeare Hotel, evening after evening in full kit, bound for the guardroom, some of my comrades would lean out of their Elizabethan windows and give me a cheer. But this rugby business turned out to be much more serious. There was a theory that rugby players made the best fighter pilots and also that established, aggressive sportsmen were the best chaps to have around for the supervising of aircrew. That is why we had Crawley; air-crew training establishments were apparently invariably commanded by distinguished athletes. And so, in avoiding rugby I had perpetrated the unforgivable. My flight-commander suspected the truth: 'You're in real trouble this time, Griffith! *I'm* putting you on a charge – personally.'

It was well-known that if your flight-commander put you on a charge you were automatically removed from training for air-crew. I was marched for the umpteenth time before Squadron-Leader Crawley. Hat whipped off. I received the impression that our Commanding Officer was a bit hang-dog. He cast a bleary eye over the charge sheet: 'Well, Griffith, you've done it this time! Mr (So-and-so) has had to put you on a charge himself. "Deliberately avoiding rugger!"'

That was the death sentence.

'You leave me no alternative but to throw you out. Have you anything to say?'

I stood there feeling desperate and dreary. And then I was inspired. I knew that the Squadron-Leader had been a Ryder Cup performer. I replied: 'Well, sir, I'm so *keen* on golf.'

I can only relay to you, dear reader, the true impression that I am left with after all of these hard years; it seemed that Mr Crawley's ginger moustache lifted; certainly his head did.

'What's—'

And I felt that he was poised to enquire about my handicap. Instead he mumbled: 'Well, don't see me again – and a – reprimand. Dismissed!'

My flight commander was understandably annoyed but I was allowed to practise golf at Stratford's excellent club. I had many a happy cup of tea with the fine lady who ran the place in those days; as well as a few holes of inefficient golf. This is not a proud war record.

However, the RAF was not finished with my ability to run fast. I was suddenly informed, without prior parley, that I had been selected to represent the Stratford-upon-Avon Initial Training Wing at some sports meeting at the White City Stadium in London. The distance to be run was called 'the four forty'. There was even mild excitement amongst my chums. Now, at the Greenhill Grammar School in Tenby, we certainly had a Sports Day but I have no recollection of stop-watches and recorded times. And somehow I am always loath to ask questions unless I desperately want to know the answer. I and a few supporters travelled to London and I was awed by the vast size of the arena. But I was used to audiences – though of a different temperament – and of course only when I was a practical master of histrionics. I wore an undervest, a pair of khaki shorts and gym shoes. Someone told me that 'the four forty' was next; I was guided out onto the track. The other athletes were already limbering-up: jogging on one spot and silently self-contained. They wore professional gear: spiked shoes – that sort of thing. I began to sense that I was in the midst of world-class. I was!

I uneasily edged up to one of the confident young men: 'Excuse me, but how far is the four forty?'

His reply was: 'Oh, piss off!'

'No,' I said, 'I really don't know.'

The young man looked at me from head to gym shoes:

'One and a half times round.'

'One and a half times round?'

'Thanks. I suppose you must go fast?'

'Very fast!'

'Thanks.'

The starting gun was fired and I shot off for the 'hundred yards'. I could hear the shouts and the unbelieving cheers. I had disrupted the calculations of some of Britain's star athletes. No one had ever witnessed the like before; that is in 'the four forty'. I led for two-thirds of the carefully measured course. Then my heart was banging and I began to hear the fast padding of feet behind me. I was still leading three-quarters of the way round when I fell on my face but – let it be understood – with my head pointing towards the tapes! I was pulled out of the way and was given mild medical attention. The whole escapade improved my popularity with the lads.

Of course, I was no more talented at receiving a Royal Air Force education than I had been at school. I lagged behind distressingly and in the RAF there was no leavening of English literature from Evelyn Ward or history from Wilfred Harrison. I remember sitting with a small group of my young comrades in the Shakespeare Hotel while they discussed my aeriel prospects pessimistically. Suddenly one of them, who was a farmer's son and who had a pronounced rustic accent, spoke up for me: 'Well, you've got to give Kitty (myself) credit; he's the only one of us to get his feet under the table!'

He was referring to my romance with Joan Stock and the fact that I was receiving some home cooking.

When the three-month course was over we suffered the ritual of celebration. This, by short tradition (the war had not been progressing for very long) involved some barbarity. The great physical achievement was to remove the heavy (life size?) statue of Lady Macbeth from her plinth on the Shakespeare Memorial and successfully charge her into the Avon River, from which she was fished out regularly by the local authorities. This was possibly an escapade by the descendants of Henry the Fifth's soldiers that Shakespeare would have happily approved of; not so, however, the Dogberrys of Stratford. On our night of celebration, not only were the local police force hiding in the bushes in front of the Memorial Theatre, but the military police to boot. My flight (an air-force military unit), led by my rugby friend, removed Lady Macbeth – and immediately the military and civil arms of the law attacked. Onward towards the River Avon swept the fighting youth of Britain: they 'pressed on regardless'. Bodies sprawled on the well-clipped lawns and finally, like an aeriel explosion on Berlin, Lady Macbeth splashed and disappeared into the Avon, no doubt disturbing the famous swans. My friend fought a noble rearguard action as the boys withdrew but finally he was overpowered and removed to the local gaol. It was no light matter; constabulary helmets had hit the turf.

Was it in Stratford's ancient town hall that Wing-Commander Leonard Crawley elected to lead the defence in person and stirringly pointed out that the survival of Britannia Herself depended on such a fighting soul and woe betide us all in Britain if we discouraged such a determined spirit? Dogberry and company were nonplussed at the Wing-Commander's irrefutable logic, but they miserably protected their domestic pride by thinly fining my chum and no further action was taken. We cadets had a whip-round and we paid up for the hero; I suspect that Wing-Commander Crawley led with a donation.

Again, unaccountably, I passed the examination and eventually found myself sitting in a vast cinema auditorium with thousands of other cadets listening to our selected fate read by a succession of officers from the stage: so-and-so: navigation; so-and-so: air-gunner; so-and-so: pilot; so-and-so: air-gunner. Then, after several hours, Griffith, Kenneth: pilot. So it was deemed.

I was posted to a small flying field on the edge of Leicester. It was owned by an air components firm named Reid and Sigrist. For the very first time in my life I flew, sitting behind a Royal Air Force instructor in a Tiger Moth aircraft. What a novelty! I can't claim that I *enjoyed* it. Aerobatics were pretty uneasy stuff. Eighteen years of ground orientation was firmly up the spout. Sometimes I felt queasy. At the end of a total of eight hours of flying in my entire life (I have just finished twelve hours flying from Johannesburg to London as a passenger!) my instructor inexplicably climbed out of his cockpit, leaving me alone in the little aircraft. It was drizzling a misty rain. He moved round towards me and spoke the incredible words: 'I think you can take her up yourself now.'

The *novelty* hadn't worn off! I swallowed my shock and said, 'Yes, sir.'

And then he fumbled inside his flying jacket and pulled out a printed form and a pen.

'Sign there,' he suggested and I duly signed, presuming that the form stated that I was risking my life of my own free will. Then my instructor peered around him through this misty rain and said, 'Visibility is a bit bad. There's the CO preparing to take off; I'll have a word with him.' And off he trotted towards another aircraft that was warming-up.

Back he came, slightly breathless: 'Yes, the CO says follow him up to a thousand feet so you won't lose sight of the field. Then do one circuit and land.'

'Yes, sir,' I replied.

Off went the CO and I revved up, did whatever was necessary and moved after him. As I pulled the stick back and eased off Mother Earth the Tiger Moth began to do something that it had not done with me before. It began to yaw strongly to the right, pointing itself directly at the obstruction of large aircraft hangars. I heaved heavily on the rudder bar with my left foot and the Tiger Moth began to ease round onto a more reasonable course. Such is the debate over death and life. Up I went a thousand feet and I began my rectangular circuit of the flying field. I felt like John Wayne – or what John Wayne pretended to be. In I came to land. I knew that I was the *first* out of those fifty young Braves of my flight to solo. In I came perfectly. Down I put the Tiger Moth; an immaculate three-point landing. And then it happened again: a formidable yaw to the right and slowly the aircraft turned to the right and I came to a halt pointing in the opposite direction to the one that should have been. Up ran my instructor, quite excited: 'I *knew* you could do it! Well done!'

He made no remark about my pointing in the wrong direction; one of *his* pupils had been the first to go up alone!

'Sir,' I said, 'the aircraft behaved as it had never behaved before. It pulled to the right both on take-off and on landing.'

'Of course,' he replied. 'It was much lighter; I wasn't in it.'

'I hope you'll forgive me for asking this, sir, but why didn't you warn me?'

He didn't seem impressed by the gravity of that lethal question.

In those days the skies of Britain were packed with aircraft. Alone above Leicester an enormous bomber was at me and as it roared past I was tossed aside by its slip-stream like a feather. What the hell was I doing up there in that sort of predicament? But what were a hell of a lot more boys doing in far worse . . .? And in spite of *Mein Kampf* we didn't really know about the concentration camps.

SIX

We were packed off to Heaton Park, Manchester, and then shipped to Canada – where the skies were emptier – for completion of our training. We sailed on a ship which had been named *The Empress of Japan* but was currently – and understandably – now called *The Empress of Scotland*. The ship was bursting with men and she hit very heavy weather. The conditions became appalling; even most of the crew were visibly sick. The few men who were still on their feet were recruited to drag others off the wet pounding deck at night. There was only one verified suicide. For some reason our ship docked in New York and we were allowed to flood out over the harbours. I remember a vast pack of us pulsating into a great drinking place and an American standing on the bar shouting: 'Everything we have is free for the British!' An airman friend next to me whose name was Eagle consumed seven hard boiled eggs. It was true that we hadn't seen many eggs in a long while. I remember, America!

Up by train to Moncton in the Maritimes of Canada, which was a vast holding depot, and from which place it was planned to disperse us to the various Advanced Schools which were part of the Empire Air Training Scheme. Moncton holding depot was built on a swamp; mosquitos moved about the place in clouds. Soon there were incredible epidemics of diphtheria, scarlet fever and measles. We were paraded in hangars and, stripped to the waist, were inspected by teams of medical officers. Down the serried ranks they would walk pointing their fingers: 'Scarlet fever, scarlet fever, measles . . .' and so on.

I escaped that fate and was posted to Fort William/Port

Arthur on the western shore of Lake Superior. It was a Royal
Canadian Air Force establishment; I was the only Limey on
the place. There were certain advantages in being with the
Canadians, like first-class food. I remember being astounded
at milk, orange juice and tomato juice on-tap – free! But there
were disadvantages; if I had once been an outsider in British
society, now I was tantamount to being a Martian. The out-
ward differences were matters like my reading reasonably
serious literature and in contrast the incredible fact that on
Fridays, as soon as we were paid, every Canadian I knew hurried to the mess and began to feverishly gamble, till one was
rich and the rest poor. I remember loitering on the perimeter
and feeling uneasy and insecure.

I had been given an introduction – a letter – to a woman in
New York City and when my first leave came up I telephoned
her and prepared to hitchhike the several thousand miles. A
Canadian Flight-Sergeant who was sympathetic warned me
that the journey was impossible. That the first two hundred
miles was down the Gun Flint Trail, that snow was still falling;
that no one else would traverse it except maybe Algonquin
Indians who were fishing in the Great Lake, and perhaps I
would encounter a grizzly bear. Well, with a small side-pack
supported over my shoulder, I began to walk southward. I can
still see the blue haze around the mountains – the blue
reminded me of cockle juice – the fir trees and flecks of snow
falling. I felt exhilarated with a space of prepared freedom
ahead of me and a mysterious objective: a well-to-do woman
in New York.

I was lucky. After I had walked some miles, a truck trun-
dled behind me; it was driven by an Indian who was collecting
fish from the Algonquins and he would take me all the distance to Duluth in Minnesota. I remember stopping at an
Indian's cabin and being shown a pile of enormous salmon in
a box outside; still frozen by the natural climate. The
Algonquins ate them through the winter; I think that it was
then very early spring.

Next day I was picked up by a lawyer whose name was Art
Eliasson. He had been visited by a woman client whose

husband was in some serious trouble in Duluth City and Mr Eliasson arranged for the caring wife to drive me southward in her very battered car. The lady was a little battered herself; middle-aged and blonde and as we clattered into a short evening it became intensely cold. Our discomfort became serious when the engine of the car stopped and the truth is that the large-bosomed lady and I clung to each other as ice began to thinly encase the car. But it was essentially a platonic union.

My blonde and now intimately related friend insisted that she took me straight to her home and cooked me a meal. It was a poverty house and there her husband, though clearly hard-pressed, was also warm-hearted towards me. I left them both, with feelings that I hope I have made clear here, after all of these many, many years.

When I eventually arrived in the centre of Duluth I realized that I was inevitably a celebrity, because of my Royal Air Force uniform with the shoulder flashes proclaiming Great Britain. America seemed to be suffering from a guilty conscience which President Roosevelt was doing everything he could to rectify. It seemed that every day the American newspaper headlines proclaimed the lonely nobility of the British, particularly represented by the RAF – 'Forty Wellington Bombers Over Europe; Twenty-Three Return'. And there was I in that blue uniform with 'Great Britain' on my shoulders . Gary Cooper couldn't have been more popular. I asked the delighted Americans where the Young Men's Christian Association was. The housekeeper of that establishment explained to me that it was full but would I mind sharing a room with someone? I happily agreed. Word of my presence raced across Duluth; amongst those who called on me was an American naval officer named Nelson. He addressed me with staccato respect: 'I'm proud to meet you, Mr Griffith. Tomorrow a unique event is taking place. We have just completed five Liberty Ships on the same day and the Dionne Quintuplets are coming down from Canada to launch them. It would be a great honour for the United States Navy if you would enter the arena with us. Oh, and tonight there is going to be a reception and ball, hosted by the American Legion.

We'd all like you to attend. I would collect you here at 7 pm.'

'Thank you, Mr Nelson!'

I took the whole wonderful fuss in my stride. Commander Nelson called for me on the tick in dress naval gear and I was as polished as I could manage. We drove to what appeared to be a pillared town hall. There were the lights and distant music. American Legionnaires hurried out to greet us and I was very warmly escorted into the foyer. Through great doors I could sense the fast tempo of a big dance band. And then an awful thing happened: the doors were swung open on a cue, I was urged through them, spot lights illuminated me, the entire band stopped playing, stood up and began a popular number titled 'Coming In On a Wing And a Prayer'. I froze as I had never frozen before – or since. My confident stride was gone. I stood there shocked and all I could think of was dear George Mills stuck in the tail turret of his Wellington as it rattled through the bloody night skies over Europe. I could only move when I forced on my brain: 'These kind Americans really mean George; never me!'

After that it was a good generous American evening. As I entered my room in the YMCA I noted the dark tousled hair of my room-mate. When I awoke in the morning the hair had not, apparently, moved. I prepared myself carefully for the five Liberty Ships and for the five Canadian sisters and for Commander Nelson and the United States Navy. I was well pleased as I looked at my reflection in the full-length mirror. At that moment the hair stirred and there was a face having its eyes rubbed. It peered uncomprehendingly at me: 'What you, Bub? The bell-boy?'

I put on my best English accent (English is best when one wishes to be haughty): 'No, I'm a member of the British Royal Air Force!'

'Oh . . .'

In we marched; me and the American Navy. There was a vast concourse of seated people. Suddenly the military band struck up – quite distinctly – 'God Save the King'; I sprang to my feet at rigid patriotic attention. But it wasn't 'God Save the King'; I was the only person out of those many thousands who was ceremoniously upright. The Americans, for some reason, use the tune of our national anthem for one of their own purposes. That's all I remember about the launching of the ships.

On to New York. There were many adventures along that colourfully varied journey. I saw my very first fireflies dancing over a meadow in the twilight. Magical. And there was a man who drove forty miles out of his planned route to try to persuade me that the Russians were not to be trusted. He became desperate that I should agree with him. All I could say was: 'What the hell would Britain do without the Russians?'

Finally I arrived at the lady's apartment in the middle of a New York black-out rehearsal. I was warmly hustled into a luxurious room. How strange it was talking in the dark; then she lit a candelabra and I discovered that my hostess was disturbingly blonde and voluptuous. It turned out that she had been one of Samuel Goldwyn's showgirls. She gave me presents including a radio and she took me out to restaurants and strange night-clubs. She was astonishingly kind to me. But no more on that subject except that I remember her very clearly.

Of course, my journey back to Fort William in Canada was also adventurous. Bear in mind my evocative uniform. I headed for the Appalachian Mountains and decided to go over the tops of them (genuine hill-billy country) instead of through them via tunnels. The country was strange and beautiful and the adventure exhilarated me. I heard the twang of a guitar and a melancholy voice. There they were on a veranda outside a wooden shack and the entire family seemed to be happily drunk. The Daddy staggered to his feet and peered at me: 'Who are you? The postman?'

I was invited to join them and share their refreshment.

'No,' I gently explained, 'I am a teetotaller.'

This fact never sank in. I was a mystery that passed by, never to return. But I stayed long enough in their friendly company to remember one of their songs. The first line went: 'Where are you going to, my old man?'

During my sojourn in Canada I made one other expedition

into the United States of America. I was given two weeks' leave and I became struck with a determination – not to visit my New York woman friend – but to search for my American 'cousins'. I could recall very little: simply my paternal grand-mother, Emily, speaking of John Ellis, living at a place named Glen Falls. Also there were a few details that hung on from my childhood's memory – that John Ellis had married a local girl when they were both about twenty-one years old and that then they had departed for the Pennsylvania coalfields; he as a Presbyterian minister. And if they were still alive they would be about eighty years old! But once 'bitten' with an idea I cannot easily stop.

I went into the Royal Canadian Air Force duty office and asked a helpful sergeant where Glen Falls was. He looked into a gazetteer and asked me which of the three Glen Falls in the United States did I want? Like lightning I replied: 'Which is the biggest?'

'North of New York State. Close to Albany.'

'Thank you, sergeant!'

And off I trekked once again, begging for transport across America. Again the journey was inevitably eventful but it must suffice – as far as this book goes – that I arrived in Albany of a pleasant evening. I found a centre for American soldiers and there proceeded to wash myself and shave. As I was complet-ing these ablutions a man rushed in: 'Are you really a member of the British Royal Air Force?'

'Yes, sir.'

'In five minutes I am interviewing American servicemen on the radio – coast to coast – across the States! I want you to join in!'

I was hustled onto a stage and put near the head of a queue of interviewees. Came my turn and I was given an emotional introduction.

'What did you do before you joined the Royal Air Force, Mr Griffith?'

'I was an actor.'

'An actor!!'

'Yes, sir.'

'That is why you are so relaxed in front of a microphone! Here – *you* conduct the interviews!'

It was American showbiz at its freest and best. I quietly conducted the rest of the interviews, which delighted everybody.

I travelled to Glen Falls by a local train. Very early in the morning I walked through leaf-laden streets; it must have been summer and it was very pretty. The first human life I saw was in a newsagent's shop. Now you, dear reader, will assess for yourself the unlikelihood of my achieving a successful search. Was this the correct Glen Falls? Had they moved elsewhere during the many intervening years? Were the very old people still alive? The newsagent was cutting open bales of newspapers.

'Excuse me, sir, but I am searching for my American relatives. I have hitchhiked from Canada. I am from Britain. Their names are the Reverend and Mrs John Ellis.'

The newsagent stared at me as he stood upright: 'You've come to the right place, son. They're here!'

Without reference he wrote out their address.

I walked down the street of pleasant white colonial-style houses and I rang the doorbell. And again. And again. A next-door neighbour appeared, and overcoming her surprise at my strange uniform, said: 'Yes, young man, what do you want?'

I told her the tale.

'Oh, my! They're away! Visiting their son, John, at Trenton. It is their Diamond Wedding Anniversary!'

'Where is Trenton, madam?'

'Oh a long way away. In the State of New Jersey'

And I knew that I was beaten; I had used up almost half of my two weeks leave in getting to Glen Falls. Then the good neighbour cheered both of us up: 'But one of their daughters lives close by. Come in and have some breakfast!'

The daughter of the Ellises was married to a builder and on my arrival in their house for the first time, I began to realize how important I was to them. I was their only direct contact with their roots since the old people had left Wales so long before. I was the object of warm and generous excitement.

And then, quickly, a strange element appeared in their conversation; they did not refer very much to the Reverend and Mrs Ellis but to the vital need to inform their son, John Ellis Junior (whom the old couple were visiting), of my arrival.

'You must speak to Cousin John right away.'

I thought that this attitude was very odd. They called Trenton and reverentially handed me the telephone: 'It's your cousin John.'

Immediately a remarkably controlled and intelligent voice began to speak: 'Kenneth, first – it is very good of you to have travelled so far to visit Mother and Father. Now it is imperative that you see them. And we are all gathered together here for their Anniversary. Now, at (such and such a time) you will take the local train to Albany and at (such and such a time) you will then board what we call a Greyhound Coach and travel in it to the Dixie Hotel in New York . . .'

And at this point I was compelled to interrupt the quietly authoritative voice: 'Please excuse me, Cousin John, but I can't do this because I only have two weeks leave and I have already taken up one of those weeks. And we are at war – I would be in very serious trouble . . .

'Now listen to me carefully, Kenneth, and please stop worrying about such matters. Rest assured that as soon as I have finished giving you your instructions I will telephone your British Ambassador and ask him to make arrangements for you to have extended leave. He is a good friend of mine. Now, from the Dixie Hotel you take what we call the Shuttle Service to Grand Central Station and at (such and such a time) you will catch a train to Trenton Station and outside you will find a large black limousine with me standing by it. Is all of that clear, Kenneth?'

I was mesmerized: 'Yes, Cousin John.'

'We are all looking forward to seeing you.'

One of the remarkable facts about John Ellis's instructions to me was his memory of the timetables; there had been no pause to make visual reference.

The journey went according to Cousin John's instructions – to the minute and that was reassuring. In due course I emerged from Trenton Station and looked about me and I suffered my first set-back: there was not the hint of a large black limousine. For some time I stood there, the subject of passing curiosity and I was beginning to feel neurotic.

A large policeman ambled towards me. He looked at my shoulder flashes: 'I see you're from the Old Country.'

'Yes, officer.'

'What are you doing here?'

'I'm waiting for my American cousin.'

'Did he say he'd meet you here?'

'Yes, sir.'

'Where does he live?'

Now this is strange but I didn't know exactly. Everything had been so pat and firm.

'I think, officer, he lives at the Trenton State Hospital.'

'Is he a doctor?'

'I don't know; I don't think so.'

'Is he a patient?'

I looked at the policeman uneasily: 'I don't think so . . .'

Long uncomfortable pause.

'What's his name, son?'

'John Ellis.'

The policeman changed his bearing; certainly he grew in height: 'You don't mean *Commissioner* John Ellis?'

'I don't know.' The only commissioners I knew of stood outside cinemas and hotels.

'Yes,' continued the policeman, 'it must be him! I believe his residence is within the grounds of Trenton State Hospital. Of course I've never met him; I've seen him from a distance. And photographs. And his name on many documents.'

From that time I was *guarded*. And then there *was* a black limousine, like a battleship. The kind policeman touched my arm deferentially.

I hastened to the well-tailored handsome man who was at the wheel: 'No, Mr Griffith, your relatives are in the back getting out.' It was the chauffeur.

My cousin John was standing on the pavement, a substantial man in his late forties and smiling; he shook my hand: 'It's very good for us to see you. Here is my father, your great-uncle who came from your home in Wales.'

Great-uncle was a small, compact, dynamic old man with thick-lensed glasses. Alan Paton still reminds me of him. The old gentleman gripped my arm very tight indeed as he said: 'Hello son; yes it's very pleasant to see you!'

Into the back of the car I went between my two relatives. My great-uncle never released his physical grip on me and now I realized that I was a very special visitor indeed. I wondered to myself: 'Why have they never even visited Wales?'

We passed through large iron gates and Cousin John said: 'This is my garden, Kenneth; I'm very proud of it. In it is every type of tree that is known to grow in the United States of America.'

We arrived at the house, which had broad wooden steps leading to the entrance. In front of the house was an open space and there were, already waiting, the celebrating family. As I stepped out of the car a very pretty old lady caught hold of my other arm and this was my great-aunt. Apart from her pretty appearance I next focused on a brooch that she was wearing on her bosom; it was the British Royal Coat of Arms.

I have an image of a servant handing Cousin John a carving set at the head of the long family table and my relative saying: 'What a pity you couldn't have got here by yesterday, Kenneth. We've had a fellow countryman of yours, William Beveridge, staying with us. He's been here with me discussing some social scheme that he has in mind for Britain.'

I had peered at the many photographs on the walls, of Cousin John with President Roosevelt. Mrs Roosevelt visited now and again. I felt confident that the British Ambassador had extended my leave.

As I was preparing to go to bed that first evening my Great-uncle John gave me some orders for the morning: 'Son, I want you breakfasted, dressed and ready to go out with me by 9 am sharp. I've got something to show you!'

'Yes, Great-uncle,'

I was ready on time and he was already waiting – impatiently: 'Come on, son!'

And the near blind piece of dynamism hurried down the steps to one of those big, black, chauffeur-driven shiny cars: 'Get in, son!'

And we were driven off without more ado; just the two of us.

'Where are we going, Great-uncle?'

'Wait and see, son!'

I remember the New Jersey countryside being very flat and it was a grey rather dismal day. I was bewildered. Finally we stopped in the middle of the country by the side of a river. There was nothing interesting to see.

'Out you get!'

He led me to a muddy place where cattle might have been drinking.

'Why are we here, uncle?'

'Do you know where this is, son?'

'No.'

'This is the Delaware River; this is exactly where George Washington crossed it. This is where we beat you, son! Right, back in the car; home we go!'

I can only ask you to believe that this is what happened and what was said by my great-uncle, John Ellis, all those years ago. He was born where I was born and though I never discussed it with him it was his astonishingly stylish way of saying to me: 'Make no mistake: I'm an American!'

His son, Cousin John, talked to me about his parents. His father was well known as a Free Thinker and had been a friend of President Theodore Roosevelt; whereas his mother, who wore the British Royal Coat of Arms, was obviously a royalist. My cousin told me that the entire family had to be very careful what they said to her on this sensitive subject. And when the Edward the Eighth scandal was at its lurid height, in America, he, her son, at dinner one evening, felt that he could dare to mention it: 'Now, Mother, what do you think of your British Royal Family?'

Her answer was simple: 'Well, John, you know I've never had *any* faith in the American press.'

And that was the last word permitted on the subject.

My cousin was Commissioner for Institutes: prisons, state hospitals, etc. He took me with him on several official journeys. The principal of one vast hospital, a Southerner, asked me, in private, if I knew much about John Ellis Junior.

'In this country such a person's fortune depends on whether he is a Democrat or a Republican; your cousin is an exception. I know of no one who *knows* which party he supports. Perhaps neither more than the other. He stays in his job whoever is in power. He is an outstanding American.'

I recall outside of the main doors of the hospital a bust of Elizabeth Fry. My other unforgettable memory of those institutional jaunts is of playing baseball when I was informed that all the other members of the two teams – except me – were convicted 'homicidal maniacs'. Perhaps there were a few male nurses sprinkled amongst us – but nobody told me.

I travelled back to Canada on this second occasion by a new route: straight up the Hudson River Road northward. I was told that it was the Millionaires' Highway; certainly the cars were too big and fast to see me and stop. I walked many miles; finally an old car – a jalopy – stopped. It was driven by an elderly Black man who, a shade apologetically, offered me a lift. He drove me to the outskirts of a small town named Ossining where he told me the prison Sing Sing was located. I said goodbye to my friend and then sat down on the plinth of what I thought was a war-memorial. Several local people passed by and looked at me in my strange uniform and I noticed that some smiled. Then a group stopped and a man asked: 'How are you?'

'Fine, sir,' and then I followed his smile which was behind my head and there I read the legend which I can only paraphrase from memory: 'At this place in the year 1776 (?) the following American Patriots apprehended the Head of British Intelligence in this area, Major André, who was duly executed.' Words to that effect. I stood up in my British uniform.

'Do you think that I am the first Britisher in uniform to have stood on this spot since that time?'

'Very likely,' and then he added, 'but you're quite safe this time!'

When I got back to the Canadians at Fort William I began my training again but I was not feeling well and reported myself sick; it was quickly diagnosed as scarlet fever and I was ambulanced to a small hospital above the lake. Indeed it was so small that I was the only patient and there was only one nursing sister in charge plus a maid.

Someone heard I was there and the first salmon that was caught out of Lake Superior after the winter ice broke was delivered to me and the sister at the hospital. My month or so of medical isolation ended and the ambulance returned. I was paraded before the Canadian medical officer who had made me feel that he thought that all Limeys were soft: 'How are you feeling?'

I gave the obligatory reply: 'Fine, sir.'

'Right. You're on flying in the morning!'

Up into the air I went and felt ill and came down again. Up I went again and I felt dreadful. The next day I tried again and now I was clearly ill. Alone in the aircraft I vomited. I believe that this is a rare occurrence; when one has critical technical operations to perform the concentration obliterates physical problems – as a rule. But I vomited. I felt very ill high above the ice and snow. My head seemed to be swelling and had the effect of my flying helmet cutting into it. Water from my eyes, rather than tears, ran down my face and was affecting my vision.

I manoeuvred the aircraft back to the flying field and in my difficulties lined it up to land. Now I must explain that I was in a specially adapted Tiger Moth: the cockpit was enclosed because of the low temperatures and in place of the usual wheels were skis so that we could land on the hard ice and snow. I began my approach and because of my impaired vision and with the glare of the snow I realized that I was going to overshoot the runway. Up again and around. Once more I was going to overshoot. Up again and around. And now I was feeling very shaky. I noticed below me that the ambulance and the fire-tender were mustering and I knew that I hadn't got the strength to go round once more; I felt that I was near to fainting. I determined to force the aircraft onto the ground with whatever runway I wasn't going to have. I felt no fear. I remember feeling curious as to what it would be like to disintegrate. I was interested. Just as I hit the ground I saw a most memorable sight; I saw a man I knew (he had a tassel fixed to the top of his flying helmet – I saw the tassel) – he was an American bush-pilot – actually bend down and hide his eyes in order not to see my apparent end. Well, I had a miraculous escape. Luck. Or the hand of God. I am an agnostic. I don't know . . .

I was taken to Toronto and then back to Moncton in New Brunswick where I was placed in a pretty hospital with good Canadian food. There, after some months, I learnt that my mates – some from as far back as Stratford-upon-Avon – had gone on to Burma and there they were dying fast. One boy, named Harry Arbon, who was a rustic from Cumberland, I think, went out once above the jungle and there met the Japanese Zero fighter aircraft and never returned. Harry was a sweet soul; totally unsophisticated, rather girlish actually. There could be little that was so monstrously incongruous. Anyway that is what I was *told* in that pretty little hospital; I never verified the story. But I also heard what happened to the others and I went into a physical decline. Finally my weight fell to below seven stone; which, of course, is danger list for a young man.

SEVEN

Well, I tell myself these days that I am a survivor. A little luck and a little native cunning. It looks as if I am going to grow old; as Harry Arbon and company did not grow old. I think that my astonishing physical decline had a lot to do with guilt. There was a period of one month – I think exactly thirty days – when I kept mentally afloat by composing a poem per day. Never before had I tried it and then for thirty consecutive days and then never again. I had thought a little about the structure of verse: iambic, trochaic, and so on. The pieces were very personal and all of them about those traumatic times. One statement went:

> They lightly presented their lives these boys
> To men who busied forms through day and day;
> To men who knew no end, no price to pay
> For schoolboy names on printed sheets of law.

I think that's how it went and that's all I can remember. Anyway, there were thirty of them and though they saved no one else's life, I think that they saved mine.

However, in that pretty military hospital there was an episode which demonstrated very briefly that even my physical strength was not entirely depleted. In the town of Moncton (didn't Lord Beaverbrook come from there?) a local family befriended me; they sat by the side of my bed. They asked me if there was anything I wanted.

'Some books to read, please?'

They soon brought along a selection of 'classic' novels, bound in fine leather. I read *The Last of the Mohicans*; it

seemed appropriate. Across from my bed was a poor chap
who had also been knocked about in some air turmoil.

'Can I read that?'

Handing it over, I warned him about the importance of the
aesthetic appreciation of a fine book. Remember that I was a
bed-confined skeletonic disaster who was giving the hospital
cause for worry. I awoke from a drowse and out of the corner
of an eye (the right one) I saw this damaged giant reading *The
Last of the Mohicans* while sucking an orange! I elevated out
of my bed and having grabbed the book I went for my com-
rade's throat. We were separated and I was forced back into
my bed. Perhaps it was the first clear sign that I would live.
The Maggs Family of Berkeley Square, London (in my opinion
the best bookshop in the world) will not be surprised to read
this story.

Lying in the grounds of this Moncton hospital I saw a four-
leafed clover. And another and another; soon I had about a
dozen. Another casualty who was with me began to search
and he found nothing. Both of us were disturbed by the
curious event – in our different ways.

I remember the wonderful sight of the Canadian autumn –
or the fall as they call it – in the Maritimes (the eastern
seaboard). As far as I could see there was nothing on the earth
except brilliant crimson and scarlet of the passing maple leaf,
interspersed by columns of pure silver from the birch. I wrote
a letter to my friend Joan, back in Stratford-upon-Avon, on
that unsullied bark.

I recall nothing of being transported, after many months in
Moncton, to New York for shipment to Britain. The bedrid-
den were put into F Deck of the *Queen Mary*; that is in the
very bottom of the ship. It was a curious experience. We lay
there in cots; the only illumination came from blue lights – it
was decidedly sinister. And, as throughout the rest of that
great ship, there came a continuous voice through a Tannoy
system from the bridge: 'You are now in the danger area!
Have your life-jackets with you.' I think that the voyage took
nine days as the *Queen Mary* ploughed north and south as
well as east to avoid the German U-boats. Of course we lads

on F Deck had little use for life-jackets. Why casualties were
allowed on the *Queen Mary* or why the broadcasting system
was not disconnected from our deep quarters I do not know.
Above us, so I was told, were thousands of American soldiers. Not that they would have stood much chance either in
that Atlantic Ocean if we had been sunk. Those passenger
liners, then troopships, relied on their speed and seafaring
cunning to avoid the German underwater sailors.

However, they were not *all* American soldiers. There suddenly appeared by my cot the boy who had lived next door to
Rhos Cottage when I was an infant, the son of Constable and
Mrs Griffiths, Dennis. He was also in the Royal Air Force, on
the technical side, I think, and mysteriously had learnt that I
was on the ship. How did he learn that? Dennis was quite
highly strung as I recall from his visits to me. He would regularly descend to me, his old friend, in a high state of tension.
Certainly F Deck was uneasy with the blue light and the pointless warnings from the bridge. Dennis was there as regular as
clockwork, but after the usual pleasantry: 'How are you, boy?'
he would articulate his extreme unease: 'I wouldn't like to be
sleeping down here boy! You know where I'm sleeping? On
the bloody deck! If anything happens to this lot, I'm off quick!
No, I wouldn't like to be sleeping down here . . .'

After several visits and a guaranteed repetition of Dennis's
Queen Mary philosophy, my fellow patients around me issued
an ultimatum: 'If you don't tell him to shut up, we will!'

I never did nor did they. Dennis was always my friend and
I would like very much to see him again. Every day he brought
me the *Queen Mary News*, a sheet published on the ship. On
one of these days he laid it on my chest and when there was a
pause in his chatter I picked the paper up. Then I noticed the
date: October the Twelfth!

'Dennis, it's my birthday!'

'Go on!'

'Dennis, I'm twenty-one years old today.'

What do you do with a man who is twenty-one years old and
is disappearing? The RAF put me into the 'air-crew stress

hospital' at Matlock in Derbyshire. Matlock was (I haven't been there since) a place of beautiful grey decay: lots of damp and ferns. And there, in one of the Victorian/ Edwardian 'hydros' they placed the young mental casualties of the air. I believe that in that hospital a number of experiments were initiated which involved various forms of shock treatment; rumour had it, within those walls, for the very first time. It was an extraordinarily free-wheeling place for a military establishment. I always had my own private room. Around me were young men suffering from what used to be described as shell-shock; they couldn't control their limbs – in particular. I drew close to a very intelligent and well-educated young man who had baled out of his fighter-aircraft and whose parachute had failed to open and who had surprisingly lived because he landed on a hayrick or tree or something deeply soft. The young man's thick hair was as white as could be. I listened to his dissertations about mysticism and about Bishop Berkley proving that a table wasn't really there. But my injured friend was a little intolerant of my lack of such metaphysical knowledge and definitely held himself above me. And in any case the hospital authorities, with their ears close to the ground, noted the direction of our interests and intervened. It was one of the rare occasions in that experimental hospital when they discouraged freedom of expression. Perhaps we were on the very edge of proving that neither of us existed . . . And that wouldn't do!

Every man was a volunteer for those medical experiments. I was asked if I would have a go at insulin. I suspect that in all departments (when I hark back to the results) we were given massive overdoses. I know that a container of glucose was fastened to my body and that I was clearly instructed that when I felt myself fainting after an injection of insulin that I must cram the sugar into my mouth with alacrity or the result might be fatal.

In that room I heard the most horrific true stories and yet I associate them with the laughter that prevailed. Except once. There was a young Scotsman whom we unimaginatively called Jock and he was an advanced case of shell-shock; he had little control over his movements. One evening in my room some-one asked Jock what had happened to him. Laughing, he told us that he had been a rear-gunner on a Walrus aircraft in the Pacific area. I believe that the Walrus was a small flying boat with a repeller (the 'prop' back to front). They were patrolling over the ocean when Japanese Zero aircraft attacked. The pilot took the little aircraft down to sea level in the hope of buzzing for base. The Japanese came at the pathetic target again and again. Jock continued to blaze back. He told us that as he sat there firing he could not understand why he was not dead. Suddenly he sensed that there was someone standing behind him as the Walrus sped just above the level of the sea. But no one could be there. Jock turned around and there was the pilot – away from his controls – and Jock, still rocking with laughter, told us that he began to speak: 'Don't lose your head, Jock! Don't lose your head!'

And Jock told us that 'the shit was running down the skip-per's leg'. The aircraft went into the sea and Jock was somehow picked up. Nobody was laughing at the end except Jock. The truth about murder broke through our protective illusions.

Everybody had his own nightmare; that was the brother-hood. A particular friend of mine was the son of a Covent Garden fruit and vegetable merchant. The father visited the hospital and he was an irrepressible cockney. When I told him that I had worked at The Strand (theatre) he would insist that I had sold newspapers outside it. His son was very like him except that he had suffered some awful trauma connected with a bomber raid on the German city of Mannheim. He was obsessed with Mannheim. My friend volunteered for electrical shock treatment. I visited him while he was confined during this period. All was quiet. And then he emerged supported by two young men. To me he had become an old man who had difficulty standing up. His obsession of terror against Mannheim was now totally reversed. Whatever had happened on that night raid he now described as a perfect event: a lovely night, an appropriate amount of cloud cover, no German night-fighters attacking and no flak. A successful, accurate

bombing mission and a peaceful landing in Old England. He
would relate this untruth to you *ad infinitum* with many disturbing details such as a photograph of his daughter wedged
in front of him by the side of his gun. I do not recall seeing a
more desperate argument put by a human being in all my life.
That is my last image of him and I hope that he recovered and
that I could embrace him.

I had to be weighed and such was my personal situation
that I was assisted onto the scales. I believe that it was the
matron who supervised this procedure and one day she
noticed that my eyes were focusing on my recorded weight. I
remember her extraordinary words: 'In future, Mr Griffith
will be weighed with his back to the scales!'

And so I was.

My gentle good friend Joan visited me at that hospital in
Matlock. I think she stayed in the town. All day she was freely
allowed in my room and she was my only outside support.

My psychiatrist (I presume that is what he was) reiterated
every day that all I had to do was to get strong again and that
then I could pick up my flying experience exactly where I had
left it. I believed this and consciously strove for that end.
And then came a Christmas when that psychiatrist went on
leave and a new one bounced in to see me: 'Well, what would
you now like to do with your life? It is within my power to
grant your wish: you can have any trade you choose in the
Royal Air Force – except air-crew – or you can go back into
civvy street. Which would you prefer?'

This was in my bedroom with me sitting up in bed.

'But, sir, I have been assured all of this long while that as
soon as I can walk out of here I can go back to flying!'

'I don't know who's been kidding who, but you and I know
that that is impossible. You have been too ill.'

I continued to remonstrate vehemently. The next day I told
him: 'If I can't return to flying I would like to return to civilian
life.'

And then the man said something which I have never fully
understood. He said: 'That's right, son; you get in before the
rats get in.'

I can't be sure, but I think that at that very time our soldiers were making the Sicily landings. Anyway I was in no position to remonstrate with that medical officer. It was one of the few occasions in my life when I have rejected a proper argument.

Not many weeks after that interesting discussion I had gained a great deal of weight and I was beginning to feel fit. Just short of nine stone (my pre-war weight) I walked out of Matlock unassisted back into civilian life. The answer to this phenomenon must be very plain. I learnt at that time about our human capacity to deceive ourselves deeply. And from that date I began to search for the truth about myself, as far as I could possibly perceive it. I travelled to Joan's home at Stratford-upon-Avon. Her good parents made me welcome.

EIGHT

I had learnt that my poor grandparents were having a very difficult time. And then a telegram arrived to inform me that Emily had died. I think that I was still in uniform when I went home. I declined to look at her corpse. I remember walking behind the coffin down the steep hill to Penally Church and daring to look at Ernest my grandfather. The near-indomitable man was being supported as he walked and was weeping. I tried to close my mind beyond that and I must confess I still do. In the church I wept convulsively. I have not wept like that since.

I returned to the theatre. My first job was to tour Britain as Heathcliff in Emily Brontë's *Wuthering Heights*. Catherine was played by a well-known actress, Miss Rene Ray. After some time a powerful actress, Miss Eileen Herlie, took her place and that did present me with a new problem. Miss Herlie was not a chit of a thing – by any imagining – and there was a scene, clearly inscribed, in which Heathcliff swept Catherine into his arms and bounded with her up the stairs. Impossible. And that sight was never seen. Nevertheless, Miss Herlie and I had a grand success. Though I was still around the nine stone mark, I was able to prove that the mind could over-rule the puny physical matter.

After months of touring and with the coming of cold weather my vulnerable constitution began to waver. I contracted bronchitis. Our theatrical company manager was from the very old school; his life had stretched back into Victorian theatre history. Initially he was a committed admirer of my histrionic ability. He said that I reminded him of Sir Martin Harvey. But as my illness gripped me he showed a sadism which I could not ignore. By this time two buckets were placed in both wings of the stage for me to vomit into. And the role of Heathcliff was arduous. I was near to collapse. The old theatre man said to me: 'If you miss one performance I'll see that you never work again!'

Of course the threat was ludicrous but I have never dismissed it. The truth is, apart from my association with Lord Bernard Miles, Mr Robin Midgley and, above everyone, Sir Tyrone Guthrie, I have never felt at ease in the British theatre. The tempering of self-indulgence by practical technicians in the cinema and television businesses has always been preferable for me.

The war was still being waged and we were to play at Ipswich in East Anglia. Arriving on the Sunday evening I headed for the theatre to install myself in my dressing-room. The place was throbbing with lights and life; an American show for their airmen was in progress. I passed through the stage door and found one of the theatrical heroes of my life, Mr James Cagney, leaning against my door surrounded by Americans. I longed to pay my respects but though smiling he looked tired. I confined myself to: 'Please excuse me, Mr Cagney.'

When I came out I noted that our stage carpenter was in animated conversation with the great Irish–American performer. I felt a small pang, but remembered that the carpenter had once been a performing member of *The Humming Birds* and that amongst his colleagues had been Mr Stanley Laurel and Sir Charles Chaplin. And I was compensated: I was allowed to stand at the side of the stage and watch James Cagney sing 'I'm a Yankee Doodle Dandy' and I watched his magnificent dancing. Let me hasten to underline – in view of my strictures on the British theatre – that I have generally doted on my fellow Thespians. It's the rest of them that I have reservations about.

We played Blackpool and I sent a telegram to Joan in Stratford-upon-Avon to the effect that if she could get there by the following Saturday morning (well before the matinée) we could get married. I had gone to see the local vicar who explained to me the law about banns being read but he added: 'If you're prepared to perjure *your* soul I'm prepared to perjure mine.'

Joan arrived and the kind man-of-God married us at Heysham Parish Church. His equally good wife had made us a wedding cake. I wore a new sports jacket and grey flannel trousers for the ceremony.

The curtain came down on the matinee and I repaired to my dressing-room; Joan was waiting there. A knock on the door and Tyrone Guthrie entered: 'How are you, dear boy? Excellent performance. I want you to move back to the Old Vic as soon as you can free yourself.'

I hadn't seen him since those days at Burnley and the Council for the Encouragement of Music and the Arts tour of Wales. I told the splendid man that he had brought us the best of all wedding presents. He also asked Miss Herlie to join the Vic.

Guthrie asked us both to go to the Playhouse at Liverpool where the Vic had set up a satellite company similar to the one that they would foster at Bristol. In the company was a stylish actor: D. A. Clarke-Smith, a youngish David Markham, and above all, Noel Willman, whom I soon began to understand as one of the cleverest creative actors that I would ever witness. I mean by 'creative' perhaps what is usually referred to as a 'character' actor. There are two distinct types of Thespians; indeed they are *so* different that they follow almost different professions. Perhaps ninety-five per cent of players (at a con-servative estimate) project their own personalities strongly into whatever character they accept to do. They go on refining this polished version of themselves all of their active lives and these players usually become the so-called stars. The public know them and they become old and often loved familiar friends. They range from Clark Gable to John Gielgud; indeed, as I have already mentioned, they comprise the vast majority of my profession. If any reader is demurring – and he or she would only demur about Gielgud (not Gable) – I would point out that Sir John in the many years that I have wit-nessed him has only given *one* attractive, highly modulated and strangulated performance. I believe that once upon a time

Gable was persuaded to play the Irish patriot Parnell, which necessitated sticking on a beard. I am certain that this valuable actor didn't attempt to *become* Parnell (apart from the beard) because he didn't have that strange metamorphic skill. But as far as the cinema public went the beard was more than enough; it almost finished his career. Never again! Of course Sir John has stuck on *many* beards, including a tragic one for *King Lear*, but I do submit that he carries the same basic mental state – or character – even if he is dressed as a Hell's Angel; of course then, the latter is very funny, because Sir John is a truthful and skilled performer. Therefore his performances are always finely timed and expertly presented. And he is not without a sense of humour.

In the other corner, however, is the creative or character actor who actually has the ability to move from his own established personality to become – to *change* into – whatever the author or indeed history has engraved. Noel Willman was a master of this art. Few players have achieved stardom through doing it – in America before the war, Paul Muni; and in Britain Alec Guinness and Peter Sellers. I believe that I belong to this special band of brothers. No! I know of no sisters; though perhaps Dame Peggy Ashcroft.

There are or have been a few fortunates who have had the choice to be either: Lord Olivier, Peter O'Toole and Fredric March notable amongst them. Understandably, they were too shrewd to turn their backs on stardom and therefore rarely failed to put their handsome faces to the fore – though regularly showing their inventive creative hands. Indeed, not so long ago Peter O'Toole played a character not unlike Errol Flynn in an excellent film called *My Favourite Year* and he hurtled the truth (as Errol): 'I'm not an actor! I'm a film star!'

Of course the great O'Toole knows the whole name of the game.

Our first play at the Vic, Liverpool, was Christopher Marlowe's *Doctor Faustus*. What a brilliant lad was Marlowe! What might he have done with the English language if some wasteful idiot hadn't run him through the vitals? Of course 'Kit' was always asking for it. I spoke the Chorus; Noel

Willman, Mephistopheles; and D. A. Clarke-Smith, Faustus. I remember after the dress rehearsal Noel Willman quietly complimenting me. Those are the words that count; from those that you would like to think are your peers. Of course Noel was remarkable; he always had such an intelligent depth of understanding: 'Think'st thou that I who saw the face of God am not tormented with ten thousand hells?'

Why did that performance alone fail to shoot Mr Willman to some theatrical immortality? I wasn't the only person to be present when he did it.

The next play was to be an adaptation by the distinguished actor, Nicholas Hannen, who was also in the cast, of Anthony Trollope's ecclesiastical novels; the play was called *Scandal at Barchester*. Noel Willman was directing and he asked me to play the ancient Bishop Proudie. I had one great adventure while acting in the play. Noel Willman had directed me so that I sat behind my enormous Bishop's desk throughout my scenes – with Mrs Proudie, the power behind the throne, looming over me. I never moved from that Bishop's chair in the planned production. But one evening someone on the stage 'dried' – forgot his or her lines – (to this day I don't know who it was). But they were a pretty cool lot of actors. I remember looking at suave D. A. Clarke-Smith and at David Markham and it was clear to me that they didn't intend to do a damned thing. They casually waited for a prompt. Nothing happened. I was the first to break as I realized that the young man 'on the book' was a dear delightful chap, but a blue-blooded English aristocrat and therefore not too conversant with the cruel realities of the theatre. So I rose to my feet and as I did so I realized that I had never even stood before as the very ancient Bishop. But I was embarked and I began to make my astonishing progress towards the prompt corner. I tell the *truth* as an actor and my Bishop's *mind* was extremely ancient. It took me a long time to disappear from the audience's sight. I recall that I broke the *savoir-faire* of Clarke-Smith and Markham. I can still see their astonishment and mouths agape as I grunted and groaned my way along the footlights. I grabbed the prompt book from the panicked young man (who is a knight!) with a 'Give me the fucking book!'

found the lost place and re-entering the arena said in the character of Bishop Proudie: 'As you were saying, Arch-Deacon—' and gave D. A. Clarke-Smith a verbal rope to hold onto. I don't recall any member of the cast so much as mentioning my act of heroism – or panic – for both qualities are much the same. And of course the audience noticed nothing – as usual.

But the changing times caught up with me when Mr Peter Grenville was appointed director of the company. It has never occurred to me to move tactically with fashion. I have only wished to organize my own very personal ideas as efficiently as I have been able to. It has always been my weak spot in one way and my strength in another. Anyway, Mr Glenville then belonged to the height of theatrical fashion. I think that he was close to 'Binkie' Beaumont who, in those days, ran the powerful Tennant (theatre) Organization. Certainly a new sheen was on the Liverpool Vic Company and I knew that I didn't belong.

The first play under the new regime was Henrik Ibsen's *John Gabriel Borkman*. Apart from my persona no longer having a niche I was slow in developing my role in *Borkman*. What with one thing and another, I presented Mr Glenville with a cue for my removal and out on my ear I went – in a quiet muffled style. But often disasters presage advancement. I was soon invited to play the young villain, Archie Fellowes, in a thriller written by a strange Tory Member of Parliament known as R. D. Smith. The play was called *The Shop at Sly Corner*. And almost at the same time Tyrone Guthrie was back at my side asking me to play in *Romeo and Juliet* for the Vic. Tyrone Guthrie always treated me with warm deference. He took me out somewhere and apologized that Romeo was already promised to another actor, would I consider Mercutio? Well, only a foolish player would prefer Romeo – but the commercial theatre called. The West End! It still meant special distinction in those days. And no doubt I was still stinging from Liverpool. Tony – as Tyrone was usually called – also mentioned that Alec Guinness was leaving the Vic for films and that his proposed roles could be mine. But explaining to the great man that being married now I needed more money, I turned away from the best of quality that the British Theatre has perhaps ever offered (the famous New Theatre Vic Season) and threw myself into entertaining villainy at the St Martin's Theatre. Uncomfortable to surmise about what might have been . . . Ever under Guthrie's wing I might have risen high in the Thespian hierarchy, but I doubt it.

The Shop at Sly Corner was a tight thriller about the entertaining conflict of good and evil. The leading character, an antique dealer by the name of Heiss, was played by Mr Keneth Kent, a justifiably well-known character of the West End theatre in those days. Keneth was an immaculate dandy. He wore expensively cut suits, usually with a decided stripe. His shirts must have been handmade and his neckbows would have been *tied* each day. He wore a personalized trilby hat always worn at the same unvulgar jaunty angle. I am prepared to swear that he wore spats above his immaculate shoes. And always a fine decorative walking stick. Were there gloves? I acted with him eight times a week for a year and a quarter and we never knew an unkind word.

It was my part in the play to sadistically blackmail him to a point where he strangles me to death. Every performance for that very long period I gave my utmost and Keneth Kent was not less than grateful for that. He was one of those actors who lived for the whole theatrical scene. The whole fashionable milieu. It was a world that a self-contained Welsh individualist could only embarrass. Anyway I couldn't afford it. And there was undoubtedly something else: much of the strange glitter was homosexual. Now I hope that it is already clear that I have no jot of criticism towards my gay brothers. Indeed when I was allowed to have a peep at all of their inspired decoration I was most appreciative. But they knew that I was a bit of an odd-man-out heterosexual and I saw little of it. And on the smart heterosexual side of the West End theatre – well again you can sense that I hardly fitted. My life's course was set. I was no gadfly; I was set on the harsh and sometimes dour track of simple survival – as an actor! How does it go? 'Hey diddle-di-dee, an actor's life for me!'

Also in the cast was Ada Reeve. Ada Reeve! She had been

one of the great figures of the British Music Hall deep back into Queen Victoria's time. A darling of the true cockneys. In our drama she played Mrs Cat, the charlady, and she performed it like the star she was. And why not? The audience was always delighted and Keneth loved things to go with a bang! What a change there has been in the British theatre in my lifetime! Sometimes I think that there is only O'Toole left. Even his world-famous disaster (*Macbeth*) became the *biggest* disaster ever – since Kean's disasters, of course. Ada Reeve's eyes would glimmer as she came off and made her way to her dressing-room. She never gave an inch but if you were a pro, did your skilful best – well she never gave me a bad moment. I am very proud that I shared the same boards. When Ada died those two great theatre historians, Mander and Mitchenson, who inherited something of her history, sent me a brooch which Ada Reeve had worn during the Anglo-Boer War. Those two caring gentlemen knew that I was interested in that war, and in Ada, and they felt that I would most value the pretty object. Such remembrances keep me afloat.

And then there was the glamorous Cathleen Nesbitt, she played Keneth's sister. Miss Nesbitt – so I felt – was never really happy in our thriller. Sometimes fate overtakes us; I suspect that Keneth wanted the aristocratic quality of Miss Nesbitt near him. But I sensed that she tended to hurry past me. Of course everyone knew that she had been a love in Rupert Brooke's life. Now there is a touch of romantic magic! It is true that while on that CEMA tour of Wales, just after the outbreak of war, a young lady who was sharing a bed with me in Aberystwyth suddenly said in a tone of awe: 'My God! In profile you look like Rupert Brooke!

But that bit of reminiscing wouldn't have carried much weight with Miss Nesbitt . . .

I had one sort of mate in the company, William Roderick. Well 'mate' is a bit too familiar, as he would have remarked. Bill was the conventional leading man: handsome and debonair. He was a satirical chap. I think that he had long before realized that the theatre was not what he had once hoped it was. He would 'send me up' in his sophisticated way and that was always beneficial to my soul. I was comfortable in his company. He made me laugh.

In due course Cathleen Nesbitt left us and was replaced by Miss Viola Lyle. Miss Lyle had acted in my first feature film *The Farmer's Wife* so already I was part of that interweaving of lives which is one of the happiest aspects of showbiz.

A close friend of Miss Lyle's was the famous actor–manager Robert Atkins. There are more theatre stories about Mr Atkins than perhaps about any other British player ever. He was a formidable heavy man with a deep resonant Shakespearean voice which he had finely cultivated over the many years. During my professional life Robert Atkins was most famous for running the Shakespeare Company at Stratford-upon-Avon and then the Shakespeare Company in Regent's Park, London. Who can vouch for all of the priceless stories? But they are ever consistent with his highly coloured character and they reflect graphically so much that is now only nostalgic history.

Came the day when the brewers who had manipulated the Stratford-upon-Avon theatre into well-endowed existence – Flowers is the name of the firm – decided that Robert Atkins' traditional days of Shakespeare had to move over for a more modern interpretation of the Bard. The grand old master was summoned before the board of Governors. Was it a Sir Archie Flower who presided? The story goes that Sir Archie paid Robert extravagant compliments, emphasizing his enormous creative achievements over the many years, of Robert's service to the incomparable Shakespeare. But now the time had come . . .

Robert Atkins stood up and responded: 'I have only one thing to say on this occasion: Flowers Ale is piss.'

Towards the end of Robert Atkins' active life, when he was still running the Regent's Park Theatre, the great memory was beginning to fail him. One evening he opened his mouth and speaking the first line of a major purple passage, dried completely. Nothing else came. But with cool aplomb he turned to a perfectly innocent actor who was at hand and said: 'Artemedorus! *thou* tellest the tale!' And Robert made a firm exit.

Viola Lyle was a kindly woman and she introduced me to Robert Atkins. Thank you.

The play ran on for a very long while. On a Saturday night after the performance I would catch a train from Paddington Station to Leamington Spa, but there was no connection to Stratford-upon-Avon where Joan and I had a flat. Joan was now a mathematics teacher at a grammar school in Warwickshire. However at Leamington, a Mr Brain, who collected the London Sunday papers in his van, would carry me home by a very circuitous route as he dropped his bundles at various villages. Though extremely tired as I arrived in Stratford at first light, I can still recall the dawn chorus and the freshness of early morning Warwickshire. Joan was a constant friend to me. Then back to London on Monday.

I led a sober studious life during the week. Having survived the war I experienced a hunger to educate myself which has grown firmly to this very time; almost obsessive. In those days (the late 1940s) I read and read about the history of theatre and about the story of acting. And I haunted the old print shops and I built up an extensive collection of theatre ephemera. It was during those wanderings that I first met Mander and Mitchenson who were then youngsters in stage-management, I think.

Once or twice I caught a glimpse of the glamorous side of my profession. Keneth Kent would take me and Bill Roderick to The Ivy after the show. What an experience that was! The Ivy was *the* place for the big fashionable winners in the theatre. Close by would be famous stars. Not for one moment did I feel that I belonged there. But I *was* an actor. And I enjoyed the experience. It is a measure of Keneth's integrity that he gave me those occasional treats.

The distinguished actor Henry Kendall had produced *The Shop at Sly Corner* and after I had been performing in it for a long while I received a mysterious note that he wanted to see me. With some unease I visited him in his dressing-room at the Ambassador Theatre where he was playing in a revue with Hermione Gingold. My foreboding was justified. Mr Kendall was offhand to me as he raised some vague unspecified

criticism of my performance. He was disconcerted at my innocent shock. I felt strongly that he wanted me to leave the play.
I suspected that he had another young man in mind that he
wanted to replace me with. But if this were true, his was a for-
lorn hope. I don't think that Keneth Kent or the management
would have approved of my going. But it left another mark on
me as I realized more and more what treachery was ever in the
theatrical air. Recently my eldest son, David, asked me very
carefully: 'Dad, don't you think that you're a bit naive?'

In human affairs I think that I have always had that over-
trusting inclination. A belief that others will do unto me what
I would do unto them. That fair play will be paid by fair play.
And here in Venice – where I now am – I have just read a *pre*-
Christian Jewish piece: 'What is hateful unto thee, do not do
unto thy neighbour. This is the entire Torah. The rest is com-
mentary.' Of course this raises the question whether Good
Jesus was guilty of plagiarism. Anyway Henry Kendall never
mentioned the subject again and in latter years he was
pleasant and treated me with reasonable respect.

NINE

Came the day when the film producer and director, George King, asked me to act Archie Fellowes in a film of the play, which he was soon to make. The great German (I presume Jewish) actor, Oscar Homolka, was coming over from America to play Decius Heiss. And just at that same time the theatre critic, James Agate, sent me a message stating that he was then employed by Arthur Rank to put outstanding talent under contract and would I telephone him because he wished to get me signed up. I spoke to the grand doyen of the British Theatre and explained to him that I was about to film for George King, and Agate said: 'Oh, we mustn't play one off against the other must we?'

Well I was only telling the simple truth, but I heard nothing more from Agate.

One or two people commiserated with me because I was going to have such a big film opportunity with a man as ruthlessly talented as Oscar Homolka. I was told some hair-raising stories about him, but once we had acted together and he had recognized that I was a serious player who was doing his utmost, Oscar Homolka became my friend. He would wait at the end of a long tiring day so that he could have me taken into London in his chauffeur-driven car.

Oscar Homolka had been a leading actor in Germany for the fabulous Reinhardt and I think that he took a cynical view of Hollywood and all that was brutally commercial – which is why he was intolerant on occasions.

In this film version of *The Shop at Sly Corner*, Archie Fellowes, the character I played, had a girlfriend, and when it came to casting her George King and Eric Lepine Smith – the casting director – asked me to be present. And there in Mr King's office was a voluptuous young woman who brimmed with quiet confidence.

'Now what is your name?' asked George.

'Diana Fluck.'

There was suppressed amused interest but not from me.

'How old are you?'

'Sixteen, Mr King.'

'What work have you done?'

'Oh, I've entertained the Americans.'

More barely concealed interest.

'Now, Diana, I think you could play this part with Mr Griffith, but I do feel that you should change your name for film purposes.'

'Why?'

'Well – "Fluck" – well, it doesn't *sound* right.'

'Why not, Mr King?'

'Tell me, Diana, what was your mother's name?'

'Dors.'

'What!?'

'Dors: D–O–R–S.'

'Oh. How do you feel about calling yourself Diana Dors?'

'Why not, Mr King?'

Diana's bosom was so well developed even during those early days that I understood that it had to be supported by adhesive camera tape. I certainly didn't peer too closely. But I sensed that the technicians were buzzing with lewd whispers and I was worried that the young girl would be thrown by the atmosphere. That her concentration would be impaired: 'You know, Diana, you must learn to ignore everything around you except the scene that we have to do. You mustn't allow anyone to upset you.'

'Oh, I'm not nervous, Kenneth. But thank you.'

It was her very first part in films.

The film was an enormous success and the truth is that British Lion, who distributed it, sold the drama on my performance. They took full page advertisements in the trade journals and featured only my name. I had reason to suspect that I was on my way.

Immediately upon the film's release in the cinemas, Anatole de Grunewald, a distinguished film maker, talked to me. He asked me a simple question: 'Can you do for me exactly what you did for George King?' And he gave me a script called *Bond Street* which was virtually a series of short stories, all happening in that expensive thoroughfare on one single day and in which the stories were lightly interwoven. My character was a copy of Archie Fellowes from *The Shop at Sly Corner*. After I had read the script, Anatole de Grunewald repeated this question to me.

'Yes, sir,' I said, because I wanted the experience and required the money; but as I answered him I was puzzling how I could make this new villain *different*. And I quickly found the key. When *Archie* demands money he says to the old man: 'I want a thousand pounds and I want it now!' But the Bond Street character says to *his* victim: 'Would a hundred pounds be too much?' It would have been difficult to play Archie for laughs, but people do enjoy horrific villains who can make them laugh through shock; the hint of insecurity in a villain can be very funny – and was. And the film gave me an opportunity to refine my screen acting; I became more consciously audacious with the choreography of my body. It may surprise the lay-person, but very rarely does a film director interfere or even advise a screen actor. Very often they have got the director's job through their technical skill; usually as film editors – film cutters. And when film directors *have* instructed me what to do, it has tended to push me into potentially disastrous situations. An actor should learn and learn and think and think for him or her self. And most film directors simply sigh with relief when they see that the player knows what he or she is doing. The battle for actors, as I have observed it, is how to survive when so many unimaginative elements are unknowingly inhibiting you.

At this period I became even a famous villain in Britain. I have known people enter a railway compartment, stare at me, and hurriedly leave. And people would ask me strange

questions. After *Bond Street* had been exhibited someone
asked me: 'How did you decide to walk in that unusual manner?' I replied vaguely: 'Oh, you know – when you're an
actor . . .' And then someone else asked me and someone else
and I didn't know what they were talking about. Well, I
thought that I had better go and look at the film to see for
myself. But by this time it had finished its major run and I
asked British Lion – the distributing company – where it was
showing closest to London?

'Leamington Spa.'

As I entered the cinema the manager recognized me and
gave me a free seat. Yes, in the film I did walk in a peculiar
manner. And sitting there I learnt very clearly a fascinating and
vital lesson for all creative actors: that the state of mind dictates the physical responses. Change the state of your mind –
become some other character creatively – and your body will
behave differently. You don't have to stick noses on or ponder
whether you will walk loosely or stiffly; the *mind*, if it is true
to the concept of the new character, will *insist* how you carry
yourself.

And then George King had another villain written for me in
a film called *The Golden Mile*. By this time I had begun to
realize that I was being pulled into serious professional trouble. I was being typecast in an evil role which in all fairness
had little to do with my own evolved character in everyday
life. I mean I was being called upon to repeat successful villain
roles that had little to do with poor young Kenneth Griffith.
And as was to be expected, the copies of the original Archie
Fellowes were deteriorating in quality. I was on the skids.
There was no Tyrone Guthrie of the British film industry keeping an eye on me. I was being passed from one unperceptive
film maker to another and my initial impact as a film actor
was on the wane. Well, one man *was* caring enough to observe
my fate and he wrote a letter about me to Sir Alexander
Korda. That man was Sir Arthur Jarrett who had sold *Sly
Corner* on my performance. One of Korda's side-kicks saw me
and talked grandly of my future but naught else happened.
Panic was in the air for me.

Somewhere about this period I was employed to play in a film called *On the Waterfront* which was being produced by a Mr Paul Soskin. Mr Soskin was a fantastic man with a formidable Russian accent. He had employed Mr Michael Anderson as the film director, who had previously been, I think, a very successful first assistant director. I remember a scene around a table which became for me one of those occasions when all of my actor's plans were quickly squashed and I was left floundering. Michael had rigidly worked out what I was to do and my contribution was annihilated. That really stings for a long while! To this very day. Of course I understood Michael Anderson's situation. It was his first film as a director and he was being overruled by a weird force – Mr Soskin. And he simply wanted to get the thing finished on time and on budget.

The film's story was about a ne'er-do-well seaman played by the unforgettable Robert Newton who was married – in the film – to a good woman played by Kathleen Harrison and they had three children: a young boy and two daughters. One of the daughters was naughty and walked out with me, one was good and walked out with a decent young man, played by Richard Burton.

We were on location in Liverpool for a few weeks and I made a tentative gesture of friendship towards my fellow countryman, Burton, but he was cool and aloof. Only in his latter years did he warm towards me. I can recall Susan Shaw, who played the naughty daughter, presiding at the head of a hotel dining table in Liverpool. Because she was under contract to the Rank Organization she was treated with near royal deference. I have witnessed young women placed in that situation often, over the years, and then 'the Company' or Fortune cuts the golden hawser and they flounder and sink. It is a cruel thoughtless piece of commercial reality, often fused to stupidity.

The studio used was Pinewood. By that time Robert Newton had become a heavy drinker; the handsome leading man that I once knew had departed. But he could still be an outstanding actor. In his often befuddled condition he would tend to take the film relationships as literally true. He would take me aside, place his hands on my shoulders and gazing so sincerely into my eyes: 'My boy, I *know* that you're going to be good to my little girl!' And one morning he collared me and detailed his powerful relationship with a lady wrestler. Robert was a big handful and it required special loyalty to stand by him in public. We often dined together in the great baronial hall at Pinewood. All around would be the self-important appendages of film making: the accountants, the producers, the fixers. In would loom Robert Newton with his eyes haughtily and determinedly fixed on my table. I have risen to assist him. Then he would mumble incantations: 'I've got the twinges!'

And louder: 'I've got the twinges!!'

On to his feet he would get and picking up the enormous bread roll basket he would send those pieces of food north, south, east and west around the dining room, now booming: 'I've got the twinges!!!'

And the masters of film finance would sink deeper into their soup and pray that this vulgarity was not happening. Kathleen Harrison was very good with him: 'Come on Robert! Stop being a naughty boy and sit down!'

Robert Newton had a death-cell scene in this film with his son. I saw it a couple of times and his performance moved me deeply; I wept on both occasions.

Now I had heard that when the incomparable twins, the Boulting Brothers, were planning to make *Brighton Rock* my name had been in the casting hat to play the principal role of Pinkie. But Richard Attenborough was close to John Boulting and he played it. Well, I thought to myself: 'There are two highly intelligent British film makers who clearly care about human problems and I am assured that they know about me, so I wrote a letter to Roy Boulting. Back came a speedy reply in which he wrote about how well he understood my *cri de coeur* and he befriended me and has remained one of the best, most constant friends, that I have ever had. In due course he was to feed me, clothe me, educate me and in general he made sure that my head was always above the water. How do you repay such a friend? I certainly love him – as I love Tyrone Guthrie, to this day – but I fear that the slice of Anglo-Saxon in Roy Boulting will not approve of my using such an unmanly word. However he will put it down to Celtic emotionalism and laugh it off.

Tyrone Guthrie never severed the line that connected us. Again he wanted to talk to me: 'Emlyn Williams has written a beautiful play called *Pen Don* – in my opinion it is far and away his best play. The leading role is a saint-like young man who leads his tribe – his family – to King Arthur's city of Avalon. I am going to direct it for Tennant's (London's foremost management) and I want you to play the part. Do you know Binkie Beaumont?'

'No, I don't.'

'Then I'll take you along.'

Guthrie gave me the play to read and I agreed that it was 'a beautiful play' and like every drama that Emlyn Williams ever wrote, it was outstandingly theatrical; now almost a lost art – the death-knell was first tolled at the Royal Court Theatre under George Devine and company.

Tyrone Guthrie duly introduced me to the famous Binkie Beaumont. The Tennant offices were high up and you ascended in a minute two-person lift. Now, as I have explained, I did not lead a normal theatrical life; though enjoying – generally – the company of fellow players, I shied away from the super social milieu; I always felt happier amongst simpler, more down-to-earth Thespians. And here was the little lift elevating me towards the antithesis of them; Binkie Beaumont was the leading chum of John Gielgud and the theatrical glitterati. But please don't misunderstand me: Mr Beaumont set a very high standard in the British Theatre – creatively anyway – it is simply that by my nature I had little in common with them. I steeled myself for the encounter. Well, Mr Beaumont, who looked an elegant, handsome man, was warm charm personified.

'What a pleasure, Mr Griffith, to meet you! Isn't it remarkable that both Mr Guthrie and Mr Williams are unanimous that you should play the part? Therefore I am delighted.'

All was verbally agreed to there and then.

'Oh, and Mr Griffith, has Tony Guthrie told you who else we have cast?'

'No, sir.'

'Well, Dame Sybil Thorndike will play your grandmother; Sir Lewis Casson will play your grandfather; Flora Robson will play your aunt, and apart from yourself we haven't got any further. Oh, and Paul Nash will design the décor.'

I realized that the significant day had arrived! A fine play by a famous author and a very distinguished cast. And Paul Nash. It was clearly seen by the powers-that-were as a very prestigious production and I was confident that I was a candidate for being the best actor in Britain.

Yes, this was the day that my life would change! Mr Beaumont then said: 'Now you know that we don't commence rehearsals for – maybe – another six months; I think that we should put you under contract – look after you – while you wait.'

'No, sir, that won't be necessary; I want to devote all of my thoughts and energy to this challenge. I will go back to the peace of Stratford-upon-Avon and quietly prepare myself.'

'Are you sure, Mr Griffith?'

'Yes, sir.'

And with a warm farewell I departed, exhilarated by Fortune who was smiling on me.

There was much in Stratford-upon-Avon that made me very happy: the kindness of Joan, Shakespeare, the Warwickshire country, the colourful local characters – particularly the antique dealers. I fished in the Avon River and played a little cricket. And I read books and educated myself. And now my creative future looked rosy; I examined every nuance of the play *Pen Don* and learnt my sensitive role till I understood it inside out. After four months I became mildly uneasy that I had received no preliminary word from Binkie Beaumont. After five months of silence I wrote him a letter. The reply was not long delayed: 'Dear Mr Griffith . . . How could we have overlooked informing you . . . the production has been postponed . . .'

Pen Don was never produced in London. As far as I remember, I stayed in Stratford numb with disappointment and shock. Of course it has always been a peculiarity of mine to withdraw from everything except the truth as I understood it. The idea of playing the game to get on is alien to my Welsh Nonconformist nature. And I have made the mistake – regularly – of expecting people like Binkie Beaumont to behave as I would have behaved, which is foolish of me.

Joan and I were still together but all was not well. I was reverting to the gypsy-type (no offence to my respectable Romany friends). I was playing any parts to make a living; a remarkable volume of rubbish. But I still had that steely determination in my soul. I was not going to give up. I think that it is true for me to write that at that period I had little else left except my fundamental reason for existing: don't surrender! Joan and I now had our son, David. Joan, understandably, murmured that perhaps I should take some other job. It was very dangerous. It would have been more positive for me if she had suggested that I died. I don't want to over-dramatize, but that was my predicament and of course hers and little David's.

Depression and fears had already overtaken me. I had enjoyed my rural life in Stratford-upon-Avon, but I was cutting myself off from the Thespians; I was rapidly drifting away from my creative work. And I didn't have the will to do something about it. My deep dread and unease was expressed in a strange compulsion; I would pack my old RAF side-pack and I would walk – always westward. On one occasion I reached Ludlow, where I had been stationed during the war – and I visited a woman who had befriended me. I stayed a few days but then pushed on into the Wenlock hills: 'When Wenlock Edge was umbered at Ashton-under-Clee . . .' and there I found a spiritual community living in a vast old farm which they called a Bruderhoff. Originally they had been refugees from the Nazis but I understood that the founders had continued westward to South and North America. This Bruderhoff had once become a staging-post for those refugees but was now a permanent settlement of its own, containing mainly British people; refugees from our modern materialistic society and perhaps some unstable, uneasy souls like myself. I stayed there; it was a hard life. I slept in a loft, on straw, I think. We rose at 4 am and after a spartan breakfast of unsweetened porridge and raw brussel sprouts we went into the potato fields for the day. During meals – taken at long trestle tables – someone would read to us; usually travel books. I recall that much of it was about the arctic or antarctic; perhaps these subjects put our own suffering into a reasonable perspective. And towards the end of meals anyone was free to speak their thoughts out loud to the diners. I was addressed several times: 'Kenneth Griffith what do you think of our community?'

'I appreciate your hospitality to me very much. My life has been getting difficult in the world outside. But I cannot accept, easily, your pacifism. At this moment millions of people – including friends of mine – are in mortal danger to enable us to live here in freedom.'

'We understand very well what you are saying, Kenneth, but we believe that we have an obligation to demonstrate that a life of peace and love can be led in the world *today*; indeed we are performing it and all of humanity is welcome to join us. Indeed, we pray that they will: the Nazis, the Fascists and the Japanese are also welcome. Here is a way of life that is working and is ready to receive all who want it.'

'I value your achievement and thank you for giving me a rest, but emotionally I cannot accept the privilege.'

They were all very peaceful towards me, I remember a young man shelling peas in a small wooden shed: 'Did you fly in one of those war-planes?'

'Yes' – without going into the humbleness of my contribution.

He got up and peered closely at my face: 'I have often wanted to look at one of you.'

Many of the members of the Bruderhoff wore what I guessed was early nineteenth-century German costume. The head of the community was called 'The Speaker' or was it 'The Thinker'? I asked if I could thank him personally before I left. He lived in a little wooden house and his rooms were lined with books; he said little and I remember thinking that I would have liked his job more than labouring in the fields. I am ever a bad team man! I walked back to Stratford-upon-Avon and rejoined patient Joan.

Roy Boulting allowed me to play many different characters. Indeed he is one of those rare directors or producers who really understand the problems and potential of acting. A couple of years ago I received an enquiry from an American: he enclosed a list of eighty-odd feature films in which I had appeared and he asked me if I could add to the list. I could but didn't; this was not necessarily discourtesy on my part, it is that I can be out of Britain for very long periods working and returning to usually hundreds of letters and then I am away again. Often I just haven't got the time or the facilities. But the point that I want to make is the volume and variety of films that I was involved in while making a living. And I hastily promise that I am not even going to enumerate those films. Most of them are no more important to me than if I had been a plumber who had to tackle continuous drainage problems and almost invariably did his best.

TEN

In 1952 Tyrone Guthrie was back at the Old Vic in the Waterloo Road. My home was still in Stratford-upon-Avon with Joan and our son David. One day I received a message from that great man asking if he and Mrs Guthrie could visit me. I can see them now sitting in our flat in Warwickshire. His very presence always lifted my spirit. He said: 'I am going to direct a play at the Vic written by James Forsyth about François Villon. Would you consider playing the poet?'

He gave me the script; it was called *The Other Heart*. Tyrone Guthrie always talked to me like that. He rejected entirely *who* a person was and only saw *what* they were. Of course, if an outstanding performer had become a so-called star, Guthrie would continue to treat him or her as an outstanding performer. But the star bit was no more than nonsense to him in his work in the theatre. There have been a few players who have clearly not liked Tyrone Guthrie; Miss Diana Wynyard was one and so was Richard Burton. But the root of their dislike was that they could not happily accept the fact that Guthrie treated a spear-carrier with the same courtesy and respect as he treated *them* – that was if the spear-carrier was trying to do his best. And believe me one can be an imaginative and creative spear-carrier.

I read *The Other Heart* and said that of course I would like to play Villon but that I hadn't worked on a stage for about four years and shouldn't I do something a little less challenging first?

'*Would* you join the company?'

'Of course, sir!'

'Good, then to play yourself in do Oberon for me in *A Midsummer Night's Dream*!'

Those were his words; as simple as that. If anyone else had asked me I would have ducked Oberon. I had played very little Shakespeare and the two previous Oberons that I had seen – both at the Vic, I think – had been Robert Helpman and John Gielgud and to my thoughts then, Oberon must inevitably be a sugar-plum fairy with much tinsel and a poetic romantic voice. And that was not what I had become an actor for. It would be better if I returned to my miscellaneous characters often performed in 'second feature' films. But Guthrie had asked me and he was going to direct it!

With some trepidation I perused the text of *The Dream* and I speedily recognized that there was a deep psychological conflict going on between Oberon and Titania, with Puck naughtily aiding as Oberon's side-kick. I raced happily but unbendingly towards the Vic in the Waterloo Road. We were weeks off beginning rehearsals.

'Where is Mr Guthrie?'

'Up in the rehearsal room with Cedric Thorpe Davie the composer.'

There they were at an upright piano.

'Hello Kenneth, what can I do for you?'

I babbled out my point of view, ending: 'And thought that I should tell you *now* because I cannot see the part any differently.'

'There was a long long silence. Guthrie fingered through some music sheets very slowly. I was a little alarmed, then: 'Jolly good idea!'

Now what went on in that man's head I cannot be sure, but I suspect that he was asking himself a few questions. Was my concept legitimate? Could I (Griffith) carry it off? And if both of those questions were affirmed, how could he make use of the new idea in the production? Guthrie was the least hidebound man that I knew; he was the most humble and the person who has had more respect for honest creative ideas than anyone else that I have ever met. What a fall there has been in the British Theatre since he left – in spite of the expensive machinery that accelerated after him.

The next significant news I learnt was about the design of

the costumes and sets by Tanya Moiseiwitsch. They were to be cobwebby green and forest-spiky. And most astonishing of all, the fairies were to be schoolboys. I had been given my gritty context and no messing about.

Rehearsals were, with Guthrie, big, exciting and happy adventures. At least for me. Initially we worked in the large rehearsal room upstairs. I thought and toiled with every piece of my being. At the end of one rehearsal Guthrie said to me, very quietly: 'Kenneth, that was beautiful; I understand everything that you are telling us.'

Those words have been a comfort to me over these many years. Guthrie said them to me and so I have – in my time – soared very high.

And then rehearsals moved down onto the Vic stage and came a day when I was speaking one of Oberon's purple pieces: 'My gentle Puck, come hither . . . Thou rememberest since once I sat upon a promontory and heard a mermaid on a dolphin's back . . .'

Of course, I had fixed myself in the very centre of the stage and well to the fore. From that uncertain gloom of the carpeted auditorium came Guthrie's voice: 'Kenneth, do a circle.'

I couldn't quite believe that he had said it. If it had been anyone else under the sun I would surely have remonstrated. Even if it had been Jesus – I suspect. But I started again: 'My gentle Puck . . .'

'Much bigger.'

And finally: 'Kenneth, the whole stage.'

Guthrie was pushing me into virtually dancing the entire role. Or rather he wanted me to move like Nature's Air. I knew that if I was to meet this concept I must learn how to achieve maximum balance. I had never had a dancing lesson in my life – except from that red-headed ballroom instructress at Colwyn Bay during the early years of the war. And came the memorable day some many months later, when we were performing this production in Johannesburg, South Africa, and the stage doorman announced: 'Mr Griffith, a young man and woman would like to see you.'

Into my dressing-room came an exquisite couple. As I

remember them they were both quietly shy and indeed somewhat fey: 'Mr Griffith, we have to come and see you because
we could not decide where and under whom you had studied
dancing. Oh, my name is Massine and this is Miss Nadia
Nerina.'

I then knew, clearly, that I was doing Tyrone Guthrie's
'circles' properly.

I can't remember much about the first night. People congratulated me, including Guthrie, and the production – which
was full of wonder – seemed to be generally well received. But
there were criticisms of the production. I remember one critic
had the shallowness to ask: 'Where is Mendelssohn's music?'
And, yes, there *was* a let-down. Guthrie called the company
together and spoke to us. He again congratulated us – we
were all assembled on the stage – and said something like:
'We're a flop. I don't understand it. This is *my* idea of what
The Dream should be. I simply ask you all to go on doing
exactly what you are doing now.'

I think that he sat down when he said it – which was
unusual. I suppose that the criticisms were more widespread
than I had realized; for Guthrie to be affected by the Philistines
was unheard of. But it was not 'a flop': we always played to
remarkably full houses.

I thought that the production was beautiful and intelligent
but I felt dissatisfied with my own contribution. Though 'the
beautiful voice' and pretty showing-off was hardly my forte, I
wanted desperately to give full value to Shakespeare's match-
less words. Everything else seemed right for me, but was I
filling every cranny of the old theatre with vocal – ah! perfection? I felt that I wasn't! I went to Guthrie who said that as far
as he was concerned, I was one hundred per cent. I then went
to our musical director seeking an opinion and advice.

'No,' he said, 'I listen to you with pleasure every night.
Indeed Miss Iris Warren (then Britain's leading voice production expert) has been to see *The Dream* and has particularly
remarked how much she admires the way you speak Oberon.
But if you like I will ask her to come again and perhaps talk to
you afterwards.'

'Thank you; I would appreciate that.'

Miss Iris Warren saw the production again and visited me in my dressing-room. I remember a pleasant woman with an impressive bosom which was emphasized by furs.

'Mr Griffith, there is really nothing that I can tell you. It so happens that you speak naturally, in the way I instruct my students.'

She then gazed at my unconvinced face: 'Of course, Mr Griffith, this is probably the first time that any actor has played Oberon while on the run.' A reference to Guthrie's 'bigger circles, Kenneth!'

And then we were going to do Christopher Marlowe's *Tamburlaine* with Donald Wolfit. Guthrie asked me to play Darius, the King of the Persians, who opens the play. Studying the play and in particular my role, I again became uneasy and hastened to see Guthrie – again well before rehearsals had begun. This time it wasn't because I was unshiftingly committed to an interpretation of the character but because I could *see* no unified character whatsoever. Darius was a proper mix-up: sometimes he talked about blood and sometimes about 'pretty things' and sometimes about pacifism. I feel that Christopher Marlowe, more than any author that I have ever read, was totally dependent from day to day on how he happened to feel; whether he had a hangover or not. On one page he would write surpassing well as if he were o'er topping Shakespeare and on the next page boring vulgar undergraduate mishmash.

I had lunch with Tony Guthrie in a pub. With him it was usually cheese, bread and beer. He heard my agonizing: 'Maybe those four years away from the stage in films *have* harmed my perception. This is the first time in my life that I don't know what to do with a part. What do *you* think I should do?'

He replied with alacrity: 'Much rather leave it *your* donation.'

And then, digesting my suffering, he laughed and smothered it which made a sort of snuffled explosion: 'Kenneth, this is how I see the play begin. When the audience arrive in the theatre the curtain will be up already and they will see enormous Persian (which he pronounced "Perseean") tents of war and beyond them hundreds of "Perseean" tents of war stretching away into the far distances of Asia (pronounced "Aaseea"). The stage will darken and the house lights will go down and then between the tents of war will appear a path of light and down that path will walk the young actor who speaks the Chorus. I think that he will be half dressed in his costume and will have his dressing-gown still on. He will probably also be finishing his make-up. [The make-up bit didn't happen in the actual production.] As the Chorus finishes his piece he will walk down into the hole where the orchestra used to be. Then a spot-light will illuminate an empty, raised, throne. At this point tall, golden armoured figures will emerge from both wings of the stage and will turn ceremoniously towards the prompt side and the audience will know that the king is expected. At that moment from the *other* side will dart the little rat-like figure of the king [my part].'

And Guthrie firmly stopped. He had nothing more he wished to say to me on the subject. Of course there was now nothing more I wished him to say. All the contradictions that had worried me in the character of Darius became valuable opportunities in the overbred, inbred, royal ruler who was obsessed with 'blood' and 'pretty things' and who was to become terrified by the new and brutal war-machine called Tamburlaine.

Anyone who truly cares about the art of drama direction would do well to ponder the above story. Guthrie had a reluctance to tell another artist how or what to do.

'Much rather leave it *your* donation.'

But once he saw that I had worried and failed, he told me what he had in mind to prepare for my entrance, and of course giving that entrance a maximum lift-off. He considered interference with the actors' creative process a big sin; but he would quickly recognize what the player had in mind, would nurture it with the utmost care and then egg it on with happiness and confidence for all concerned. Some have said – and still do – that he would egg one on to go too far. But never too far for me. Either as a player or as a member of the audience.

The entire company for *Tamburlaine* assembled. Were there forty-odd of us? On the first morning Tyrone Guthrie said: 'Please be patient with me; today I may not know everyone by name, but tomorrow I will.'

The centre of the pulsating excitement was the famous theatrical character Wolfit and, of course, our director. What would happen? Well everything progressed in a pretty civilized way. Donald Wolfit's personality breathed over everything; but it would have been worrying if it hadn't; here was a truly big actor tackling an overwhelming part. And supervising everything was our very tall thin leader. Guthrie took up an unusual vantage point for himself initially. He sat bolt upright on a chair perched on the very centre of the stage, at the footlights. I can hear Wolfit's voice now, coming out of that florid actor's face and certainly Guthrie was being nothing less than supportive.

The first rift in the concerto came through the actor David Green – who has now become a successful film director. David is large and was not lacking in confidence. He was extrovert. At the end of one period of rehearsal he – as far as I remember – put a hand on Wolfit's shoulder and in making some comment called our leading man Donald. Well, 'Donald' swung around (as only he could) and hurled the following words: 'Macready [a great actor–manager] said – but I don't suppose that *you* would have *heard* of Macready – but all of that is lore to me: "Speak your cue and keep at arm's length." And that is what I believe in to this day!'

We were all enormously impressed to hear exactly where the line was to be drawn. But it is a measure of David Green's tough character that the thunderbolt was carried by him like water off a duck's back.

And then a political question cropped up at the Vic. The General Secretary (the boss) of the actor's trade union, Equity, was a remarkable man named Gordon Sanderson. He had light red hair, was very pale and he worked like a well-primed dynamo. The players of the company were suddenly informed that Mr Sanderson wished to address them personally to give us some important news. Up to the big rehearsal room we climbed and there was our General Secretary behind a table with his assistants and a collection of documents. He was always brusque. Was he an Honest Marxist? He informed us that Equity had negotiated a new, improved contract and he shot out to us the legal details. A show of hands, signifying agreement, was demanded. And at that point I intervened: 'Excuse me, Mr Sanderson!'

He flicked his pale eyes in my direction: 'Yes?'

And he proceeded to apparently preoccupy himself with his pile of papers. He had suffered a little trouble from me previously, but I was not thrown by his psychological lawyer's tricks. I spoke loud and very clearly: 'Sir, I have recently signed a contract with the Old Vic management for one year and I am certain that I do not want that solemn agreement changed by one word until it has expired and then maybe has to be renewed *unless* the Old Vic management is totally happy with your new arrangements.'

You see, as I keep reiterating, I am an impossible team man. I really can't help it.

'Well – Mr Griffith – you can either simply vote against what we have achieved for you all, or abstain. Now let's get on with the business!'

'As long as you understand, Mr Sanderson, that I am not going to be a party – in any way – to my written promise to the Vic being broken unless *they* want me to break that promise.'

Somewhere in the rehearsal room was Donald Wolfit; you always knew if he was present even if you could neither see him nor hear him. A second Equity meeting was then announced for a week or so ahead.

While waiting for this second meeting I whizzed around most of the company (particularly the junior members) asking them all the same question: 'Do you believe that we players are *compelled* to belong to Equity? That it is a closed shop?'

'Oh, no,' came the unanimous replies.

I even went to our good-hearted and bright Equity deputy,

the actor and director, Mr John Blatchley, who also replied: 'No, no my dear fellow! We are creative people; we don't *have* to join. But we *must* support Equity; look at all the good they have achieved for us!'

I of course conceded that Equity had done much good – but that was far away from the point.

The second Equity meeting arrived and this was a grander, more formal affair: the trade union officials were on the stage of the Vic and we Thespians were in the stalls. An unhappy symbol of perhaps what I was objecting to. The whole legal negotiations were repeated by Mr Sanderson but more fully, and as the final endorsement drew near I again intervened: 'Forgive me for disrupting the smooth flow of this event, but I am a very troubled man. I think that you union officials should be aware that in many ways – but not in *every* way – we artists are very innocent and we can sometimes happily vote without realizing all of the implications . . .'

Mr Sanderson offhandedly urged me to get to the point.

'Mr Sanderson, please forgive me for asking a very simple question. But it is relevant to my worry about decisions being made for me which I do not approve of. My question is: do we actors and actresses *have* to belong to Equity?'

There was an awkward silence on the stage which was counterpointed by heavy strides at the back of the auditorium. I sneaked a glance and there was Donald Wolfit striding up and down and clearly in an emotional state.

'Oh God,' I thought, 'he's angry with me for nicking the limelight.'

And then from Mr Sanderson – on the stage: 'Yes, you do have to belong to Equity. Everyone knows that!'

I turned and addressed my uncomfortable but honest colleagues, one by one: 'Did you know that Bob?'

'No.'

'Did you know that, Rupert?'

'Nope.'

I publicly went through a fair proportion of the cast whom I had questioned previously ending up with our Company Deputy who had slid very low in his seat: 'Did *you* know, Mr Blatchley?'

'Well, I hadn't realized – fully – that it was – exactly – compulsory . . .'

'Now, Mr Sanderson, here, in front of my colleagues and before you officers of Equity, I publicly resign from the union. What are you going to do?'

There was a whispered conference on the stage.

'Mr Griffith, you can't resign from Equity; if you stop paying your subscription – you will simply be accounted as in arrears.'

'But I'm telling you now, I'm out! I'm not a member of Equity any more! What are you going to do about it?'

Another whispered chat: 'Then we would consider calling the company out.'

'Out!?'

'On strike?'

I again addressed my comrades in the stalls: 'Did you all hear that? I've made my point.'

And so the meeting continued and the players accepted their improved contract.

And then Wolfit, in an excited state bounded up to me: 'My boy, *you* should join the Society of Individualists! I will speak to you later!' and he was gone. There was no smile on his face.

'Wow,' I thought, 'he's gunning for me. I'm in real trouble!'

That evening Donald Wolfit came to my dressing-room with a folder of information about The Society of Individualists. It was pretty right-wing. The great actor was now beaming at me: 'If you so choose, Kenneth, I will nominate you personally. You're a credit to the Profession.'

And out he went. I never mentioned the subject to Donald again but I received my reward. He always treated me as a friend *and* the greatest accolade: as a professional peer. As for the Equity business, well, the last thing I wanted was to give the Vic a problem so I made a compromise: I would continue to be a member of the union – which I am glad to be to this day – but my membership card must be endorsed: 'Under Protest'. I've never checked; I hope that they did it. Equity has since proved to be a good friend to me.

Of course Donald could also be vulgar. Whether I would

dare write that if he were still alive I don't know. He was a tremendous egotist. Sometimes I got the impression that he really felt that the play had temporarily ceased to exist when he had left the limelight. As Zenocrate (Tamburlaine's queen) died and Miss Jill Balcon spoke her last words I have observed Donald picking his teeth. But oh, he was full value.

After the curtain came down on the first night of *Tamburlaine* and Donald and the rest of us received powerful applause, our leading man remained on the stage – dead centre – clasped his hands, looked upwards and said: 'Kit Marlowe, we've done yer proud!'

There are some who will swear that he said: 'Kit Marlowe, *I've* done yer proud!' But I refuse to believe that my ears deceived me.

Eventually we left the Vic for the Provinces and arrived at the Shakespeare Theatre, Stratford-upon-Avon. Nothing could be happier: that beautiful bit of England and Marlowe in Shakespeare's home town. I remember calling on Donald Wolfit at the Arden Hotel (I think it was) and giving him a biography of one of the great actor–managers. All seemed very well; but disaster was hovering over Warwickshire. Donald announced that he could not play the next Saturday matinée 'because I am lunching with my Queen'.

Tyrone Guthrie enquired further.

'I have been invited to lunch with my Queen at the Palace.'

Guthrie said: 'I'm very sorry Donald but you have a prior appointment with your audience in the theatre.'

'Under no circumstances can I reject my Sovereign's command.'

I have no idea how many other guests there were 'at the Palace', but Donald was adamant. And so was Guthrie.

'Donald, if you don't play on Saturday I'll have to sack you.'

'You may do as you please, Tony!'

And Donald had his royal lunch and Tony fired him. It was nearly as big a drama as *Tamburlaine* itself.

Back in London, I was about to enter the Old Vic stage-door as Donald Wolfit came out of it: 'Oh, Mr Wolfit, I am deeply sorry that you are leaving.'

He gazed at me with that astounding penetration. In silence formidable emotions were pulsating and then suddenly: 'My boy, I have done this for *you*! Someone had to make a stand against *them*.'

And his index finger at arm's length was pointing upwards towards the administration offices of the Vic. And then, placing his hands on my shoulders: 'No, my boy; I did it for *you*!'

I felt an uneasy burden of responsibility and I was also aware of a small group of fascinated pedestrians standing around us on the pavement. Well – they were viewing, for free, a big theatrical drama and they were very close to the great Donald Wolfit who was addressing an actor friend.

'Thank you, my boy! A good day to you.'

And off he strode.

One of the greatest moments of my life was walking on the eastern side of the Haymarket some years later, when a voice carried across the roar of the traffic from the western side: 'My boy!'

Whether he bounded across to me or I scurried to him I cannot recall, but as Wolfit asked after my health and the eternal Thespian's enquiry: 'What are you *doing*?!' I felt enormous pride which still warms me *emotionally*, as I sit here in the Mediterranean heat of Sicily, where I am now pencilling these memoirs.

But my own tragedy was at hand. Tyrone Guthrie had begun to share the directorship of the Old Vic with a Mr Hugh Hunt who was, I believe, a brother of that John Hunt who had something to do with the first scaling of Mount Everest. We had met before and on that occasion Mr Hunt had made a firm professional promise to me and when in due course I discovered that he had overlooked that promise, I wrote him a plain-spoken criticism. I received an angry and priggish reply. How dare I address him in such a manner? And now Guthrie was taking me into the director's office to meet this Mr Hunt once again. I said nothing about our previous encounter – maybe two years before – and neither did he. The meeting was friendly and I felt very much that bygones should be bygones and anyway I knew that Guthrie would protect my interests. But the clouds were blacker than I had supposed. Soon Guthrie told me that he was resigning from the Vic and that his power would be vested entirely in Mr Hunt. But that he (Guthrie) had expressed his wish that I would play François Villon; it was a verbal invitation from Guthrie to me. And so began one of the most humiliating experiences of my life. Hunt was not the sort of man to talk to me openly and fairly as Guthrie would have done. Doubts about my status in the company simply seemed to permeate the theatre. And then it was announced that Miss Irene Worth (who had played Helena in *The Dream*) would play the leading woman in the Villon play: *The Other Heart*. It just became bloody uncomfortable. And then it was somehow arranged that Miss Worth and Hunt would travel to Pinewood (I think Roy Boulting supplied the car) to view a fine cut version of the film that I had most recently acted in, *High Treason*, and from my performance in that film to judge whether I was fit to play Villon. The young man I played in *High Treason* was a far-call from the tear-away French poet and for me a very painful drama was in motion. My dear friend, the distinguished film editor, Mr Max Benedict, supervised Miss Worth and Hunt at Pinewood Studios. I was quickly put out of my misery when I learnt that Mr Alan Badel would play Villon. My one consolation was a long affectionate letter from Tyrone Guthrie stating that if he had remained at the helm there would have been no other actor in the world that would have had precedence over myself. I am being honest when I write that I would prefer not to have played Villon but with Guthrie's admiration, than to have played it with such people as Miss Worth and Hunt, but without Tyrone Guthrie's support. However, also in the letter from Guthrie was advice that I should *not* have taken: he urged me to stay in the Vic company and if necessary to accept a supporting role in *The Other Heart*. Because Guthrie asked me to, I did this. It was a sickening experience and I began to spiritually sink. However, life is a long race and I have regained several 'new winds' since that miserable greying period.

Of course I still had to carry on with Oberon in *The Dream*, and now under Hunt's direction, *Macbeth* was to be done and these three productions were to be taken to South Africa.

ELEVEN

Well South Africa approached and of course the school-boy fairies could not go, and in came the young ladies. Amongst them was Lady Olivier, but at that time, simply Joan Plowright. She was a jolly, intelligent, good-natured girl. And playing Mustardseed was Miss Doria Noar who has remained a significant and valuable influence in my life to this very day. Indeed to come to the point: Doria is the mother of my beloved daughter, the actress, Eva Griffith.

My marriage to Joan was already in disarray. The most painful part of looking back at my life is to consider the reality of my leaving – in due course – three wives! And a child or children were always involved. I recall arguing with friends during the first years with Joan, that the irregularity of an actor's life was no excuse for the breaking up of marriages. Well, with hindsight I now believe that the endless uncertainty does put an abnormal strain on such relationships and that the relationships are therefore in greater hazard than the average marriage. But insecurity was not the fundamental cause of domestic failure in my case. It seems to me now that I was, long ago, given the hint of personal salvation when Evelyn Ward pushed me into the school play and when Frederick Coles wrote: 'If this boy chooses to make the stage a career . . .' Until then I was a vague lost soul. It seems to me now that that hint of possible creativity was all that I possessed to hold off oblivion and on the positive side that I might even make something big or communicate something worthwhile. I plead to my judges that I had *nothing* else except this unformed idea and that even when my efforts to succeed were a dismal shambles, anyone or anything that put the dream in jeopardy was expendable. And I believe that if I had in any way succumbed to a more regular life or had stopped giving that dream a ruthless priority I would have shrivelled into a little grey man and indeed disappeared. No one can be sure what my children – or the ladies in my life – would have felt about the disappearing Daddy. Today, in spite of the injury that I have inflicted on them, we are all good friends – with the possible exception of Joan – and I am a person that they all value, with their individual reservations. As I keep thinking to myself, life is a very long race and the varied fortunes of each lap mean less than one's position at the winning post. And I am not writing, primarily, about fame and fortune but rather about what we do with our talents and who we define ourselves to be. In short, I am claiming that I had the choice of either running the race or dying. We all have different sets of demons at our heels.

Joan and our son David came to say goodbye to me at Waterloo Station which was en route for Southampton where the ship for South Africa waited. David, strangely, doesn't remember, but I caught his fingers in the heavy carriage door. I already believed that the marriage was over. Joan, as always, behaved with dignity and courage and with patience and kindness though I have some idea of how deeply she suffered and was to suffer.

The arrangements for the Vic Company on that great liner were curious and divisive. No one, under Hunt's direction, would think of explaining to the body of Thespians any human problem in a human way. I presume that a debate had taken place as to our Old Vic status while travelling: the great company couldn't sail into Cape Town to a civic reception and lunch with the bigwigs while living cabin class. So the principals of the Vic travelled first class and the others in less comfortable accommodation. It must have irked the new administration to feel compelled to include myself in the posher end of the ship. But I shamelessly enjoyed it; indeed the awful truth is that I had bought a tailormade *white* dinner jacket for the tropics. I was determined to be fancy-free. However, I got my come-uppance speedily. On the first night that we formally met the sun's heat I donned my striking gear. I strolled onto the deck and nonchalantly watched the flying fish at play. And then was tapped on the shoulder by another first-class passenger: 'Would you bring that chair over for my wife?'

I rather gallantly heaved the thing across the promenade deck. There was a whispered debate between the passenger and his lady: 'Oh! please forgive me, sir. I am most awfully sorry.'

'That's perfectly all right,' I replied, using my actor's skill. I did look uncommonly like a deck steward!

Also Doria Noar (Mustardseed) observed me from the cabin area paying court to a delightful young Scottish lady in the first-class area and when I had the barefaced cheek (to be as kind to myself as possible) to call on Doria in her humble quarters, wearing my white dinner jacket, Doria refused to open her cabin door. This scene prompted Robert Shaw (later to become a wealthy and famous actor in Hollywood until his untimely death) to mimic me loudly: 'Oh, dear Doria, please let me in. I promise not to do it again!'

Suddenly the cabin door opened and Doria plunged at me with a pair of scissors. I ducked the thrust but a blade caught my ear and the blood poured over my white shoulder and down the satin lapels. I can only agree that it served me right and that that piece of sartorial ostentation was always doomed.

The ship called at the island of Madeira which has remained for me far more beautiful than Las Palmas and all of that lot. I went ashore with the young Scottish lady and I was overwhelmed by the profusion of sweet smelling, tropical flowers. Amongst the innocent romantic experiences we had in the town of Funchal was the occasion when we turned a corner and entered an ancient street with gutters on both sides and men leaning in relaxed poses against the walls. As the very white Scottish lady and myself entered the top end we realized that everyone was having a piss but both of us, having the indomitable common quality of being British, continued advancing. The street was a public urinal and as we passed down, the Madeiran men succeeded in gallantly raising their hats. Also there were ladies in the street who leaned out of the top half of stable-doors. They also smiled at us and gesticulated.

One lady – a little older than the rest – came out and chatted to my lady friend in a most enthusiastic and complimentary manner; but we simply smiled and progressed onward – never hurrying one bit.

That evening, back on the ship, Robert Shaw and Rupert Davies (later to achieve national fame by playing Maigret on BBC television, and who was popularly known as 'Pud'), told me that they wanted to have a confidential chat. Bob Shaw was the spokesman.

'Dearest Griffith, Pud and I have had a marvellous piece of luck this afternoon and as we want to share it with someone – well – we have chosen you. A famous wine-grower in Funchal befriended us and offered us this bottle of very rare – and old – Madeiran wine. "From the time of Napoleon," he said. We are now going to drink it and since none of us will have such an experience ever again, would you like a third?'

'Well,' I replied, feeling warmed by their friendship, 'I wouldn't mind.'

'It cost us six quid.'

'Oh . . .'

'So that would be two quid from you.'

I remember Pud eyeing me silently. I handed over two hard-earned pound notes to Robert and I sipped the liquid appreciatively. All four of their eyes were now silently fixed on me and, too late, I began to suspect the very worst. Many years later Shaw was to distinguish himself in a famous film called *The Sting*. Of course I wisely kept quiet, keeping an honest and trusting expression on my face and sipped my losses.

Cape Town, as dawn approaches, from the deck of a ship, looks like magic land, with the myriad twinkling lights beginning to ascend Table Mountain. Eventually we went ashore to a civic luncheon. Now the Old Vic Company, like the Ford Motor Corporation I suppose, was breaking up into its self-inflicted social strata. It is a sad reflection of our human frailties that the winners within Hugh Hunt's regime generally stuck together, never seriously associating with those who would appear to be beneath them. The élite were Irene Worth, Douglas Campbell, Paul Rogers (a decent kindly man), plus slightly lesser-lights. People like Pud and Bob Shaw didn't join because they had a high degree of independent self-respect. As for myself, I was markedly well outside the pale.

Anyway at that civic luncheon I sat far away from the top table with its gushing and inhibited chat. I must have been glowering a trifle (not a pleasant trait) because a young journalist appeared over my shoulder.

'My name is Danie Van Niekerk,' and he named his paper.

'Are you bored, Mr Griffith?'

'Yes, I am.'

'Would you like me to show you a bit of our coast?'

And the young Afrikaner hustled me out of the dining-room and later took me to the seaside house he lived in with three other bright young Afrikaners. In due course, I moved in with them while playing in Cape Town, to avoid the deadening effect of living in a hotel and for the pleasure of sharing their much maligned culture. A couple of years ago, I received a letter from the managing director of the Tafelberg Press – perhaps South Africa's most prestigious publishing house; yes, it was from Danie Van Niekerk and about six months ago he took me to lunch at the Mount Nelson Hotel in Cape Town. I remarked that he hadn't changed; certainly got older but with the same detached, slightly aloof, quizzical look.

Robert Shaw had confided in me about his passion for one of my fairies, Miss Jennifer Bourke. Well, for reasons just stated I wasn't exactly poised to aid and abet Robert over any matter; at least not before giving him a bad time: 'No, Shaw, you don't stand an outside chance there! Now, I happen to be in a position to *know*.'

I can see him glowering at me across a table as I provokingly prattled on, but he said nothing further. Bob and Jenny were eventually married, but sadly I was not present.

The Old Vic Company travelled northward to the Transvaal and Johannesburg by train; a long intriguing journey. Doria and I were openly consorting and I have always suspected that it was Mrs Mara, the wardrobe mistress, who huffed an objection to our manager, Robert Quentin. Anyway it is the only explanation I have ever suspected for Robert

Quentin unexpectedly appearing before me: 'Kenneth, I happen to be on my own; would you keep me company by sharing my compartment?'

I have always been an innocent mug at any hint of human friendship. I swallowed my astonishment: 'Thank you, Robert!' and I lugged my belongings up the train. I remember that we had a long and interesting chat, and though a trifle uncomfortable in the shadow of the establishment personified, I enjoyed it and perhaps even contemplated that this was another world in which I could dally, beneficially, occasionally. Now, there had been some doubt as to whether there would be a proper meal served in the train during that first evening, puffing northward. So Robert Quentin had responsibly organized a vast quantity of sandwiches and other good things which were packed into an enormous hamper; we were a numerous company. And then we learnt that South African Railways were, most certainly, serving a five-course meal in the marvellous old dining-car.

'Oh, dear,' said Robert, 'our sandwiches – what a waste!'

Every so often the train would stop in the star-laden African night and immediately dark African faces would appear: 'Please baas – money please; food please!'

My face lit up like a Christmas discovery: 'Robert! I've got an idea! Let's give our sandwiches to the Africans at the next place we stop!'

'What an excellent idea, Kenneth!'

And I felt like a rating who had been taken under the wing of his commander. The train hissed to a steamy halt and sure enough there was the bustle of Black Africa in the night.

'No, Robert! Please don't bother! It was my idea and I know where the hamper is!'

I ran along the corridor of the train, caught hold of the enormous container and heaved the thing to the connecting platform.

'Here chaps!' I yelled excitedly into the night. 'Grub! Food! Sandwiches!'

The Africans got the gist of what I was yelling and clamoured below me and I pushed the great box towards their uplifted arms. Down it was hastily lowered. My, it was heavy! Very heavy! I watched full of warm goodwill as they dragged it some distance away and began to raid the contents. There were shrieks of delight and screamed thanks in my direction.

'Good baas! Good baas!'

I felt tremendous as I returned to Mr Quentin's compartment.

'Ah Kenneth! Did it all go well?'

'Yes, Robert; they were extremely happy about it all'

'Good! Dinner's been called; let's go and eat.'

Robert Quentin and I sat at the same table in the dining-car. I felt a little conspicuous. I am more than capable of being paranoid. I felt the eyes of Miss Worth and company disapprovingly on me from one direction and 'Pud' Davies and Robert Shaw, equally disapproving, from another. Had I sold out?

'Now, Kenneth, what shall we have? Wine?'

And suddenly Mr Quentin froze. What could it be?

'Kenneth, you didn't give the natives the unemptied basket, did you?'

'Yes, Robert; there was no time to unpack it. And I could see that the container wasn't valuable.'

'Oh my God! Not valuable! All of our liquor: whisky, gin, the lot was in the bottom! Oh God!'

I had innocently given away the entire supply of alcoholic refreshment belonging to the Vic's top brass for the three-day journey! It was the end of my humble entry into that particular top drawer. But over these many years I have nursed the hope that somewhere south of Kimberley, a small underprivileged African tribe still tell the tale around the crackling fire, of the night that this astounding White fellow handed out a couple of hundred expensive sandwiches but above all: a wide selection of White man's best booze.

We opened with *The Dream* in Johannesburg. Now I don't remember anyone warning me, but Johannesburg is over six thousand feet above sea level and this fact is one of South Africa's many secret weapons. Foreign athletes, who normally live only a small distance above sea level, find themselves fighting for breath after any exertion in Johannesburg and this continues for a week or so till acclimatization intervenes. Well, my Oberon was an athletic exercise all right and I remember on that first night there, after belting out a soliloquy, holding onto a pillar in the wings and rasping for breath. But I don't know why – whether it was because I *had* to make a superhuman effort – but *that* night I *did* it. I mean I played Oberon that night as I had always imagined it should be played. I hit the top notes – as it were – like the genius I wanted to be. I sat in my dressing-room wishing and wishing that Tyrone Guthrie had seen and heard me; but he was six and a half thousand miles away. I wouldn't have cared if Hunt had seen me or not. And as for Robert Quentin – well my opinion was that he wouldn't have recognized Edmund Kean even while the lightning was flashing. And the next morning, to my intense satisfaction, the South African newspapers acknowledged my achievement. They stated exactly what I felt I had achieved that night. It wasn't so much the printed praise as the confirmation that there are other human beings who care and recognize. It is almost enough to know the truth about oneself – but not quite. Of course in Johannesburg there are many Jews and I have learnt during the course of my life to expect an unusual degree of perception from those astonishing people.

The editor of one of the English language papers – I think that it was *The Sunday Times* – got in touch with me on the strength of my performance and took me into his generous company. His name is Joel Mervis and though he has now retired from the helm he is still much respected in South Africa. I recall being taken to a very grand Jewish wedding and being given a trilby hat to wear, which, because of my evil young men in films, always made me look sinister.

And then I was asked to address an 'international congress of women' at the old Carlton Hotel, on the subject of: 'The Old Vic in Africa' and as the time drew nearer I could sense a rebellious conflict scurrying in my brain. I got up in front of the assembled ladies: 'I have been in South Africa now for two months and after the emotional impacts that I have experienced, I find myself incapable of talking about anything as unimportant as 'The Old Vic in Africa'. I apologize most humbly. But if you would like me to tell you what it has been like for a youngish actor [I was then about thirty years old] to arrive in South Africa, in total ignorance of South Africa's racial problems, I would feel privileged to do so. However, if you feel that this is not the occasion to do so, I will withdraw apologizing all the way.' I was encouraged to continue. And the press was present.

I spoke about the contrasts and conflicts that I had observed. Of how I had been taken out to dinner the night before by the chief of the Rank Organization in South Africa – 'here in this Carlton Hotel' – and perhaps never eaten so richly before, but that as I strolled back to my hotel afterwards, a young Black boy had emerged from behind rubbish bins: 'Please, baas, I hungry.'

And that at that same dinner-party there was another guest – White of course – who had a bandaged head.

'What happened?'

'Oh, I was at Vereeniging.'

'What happened there?'

What had happened was that a political movement of mainly British-blooded, Second World War ex-servicemen, calling themselves the Torch Commando and which was apparently led by the famous Second World War air-ace, 'Sailor' Malan, had gathered at the town of Vereeniging as part of their demonstration against the Afrikaner republican nationalists. And there, at Vereeniging, those Afrikaners had attacked the Torch Commandos while the South African police (almost entirely Afrikaners) had looked on and, so I have been told, refused to intervene. A touch of the Anglo-Boer War.

Looking back at my words to the responsible gathering of women I am fairly certain that I attempted no categorical judgement. I had been shocked by a vastly different set of circumstances than those that pertained in Britain – where, at that time, we had no serious racial problems of our own – but nevertheless I went little further than to express my bewilderment and uneasy distress. But in those two elements that I spoke about – the British–Afrikaner (Boer) conflict and the division between Black and White – lay a great deal of my future. I couldn't have guessed then that I was heading towards being the author of several films on those two difficult subjects and to be the author of a book (*Thank God We Kept the Flag Flying*) which dealt partly with the dreadful cause of the Second Anglo-Boer War or, as my Afrikaner friends and I prefer to call it, 'The Second War for Independence'.

I think that it was this event – the public exposure of my sociological emotions – which led Joel Mervis to invite me to write my views in his newspaper. I was told that the piece was reprinted in the Black journal, *The Drum*. Perhaps there was something in my contract which prohibited such expressions of belief, but I was in no mood to appease the smug respectability of our management. Coming face to face with our company manager, Mr Quentin, I jollily remarked: 'Well, Robert, seen my red propaganda?'

It was one of the few occasions that I have observed Robert lose his *savoir-faire*. He must have been a good RNVR officer. Of course I am not a red nor ever have been; I am a convinced, though often confused, democrat.

At that very time in South Africa the Marxists were beginning to disturb the equilibrium of Johannesburg. 'Solly' Sachs, the leader of the garment workers' union was on trial for some transgressions and I paid close attention to his arguments and to his defence in court. I remember that he was accused of allowing a Black female servant to wash in his bath. Mr Sachs simply said that he was only too glad that she *wanted* to use it. Of course the airing of such laws began to make the Nationalist government of South Africa look ridiculous to the world outside and today, sinister. But even then, in 1952, I was not ignorant (as most of South Africa's critics are) of the unique predicament that prevails south of the Limpopo River. Even then I was aware of the hypocrisy of the world in general. During our British administration of South Africa and indeed throughout the whole Empire, no native servant would be allowed to use the White master's bath or to sit at his dining-table or be treated as an exact peer under any circumstances. And that applied to every imperial power on this earth. And even to – almost all – White Americans in relation to Black Americans. The new dimension that the Afrikaners introduced was to put into written law what had previously been – generally – unwritten. The Afrikaners put on the table, face upwards, what had previously been held close to the chest. And the Afrikaners called this new arrangement 'separate development' or, in their own language, 'apartheid'. They believe, with the Black African evidence to support their conviction, north of their territory, that the two deeply divergent cultures cannot both survive within one unified government. The outside world – whilst they had a heavy and direct vested interest – also knew this. But as the imperials withdrew their particular investment, they veered towards the material and strategic value of the Third World and the liberals and Marxists quickly stepped into the vacuum. Thus, hypocrisy and shallow selfrighteousness has spread on a monumental scale – all at the expense of, mainly, the Afrikaner, who has nowhere else to go and doesn't want to go anyway. The Afrikaner has been in Southern Africa for some three hundred and forty years. And when he trekked northward during the 1830s he began to control and then stop the massive bloody anarchy that Black tribes were inflicting on other Black tribes. The Zulus call this Black holocaust the Mfecane. The Afrikaners cannot reopen that old box at the behest of the world outside who they know are mainly driven by self-interest and by their own old guilty consciences. Today's White government (written in 1985), at worst, is not as blameworthy as the old colonialists. The Afrikaners are today fighting for simple cultural survival; we British imperialists – and the rest of them – were fighting for simple exploitation.

Well, the shade of Solly Sachs isn't too pleased with the above paragraph because it crosses his Marxist – and idealistic – cause. Nevertheless, Solly and I became friends because we were both serious emotional men. Solly came to see *A Midsummer Night's Dream* and I am proud of the fact that he singled me out to be the Thespian he wanted to get to know.

During his later exile in Britain he visited me regularly. A powerful passion.

One evening after a performance in Johannesburg I received a message from the stage-door that a gentleman wished to see me. Into my dressing-room limped a stranger with a heavy moustache: 'Hello Ken; you don't remember me?'

And through the haze of years I began to perceive the handsome, patrician, young man from Sandy in Bedfordshire; the middle son of the Reverend Strong, Peter. I was very glad to see him. Rumours had filtered through to me over the years: a very skilful fighter-pilot and then a terrible flying accident, somewhere in northern Africa during the war. The slight limp. And I believe that the moustache covered a scar. I had also heard that he had spent – was it? – two years in military hospital.

'Ken, I am running a flying business at Ladysmith in Natal. I fly into Basutoland. I want you to visit me and I will take you into that country and you will see things that you have never seen before and will never see again.'

I promised my old friend that I would join him at my first opportunity. What has always paid me my best profits is my anxiety, my compulsion, to push in through every adventurous door that has appeared before me. (Of course nothing stupid like cigarettes or drugs or too much alcohol.) I would suffer a feeling of failure if I didn't; that is the driving force.

And then our outstanding company played at Durban and afterwards was due to chug northwards to Bulawayo and Salisbury in what was then called Rhodesia. Now somehow I had managed to extricate myself from *The Other Heart* which we had also taken to Africa with us, and this fact presented me with spare time. I planned to – and did – make full use of that spare time. Peter Strong in Ladysmith hovered formidably in the air. Robert Quentin made one of his rare approaches to me: 'Kenneth, now that you and the girls [my fairies] have a little time off I would be most grateful if you would escort them on the train up to Rhodesia. It is a very long journey and they may need some protection.'

Several thoughts, I recall, went through my mind: 'It would

take a tough bundu-basher (a potential South African front row rugby player) to get out of line with any of those fairies. And if one did, who was I to start trading gentlemanly violence? And secondly: Peter Strong and Ladysmith (through which place the train would pass on its northward journey) and Basutoland.'

'Sorry, Robert, I can't do that.'

'Why not?'

'I have other plans.'

'But I don't think that they (the fairies) could manage without a man as escort.'

'Come on Robert; I think that you are exaggerating their vulnerability.'

Mr Quentin's very worst fears about my character were thus confirmed.

Doria didn't mind my stepping off the train at Ladysmith one bit – as long as she came with me.

'No! Peter and I are old friends and we are going on a rough trip; I don't want to be handicapped!'

When the train stopped at Ladysmith, Doria kept putting her luggage on the platform and I kept shoving it back on the train. I remember feeling a bit mean but I was determined that this visit was to be about men's business with no female lagging behind; no nonsense! Peter appeared as I finally managed to bundle Doria and her gear back onto the train as it began to trundle northward with Doria glaring at me through a window. I think that Peter was impressed by my apparent lifestyle. Little did he ever know!

Getting off that train at Ladysmith was to change the course of my life. It was to open an unthought-of road for my future and it was, in due course, to save me from the Hugh Hunts and later on the Peter Halls of this life. Doria is my dear friend to this moment but in retrospect my selfish instinct to give Peter Strong's invitation its uninhibited head was wise. A new and better life was beginning for me. Perhaps that childhood fantasy of becoming a soldier to enable me to see our strange British Empire was my first, very early intimation of what could lie ahead for me. Peter Strong was leading me

into a small, very famous town of the Empire. I knew little
about Ladysmith, but I had heard of the siege during that
musty Boer War. The Boer War to me then was an inexplicable conflict which had happened some twenty years before I
was born. But ghosts have sprung to life for me and I have
always striven to understand them, and I think that it is true
to write that the impetus of my great curiosity about them is
an inner conviction that those ghosts have many answers to
our contemporary and future problems. Well, in Ladysmith
and beyond, I was about to meet the genuine drama. The
dead soldiers and the awful suffering that they had endured
were about to look at me and wink and smile and perhaps
even hope that I would speak for them. The poor innocent
British 'tommies' and the shaggy strange ghosts of Dutch and
Huguenot farmers: the Boers. Perhaps all of them hoped that
I would be interested enough in their old strivings and suffer-
ings to listen carefully and perhaps even *say* something about
it. Certainly I had the histrionic ability to put their case effectively. My longing to share the past and to use my power of
communication were about to touch each other.

Peter Strong had married the Canadian woman who had
nursed him after his flying accident. They had an infant son
who was also named Peter. I stayed with them in their house
in Ladysmith. My schooldays' friend walked me around the
old defences of the town and he showed me the uneasy battlefields. Peter knew many facts about the siege and in his
English manner described some of the brave and terrible
events. He told me that a year or so before my visit he had
piloted a man, who had once been famous throughout the
Empire, over the site of his Boer War exploits. The occasion
was the fiftieth anniversary of the relief of Ladysmith and his
passenger was Bugler Dunne who had sounded the advance
when British troops had hesitated in the face of decimating
Boer rifle fire on the edge of the Tugela River. The British soldiers were attempting to cross that river to relieve Ladysmith.
They failed but Bugler Dunne had performed his terrible and
questionable duty. His bugle was damaged in the mêlée but
her Majesty, Queen Victoria, had presented him with a new

one. Peter had flown the now old man over the exact site of his childhood's military fame.

And then Peter flew me into Basutoland. It was not less than an astounding experience. Basutoland (today's Lesotho) is a totally mountainous area; as far as I recall the peaks go up to ten thousand feet. Until Peter arrived no aircraft had ever landed in the country. Just before the Second World War a man named Rivers-Thompson had dared to fly over it, or rather between the mountains, and he had succeeded in dropping a parachute with a bottle of beer attached over a Basuto village called Mahotlong. But that was all. Peter piloted his twin engined Rapide aircraft between the vast walls of mountains. I sat in the co-pilot's seat. Peter quietly concentrated, flicking his eyes sometimes to our starboard and sometimes to our port – to judge the distances of the cliff faces. Sometimes he glanced at his wrist watch. Sometimes visibility was not good; there was cloud about. We flew towards Mahotlong. At the lip of the chasm Peter used the rising air to – as it were – lob the aircraft onto the flat top of the mountain. This unbelievable manoeuvre I lived through several times. The District Commissioner of Mahotlong showed me Rivers-Thompson's bottle of beer in a glass case. Recently some sort of flying field has been formally opened in the vicinity; I have *meant* to write an appeal for a memorial to Peter Strong to be erected there, but I haven't done so yet.

Peter did show me many strange tribal occasions. On one mountain-top landing, a Basuto tribesman came galloping up on his pony and pranced around and around the aircraft. He had a rifle across his back. On his head was a wonderful fur hat with the face of the small animal at the front. I asked Peter to enquire in the Basuto language if the man would sell me his hat.

'No!' replied the horseman, 'I hunted the animal and I made the hat. I keep it!'

'Please tell the man, Peter, that I have travelled many thousands of miles from the United Kingdom of Great Britain and that I may never come back to Basutoland again. I would like to take his beautiful hat back with me to London.' The Basuto stared at me for quite a long while and then suddenly he thrust the hat towards me: 'Seven and sixpence!'

I paid up eagerly but unfortunately, in due course, I lost the hat in the River Thames.

Peter had business in Maseru, the capital of Basutoland, and I was left on my own for several hours. I wandered outside of the town and stood on the edge of a large escarpment. Far below me I watched Basutos digging rectangular holes in the earth. As I watched, the men began to move away with their picks and shovels over their shoulders. I clambered over the edge of the escarpment to cut off their retreat. I asked the leading Basuto: 'What are you doing?'

He shook his head and walked on but finally a large black police sergeant said: 'Today we kill six people; we bury them here.'

'Why are you killing these people?'

'All guilty of witchcraft. This big hole is for husband and wife.'

Later I probed this disturbing issue. I was told that the cause lay in the breakdown of the old tribal system. The young Basutos were travelling into the Republic of South Africa where they could earn more money and when they returned to Basutoland from the relative sophistication of Johannesburg and a Chief ordered them to do some job they would reply: 'Not for an old man in a blanket!' And the old man, noting his power waning, would call in a witch doctor who could order murder. The consumption of vital parts of a human body would be devoured by the Chief, believing that the essence would be transferred to himself. And so the European concept of law and order would intervene; there would be a formal trial and then the noose. Southern Africa is a terrible and complex issue. Two diametrically opposite cultures riding out an impossible sea. Neither can quietly accept the other. A thousand years – to be optimistic – separated them.

Peter Strong had won the contract to carry His Majesty's Mail and had lowered the time of transport of letters from within Basutoland to Ladysmith from about one week to forty-five minutes. He also transported 'slaves for the mines' as he heavily put it. That is the collecting of Basutos from the interior for the Union of South Africa railheads. I flew with him on these jaunts. There would be the men assembled on a mountain top and they would file into our astounding contraption that flew. Formidable men who would giggle with nerves as they awaited the nightmarish experience. Peter Strong would perform his cockpit drill and then say to me: 'Ken, walk down and reassure them.'

I even held the hands of normally brave men. Back at the flying field outside of Ladysmith, I remember Peter's engineer (whose name is lost to my consciousness and who had served with him in the war, I think) talking to me passionately about 'the Governor'.

'Peter may speak about "slave running", but I'll bet he's never told you about the endless mercy flights. He's never refused one; he's gone up in impossible weather.'

I travelled with my hero friend on one of those expeditions. Into the centre of Basutoland we went and lobbed onto a flat mountain top. The poor young woman seemed to be dying of tuberculosis and again Peter was satisfied when I sat by her side and held her hand. She was too ill to feel fear, I thought. Before the aircraft took off I wandered towards a gathering of tribespeople. The women were near naked and their bodies were painted a yellow ochre colour. Odd, astonishing impressions are left in my head.

The sight that hit my brain most forcibly around Ladysmith was the many small iron crosses on the isolated kopjes (hills) which often read: 'To a Brave British Soldier'. Poor lonely sods; the reality of empire. I have never forgotten them and they have been a fundamental inspiration of much of my life since.

I made my way across to Johannesburg for my journey to Rhodesia where I was to play in *A Midsummer Night's Dream*. But I suddenly discovered that I had been over-optimistic: there was no train to get me there on time. I telephoned an air-hostess friend: there was no aircraft scheduled. Could I charter one?

'Not easy.'

In the middle of my growing panic a lawyer acquaintance said: 'I'm driving to Warm Baths today.'

'Where's Warm Baths?'

'Well, it's on the way. Not far, but on the way.' And so I commenced to hitchhike to Salisbury in central Rhodesia to open as Oberon before the Governor General.

I arrived at about midday of our opening night. Even then, when I felt a little less responsible than I do today, I was not proud of my unprofessional risks. However, I went through the piece that evening, before the bigwigs, with stylish alacrity – until I was poised to enter the stage and speak: 'Welcome, good Robin. See'st thou this sweet sight?' when Joan Plowright (now Lady Olivier) firmly goosed me. What effect this last-straw ordeal may have had on me I cannot be sure, but I reached dead-centre stage and fell flat on my face and was carried off. I recall hearing Paul Rogers making a speech to the High Commissioner *et al* which included a reference to my 'old war wound'; all things considered it was a wise West of England decision on Paul's part.

As our tour of South Africa ended a bright and worthy young South African impresario named Leon Gluckman asked me to stay on and act in a play by Clifford Odets called *The Country Girl*. I wanted to do this and the appropriate application for an extension of my visit was made. But I was already a marked man – presumably because I had spoken up for the Black Africans – and I was instantly rejected. The formal instructions to me were not without humour; they read: 'You came in with the Old Vic scenery under bond and you will go out with that scenery under bond.'

Years later I was told in Pretoria that I was the first foreigner to be ordered out of South Africa for anti-apartheid activities. And be it remembered that this was years before the liberal do-gooders had begun to bleat their often shallow chorus with the likes of Winnie Mandela and good old Des Tutu.

TWELVE

B ack in England I returned to Joan and our son, David. It was a traumatic domestic time. Joan had done no harm whatsoever (her wish that we could achieve a more conventional stability was hardly a fault – even though it unnerved me badly). I think that I was afraid of failure and horrified at it being measured against middle-class standards. I had been hit spiritually by Hugh Hunt and company and I knew that I could only hope to survive if I strove for a gypsy level of freedom. I knew that the little disappearing grey man was just around the corner. And Joan had an extra-sensory capacity that was alarming; she always knew what I was thinking – and doing – even when I was far far away. Yet she never berated me; she simply did everything possible in a quiet reasonable way to hold our marriage together. We jointly came to a civilized decision: we invited two friends to have supper with us – the distinguished film director, Lindsay Anderson, and a Jewish friend, Peter Osborn (who had volunteered to work for a Quaker organization), and then to tell them about our crisis and to ask for their advice. Joan and I admired these two men very much. We quietly told them the truth as we both saw it. I recall the evening as being pleasant. At the end Lindsay said: 'If that is the case I think that you should separate.' Peter quietly concurred.

This judgement shocked me; I had hoped for a miraculous solution from our two good friends. The next day I packed a suitcase and walked out. Joan said goodbye.

My legs dragged as I headed towards a new life. I was deserting an extremely good woman and a young son. But the truth is I cannot honestly regret my act – nor was it to be the last of such acts! – because the alternative would have been worse, I believe, for all concerned. I have often wondered if my marriage to Joan could have survived under a firmer social structure: conforming to the class rules and to the Church. I don't know. Lindsay Anderson and Gavin Lambert the film writer and historian gave me a temporary home. I wrote to Tyrone Guthrie and he offered to do anything he could to help and being who he was he meant it. But there was nothing anyone could do except offer a little love. The wind was now flapping in my sails.

After a short while Doria and I began to live together. She had found a small mews cottage close to Sloane Square. Doria is an indomitable person. With little money she kept us fed and in spite of the trauma there came many laughs and we began to generate new and lasting friendships. Our two 'spear carrier' friends from Johannesburg, David Phillips and David Benson, arrived in London and lived with us. Between everyone we paid the rent and, though crowded, a memorable community was formed. David Phillips, being the most responsible of the team, carried the main burden.

John and Roy Boulting were preparing their film, *Private's Progress*, and normally I would have been earmarked to act in it from the beginning, but unfortunately I had upset Roy (my particular friend and supporter) through a sin of omission and therefore I had not been asked. This made me sad for two reasons: I needed his affection *and* the continuing work. When all seemed lost the phone rang and Roy said: 'Kenneth, we're making a film about Britain's contemporary questionable spirit – as reflected in aspects of army life – a comedy. I have to tell you that the better parts have gone; but there is a small-ish part of a somewhat backward chap. Perhaps you'd like to call round and pick up a script.'

The re-offered hand of friendship overwhelmed all else. Having read the script I returned to the Boulting Brothers: 'Roy, John, I would very much like to play in *Private's Progress*, but I was wondering if you could consider doing me a favour?'

'What favour?'

'Well, I've looked at the part very carefully and the truth is that you could cut every word that my character speaks and it wouldn't even affect anything that anyone else says.'

'Well?'

'I was wondering if you would allow me to cut *all* of my lines but still to place me in the same position in the groupings that I would have had if I was speaking?'

I think that it was John: 'Why are you always so difficult, Kenneth?'

'Well, I would like to make the character *so* backward *and* shy, that he really can't speak – but he *does* think.'

'Ohhhh . . .' (extreme Boulting exasperation) 'I suppose you can – but you *are* difficult, Kenneth!'

'But I would just like to retain the last line that my character has been given in the script: "Please sir, how do you get a medal? 'Cos I haven't got one yet!"'

'All right, dear boy, I'm sure you know what you're doing' – spoken with ill-concealed Boulting doubt. And that performance edged me into film comedy. And survival was the object of everything I did in those dodgy days.

At Shepperton Film Studios the old Boulting Repertory Company assembled. I think that the cast of *Private's Progress* generally extended into its prophetic sequel *I'm All Right, Jack* and they were: Jill Adams, Richard Attenborough, Ian Bannen, Liz Fraser, Irene Handl, William Hartnell, Sam Kydd, Margaret Lacy, John le Mesurier, Victor Maddern, Miles Malleson, Dennis Price, Cardew Robinson, Margaret Rutherford, Peter Sellers, Olive Sloane, Thorley Walters, Ian Wilson, myself and the newcomer, Ian Carmichael, who was personifying the innocent face of England – already disappearing as the last of British ethics disappeared; strangely enough hand-in-hand with the disappearance of the Old Empire. I have probably missed out a few old friends, but isolated here at the western extremity of Ireland, where I now am . . . well there we are.

Those Boulting films were a special experience. All of it reflected from the unique character of the identical twins. They were very careful who they cast; everybody had to be a talented honest player and – I honestly believe – everyone had to be someone that they liked and respected. And then, of course, the Boultings are remarkably intelligent and perceptive about everything that really counts on this earth: drama, politics, the human condition and cricket. Every department reflected their professional and personal standards. In the cutting room: Max Benedict (one of the best human beings that I have ever met) and Anthony Harvey (who, though living in America, is still my chum). I enjoyed hanging around these two men in their workplace. Bob and Chuck, the property men at Shepperton, were essential on a Boulting film and if there was a hierarchy of importance poking through the roof of the essential democracy that prevailed, Bob and Chuck were very high up and never far behind the producer's throne. I must admit that a warm glow embraces me and tears prick my eyes at the very remembrance of those exclusive gatherings to make a Boulting film. Would that such civilized acting opportunities still presented themselves these days. And to add to my joy, Roy would usually drive me to Shepperton in his Rolls-Royce and bring me home.

But between one thing and another I felt compelled to let go of my finger-tip hold on the Drama. I was shaken by the domestic tragedy with Joan and our son and now Joan was ill in hospital. I went to see her but as always she did not complain or accuse; she was like a saint towards me. I couldn't quite cope with myself so I released my focus on acting and I began to work with two friends of my own age, Derick Bolton and 'Ricky' Richardson, who ran a philatelic and postal history business from a shop in Broad Street Station. They didn't pay me a salary, but I was useful to them when they were both out on business and I was allowed to conduct my own limited buying and selling of postal history which I had become enormously interested in – and still am. Postal history is not simply the adhesive stamps but the entire used envelope: the postal markings, the various endorsements, indeed everything to do with the history of that envelope. And I was good at it. I had – and have – a living interest in every aspect of history and to examine and assess the stories of envelopes (or covers as we postal historians confidently call them) from every corner of this world and over several centuries (because there were envelopes long before stamps) was – and is – a great educating excitement for me. I recognized the postal histories and was able to communicate those stories to potential customers. My big problem was that I had no capital; in truth I was skint. But I managed, with Doria, to eke out a living – barely. We had to leave our mews cottage and we were given refuge by a friend of mine, Mr Geoffrey Jackson, who ran a preparatory school in the Harrow area. But it was not exactly Harrow Public School. Geoffrey was one of the great characters of my experience. His school was two or three Tudor style houses adjacent to each other; it was ramshackle but everyone wore academic gowns and I might swear that Geoffrey occasionally wore a mortarboard! He had an irrepressible sense of radical humour which understandably was not shared by his intelligent wife. Geoffrey was also a wholesale foreign stamp merchant and that is how we met. He learnt about my financial pressures and he enthusiastically offered Doria and me a room in one of his three houses. Mark you it was tough. Basically Doria and I shared a camp-bed (but we were both very slim in those days). At the end of one outstanding week I had sold some of my postal history items for twelve pounds! Riches that we were unaccustomed to; usually we were scraping the bottom of the basket for survival. Doria was apprehended in the local greengrocer's for nicking a cabbage. She and I have a bond which cannot be dissolved. I believe Geoffrey emigrated to Chicago and I thank him and I hope that his genius met with great success in that windy city. I doubt whether Al Capone could have got the better of him.

Eventually I moved from my friends, Richardson and Bolton, to one of the most astounding characters in the foreign stamp trade: Mr Frederick Beach, whose Aladdin's Cave shop was in Fetter Lane, which is just off Fleet Street in the City of London. Freddy was a large round man in his fifties, I guess, with a fine shock of silverish hair. He sat perched on a high stool behind his counter, dispensing his wisdom and humour to all who entered. He tended to be right-wing politically; I remember Mr Fenner Brockway, the great humanist and socialist, entering Freddy's territory, to buy foreign stamps for his son and Freddy dishing out his firmly held conviction that Britain was on the downward slide because of Socialist policies and because of the sinister bullying tactics of Britain's trade union movement. Well, in those days I leaned towards the Left and I had the cheek to lend humble support to our great socialist visitor. But of course Mr Brockway was quite capable of looking after himself. Freddy never got cross with me over anything and he chuckled over my innocent idealism. Now, today, after I have observed the universal hard reality of human behaviour, I tend to agree with Freddy's Tory sentiments, but I would still lend support to Mr Brockway because he was one of those honest, intelligent, caring socialists, who really meant and felt what he said from the heart of his heart. But such quality doesn't grow on trees.

It was in that wonderful shop that I first noted the military postmarks and censor hand-stamps on envelopes which had emanated from South Africa during the Transvaal's and the Orange Free State's Second War for Independence (the Second Boer War) against us British. And I decided to collect them and study them. Freddy helped me to begin this interest and to educate me. Other dealers would advise me, and help me, and what a Dickensian collection they were – all held in considerable awe by the aficionados because of their knowledge and authority: Mr Houtzamer, Mr Johnson, Mr Agabeg and Mr Freshwater.

And it was out of the possession of these Boer War envelopes and postcards – and even letters from such men over whose graves I had pondered those six thousand miles south of Fetter Lane – that my empathy for the old soldiers became sharply focused. From the ghostly anonymity of the iron crosses on lonely kopjes to the old soldier's personal efforts to communicate with loved ones. Life was knitting my varied experiences into one tapestry. Apparently by accident – but I sometimes wonder . . .

During that period I had nothing to do with the drama business. Freddy Beach would sometimes challenge me: 'What are you doing wasting your time here? If I had your talent I wouldn't be here!'

One day, on top of a London bus I met the actor, Alan Tiverton, who talked enthusiastically about my histrionic ability and then: 'What are you doing now?'

When I told him, he expressed shocked sorrow. I remember his warm kindness vividly.

THIRTEEN

After a year or so of postal history dealing, my sometime agent, John Redway, received a telephone call from the distinguished theatre director, John Fernald, who was later to become the Director of the Royal Academy of Dramatic Art. He explained that he was shortly going to direct Dostoyevsky's *Crime and Punishment* for BBC television and that whenever he came to think of casting Raskolnikov, Kenneth Griffith came to the fore in his mind.

'What has happened to him?'

'He's been ill,' replied John Redway.

'Is he better?'

And like a good agent: 'Yes.'

'Can I see him?'

And so I met John Fernald at the BBC's Television Centre. He explained to me that the production was going to be the biggest and longest running drama that had ever happened on British television (about three hours) and that Raskolnikov would appear in some twenty different sets.

Now it has to be understood that in those days television plays were done live. There was no safety net. And therefore whoever took on Raskolnikov had the toughest job in the history of television.

'Do you think that you could do it, Mr Griffith?'

'Yes, sir!'

There was a longish pause: 'Would you mind coming to see me again tomorrow?'

And as I entered his office the next day Mr Fernald said, with his youthful spirit to the fore: 'There's no point in messing about; I want you to play Raskolnikov!'

The British Broadcasting Corporation then made one of their spine-chilling bureaucratic decisions: 'Because the cast and the production is so large and therefore so expensive, the rehearsal time will be cut to exactly two weeks.'

Well, I was now heading back towards the Drama Job in no small way and I came to a serious but highly dangerous decision: I would not learn one word of the enormous role until I was actually rehearsing with John Fernald. What I would do in the interim was to read and read Dostoyevsky's great novel; but this decision did mean that I would have to learn – memorize – the long complicated text in two weeks before appearing before the British television public in live, intimate close-up. And in those outrageously cavalier – or, more accurately, bureaucratically ignorant – days, we did the big weekly plays on a Sunday evening and repeated it on the following Wednesday. My main memories are of scraping the cash together to pay for my bus fares and for my lunch money. And then being in the studio on that Sunday evening waiting for the great production to begin. I think that I was only a wafer from a breakdown. I lay on a bed on the set with some dear forgotten actress holding my hand as I kept muttering, 'It shouldn't be allowed.' I remember Mr Fernald hurrying everywhere in a good-tempered attempt to hold the production together and then dashing across to my poor body: 'Dear Kenneth, we've had a small set-back: the number one crane camera isn't functioning, so early on we'll (meaning him and his technical team) have to improvise a bit. Don't worry!'

And then began the awful count-down, like the commencement of a grand-prix motor race. No one who has not experienced those live plays can begin to understand the tension and extreme fear. Courage is needed in abundance. Long live the Thespians!

Suddenly the senior floor manager stabbed his finger in my direction: we were transmitting. I began to move forward through old Saint Petersburg under an archway where a hurdy-gurdy man was playing in the shadowy light (the actor was Wilfred Lawson's brother) . . . Raskolnikov was on his way to murder the wretched female moneylender. Inside my shabby student's coat I gripped the murder-axe. I could not remember the first words that I would be called upon to speak. Only one thought passed through my head: 'I am a little sailing boat on a great ocean at the mercy of the wind.' Of course it was not to be like that: as I moved into the production the creative skill took over and I became even arrogantly authoritative. It is a common phenomenon which other performers will recognize. I played scene after scene, dashing from one set to another; there were two men on duty the entire evening to keep a pathway clear for me. The quick changes! And then the last lap was clear ahead. I mounted the stairway towards Sonia's little room. In front of me and staring very close was a camera. I turned to the right and entered her small white cell; there awaiting me was another camera. Sonia, played by the sensitive Canadian actress Frances Hyland, asked Raskolnikov the great critical question of the whole massive drama: '*Why* did you kill the old woman?'

The demanding camera edged towards my face, peering for the reply. And horror overwhelmed me: I didn't know what to say! The camera – not to mention Miss Hyland and the television watchers throughout Britain – waited in silence. Frances was holding my hands and she repeated the question. Nothing! The camera continued to stare implacably. Frances put pressure on my hands and carefully asked the question again: '*Why did you do it*?'

My brain was working. I thought: 'I know why I murdered the old woman but that isn't what I'm supposed to *say*.' I could register Frances's eyes on me and the pressure of her fingers. I thought: 'I have no choice; I'll simply tell Sonia why I did it.' And I commenced the reply and the play miraculously proceeded towards its great climax. What had happened was that in the text Raskolnikov replied to her question with a lie: 'To steal', because in his intellectual arrogance he believes that she couldn't understand the true reason and Sonia, in her purity of spirit, ignores the lie as an irrelevance and repeats the question. Raskolnikov then tells the truth and thereby finds himself on the road to absolution and salvation. I had simply forgotten the lie. Those occasions to an actor are a nightmare.

To me it seemed that Britain must be talking about my lapse. The play had ended and a great exhilaration was sweeping round the studio. People embraced. John Fernald ran towards me: 'Wonderful! Wonderful!'

'What about the disaster?'

'What disaster?'

No one seemed to know about it except Frances Hyland and myself. It had been simply one of those tremendous dramatic moments: the agonized inability of Raskolnikov to tell God's simple truth.

When it was all over – including the repeated agony of Wednesday's performance – and the national press had extravagantly sung our praises, I received a cheque for my work; it was forty-five pounds sterling. From our little room with its welcome but miserable camp-bed I composed a letter to the priggish uncaring rulers of the British Broadcasting Corporation. I am not the sort of chap who keeps copies of his letters, but at worst I am only paraphrasing mildly: 'You exist on the poverty of my profession. If my profession were, generally, not so hard pressed and desperate for opportunities to demonstrate and exercise our talents, few of us would agree to entertain the British nation for such a pittance. I am still poor, but please do not offer me any more work; it would only waste your time – and mine.'

Shortly after that the BBC, in some small spasm of shame, doubled all actor's salaries; which still left those salaries miserably low, for the national reponsibilities which were entailed. And the BBC took me at my word; I was not offered another job by them for some years. I am glad that the BBC has recently (1985) been shaken to the very top of its ivory tower.

After *Crime and Punishment* had been transmitted Mr and Mrs Roy Boulting invited me to one of their happy parties at their home in the King's Road, Chelsea. Roy was talking to the American actor, Richard Widmark; they had been talking about my playing of Raskolnikov. Roy called me over and introduced me to Mr Widmark: 'And Richard, what do you think Kenneth was paid for that extraordinary achievement?'

'Well, I have to confess that I am aware that the BBC pay artists very badly.'

'Even so, what do you think?'

'Two thousand pounds?'

'Forty-five quid!'

And then John Fernald arranged to put our *Crime and Punishment* onto the stage at the Arts Theatre in London. Frances Hyland couldn't do it because – I think – she was going to New York to play Juliet in a Guthrie production of the love story. I missed her; a few years ago we met again in Dublin and she told me she always knew that I was a little in love with her. Oh, what a carousel it is!

I was marked for life by a review that Harold Hobson wrote in *The Sunday Times*. Some while before, John Gielgud had appeared on the London stage as Raskolnikov and the critic wrote: 'Which would you rather see: Bristol Rovers (me) play brilliantly or the Arsenal (Gielgud) play badly? I'd travel to Bristol any day.'

Oh boy! it has irked me all of these years. I had seen Gielgud play the Russian; it was the same eternal, strangulated highfalutin performance as ever. Whether Hobson was correct or not in his opinion, 'brilliant' is brilliant and 'badly' is badly. I have felt that I should have been transferred – if there was any justice (!) – to Arsenal and Gielgud, presumably, to the Second Division. But it was not to be. And now I follow a different profession – or rather a different emphasis of it – where I reside in a class of my own. And whether I am loved or hated no one can honestly argue about that.

However, I was then back in the acting game and began to scramble a living. The general pattern seemed to be a series of miscellaneous decent television plays and a real mixed bag of films; sometimes with merit, sometimes unadulterated rubbish, and always the Boultings would find me something to do in their enlightened satires. I was earning a living. I get cross when critics occasionally explode: 'How could Miss (or Mister) So-and-So demean herself (or himself) by appearing in this poor stuff!?' Well, let me settle the outraged question once and finally: they did it to pay the rent and buy the food.

Most players know a hawk from a handsaw but even more clearly they know that they must sleep and eat with as much dignity as often-half-baked employers will allow.

One day I was doing a bit of film rubbish which involved me running across houseboats moored on the Thames at Chelsea. I spotted one for sale and I got home and told Doria that we were buying it. She was very pleased and since it was a queer little landing craft we called our boat *The Coot*. It was a happyish hazardous time. When the Thames was ebbing and flowing (very regularly) the little home banged about on the curve of the mighty river. Often Doria would feel seasick but because of some odd quirk in her nature she would never walk to the landward end, where presumably her nausea would subside, but she always hung out of the river end till she had sicked everything up. Doria can be wilful if not wayward in a perverse sort of way; I can communicate no better example of what I mean than the above fact.

Also we were known to entertain on *The Coot* and it has happened that as I was sitting at the dining-table have noticed one or two of my precious postal history items float by under my feet in the open bilges. We stayed aboard our boat for about a year; it was not a peaceful relaxed time. Occasionally we would sun ourselves on the river end of the craft and, in the summer time pleasure boats stuffed with tourists would motor by, not only causing a severe undulation of the water, but some cockney oaf would bellow through his megaphone: 'Now ladies and gentlemen over to our right is a very strange colony of artistic types; them people actually *live* on them boats!'

And the least I could do in retaliation was to project an embarrassing rejoinder with all of the articulation and power of my Old Vic experience. It was with some relief that we moved to a nice little basement flat in Markham Street, Chelsea. We were struggling up in the world.

The truth is that Doria and I were living what could be described as a Bohemian life. In those days Chelsea was still an artists' area; painters still inhabited working studios. We felt privileged to be a little part of it; this of course was well before the younger stockbrokers and then the pop world began to despoil the place and finally create a haven for the pseudos and Sloane Rangers. It is another sad strand of Britain's miserable decline. Was that a sour note that I have just played? Markham Street was a more comfortable time. On the corner, at the King's Road, was the Chelsea Arts Cinema and when the queue reached our gate we knew that we would have to hurry if we wanted to get in. Doria was something of a troublemaker and I have uncomfortable recollections of her stirring it up during such cinema visits: 'Griffith, that man was behind us, now he is in front!' And I would wish that nothing had happened or would happen.

Sometimes with Doria I found my lost youth again or perhaps it would be fair to say that I found my youth for the first time. The nice little flat was in a classic Georgian basement and one day I went out because we had had a small difference of opinion or to buy some trifle and shortly after my departure our dear and eternal friend, Max Benedict called, wearing his customary grey trousers, tweed jacket, tie and the carefully rolled umbrella. Max always upholds certain of the old conservative standards, which he originally learnt from his heritage of the long-gone Austro-Hungarian Empire in Vienna (Max grieved the passing of Franz Joseph). Anyway there he was at the door politely knocking. Naughty Doria had turned the key, simply to annoy me, and then proceeded to do a Yah! Yah! dance naked in front of the very slightly opaque glass of the door – thinking that it was me! I returned at that moment just in time to stop Max from virtually hurrying elsewhere. The whole subject was so peculiarly improper that this is the first time ever that it has been stated openly. I recall it simply as one example out of many from those days of naughty innocence.

Eventually Doria and I like a couple of nomadic Bohemians found an inexpensive – probably unique – corner of Belgravia: Dorset Mews, wedged between Belgrave Square and the Coal Board and not five minutes walk from Hyde Park Corner. This was to be our adventurous home for several years. Here we cultivated a humble but historic Thespian centre and a fair slice of what was left of genuine theatrical excitement would be generated from that place. I ploughed on with my television plays and miscellaneous films. Looking back at the time, highlights for me were when I met and became close friends with a couple of great actors. Such rarities have given me a new dimension to life: they have made me comprehend that the days are funnier, deeper and more vital than I had previously recognized them to be.

Amongst the catalogue of routine jobs that paved my path at that time was a film called *The Naked Truth*, and also in it, playing his first leading role, was a chap named Peter Sellers. I had met him once before while walking up Shaftesbury Avenue and David Jacobs introduced us; Peter was then becoming well known through his radio work. I remember that he was warm and smiling towards me. It was the beginning of a friendship which only wavered once, and briefly, to the end of his invaluable days. If you were acceptable in Peter's mind, you entered a world of profit and delight, occasionally punctuated by an opportunity to share his despair. I suppose that he could be called a manic-depressive, but for me, most of the time, it was vivid fun and more laughs than I have been given anywhere else. But there was much more to Peter Sellers than humour. One day after lunch, I joined the key members of the film unit at the daily 'rushes' – the viewing of the previous day's work. Of course, on those professional occasions everyone stares critically at his or her own contribution. I cannot now recall what exactly distressed me about my own performance but as soon as I could escape from the little viewing theatre I hastened to the deserted 'sound stage' (where we filmed) in a state of shock and muttering to myself: 'Never do *that* again! Never do *that* again!' But the sound-stage was not quite empty. Peter Sellers was already there, prowling, with a terrible scowl on his face. Full of shame I edged towards him and muttered contritely: 'What did you think of the rushes?'

He snarled an angry: 'What do you think I bloody-well thought? Dreadful!'

I felt that I deserved this extreme flagellation but was taken aback at the merciless degree of his vehemence.

'Well,' I mumbled, 'I'll never do *that* again.'

'What?'

'Well, at least I saw what I did and I've learnt a hard lesson.'

'What?' repeated Sellers.

'Well I *know* I was dreadful in that dressing-room scene.'

'Dreadful?' he roared. 'You were bloody marvellous! *I* was dreadful! And you being so marvellous has made it worse, Kenny.'

Whoever was right or wrong it was clear that both of us cared passionately.

One day, while working on that film, he began to tell me about his discontent with his agent. Of course it should be understood that Peter was very often discontented with the standards of almost everything. And I began to express my appreciation of my agent, John Redway: honest, enthusiastic, hardworking, etc., etc. Well, Peter was feeling very down: 'Would you like me to drive you home, Kenny?'

'Thank you, Pete.'

Into Dorset Mews he came, feeling very sorry for himself. Suddenly: 'Here Kenny, do you think John Redway would be interested in looking after me?'

'Yes,' I replied as coolly as I could; Peter Sellers was already a very valuable client to have.

'Would you ask him, Kenny?'

'Yes, Pete.'

'Now.'

I picked up my telephone and dialled John Redway's number: 'Yes, Kenneth, what's the trouble?'

John could be a little impatient with me.

'No problem, John. Mr Peter Sellers is with me and wants to know if you would look after his business?'

There was a palpable silence: 'Are you serious, Kenneth?'

'Yes, John; he's with me now; in my house. Indeed he'd like to speak to you himself.'

And when Peter moved his business over to John Redway he took his personal manager, Dennis Selinger with him. And that is why Dennis Selinger is my agent today for what little conventional acting I have time to do, which isn't much. And that is how I came to meet one of my best and most loyal friends over these many years. Incidentally, we have never ever discussed that curious event which certainly has affected Dennis's life radically. Perhaps he never knew about it till he reads this . . .

And then the Boulting Brothers made their monumentally prophetic and hilarious film, *I'm All Right, Jack*, a saga of where Britain was heading for – downhill all the way – and why. Not only did the Boultings pillory our awful trade union movement but they also belaboured our inefficient and corrupt 'unacceptable face of capitalism'. The whole team was there; it was a grand reunion. Of course Terry Thomas was there, rising fast in the film world with his series of monstrous, lovable English villains. He had also acted in *The Naked Truth*. I had truly learnt to admire him; not only as an actor but because of the depth of his kindly no-nonsense sincerity – towards me anyway. And Peter Sellers was there in the person of his Fred Kite, the trade union leader: a Hitler moustache but a convinced Marxist, carrying his dream of power with a minimum of brain. Perhaps my favourite scene in the whole cannon of international cinema is when Ian Carmichael calls on Fred during the disastrous strike. Fred's wife (Irene Handl) has walked out on him and he is in a domestic mess. However Fred is basically a nice hospitable chap: 'Do you imbibe? I have a very nice bottle of Australian type sherry.'

'Oh, thank you Mr Kite.'

We cut to an hour or so later and both are a trifle maudlin and his visitor is helping by darning a pair of Fred's socks while sitting on the sofa: 'Tell me, Mr Kite, have you ever *been* to Russia?'

'Sadly, no. But I often think about it. All them cornfields and ballet in the evening.'

Incidentally, I haven't a script in front of me; it is like the rest of this book, simply as I remember it.

The highlight of my own experience on *I'm All Right, Jack* was in a scene where my mentally backward character (we were the same people that we had been in *Private's Progress*, but now in civvy street) goes up to Mr Kite's office to report the frightening fact that Stanley Windrush (Ian Carmichael) was happily putting in an honest day's work. Fred Kite hears this appalling story which cuts across everything that the British Trade Union Movement stood for and nodding approval to his cronies (which included Cardew Robinson) says of my character: 'A promising lad, this!'

And when I had performed my short sycophantic piece, Peter Sellers clapped his hands in applause. I mention this memory because of *his* opinion in front of the team; what an accolade! Peter Sellers always treated me as a peer and, for me, his opinion was one of the few that truly counted.

The film technician's trade union, the ACTT (Association of Cinematograph Television and Allied Technicians) got wind of *I'm All Right, Jack*'s message and some of the brothers stopped working. Immediately the Boultings pretty well ordered us out onto the lawns of Shepperton Film Studios to play cricket. But after a few days we went back to our work and the glorious film was completed. Roy has told me that he and his brother John also had trouble with the potential financiers of the film; few people want any boats rocked. There is a great scarcity of principled brave people.

And so the endless gamble of an actor's life proceeded. Hoping against hope that a reasonable proportion of creatively worthwhile scripts and roles would come one's way. Amongst my motley assembly line appeared a play by the Scottish painter and writer, James Forsyth, which was titled *The Pier*. Now James had written *The Other Heart*, the play about François Villon, which had been such a sickening tragedy for me at the Old Vic. However, this was a drama for television and I was to play what could be described as the principal character. To some extent all of James Forsyth's plays are about good and evil; certainly James is not interested in piddling themes. This was a play about a gang of Teddy Boys who centred themselves on Brighton Pier and I was the leader of this gang; therefore it could be argued that I at least *represented* the Devil. Mr Peter Zadek (now one of West Germany's most celebrated drama producers) was the director and the whole enterprise was to shift the course and size of my life.

We rehearsed in a big basement Irish Club on the edge of Canonbury in Islington. Amongst the largish cast was George Rose, an old friend and certainly and clearly the best Shakespearean comic that I have ever seen. Also I had as my gang, about ten young men, all good actors. One of them, however, was not an actor, but the emerging playwright, Michael Hastings, who was associated with the Royal Court Theatre; Michael I understood wanted to have some practical experience of the business of acting. Well, I think that we all admired his cheek and we gave him credit for his influence and initiative and therefore he was warily welcomed into the Thespian circle.

On about the third day of rehearsal I addressed the director, Mr Zadek: 'Here Pete, where's the missing chap?'

'I really don't know, Kenneth. I have received a number of messages, but it's all a bit of a mystery. I understand that he is expected this afternoon.'

My gang was incomplete; there was one short and I had a small scene with him. Well, the rehearsal continued into the afternoon and there I was in full spate when the two swing doors which led into the club-cum-rehearsal room burst open and what appeared to be a tall young tramp was standing there: 'Sorry I'm late, darlings!'

And down the steps he came onto what was meant to be the dance area where we were rehearsing. As I remember it, the young stranger advanced unhesitatingly on me, picked me up, gave me a kiss, put me down and said: 'I think you're fucking marvellous!'

My feelings are most truthfully described by the word 'astonished'. Yes, I was a sort of leading man but my feelings – which included my ego – were touched by a directness and penetration unprecedented in my life's experience. He was the missing young actor and his name was Peter O'Toole.

Before O'Toole had arrived on the scene I had addressed my very first 'old actor' remark to George Rose. The young men around us – my gang – I liked; good blokes, but they were a new phenomenon. After they had completed their various histrionic pieces they all retreated to an adjoining room where they either gossiped eagerly about the next television plays that were going into production or they played on a 'pin-table'. Because of this new dimension of our burgeoning pop times, I had turned to George Rose with a little fear and a little sadness: 'What's happening to our profession, Georgie?'

'Don't ask me, darling,' came the reply, much in the spirit of Pontius Pilate.

But this astounding newcomer, O'Toole, was different and I registered the fact that very afternoon: he retreated to an ill-lit corner and with his long legs stretched out on either side, his eyes never left every move I made, as he stared over the back of a chair. Mr Peter Zadek said: 'Right, now, Mr O'Toole. Let us run your scene with Mr Griffith.' And as the actor happily strode across to where the set had been chalked out on the wooden floor, I suffered a mild premonition. 'Right,' said Mr Zadek: 'Begin.'

Well – boom – and the scene ended. I stood there with the happy young man, Mr O'Toole, knowing that I had just encountered the most formidable competition that I had ever dreaded to meet. He was word perfect and there was the scene *done* - boom! Later I casually mumbled to Peter Zadek: 'That O'Toole chap – is – very good.'

Wow! That was a memorable day in my life. As a matter of fact, some twenty-nine years later, at this very moment of writing, I have moved from the velvet warm shadows of Sicily and I am sitting in the eastern room of O'Toole's house on his estate at the western tip of Ireland, while he is in the other end of the house, also scribbling *his* thoughts onto pieces of white paper. Life is incredibly strange and moving at times. There is no human being between this room and his. The only sounds are the soughing of the wild western wind and the occasional melodious shriek of the curlew. The millions of fish around us, of course, we do not hear. On a windy walk this morning O'Toole told me that the white topped waves were called in this part of the land: 'the flowers in the fisherman's garden'.

Well, we all moved up to Manchester to perform the play

live! I arrived in the big television studio and went to my dressing-room which was number one, on the stage level. On the seat of my dressing table was a banjo. I went out onto the stage and addressed the stage manager: 'Oh, excuse me, but there's a musical instrument on a seat in my room.'

'Oh, I'm sorry! It belongs to Mr Formby; I'll come and get it.'

'George? – Formby?'

'Yes.'

'Oh, leave it where it is; then I can pay my respects to him.'

I didn't wait long and in came the unique Lancashire entertainer: 'Eee, I'm sorry!'

'No, Mr Formby, I asked specially that it should be left there so that I could have the pleasure of meeting you.'

He exploded that enormous smile: 'Eee, I think you're good too!'

I again went to the floor manager and thanked him for his co-operation: 'And where's that chap O'Toole dressing?'

'Oh, he's up on the fourth floor in the big dressing-room with the other young men.'

'Would you be a dear and do me another favour?'

'If I can.'

'Would you go upstairs and ask him if he'd like to join me in dressing-room number one – where he belongs?'

I retreated to my room and very soon O'Toole came through the door carrying his bits and pieces. There was not even a split moment of false protestation, such as: 'Oh no, I can't really!' It was very businesslike and quick: 'Thanks. Now which half of the mirror do you want?'

Peter O'Toole is one of the five people who have radically changed the course of my professional life – and for good. I am tempted to add to that precise number but won't. And I will leave the reader to guess who the others are. Before I met him he was unknown to me. He was already a member of the Bristol Old Vic Company but his talent had not yet begun to seep through to me in London. I knew that talent clearly from his first cough. And for me it was not simply a matter of recognizing a dynamic actor. A man (or woman!) is not divisible from his or her work. The work is a true reflection of the quality of the workman. So what sort of human being lay inside this explosive theatrical pirate? I was, and to some extent still am, a struggling inner conscience – of a darkish hue – battling to explain and communicate. O'Toole, when he came to deal with the common facts of this life, plonked them loudly on the table face up. Once or twice over these twenty-nine years he has caught me being – to put it kindly (I hate flagellating myself) – inconsistent, and he has wagged his finger at me. I have never forgotten those gentle rebukes and he has mentioned those shortcomings no further. Mark you, he has remembered them, because he has a prodigious memory. But that is only one aspect of his nature; the big overwhelming contribution that he has donated to my welfare is the importance of painting my life large. I hope that you will recall my sad experience of drawing a teeny naked woman in a corner of my vast piece of paper at the St Martin's School of Art and of Tyrone Guthrie's urging me to do my Oberon circles bigger. O'Toole burst through my dangerous miniature beginnings and by example urged me to go all out for the roof of the Sistine Chapel. And I believe that in my own films I have had a fair stab at it.

Of course everything that O'Toole does has to be large top-class drama. He is the antithesis of the mumble-mumble school of acting with its frigid intellectuality (perhaps 'pseudo' should lurk as a prefix) which has captured the once robust stages of you-should-know-where. *Before* O'Toole even went into rehearsal for his world-famous scandal of *Macbeth* (which he prefers to call 'Harry Lauder') he hissed into my ear: 'It will either be an *enormous* success or an *enormous* disaster; I *promise* you one thing faithfully, Griffith: it will not be "good".'

I thank my hero from the bottom of my heart. Almost alone he fights to keep the old flame alight. The truly big-boys: Garrick, Kean, Macready, Irving and Wolfit are certainly keeping his roaring place amongst them in good order.

I was also shocked and impressed by a person who, because he picked his nose in private, insisted upon picking it also in public. 'No deception' was a constant rule. Of course, the Irishman has his personal, private concerns; he often explains these by pulling an imaginary zip-fastener across his mouth. For me he is a human, broadcasting revolution.

My young friend (there's about ten years in it) urged me to visit him in Bristol and take a look at what work he was doing there. Down I went and stayed with him in his long straggling old mews house. With my Protestant Methodist background every minute was a startling revelation. The impressions were valuable and lurid. A quiet area was O'Toole's woman-friend Isabelle Dunjohn and a young journalist on the Bristol newspaper named Tom Stoppard. Tom, very properly, doted on O'Toole; he also had the perception to know that there was a very formidable eagle in the offing.

FOURTEEN

During those days Doria protested (probably she was humouring me) that she didn't mind my carrying-on with other women. And one evening I was strolling up the Haymarket in London with my old friend Oscar Quitak (we had been dining at that blessed theatre club, The Buckstone) when we saw two young American ladies, having just come out from seeing a play *The Flowering Cherry* and quite clearly not knowing in which direction to turn. I said: 'May we be of any assistance?'

The darker-haired one answered: 'Well, you may think us silly, but we saw *My Fair Lady* in New York and in it they sang about Soho Square. And we thought that we'd like to see it.'

'Oh, as a matter of fact, Mr Quitak here and myself happen to be walking in that direction (which was a brazen lie; we would have turned due west towards Hyde Park Corner) and we would be delighted to escort you.'

'Well, thank you; that is very kind of you.'

They were both delightful people. I was immediately much taken with the one who had spoken, whose name was Alexandra MacCallum. And the long and the short of it is, we became much attached to each other over the following days. Finally Alexandra had to depart for Europe on a prearranged tour. To my mild surprise she urged me to go with her but I explained that I couldn't: that I was about to begin another 'telly' play, that I couldn't afford to go and off Alexandra went.

Soon after her departure the letters began to arrive and I missed her company more and more. (My Nonconformist

Welsh guilt is punishing me at this very moment.) One letter informed me that she would be attending an orchestral concert in a grand theatre in Stockholm on some specific night. I have always been tenacious. I succeeded, on the telephone, in not only speaking to the manager of that theatre but persuading him to bring Alexandra to the telephone from the auditorium. Another letter arrived listing her various places of call along the southern coast of France and then into Italy: somewhere on the fifth, somewhere else on the sixth and seventh and Pisa on the eighth – that sort of information. Having read the letter I hurried about the West End of London attending to my miserable business. It was a hot dusty day. Gradually I began to focus in my mind on 'Pisa on the eighth'. How could Alexandra, and an American to boot, pass through Pisa without visiting the Tower? Impossible! And as it was in a field I could keep the upright cylinder under non-stop observation. That was the theory and off I set on my romantic adventure: in the ship across the English Channel and then on trains across Europe.

In those days my face was pretty well familiar throughout Britain because of an unknown number of films and television plays. British travellers on the train began to befriend me and of course asked me where I was going: 'Florence?' 'Rome?'

'No, Pisa.'

'Oh!'

And I told them about my mission to find Alexandra. When the fine Italian express slid into Pisa station and I clambered onto the low-slung platform, I had quite a gathering of new friends lining the train's corridor and acting as a well-wishing farewell committee; they waved and tapped the windows: 'Good luck!'

I waved back and the great conveyance quietly moved southward.

Alone on that Pisa station I was suddenly hit by the loneliness of my eccentric position: I didn't speak the language; I hadn't got much money; perhaps Alexandra had changed her plans. Perhaps she had passed through Pisa the day before or was postponing her visit until next week. But I was clearly committed; I picked up my piece of luggage and moved into the tunnel which stretched underneath the railway tracks towards the station's exit. And in that tunnel began a series of curious, indeed unreal occurrences. As I walked through the relative gloom, amongst those strange Italians, I saw and especially registered a tall, lean saturnine man coming towards me. His eyes were fixed on me; he stopped: '*Scusi*, Signor Griffith . . .'

Astonished, I interrupted him: 'Signor, I am very sorry but I cannot speak Italian; only English.'

'Ah,' he continued as if nothing extraordinary was happening, and then in the English language: 'Ah – about this Raskolnikov you act in Britain; I think it was a revelation. I want to ask you for a long time; do you believe that his mentality . . .'

And off the Italian went on a lengthy detailed dissertation about what I had deeply felt was Dostoyevsky's intention. I became embraced by the Italian's depth of feeling and I anxiously confirmed that his perception of what I had tried to convey was correct.

'Thank you, Signor Griffith; it has been a great pleasure talking to you.' And raising his hat he turned to leave me.

'Oh? Signor, excuse me, but do you happen to know where the left-luggage place is?'

'Certainly, Signor Griffith!'

And he retraced his course.

'There!' and he was pointing down a very short broad passage at the bottom of which was a counter, behind which lounged a few men. And raising his hat again, the Italian intellectual was gone.

'Excuse me,' I announced to the baggage personnel and in my clearest English, 'I am very sorry but I don't speak Italian. Please may I leave my suitcase here?'

I was eyed, but no one budged. Now when faced with insolence, I have always tipped into razor-sharp behaviour. I banged my case on the counter: 'Mate! Move!'

Before I could register what effect my declaration of conflict was having on my Latin brothers, a soft English voice said – and very close to my left ear: 'Can I help you, Mr Griffith?'

And there, breathing very gently, was a pretty blonde lady. It was more than astonishing. The first thought I had was: 'There was no one in the corridor; and I couldn't possibly have missed such an attractive person if there had been'.

'Yes, thank you.'

The blonde turned on the now impressed men and whipped across a sentence in the native lingo and then sweetly back to me, specifying the cost; she picked out of the palm of my hand the required coins and she gave me the receipt.

'My name is Bubbles [and I have sadly forgotten her surname – but Bubbles never]: where are you going to?'

I, of course, was thrown off balance a little by the whole sequence of extraordinary events in a foreign land.

'Oh, I don't know exactly. I hope to meet a friend here tomorrow. I must look out for a place to stay tonight.'

'Where are you meeting your friend?'

Well, the answer to that question needed a lengthy explanation and as I told Bubbles the story of Alexandra and her written words: 'on the eighth I will pass through Pisa', again, as on the train, I witnessed the effect it had on the listener. I became transformed into something special.

'Goodness!' said Bubbles – 'Look, I am staying with dear friends at Pisa Da Mare and I know they would like you to stay too.'

'Oh no!' I said, 'I couldn't possibly.'

'Yes,' said Bubbles.

'No.'

'I tell you what,' she argued, 'since you're embarrassed, I'll telephone them and ask them. How's that?'

'All right,' I conceded.

Back she came smiling: 'They're coming to fetch us in a car.'

They were a polite, well-mannered cheerful lot. Bubbles was an air-hostess. Were the others Al Italia air crew? I have no recollection but they could have been. The house was very pleasant and located, as far as I remember, in a pine forest close to the sea. I was given a pleasant room and that evening there was a jolly dinner party.

The next day Bubbles and I were on the streets of Pisa by

eight. We sat under a sun umbrella and I will swear that I secured bacon and eggs. As we sipped our coffee I became a little uneasy: what if Alexandra had already arrived and decided to take an early morning stroll, and saw me with Bubbles supping cappuccino in the shaded sun? So I excused myself: 'Well, I'd better head for the old Tower!'

Sweet Bubbles escorted me through the streets of Pisa; we turned a corner under an ancient Roman arch and there, to my forward left was the basilica and one of the acknowledged wonders of this world, distinctly leaning and reasonably on its own. I thanked my mysterious good friend, said goodbye and began my walk towards my lunatic vigil.

I began my task by quietly walking around the astonishing renaissance construction. There were few people about. My eyes easily missed nothing. I coughed in a controlled manner, paid a few coins, received one of those myriad Italian tickets and slowly tramped to the top. Took a reasonable dekko at the scenery and descended. I was controlling myself very well. After strolling round and round the edifice once again I lay down on the grass and perused the increasing number of people. First sellers of fruit appeared and ice-cream merchants. The sun rose higher in the sky and tourist coaches were in the offing. Yes! There was a preponderance of Americans. Our recent enemies, the Germans, were thinner on the ground in those days. The sun began to get bloody hot; I noticed that one of the Italian vendors had actually retreated with his wares into the fine spray of a nearby fountain. Not a bad idea. Then I noticed that a crowd of teenagers, most of them reading books, had pulled back into the diminishing shade of what appeared to me to be a very high privet hedge. I held-out like a good Brit for a while and then calmly pulled back to that dark line of protection. After a while I became aware that these young men and women, who were now lying close to me, had taken an interest in my behaviour; there was a certain amount of nodding and nudging in my direction but I couldn't understand the *sotto voce* chatter because it was in the Italian language. I certainly got a mild touch of the needle. Suddenly one of the young men, urged on by the giggling others, edged towards me and started off: 'Signor – Sir – my friends and I see you for a long time. You walk round the tower, up the tower, down the tower, again around the tower. You lie on the grass, looking at the tower. Why do you love the tower so much?'

I eyed the students – for that is what they were (all from the University of Pisa as it turned out) – with little confidence. But I had been asked a direct question and ploughed forward with a direct answer: 'In London, one evening, I met a young American lady named Alexandra MacCallum . . .' The giggling continued and my tale was rapidly translated into Italian by a couple of my audience to their less-gifted chums. But as I progressed the hilarity ceased and the translators became swifter and more intense. By the time I came to the end and to the immediate moment, with my eyes still flicking around each visiting tourist, the youngsters gazed at me with rapt attention. They quietly chatted amongst themselves: 'Signor, what is your name?'

'Griffith; Kenneth Griffith.'

'Please, what does the Signorina MacCallum look like?'

'Ah, she has dark hair. She is nice-looking. She dresses nicely. She has horn-rimmed squarish spectacles!'

'Ah, Signor Griffith, we will help you find the Signorina MacCallum!'

'Well, that is very kind of you. Thank you.'

I now felt that I was getting into potentially deep water. What if Alexandra had changed her mind about me? I mean it wouldn't now be a matter of a little friendly note. There I would be – perhaps even larger than life. And what if she turned up holding another man's arm? Such things have certainly happened. And on top of all those potential hazards I had a largish group of enthusiastic assistants. Could be tricky! I thought to myself: 'If Alexandra doesn't seem knocked out by my apparition, I will suggest a glass of something and depart for Blighty. And if there's an escort? Well I'll play that one off the cuff.'

I addressed my helpers: 'Friends, of course we must face up to the possibility that Miss MacCallum will not come – perhaps never come . . .'

'Signor Griffith! She *will* come! We *know* she will come!'

The hours passed and the sun poured down from on-high. We crowded around the fountain.

'Signor Griffith!! Is that the Signorina MacCallum?'

'Ah – no; sadly not.'

'Signor Griffith!!'

'Ah, no.'

Midday passed and lunchtime arrived.

'Dear friends, please, you must go now. The visitors are all going for their meals. Please – thank you – but I want you to go and eat now.'

'No!! We will stay *all* day until you find the Signorina!'

I began to feel a bit desperate and dismal. The crowds had gone but the heat hadn't. Suddenly, in the far distance (my eyes were abnormally sharp in those days) through the distant Roman arch, I saw Alexandra walking all alone. I allowed her to approach fairly close before I spoke: 'Friends, there is the Signorina MacCallum!'

'Ahh! Oh, Signor Griffith, she is very beautiful!'

'Friends,' I announced, 'I am an actor. When the Signorina is opposite to us (Alexandra was on the far side of our road) I will project my voice across to her. She believes that I am in London, and since she is a little shortsighted she will wonder where the voice came from!'

'Ahhh! It is a very good joke!'

Alexandra came opposite to us and I carefully projected – clearly but not loudly – 'Alexandra!' I have never in my whole life seen such a reaction; she stopped, momentarily paused and then very slowly turned around the full three hundred and sixty degrees.

'Ahhhh,' said the young Italians. And I walked across the road and greeted my friend. Then Alexandra came back with me and I introduced her to my loyal and extraordinary search party. It was a happy time. I travelled to Florence and Rome with Alexandra and in Florence, on that very occasion, we experienced the Michelangelo/*David* adventure: 'It is very simple; all you do is knock off what you don't want and leave on what you do.'

Incidentally, years later, I was in a Chelsea pub, close to the River Thames when a pretty lady came up to me: 'Hello, Kenneth; how are you?'

I knew her face but where?

'We met in Pisa.'

'Bubbles! How are you?'

'Did you find Miss MacCallum?'

'Yes.' My delight in seeing Bubbles again was clear but after nostalgic talk she was gone and we have not met since.

The confused mists of time have swamped me about what happened next – I mean to Alexandra and myself in Europe. But I travelled alone to meet Peter O'Toole and Isabella Dunjohn in Zurich. In Zurich, with O'Toole, I met a few memorable people and there demonstrated that I was ever confused between romance, love and sex; but please let that pass. It would be impossible for Freud to sort my problems out. Or God have mercy. In Zurich I met an Indonesian lady who played the guitar and who wore saris which she called sarongs. I remember her with gratitude and affection and some alarm. As we walked through the magnificent public gardens of that very fussy city, my new friend would pick great bunches of magnificent civic flowers and when I nervously remonstrated, she loudly accused: 'Oh God! You are so *bourgeois*!' But overall she was a dear.

And then I met the distinguished playwright, Fritz Hochwelder, and we became friends. I think that he was Jewish and had come from Vienna during the Nazi obscenity. I knew one play that he had written which was produced in London at the Theatre Royal, Haymarket. It was called *The Strong Are Lonely* and Donald Wolfit had played the leading role.

Hochwelder loved the English language and he was one of the very few people in my life who have positively asked me to read to them. We would spend evenings in a vast low-ceilinged room in the old part of Zurich. The place seemed to be so elongated that all of it was never illuminated clearly. Great wooden beams and books and books.

'Read to me, Kenneth!' he demanded, in a deep resonant voice with its Viennese accent. Hochwelder was an abnormally short man but full of muscular power and around the ancient fireplace we would sit: 'Oh! for a draught of vintage full of the warm south.' Of course I would speak the glorious words with as much fineness as I was capable of; my companion would gaze into the fire, his head in his hands, wrapped in his volatile intelligence. Hour after hour. The artist enjoys the willing ear. Or eye.

One dark evening he announced: 'Kenneth, read me *Hamlet*!!'

It was as if the time had arrived! This was to be the climax of the story: 'How all occasions do inform against me . . .' And suddenly Hochwelder went berserk. He leapt to his feet in the eerie room with a roar: 'Aahh!' and he began to leap through the semi-darkness: 'It is impossible that a human being wrote *Hamlet*!'

And as the small mass of athletic muscle sailed close to my startled person, his hand shot out and the book was gone: 'It is *impossible* that a human being wrote *Hamlet*!! No human being ever wrote *Hamlet*!'

It was even the despairing rage of another creative writer who perhaps was injured by the towering, impossible competition. That night Hochwelder gave me one of the few meaningful, potent commentaries on William Shakespeare that I have ever experienced.

One evening before departing from Zurich we participated in a party: O'Toole, the Indonesian lady, Hochwelder and a strange young man who wore dark glasses, plus a few others who should not be named. There was music and singing (mainly from O'Toole who has a bottomless reservoir of ballads, and from my new sari-clad friend). Yes, there was much boozing and no doubt some 'How's-your-father'. But I am rarely – even over the years – a heavy drinker. I make my own contributions to self-survival; which fact meant that I was the first person to stand upright on the following morning. Through the debris of celebration I threaded, out into the front garden of our detached house. Already a woman was attending to some domestic duty next door. The light was painful and the neighbour addressed me with that pronounced hoity-toity Swiss-German accent: 'Please remember, while you are here, not to be so happy!'

She must have been referring to our nocturnal jollity. I replied: 'Madame, I promise to remember that I am in Switzerland now and I will do my best not to be so happy!'

The Swiss lady was pleased with my simple honest reply.

The young man with the dark glasses turned out to be a schoolteacher and though I had alienated the affections of his lady-friend (oh fickle woman and faithless man) he treated me with friendliness and he invited me to visit his small school in the so-beautiful Swiss countryside. He drove me there on the back of his motorbike, amongst the mountains. He taught mentally retarded children and I was privileged to sit at a desk amongst them. My young Swiss friend played to all of us in the class on his ocarina (an 'egg-shaped musical wind instrument' according to the *Concise Oxford Dictionary*) and everyone shouted with delight. Then the boys and girls sang for me and the schoolteacher translated each song's title into English for my benefit. One piece was called 'Twenty Thousand Wanderers' and it had a rousing repetitive chorus after each verse. I didn't understand a word of what it was about. The children sang with great happiness. I raised my hand: 'Please, what is the song about?'

'Oh, it is about twenty thousand refugee wanderers who reached a Swiss mountain pass during the Second World War and there our Swiss border guards refused them entry and turned them back.'

Were they Jews? And what was their fate? I think that my Swiss friend told me this story with sad irony. But the faces of those innocent Swiss children laughing as they sang the jolly good tune was a sight that I shall live with till I die. Outside the little village school on the lush Alpine grass amid those fabulous flowers was a great white decorated marquee; an evangelist was conducting a Christian revival service in it. I mention this as a purely incidental memory of that day.

Off O'Toole and I went on a Continental jaunt and first we

attempted to penetrate the Italian Alps with, ominously, O'Toole at the steering wheel. Now few people can have suffered (I hastily emphasize that I am referring to his salad days, not the sobriety which he exercises today) this experience as I have. Mr O'Toole was then *learning* to drive and even on the flat fenlands of Cambridgeshire, with his flashes-of-lightning temperament, one's nerves were tested to the limit. But very high up, on a sharp bend of – was it the Brenner Pass? – O'Toole cursed: 'What's wrong with the bloody gears!?

As calmly as I could I said: 'O'Toole, that isn't the gear lever you're holding, that is the hand-brake.'

May God strike me dead as I sit here in Connemara if that is not the simple historical truth. And I am confessing that I, his co-driver as-it-were, am no Nikki Lauda – or Fangio as it was at that time. But!!

In due course we entered Italy and found a memorable boarding house virtually hanging over Lake Como. It cost astonishingly little to stay in (we both had astonishingly little to spend!) It was pretty and immaculately clean and the food was superb; particularly the trout out of the great lake. Unfortunately our idyll was marred when O'Toole garnered some domestic news which deeply distressed him and this led him to hitting the Italian wine unmercifully. And in this explosive state – he was hopping about with misery – he announced to me that the time had arrived 'to end it all'! Well it was night time and off he dashed, with me in pursuit. Along the road above the lake he pounded (it should be borne in mind that he is a least six feet two inches, while I am barely five feet eight inches). Up onto the wall leapt O'Toole. 'Ah!' Below were the dark sombre waters. If memory serves me well I got a quick glance: 'Griffith! It's got to end!'

And into the dark waters went O'Toole – feet first!

'My God! I can't swim a bloody stroke!' flashed through my awed brain. At that moment *Lawrence of Arabia*, *The Ruling Class*, *The Lion in Winter*, *My Favourite Year*, to mention only a handful, were in mortal jeopardy. However, fate is fate, and at that particular point – unknown to either of us – Lake Como is only two feet deep! Yes, into the water O'Toole plunged but only to jar his poor young legs with a monumental shock. Astonishingly nothing fractured and there was instant sobriety and O'Toole's private grief subsided – to some extent.

Across Italy we adventured, heading for the romance of Venice, which neither of us had viewed before. I was not in a good mood; it had something to do with Alexandra and my uneasy conscience. We arrived at an unattractive area in the little car and we were told that *this* was Venice and that we had to leave our transport there. My ignorance of the reality of Venice fed my bad temper. We were loaded into a motorized barge and off it chugged. The water and scenery were grey and miserable; we turned a corner of that channel and there, suddenly, was the breathtaking unparalleled magic. I suppose that it would be ideal for everyone to enter Venice for the first time in my state of abject ignorance. But a couple of months ago – is it now the eighth visit? – Venice was still scarcely believable.

Just off St Mark's Square we found a couple of rooms which were owned by a lady who was stark staring mad. But they were very cheap and bang in the middle of the old fantasy. A few nights ago, Mr O'Toole and myself sat in front of a turf fire and confessed that over the intervening years we both wandered, separately, to that doorway of our then humble digs. He unavoidably carrying the aura of international fame and even I – well – doing reasonably well in my own particular different game. The doorway is now rather posh.

Eventually O'Toole and I regretfully moved out of Venice on our Grand Tour. O'Toole, who is an intensive student, wanted to see a famous sixteenth (1585) century theatre at a place called Vicenza. We arrived in the city and found the place to be astonishing. I learnt for the first time what 'Palladian' meant.

O'Toole and I arrived at the famous Theatre Olimpico. What a treasure! It is as immaculate as it ever was. Still on the stage is the early eighteenth-century set, designed so that you can actually walk up the strongly perspected streets. Around the walls of the circular auditorium were plaques on which were inscribed the comments of previous visitors: Napoleon and the Old Brits – Shelley, Keats, Byron and company. Between us and the stage was a fine chain barrier. While gazing in awe at this precious piece of humanity's theatrical past, which for some mysterious reason humanity had not dismantled, a dapper gentleman appeared and after gazing at me, exclaimed: 'You are the English actor!'

'No, sir, the Welsh or British actor, but not the English!'

'Ah, I am very proud to meet you.'

'Thank you. My name is Griffith and this is Mr Peter O'Toole; another British actor – from the Old Vic.'

I didn't emphasize the 'Bristol' Old Vic.

'Ah! said the Italian, deeply impressed – the Old Vic! I am the curator of this beautiful theatre!'

O'Toole was now hissing into my right ear: 'Griffith, ask him if we can *walk* on the stage!'

O'Toole has always urged me to push forward more aggressively in life than I have felt inclined – that is unless I felt that a big issue like Ireland or Israel or South Africa was at stake.

'Signor, would it be possible for my friend, Mr O'Toole and myself – bearing in mind that we are actors – to actually tread on the boards of your magnificent stage?'

'Ah, Signor Griffith, sadly this is strictly forbidden. But (and he delicately reached for a hook on the chain barrier) in your case, I make the exception.' The good curator spoke his English with an Italian accent overlaid by an American influence. O'Toole and I tremulously 'trod the boards'. I noted that my beloved Irish friend was wiping a few tears from his eyes: 'Marvellous! Bloody marvellous!'

Suddenly the curator, with unsuppressed emotion: 'Mr Griffith! Will you and your friend from the Old Vic please honour this stage by speaking some – Shakespeare! – on it?'

'Oh!' said I; the request was awkward, bearing in mind the kindness and admiration that we were being shown. 'Well – ah – Mr O'Toole and myself haven't anything prepared and being —'

O'Toole was again hissing in my ear: 'Yes – tell him yes! Of course we'll do something!'

'But what, O'Toole?'

'Well you remember Oberon, for God's sake! I can manage Puck!'

'What?'

'Look, *you* do your Oberon and I'll fill in with Puck.'

'Are you sure, O'Toole?'

'Of course I'm bloody sure, Griffith!'

'Oh . . .'

And so I agreed.

'Thank you Signor Griffith; but before you start I must send for my fellow workers.'

When the museum staff were seated expectantly I launched forth encouraged by winks from O'Toole: 'But we are spirits of another sort . . .' and when Puck's cue was spoken: 'We may affect this business yet 'ere day', the great actor was there like lightning: 'Up and down, up and down; I will lead them up and down . . .' Of course he has never played Puck in his life – he's a very big lad; but there he was dashing around the stage suiting the action to the words. When we had completed our extraordinary performance and the ecstatic applause had subsided a little, O'Toole held up his hands: 'And now friends I'll follow up with a little piece of *Hamlet*.' And I have no recollection that he even offered me the role of Laertes.

FIFTEEN

Somehow, during our travels, O'Toole and I met up with Alexandra MacCallum, back in Switzerland; she was staying at a hotel predictably called the Beau Rivage. I had been rather ill; I had climbed high up an Italian mountain which hung above Lake Como and immediately afterwards I was hit for six. Reminiscing in Ireland, just a few weeks ago, O'Toole suddenly announced, out of the blue and after all of these many years: 'It was some fever on that mountain that got into you.'

Anyway, there I was at the Beau Rivage with Alexandra, with O'Toole grinning in a friendly, interested way. Alexandra assessed my sickly condition and stated: 'Now what you need is a large beef steak,' and she promptly ordered one which was carried to her room. Well, I am an instinctive vegetarian and this meat was underdone. 'You've got to build up your strength,' continued Alexandra and I ate the awful thing; which says a great deal for my American friend's influence over me.

I returned to Britain, and Alexandra remained in Europe. I had decided that my close relationship with Doria must be severed. I was – as I have been most of my life – in an emotional mess. I felt that I should go to America, and there begin to build a stable relationship with Alexandra. The years of continual turmoil had frayed my edges; Alexandra and California appeared to be a new open road. I was on the dockside at Newcastle as Alexandra arrived on the appropriately named MV *Venus*. We went to the Edinburgh Festival together, and then she returned to California.

Back in London I learnt that Doria was ill; indeed she had

been taken to St George's Hospital at Hyde Park Corner. It was not far away and I ran. Hospitals make me feel queasy – as Alexandra's beef steak had done and for the same bloody reason. I was told that Doria was about to be operated on and the official gave me directions to her ward. I blundered into the labyrinthine ways: the white tiled corridors, the chemical smells, individuals hurrying on their business of life and death. I was directed into an enormous lift and there amongst the white clad servants of our sickness was a trolley on which was clearly a prone human figure which appeared to be entirely covered with a white sheet. I tottered out of that frightening lift. Some helpful person pointed the way: 'Down there on the right.' I pushed myself forward. Was Doria dying? Suddenly from out of the great swing doors more masked figures in white emerged pulling another of those mobile tables, on which was another horizontal body. I threw my eyes to the ceiling and breathed deeply and at the same time impossibly attempted to avoid inhaling the ether. And then the most alarming experience took place; while leaning against the white tiles and believing that all was up with me a voice shrieked: 'Griffith!'

'Ahh!' I focused in agony on the trolley and there between the top of the sheets and the white mob-hat were a pair of eyes piercing me. The sheet moved and the mouth said: 'Griffith, there's cold chicken in the fridge and chocolate cake. Are you all right?'

'Yes, Doria,' I croaked.

'See you soon,' she said. And the operating team peered at our scene curiously. I mumbled to some surgeon or other: 'Doria's very eccentric.' I can recall nothing else until I was eventually sitting by Doria's bedside, holding her hand and saying: 'Of course I'm not going to America.'

I viewed the whole trauma that we were all in and for better or for worse decided to stay in Britain and to continue my life at Dorset Mews. I painfully communicated this decision to Alexandra and in retrospect I sense that all was for the best – particularly for Alexandra.

Peter O'Toole concluded his work and explosive living at

the Bristol Old Vic and he said to me: 'Griffith, I have one or two places in London where I can kip down but if you can manage it I'd like to stay with you and Dobie [Doria].' He moved into our small spare room and Dorset Mews was never to be the same again. When O'Toole refers to 'living in a box', he is harking back to those young times.

Material survival through acting was the due process. Looking back I can see that I was not behaving as a wise ambitious actor should. I did nothing to win influential theatrical allies or influence them. Of course I had a few outstanding friends in the theatre and films; indeed the best in Britain: men like Tyrone Guthrie and Roy Boulting. But they were my friends because we mutually liked each other and admired each other's professional standards. My not very conscious attitude was: 'potential employers should know by now what I can do; leave it to merit'. But of course ability is not enough. Thespians are almost completely in the hands of producers and surprisingly producers are usually strangely ignorant about the potential of players. It always was so and still is. What producers can recognize is success. Edmund Kean was hungry and rejected for eight years and then, almost by accident, in an emergency, he was turfed onto Drury Lane's stage. He was a sensation that night as Shylock and then and only then did the impresarios recognize his frightening strength as an actor. Of course Kean rarely respected managers and what-have-you afterwards. And that attitude has always tended to prevail amongst great players to this very day; tough great players are now nearly extinct – at least in our English speaking world. And, here in Britain, during our wealthy, subsidized, institutional times the grey barons in power are not too anxious to recognize and promote the potentially great performers. This is a combination of puritanically presenting *their* interpretation of the play, which is closely married to the other numbing reason: the promotion of their egos. There are exceptions, of course, but for obvious reasons the less egotistical producers are not running the Royal Shakespeare Company or the National Theatre. Mark you, ego can manifest itself in many ways. And I am certainly not against ego *per se*; but when it injures or limits the potential of a player's capacity

to reveal and excite the playwright's ideas, I am against ego.
The directors of our institutional theatres have metamorphosed
my profession from big oil-painters to often little insipid water-
colourists. I resent that.

But Doria and I were happy enough. The acting bits have
become a long haze. I have just come across an old *TV Times*
and on the front cover is a photograph of Mr Jack Hawkins
and myself playing roles in – presumably – a television film; I
haven't the slightest recollection of doing it. I am certain that
I performed the role to the utmost of my ability but most of
what I was called upon to do was, sadly, forgettable. But it
probably entertained and that is something. There were occasional challenges, of course, and they made me feel that my
creative talent was not being used in vain.

O'Toole was also being wasted initially. Though his
achievements at Bristol had been communicated excitedly to
London, no one seemed to be jumping at the opportunity.
O'Toole of course was positively a young carousing man of
the theatre. In those days he drank beer to powerful effect and
when he felt it was necessary he put up his fists and brawled.
However, never once, drunk or sober has he said one word out
of place to either Doria or myself. Today he is usually
reserved, wise and quieter than me. He gives me great humorous support; curiously he often has the active continuing role
of my *elder* brother! But Dorset Mews was different. In the
middle of the night I would hear the Irish roar – at Hyde Park
Corner, but coming nearer. I often put my head under the pillow and tried to forget. One morning, getting up very early to
depart for a film studio, I found the living-room floor littered
with hungover men from the previous night. O'Toole
appeared: 'Oh, Griffith, I want you to meet Father ——' and
he gave one of the prone figures a prod with his foot.

Well, it was early in the morning and I didn't want jokes:
'Oh, come off it, O'Toole!'

Peter bent down and picked up a Roman Catholic's dog-
collar: 'What's this, Griffith, a bunch of bloody grapes?'

'Oh, I beg your pardon, Father!'

*

I was blacklisted from BBC television plays ever since I wrote that letter after *Crime and Punishment*, accusing them of living off 'the poverty of my profession'.

One day the telephone rang in Dorset Mews: 'May I speak to Mr Kenneth Griffith?'

'I'm Griffith.'

'Oh, Mr Griffith, my name is John Jacobs and I'm directing a television play for the BBC. Now I know that you have a difference of opinion with them but I want you to be in this production very much. May I visit you?'

Well, I was astonished at such unprecedented courtesy from a BBC man – but then I think that Mr Jacobs was a freelancer who was temporarily working for the Corporation.

'Of course you can, Mr Jacobs.'

In due course he arrived, smiling, intelligent and friendly. On the settee lay the long figure of the disgruntled O'Toole.

'Oh, Mr Jacobs, this is Mr Peter O'Toole.'

'How are you, Mr O'Toole?'

'Fine,' with a trace of irony.

'Mr O'Toole is probably the greatest actor in Britain today.'

Peter, who was out of work, I think, said 'Huh' as he exited.

Mr Jacobs gave me an oblique look: 'Very amusing, Mr Griffith,' and then noting my demeanour: 'Are you serious? About him?' nodding towards the closed door.

'Absolutely serious. I don't joke about such important matters.'

'Good Lord.' And then he began to sell me the idea of being in his production. The BBC's rate of pay to actors had been doubled (which still made it abysmally low) and I liked John Jacobs, so I returned to the awkward fold.

After John Jacobs' production was behind us he talked to me of the virtues of the BBC. He told me that he was going to direct a play for them about the remarkable French artist Gaudier-Brzeska. This young man, on the eve of the 1914–1918 war, had sworn that he would not fight: he did and was killed, I think, very quickly. Mr Jacobs, underlining the support that he was being given, told me that the BBC were sending him to Paris to search for the most suitable actor.

Yes, I was astonished and impressed. And it was not to be the end of the story for me – or O'Toole.

When I had visited the Edinburgh Festival with Alexandra MacCallum we had seen a play written by a then unknown Willis Hall called *The Disciplines of War*; it had been performed by university students. I thought that the whole thing was outstanding. On returning to England I had advised Roy Boulting to buy the film rights and had told Peter O'Toole that the central cockney character was a winner for himself. Nothing happened. A long time later I learnt that the Royal Court Theatre – then at its revolutionary zenith – was going into production with a play called *The Long and the Short and the Tall* and it dawned on me that this was the same play that I had seen in Edinburgh; simply the title had been changed. But Albert Finney was to play that sparkling cockney part. One day I got home from work and O'Toole was elated: 'Griffith! Fantastic news! Finney's ill (I think O'Toole specified the complaint) and they want me to read for the part!'

I immediately got onto my radical horse: 'What do they want you to *read* it for? Your fame at Bristol should be sufficient. Didn't they bother to go across to see you act!?'

What always riles me is the priggish judgements that certain directors and producers must make. Rather like a school-teacher marking a pupil's examination paper. All right if the player is a beginner and unknown. But not a man who has distinguished himself playing principal Shavian and Shakespearian roles. The thought of George Devine, sucking on his pipe, judging O'Toole reading a contemporary play made me aware of nausea. But O'Toole answered my anger with the only charitable remark I have ever heard him make about the British Theatre's Establishment: 'Well, Griffith, it's a big responsibility; they have to be sure.'

I was dumbfounded then at his humble attitude and I still am. However, I am glad to report that he has not repeated it since.

The telephone rang in our little living room at Dorset Mews. It was a foreign call: 'Is that you, Kenneth? John Jacobs here. I'm in Paris; bit of a problem. I'm here looking for an actor to play Gaudier-Brzeska – but anyone suitable doesn't speak English.'

'Oh dear!'

'You remember that chap O'Toole who was in your house?'

'Yes, he's here now.'

'Oh, good. Did you really mean it when you implied that he was a great actor?'

'John, I told you before and I repeat it; I don't joke about such matters. O'Toole is something very special.'

'Well, Kenneth, if you are only half right he would be perfect for Brzeska.'

'Listen, John – very carefully – do yourself a good turn and accept my word.'

'Can I speak to him?'

'Yes, I'll get him.'

In actual fact there was no need to leave the room because O'Toole was draped along the settee. I hustled him into the corridor: 'Listen O'Toole, that is John Jacobs calling from Paris; he's doing a telly about a brilliant French artist named Brzeska; he wants to talk to you. Jacobs is a nice bright man.'

O'Toole picked up the phone and I listened in a state of considerable excitement: 'Morning Mr Jacobs – yes, yes, – well, I may be doing an important play at the Royal Court – very soon – I don't know . . .'

I couldn't bear the silence: 'What does he say, O'Toole?'

'He's offered me the part.'

'Ask Mr Jacobs for his number; tell him you'll phone back in ten minutes. I want to talk to you.'

Peter wrote down the number and hung up. I asked: 'What has he offered you?'

'He said that the part is mine if I agree to do it now.'

'Good! Listen to me very carefully. This is my firm opinion. Always back the man with courage and style. You've not had a leading part on television. John Jacobs is no fool; he thinks highly of this play. I haven't read it of course but it must be right for you. Phone back and accept.'

'What if I lose the Royal Court play?'

'A risk well worth taking.'

Peter O'Toole learnt early in his life to look at every issue and everybody suspiciously: 'Why do you say that?'

'Of course it's a risk, but if I read the Royal Court people correctly, the fact that you are demonstrating your independence of their patronage will make them want you very badly. It *is* a risk – but you'll have the television play. Tell Auntie Devine to stuff it!'

O'Toole paused and then: 'Yes, you're bloody right!'

He phoned John Jacobs in Paris, accepted the Brzeska play and then, with *The Long and the Short and the Tall* under his arm, he charged off westward across Eaton Square. Many years later – indeed not so long ago – a secretary from the Royal Court Theatre at that time told me that O'Toole had carried out my advice to the literal letter; he plonked the script down and said 'Stuff it!' and made an exit. Well, I didn't mean him to be so undiplomatic, but it did have the maximum effect. When he got back to our home, the Royal Court was phoning: 'What did you mean Peter?'

'I'm doing a television play!'

'When?'

'Starting in two weeks.'

'What if we were to delay our rehearsals till you've finished the television, will you do our play then?'

'Is that a firm offer?'

'Yes.'

'Done.'

I watched O'Toole perform the Brzeska play – live of course – with Doria. He was not less than magnificent. As it ended I stood up: 'I only hope that I am as good as that!' It is the only time that I have had such self-doubt concerning anybody else.

On O'Toole went into the Royal Court. He would come home from rehearsals full of praise for other actors in the cast. I remember him going on about Robert Shaw, whom I had got to know well at the Old Vic. I found it difficult to believe that Bob was as outstanding as O'Toole was suggesting. I also felt a little out of it. Here was a young shooting star telling me every day about the remarkable talents of other young actors; yes, I did feel out of the main stream – which indeed I was. Hey ho!

Doria and I were at the first night and I observed O'Toole ruthlessly hammer home every fraction of his opportunity. The truth is I felt that it was like a one-man show. He may have admired the others but this was his opportunity to demonstrate his enormous size and he was merciless. Peter O'Toole knew about the reality of showbiz; he knew where he wanted to go and he was not going to fumble. He succeeded in winning hands down and most vitally drawing attention to himself. Shortly after this he announced to me: 'Griffith, most of our business is a monumental shit-house and I'm going to be a big shit-house keeper!' Of course the metaphor was largely true but it should be examined beyond those terrible but accurate words. If one examines two of the Shavian productions which he has been responsible for: *Man and Superman* at the Theatre Royal, Haymarket and *Pygmalion* at the Shaftesbury Theatre, you can see the loving admiration for the challenging playwright, for his fellow players, and the striving for his own highest hopes. And that achieved in the middle of a rapidly declining British commercial theatre.

To live in Dorset Mews after those two O'Toole performances (the Brzeska play and then the Royal Court exhibition) was an extraordinary experience. I do not exaggerate. The phone rang continuously and often from the most powerful people in our drama business. O'Toole's reaction to this distinguished pursuit was similar to the great Edmund Kean's; very often when a large potential employer asked me if they could speak to him, he would request of me: 'Be a darling, Griffith, and tell him I'm having a kip.'

It gave me some vicarious pleasure to say what I had never had the opportunity to say on my own behalf. Of course I slightly reworded the instructions: 'Mr O'Toole is having a much-needed rest, sir.'

Peter's career was quick and upward. His first film for the cinema was *The Savage Innocents* and it was made at Pinewood Studios. That splendid actor, Anthony Quinn, played an Eskimo and O'Toole was cast as a North-West

Canadian Mounted Policeman. O'Toole, speedily moving away from a grave shortage of ready cash, showed me his contract: 'Look at that, Griffith! Two and a half thousand quid!' And then he pointed to another item: 'Car provided' and again I was pleasantly impressed. However, I also noted that adjacent to the promise of transport and, in parenthesis, was the ominous cunning legal afterthought: 'when available'. But when I am in the company of a soaring spirit I am reluctant to inhibit the rare free-wheeling. I said nothing beyond my enthusiastic noises.

Came the morning of O'Toole's first day *ever* on a feature film and I was up very early to go to Beaconsfield Film Studios, and in the bitter grey of pre-dawn I felt a mild unease because I had not heard Peter stir. But up to a point I would not intrude to be my brother's keeper. Just as I was leaving Dorset Mews, significantly to catch a miserable train (little doubt), the telephone rang: 'This is *The Savage Innocents* Production Office at Pinewood Studios. Is that Mr O'Toole's residence?'

'Yes.'

'Oh, sorry to trouble you so early, but Mr O'Toole was due here half an hour ago for make-up (I think he was doomed to wear a beard). I wonder if you know what time he left?'

I replied with a spontaneous lie: 'Well, this is a very large house (it was a minute mews flat), but I'll try to find out.'

I took about a dozen steps to the door of O'Toole's 'box' and knocked.

'Uh? Come in.'

'O'Toole, it's the production office at Pinewood; you were due there half an hour ago' (and it was a good hour and a quarter's drive from London).

O'Toole didn't turn the proverbial hair: 'Did my car come?'

'No, O'Toole.'

'Be a darling, Griffith, tell 'em "no car, no me".' And he put his head back under the pillow. I walked to the phone and quoted my friend with some pleasure. All I heard on the other end was: 'Oh my God!'

Now I knew the mentality that lay behind that sub-statement

re O'Toole's car: 'when available'. But it is a rash person who plans to mess about with my Irish friend. Quickly a Rolls-Royce appeared in front of Dorset Mews with a lady in it, apart from the driver, to supervise Peter's entry. And the Rolls from then on was *always* available – to this very day. As for me, well, I have no serious complaint and I rarely travel to work any more without transport being provided, but from the pages of this book you can learn more about the acting game than three years at the Royal Academy of Dramatic Art – a lot more . . .

Doria was devoted to O'Toole, as – I must say – she was devoted to me. During the course of each week Peter would hide his used shirts, socks and underclothes and I observed Doria search for them and then wash and iron them with mine and replace them in Peter's cupboard. This was a magic routine. Nothing was ever discussed; it was a magic circle.

One day, while I was out, O'Toole, much the worse for wear, reached our front door and could go no further. Doria heaved the heavy, grunting body up the flight of stairs, accelerating towards the end because police sirens were approaching. She pulled Peter into the living-room just as the officers of the law swept into Dorset Mews: 'Have you an intoxicated gentleman inside, madam?'

'Certainly not!'

'May we search, madam?'

'Not without a search warrant!'

I understand that in the background, as little Doria stood stiffly at the door, could be heard an incomprehensible mumble. But the officers retreated. However, came the day when the landlord summoned me (we were part of the Grosvenor Estate): 'Mr Griffith you have been a very good tenant, but the fact that the Black Maria called at Dorset Mews on four separate occasions on one day looking for your friend Mr O'Toole is more than we are going to put up with. If he doesn't mend his ways I am afraid that you will all have to go!'

Well, I saw the landlord's reasonable point and assured him that our behaviour would be exemplary in future. However, sometimes O'Toole would telephone us when he had gone too far: 'Where are you, O'Toole?'

'Ah ha!' and he would hang up.

Then Doria and I would put on our coats and travel on a thirty-eight bus to Piccadilly Circus and walk to the Salisbury pub in St Martin's Lane and there begin our negotiations to get our friend safely home. Not an easy journey.

On seeing us, O'Toole would wail: 'Oh, God, I'm so fucking predictable!' Of course the last thing in the world that he desired was predictability. He was only predictable after he'd had a few jars.

When Miss Sian Phillips became the lady in Peter's life it settled much of the restlessness. They were devoted to each other. Sian, being a very wise woman, understood many elements in Peter's complex character that nine hundred and ninety nine women out of a thousand would not have a vague clue about. Stability began to appear. One day, while I was rehearsing a television play in Cardiff, Sian and Peter appeared to tell me that they were going to get married. As soon as I could I isolated Sian and walked with her round and round Cardiff's Civic Centre – which incidentally is an extraordinary edifice; sort of miniature mock Hapsburg.

'Sian, you *can't* marry him!'

'Why not!?'

'Well, he's – he's not like the rest of us.'

'Peter is the most normal man I've ever met!'

My mouth opened and shut: 'Well, Sian, your definition of "normal" must be different to mine.'

I was staying with friends in Cardiff. A very decent Welsh family: Mr and Mrs Herbert Davies and daughters. During the evening of the above conversation with Sian, I was partaking of the evening meal when we heard striding footsteps. Into the dining room thundered O'Toole with Sian jogging behind: 'Evening all! All right, Griffith – you twisted bloody Welshman! Never mind Sian – tell *me*!'

And as I debated with O'Toole hour after hour the subject of his shortcomings – so I presumed – as a *bridegroom*, I felt very sure of my authoritative knowledge, because I was well

aware that I had failed in one marriage and that my relationship with Doria had also wobbled badly. Experience! Well, the
argument continued unrelentingly until the early hours of the
morning. Initially, the Davies family were fascinated observers,
but one by one they staggered off to bed. I became reconciled
that I would not be working on the text of my play that night
and I believe that I got the better of the debate but largely
because I remained sober while O'Toole continually refuelled
himself from a bottle of whisky. As dawn came up he received
the message of our respective mental states and he staggered to
his feet pointing the now empty bottle at me: 'All right, you
miserable little Welsh bastard – I'll catch up with you if it's the
last bloody thing I do in my life!' And he staggered off into the
Welsh dawn – which is different to any other sort of dawn.

It was not a completely satisfactory visit to Wales for me in
other ways. I think that I was acting in a play about the bomb
plot to kill Hitler which had been written by our splendid
Welsh nationalist, Saunders Lewis, and which was being
directed by his devoted disciple and fine writer himself: Emyr
Humphries. Into the rehearsal room appeared an advance
copy of the *Radio Times* and I casually glanced at it to see
how the feature billing had been arranged. Was I at the top? It
was a distinguished cast. I found the page and froze with
shock; I wasn't featured at all!

Donald Houston, who was one of the cast noticed my stiff
manner: 'What's the matter, Ken?'

'Oh, I've just seen the *Radio Times*.'

'Oh my God! I wondered if you'd seen it; it's bloody dreadful!'

'Now such an omission is not simply a matter of wounded
ego; how a player is billed is significant not only for the
player's public image but for his professional status also. It is
a professionally serious matter.

Dear Donald Houston continued his comforting words:
'Look, I've already asked Emyr [the director] how he could
have done that to you and he explained that your agent was
the only agent who didn't ask for feature billing. But I told
him that that was ridiculous.'

It all became fairly clear to me: the person handling my television work was new on the job and Emyr Humphries had only recently moved from being a writer and lecturer to the harsher world of BBC drama. In fact he is an unusually considerate and thoughtful man.

'Look,' pressed Donald, 'I know it's a serious matter, but why don't you come home with me to Tonypandy [in the Rhondda Valley] for the weekend? We'll have a great time.'

Well I knew that I had just been offered the ultimate accolade from a Valley man. Very moved, I accepted. I hadn't forgiven poor Emyr and when at the end of the afternoon he suggested that we ran through a scene 'just once again' I replied haughtily: 'I'm afraid not; it's 5 pm and Mr Houston and I have an appointment in Tonypandy.'

As Donald drove me westwards across South Wales to his old home he said: 'Oh! I should have told you. I have to go this evening to Tonypandy Opera House to attend a local production of *Oklahoma!*. Of course you don't have to come.' Of course I wanted to go!

In Donald's terraced Welsh home I immediately regained my sense of proportion. His grandma welcomed me and I sat by the side of a coal fire in a genuine miner's cottage. I felt very good indeed. Donald bustled me along: 'Come on, we mustn't be late. You don't mind if they make a bit of fuss of us, do you? Anyway, they will!'

We were received by the manager of the theatre and guided through the packed house to our front-row, dead centre seats in the dress circle. 'If there's anything you want . . .' The show was excellent; needless to say the singing was special. I was enjoying myself. The first half ended and as the house lights came up our friend the manager hurried on, holding up his hands to discourage people from leaving their seats: 'Ladies and gentlemen, last year I said from this stage that nothing could surpass the performance that we had witnessed then, but having seen the first half of *Oklahoma!* tonight I know that you will all agree with me I was wrong. Tonight is superb. And one more thing. I know most of you already know – in our midst is our own son, whom we all love and are very proud of: Donald Houston!!' A spotlight focused on Donald as he got to his feet and everyone cheered as Donald waved. And as he sat down the manager raised his hands again: '*And,* he has brought with him tonight his friend, another distinguished Welsh actor, whom we are also very proud of: Mister Kenneth *Edwards*!' And I stood smiling and dazed in the spotlight. I noticed that Donald had collapsed onto the floor and was hysterical with laughter and tears. He dragged himself to his feet: 'This is certainly your Black Friday.'

Well Sian Phillips and Peter O'Toole got married and it lasted for twenty valuable years and produced two daughters. I viewed their life together with envious awe. I have often miscalculated, but my doubts about their formal union was my biggest mistake. However, a few years ago, on the eve of their separation and eventual divorce, Sian suddenly said to me: 'Oh, isn't he strange?'

And I virtually jumped as I replied: 'Sian, don't say that to *me*!'

But for most of those years that marriage was as firm as Dame Sybil's and Lewis Casson's.

I had been filming at Beaconsfield Studios and we were rehearsing a scene when an assistant director said: 'Mr Griffith, there's a telephone call for you.'

'Oh please take the number and I'll phone back.'

'It's Mr Peter O'Toole.'

It was the director who intervened: 'Kenneth, go ahead and take it now.'

I took the call in the production office: 'Griffith, Sian and I are flying to Dublin to get married next week and we've booked three seats. You're best man.'

I was enormously pleased but all I could say was: 'Peter, you know where you're calling me? Beaconsfield Studios. I'm on this film for another five weeks – every day.'

'What?'

'Well, I can't go to Dublin!'

'You mean to tell me Griffith that you won't leave a bloody film for a couple of days to be with Sian and me when we get married!!?'

'I can't O'Toole!'

'Right!'

And his phone went down with a bang.

There is a great deal about Peter O'Toole on these pages because his spirit has overwhelmed my life. And I don't regret that fact one scrap. Indeed he has been, and continues to be, one of the most valuable influences in my experience. My own career as an actor was not flying to the heights that I believed I should go. I was a leading television actor and I often made a mark on films but I was not emulating Edmund Kean which I had long felt that I should. I was not stretching myself and therefore suffered an underlying frustration. But my friend, O'Toole, *was* emulating Edmund Kean and while doing so he was also instructing me by example to move out and start fighting. He was the most recent influence to prod me out of my circumscribed Nonconformist Protestant mentality. There was Tyrone Guthrie urging me to make my Oberon bigger; there was the miniature naked lady in a corner of a large sheet of paper at the St Martin's School of Art and now there was O'Toole *living* the big size, under my nose. Of course whether I should have walked off a film set for a couple of days to support my friend in Dublin is another matter. Priorities.

O'Toole went to Stratford-upon-Avon. For the first-night of his Shylock he sent me a ticket: ten rows back, dead centre. I was rehearsing a television play on that day and I sped northward as soon as work was completed; I wouldn't see much of O'Toole's performance. I scrambled into the theatre waving my ticket and stood breathless at the back as O'Toole made his final exit and I heard him say – as Shylock – 'I am content' and I heard the great applause. If you have a great actor playing Shylock – and it should always be a great actor playing Shylock – how can the play continue any further with those wet, shallow Christians? I don't remember anything else about the evening.

I remember the Dirty Duck pub at Stratford-upon-Avon. O'Toole was now a dashing hero to many. He would sit in the bar surrounded by admirers and preach the Word. Every so often he would cut a slice off and hand it to me: 'Now what do you think, Griffith? You tell them, Griffith.'

What a perilous journey life is – particularly for artists on the open market. And most particularly for us Players, who are almost totally dependent on that mishmash of potential employers. We Thespians have our respective talents to offer, but our success, or lack of it, is only casually equated with our true worth! O'Toole is some six feet plus in height, beautiful in appearance, highly intelligent, with a piercingly perceptive imagination and a devastating preoccupation with the Drama; how could he fail? But even he never risked leaving his talent on a marble slab to be bought or rejected. He went forth like an evangelizing William Booth to provoke and change things. However, in doing this he has upset many of the powerful mediocrities who run companies. And there is no greater proof of what I am writing about than the fact that he has been nominated seven times for the American Oscar – more than any other player ever – and has never won it once. They clearly *have* to nominate him – you cannot ignore a person who, as an actor, is in a class of his own. But so deeply do they resent his independence and his cheeky refusal to show respect, where rarely any respect is due, that they would go to the very lengths that they have to, to deny him the First Prize. But, presuming that film – I mean the negative and prints – physically last long enough, *posterity* will give him the Oscar. And even without film as the moving vocal proof, the truth will out. No film exists of Edmund Kean on the boards, but every actor with vision knows the truth about that glowering thunderball.

SIXTEEN

Well there I was in the lightning and shadow of my magic friend. What was to become of me? Pondering back I don't think that it occurred to me that, in due course, I would *not* explode in front of the public as Shylock, Iago, Richard the Third, Hamlet and company. But in the meantime I soldiered on in my television plays and with my endlessly varied feature roles in a very mixed bag of films. And then – out of the blue – a small event came my way which carried the germ of my ultimate personal and professional salvation: I was invited to be interviewed on the BBC's rightly renowned *Tonight* programme. Mr Cliff Michelmore conducted those proceedings, who, incidentally, has never been bettered, and Mr Derek Hart interviewed me. I chose to talk about the Second Anglo-Boer War, which had become an ever growing interest to me, ever since I had seen those metal crosses on those Southern African hills, inscribed 'To A Brave British Soldier'. My fascination with history as the very root of immediate and contemporary and pending issues had fermented inside me since I was a child: my grandfather talking about Mr Flynn having 'the roof of his house' being 'burnt over his head' in Ireland. To me even then I was being given a bit of jigsaw truth about Ireland. Where were the other multiple pieces? And I had begun to realize, as I garnered those pieces, by reading and talking and listening, that I understood those truths which even our political leaders seemed to be ignorant of, and sometimes – horror upon horror – were apparently disinterested in, or, even worse, *preferred* not to know! And as I went on peering at our British history, in particular, I became more and more critical of our imperial role; indeed any country's imperial role – and of what horrors those imperial roles inevitably led nations into. By the time that the interview on *Tonight* cropped up I was very clearly on the side of the Boers; on the side of Kruger, Steyn, De Wet, Smuts, DeLa Rey and Louis Botha, and I was *not* on the side of the greedy diamond and gold barons who represented the practical material side of British imperialism.

Mr Hart – again what a humorous intelligent interviewer (why do we have to decline in our British standards?) – asked the initial question and I was launched on one of my dynamos. I believe that I actually produced letters that had been written by soldiers during that Anglo-Boer War. Mr Hart attempted to interject after a while and I remember saying: 'Half a tick' before continuing. I remember the look of astonished amusement on his face but nothing could daunt me once my sermon was under way. I don't think that I can help it; short of a bullet or something equally lethal. Suddenly I heard Mr Michelmore shout across the studio: 'Cancel the Spanish dancers; ask them back tomorrow. You carry on, Mr Griffith.' And I did.

Now, unbeknown to me, fate or nemesis was lifting a pointed finger in my direction. I don't think that I have ever had the opportunity of telling – and thanking – Mr Michelmore or Mr Hart how they had intervened in my life and nudged me off on a revolutionary path. I tell them and thank them now.

Two men responded to what I had to say about the Second Anglo-Boer War and the way that I said it. Significantly, they were perhaps the most outstanding liberal spirits that BBC television has ever had – the world is darker now – Mr (as he then was) Huw Wheldon and Mr (ditto) David Attenborough. Huw Wheldon was managing director and David was head of BBC2. Those two men first broached the subject: 'Kenneth, would you make a film for us on your enthusiasm?'

Well, of course, I was very pleased to know that such men of quality had that confidence in me. I also felt that new ground could be broken in the style of television communication.

I replied: 'I believe that if a person knows about something that happened in the past, cares deeply about it and has the ability to communicate what he knows and feels, and does it on the precise historical spot, old ghosts will rise and will enter the camera. But,' I pointed out, 'I don't think that I am the person to do it; I'm not a writer and I am a film actor not a film *maker*.'

Somehow I was fairly adamant about my apparent limitations. I think I urged that Malcolm Muggeridge was the man to do it. Once again in my life I could not easily see what I was capable of. I reiterated my doubts and finally I was told: 'We'll pay you to try. And you can go anywhere you like in the world and do what you like.' That did it! I felt a little guilty – rather as if I were a confidence trickster – and accepted.

'Excellent, Kenneth; what would you like to do?'

My mind flew to my old friend, Peter Strong in Ladysmith, Natal, South Africa and all of those iron crosses inscribed 'To A Brave British soldier'.

'A film about the siege and relief of Ladysmith.'

'Good!'

I simply thought that I would see my friend again and bathe myself in the remnants of those sad atmospheric, far off days of conflict.

The BBC was extremely courteous to me. I was asked if I had any preference for the director of the film. 'No, I haven't.'

It all seemed a little unreal to me. I had formulated nothing about the style of the proposed film except my basic concept that if I could hold people's attention – with a serious subject – in a kitchen or an office how much more effective the story could be in, as in this case, the hills around Ladysmith, where the terrible drama had been actually fought. I was then asked if I would have lunch in a VIP dining room at the BBC with a young director named Lawrence Gordon Clark who was on their staff. 'Of course I would.'

Mr Clark was tall and lived in Chelsea. He struck me as an interesting example of upper middle-class respectability married to the tempting Bohemianism of that particular part of London. I liked him, so I informed Mr Gordon Watkins, who was the BBC's intermediary for the proposed film: 'Yes, Mr Clark seems fine; who am I to judge?'

Then I was asked how much money I wanted to research, write and finally tell the story on location in Africa. I asked my agent – the person who managed my acting work – what was my average weekly earnings as an actor over the past three years, that is my average weekly income whether earning money or not earning money. So assessing the number of weeks it would take of my time, I submitted a figure. This suggested sum, whatever it was, was received with horror by the BBC. I can recall the words: 'We've never paid *anyone* that sort of money!'

Now, believe me, it wasn't much. I mean I wasn't a film star! I was a hard-working actor living simply, in a small flat. I also recall David Attenborough explaining to me, in a motorcar, that he only had so much money in a bag each year. With his honesty and simplicity he actually held out an imaginary bag: 'And I've got to spread that money over so many projects.'

'But, David, no one could suggest that the sum I am asking is excessive – for a man who has to keep a relatively simple home going!'

Mr Attenborough returned to the limitations of his imaginary bag of money. We had arrived by this time at the BBC's Television Centre and I pointed at the great posh building.

'Why do you have so many office people up there? Why don't you reserve more money for actual programmes, which is what television is all about? Is it true that you have twenty thousand on the staff?'

Suddenly David seemed to leap to my puzzled side of the argument: 'Twenty-SIX thousand!' and I swear that there was a flash of outrage in his eyes.

'Well,' I said 'I simply can't do it; I've got to make a living.'

'Look, let me examine the problem; we'll solve it!'

Though life wasn't easy on that day, how I miss being associated with a man of such well meaning human standards. And Sir Huw, who was ever supportive and inspiring. Today there is no one comparable in British television, or, if there is, would he give me an encouraging word? I would be very grateful.

The idea that David Attenborough and the Corporation came up with was that I should feed Lawrence Gordon Clark all of my research material and information and that *he* would write the script. I would then be free to earn some money by acting and the BBC would pay me my requested weekly wage for the limited time that we were to be in Africa. Well, I weighed up the proposition and too easily – as it turned out – agreed. Still, at that time, I had failed to see the deeper significance of what was being offered to me. I still basically thought: 'OK, it's a wonderful paid holiday in a place that I very much want to see again. And I will be with my remarkable friend, Peter Strong.' I handed over to Lawrence Gordon Clark a crate of highly relevant information and hissed excitedly into his ears the dramatic story that we were now commissioned to tell. And I got stuck into my television acting again. Eventually Lawrence's script about the siege and relief of Ladysmith arrived, but I couldn't immediately read it. When I was doing a play, nothing else *could* exist. I lived and was prepared to die for each of those plays. I remember an odd quick meeting in Lawrence's Chelsea pad. I remember his stylish dark striped suit and his long hair. I was happy and looked forward enormously to the adventure.

We were to leave for South Africa on a Saturday aboard a VC10 aircraft. I think that we were given a week's reconnaissance time and two weeks for filming. The cameraman was Mr 'Ernie' Christie, an internationally famous daredevil news cameraman photographer. On the day before we left Britain – the Friday – I performed a television play, for the BBC. Therefore it was on the aircraft, humming southward, that I read Lawrence's work. The first thought that I had was how well he had done his homework; how well he had digested what had happened around Ladysmith towards the end of 1899 and the beginning of 1900. But my second thought was more onerous: 'What has this script got to do with me *personally*? Nothing!' It was a typical, well-written, objective BBC television documentary script. What was my specific commission from David Attenborough? 'A film on your enthusiasm.' The enthusiasm that I had displayed on the *Tonight* programme. There was none of that in Lawrence's script; how could there be? It was either the objective facts or it was *Lawrence's* attitude to our Ladysmith story.

Now, on that VC10, for the first time, my decks were cleared to face up to what I should be trying to do and then and only then did the full enormity of my responsibility hit me. I was supposed to speak for those old soldiers, both Boers and

Britons, most of them long dead. I was commissioned to be their advocate. Yes, I knew what I felt about the old soldiers and I knew what had happened to them, but I hadn't given the style of telling about them any serious thought. I had unthinkingly assumed that I could somehow fulfil my commission with whatever Lawrence had written. I decided not to say anything to him about my sudden ominous worries until I had thought and pondered what my alternative could be.

When I first arrived in Ladysmith on this BBC visit, I hastened to find my old friend Peter Strong: 'No, he doesn't live here any longer. He went with his family to Canada.'

And then someone chilled me: 'I think he died in Canada.' And so it turned out, Peter was dead.

We stayed at The Royal Hotel, Ladysmith; an historic place which had often featured dramatically during the siege. I now had with me, in my room, the crate of research books and other material. Each day we travelled to the different sites connected with those distant lethal days and the truth is that my terrible obsessive energy in pursuit of the fulfilment of an idea had taken over. Few who have worked with me over the intervening years have not resented my unstoppable drive. Memories come tumbling into my head: pushing on – though no longer young in years – at the battlefield of Plassey, with a monsoon beating us into the deep mud, two stalwart and affectionate Indians on each side of me preventing me from going horizontal; on a sand mountain in the Negev Desert of Israel, enveloped by an unmentionable heat, working on remorselessly and saying to my film-crew colleagues: 'Look lads, I'm sixty-two years old; if I can do it, so can you.' Very trying, and mutiny was in the blistering air.

You see, as an actor or a painter, or a composer or a writer you can attack your work as you feel you should; but in filming you are part of a team. How do you hold back? Does Stanley Kubrick have to check himself? I doubt it. Did David Lean? But they have a lot of money to spend and that can convert men and women to a remarkable degree; I have relatively little money. I can only appeal to such amorphous anti-union qualities as loyalty to the work-in-hand and professional respect.

Lawrence was suffering the first spasms of my headlong energetic push. He and I explored the old battlefields and already I was tending to lead our expedition, which behaviour on my part, in all fairness neither of us had foreseen. We visited the area – far over to the west – which had been the centre of General Buller's attempt to relieve Ladysmith during January, 1900. Our first objective was to locate a place known as Spearman's Farm, which had been the pivotal point of British operations and where we would want to do some of our filming. It is a fairly wild bit of country and Lawrence and I were on the edge of getting lost, in spite of our map. We eventually found a large farm, tucked away in the distance, and I volunteered to walk to it and ask for information. I walked through cultivated fields where Black Africans were working and finally knocked on the front door of the farmhouse which was opened by a handsome middle-aged man with closely cropped thick white hair. He greeted me in Afrikaans and then, realizing my linguistic limitation, in English. He was a Mr Pretorius, a direct descendant of the great Voortrekker leader after whom the capital city of Pretoria is named. Later I learnt – from low-voiced people of British extraction who lived in Natal – that my new friend was also the Commandant for the Ladysmith area. Immediately I was invited in and, as always with Afrikaners in my experience, coffee and cake were produced like magic. Afrikaner homes are similar in spirit to British homes before the Second World War: formal, warm-hearted and totally hospitable.

'This *is* Spearman's Farm,' Mr Pretorius told me. I hurried to fetch Lawrence Gordon Clark.

Mr and Mrs Pretorius were able to explain everything about the history of the area to us. Up above their farm was Mount Alice from which elevation Buller's artillery fired across the Tugela River and bombarded the heights beyond Taba Nyama and eventually, after moving those guns north eastward, the sinister dominance of Spion Kop.

Mr Pretorius then told Lawrence and me a story which all White South Africans should remember – if not Black South Africans! When the Anglo-Boer War occurred, Mr Pretorius' father and family lived a few miles away at what was understandably called Pretorius' Farm, and at that time his best friend, a Mr Spearman, lived where we were then drinking our coffee. These two men, the Boer, Pretorius, and the Englishman, Spearman, had been children together and were apparently inseparable. But the Boer Republican forces pouring southward and surrounding Ladysmith threatened their idyllic life.

Mr Spearman and Mr Pretorius hurried towards each other – the invading Boer Commandos were near at hand! Mr Spearman said that he was hastening south to join the British volunteer soldiers at Pietermaritzburg: 'Farewell!'

Mr Pretorius then made his way to this Spearman farm and here collected all of the furniture and the livestock and as decently as possible sold everything. Then he too volunteered to fight – on the Boer Republican side of course. Did they ever inadvertently aim their rifles at each other? It is possible. Both of these men survived the awful war and two and a half years later, with the coming of peace, they both returned to their war-ruined homes. Again the two old friends embraced and the Boer, Pretorius, led the Britisher, Spearman, to his farm and heaving up a large flagstone pulled out a pouch containing gold coins: 'I sold your possessions – here is the money – I didn't want the British soldiers to ruin you – or the Boer soldiers . . .'

A couple of days after our Pretorius adventure, I suddenly said to Lawrence Gordon Clark: 'I know how our film should begin!'

Lawrence already had mixed feelings about me and his reply was coldish: 'What do you mean – you know how it should begin?'

After all, he had *written* a beginning. Well this was the time; I pushed on: 'Ernie Christie has an aircraft [Ernie, our cameraman, flew everywhere] so we can begin the film with an aerial shot travelling along the Tugela River from east to west and finally home in on the profile of Spion Kop. Cut to a ground shot of one man [it would of course be me] clambering up the southern side. Cut to the climbing legs of the man; you don't see his face and the man begins to speak and the first words that he [myself] must say are "In Liverpool football ground." That will stop them switching off! "In Liverpool football ground there is a very large grandstand. Liverpool Football Club inform me that it holds thirty thousand men. If next Saturday you ask any one of those thirty thousand men what is this grandstand called they will say The Kop; and if you then ask them *why* is it called The Kop I doubt whether any of them will be able to tell you. Well," and at that point I suddenly turn my face to the camera – having stopped climbing – "I can tell you because I have just climbed the inspiration of the grandstand in Liverpool; climbed it here in the old British colony of Natal, in South Africa. Question: why is a football grandstand in Liverpool named after a mountain here in Southern Africa? Thereby hangs a strange and terrible tale!"'

I had just composed my very first professional words and indeed was visualizing how to tell one of my stories on film. Though I hadn't seen my ability before, it was now clear to me that such storytelling was an immediate part of myself. Lawrence wasn't too pleased and I can understand his annoyance.

'And after that opening sequence you can slap on the title: *The Widow's Warriors*.'

It was still coolness from Lawrence.

'Look,' I explained, 'I was given a clear commission by David Attenborough and from Huw Wheldon: "Communicate your enthusiasm". It is true that no one considered the implications of that request – certainly not me. I've just kept my fingers crossed and have blindly hoped that all would work out in the end. If the BBC had been prepared to pay me to write the script, this situation wouldn't have arisen.'

Lawrence was pretty cross; eventually: 'What do you propose, Kenneth?'

'Well, since we are about to start the actual filming, I think that at the end of each day we must decide what sequences we want to do on the following day and I will write them and deliver them to you before you go to bed.'

And that is what I did. It was a hair-raising way to make a film, but I did know about the subject and I did care about it very deeply.

Lawrence Gordon Clark began to soften his antipathy towards me when he twigged that something very unusual was happening. That the presenter (even that still commonly used word has the shroud of death over it) was really telling his personal deeply felt truth. At Spearman's Farm one afternoon we were filming over British soldiers' graves and Lawrence noted that tears were on my cheeks, and at the end of the take he grinned and said: 'You're bloody clever!' But unfortunately he didn't put his arm around my shoulders. Well, he is very English.

Ernie Christie, our cameraman, was someone very special. He was the complete man of action. He was famous for dangerous newsreel jobs. That is how the BBC knew about him. His flying ability was startling. We wanted shots from the air of the top of Spion Kop. Ernie went up and did tight aerial turns around the summit with one hand on the controls of the aircraft and his other hand operating the camera; he filmed the top of the mountain in that manner. Ernie must have been very strong and certainly very courageous. However, when it came to the easier part of film photography, when the camera has to be placed in a fixed position on a tripod, I noticed that Ernie was fumbling; his hands shook. I don't think that Ernie had any experience of our degree of prearranged directed photography; indeed, when back in Britain, I learnt that some of those relatively easy set pieces were out of focus. But not the hair-raising ones.

Many years later I was sitting innocently in front of my television set in London and one of those massive Chinese Cultural Revolution marches paraded in front of me. The half-baked Chinese (and I have to point out that we British also have more than our share of such people) were shouting and getting very aggressive on the streets of Peking as they waved their tragic little red books. Suddenly one of the oriental revolutionaries pushed a European cameraman. This photographer, holding his camera high above his head – yes Ernie was very strong – charged at the young man, lambasting him with his free fist. I got to my feet aghast at what might happen, blurting out: 'That is a friend of mine.' But no one else in Peking chose to go for

Ernie. Yes, you monkeyed about with Ernie's camera at your peril!

Last year while with some film men in Johannesburg, South Africa, I asked: 'How's Ernie Christie these days?'

Everyone stared at me in an electric silence: 'Haven't you heard about Ernie, Kenneth?'

'What?'

'Ernie believed that his wife was having an affair with another man; so he got into his aircraft and aimed it at her bedroom high up above the city, and flew it in.'

Unfortunately, or rather fortunately, the lady and her lover were not at home. Of course Ernie Christie died in the explosion. I knew from the first moment that I met him that he was a man of consummate style.

We filmed on towards the completion of our story and one morning at breakfast Lawrence smilingly announced: Well, back to London tomorrow!'

'What?'

'Our date of return tomorrow.'

'But, Lawrence, that is impossible; we haven't filmed the Naval Brigade sequences. We need one or two days more!' (The Naval Brigade was an essential part of the drama of Ladysmith's siege. British sailors at Durban, learning that the Boer artillery outranged the British artillery, heaved their warship guns onto the land, quickly built gigantic wheels for them and hauled them northward, getting into Ladysmith a few hours before the Boer Republican forces surrounded the place.)

Lawrence was adamant: 'We cannot stay in Africa any longer; they would be extremely angry at Lime Grove!'

I wheedled Lawrence: 'Look, I've been in this lousy business longer than you; all that matters, in the long run, is whether the film is any good. If we hand over an inadequate film to the BBC that was completed on exact schedule, they'll never forgive you. If, however, we hand in a film that went two days over but is first-class, you'll be on your way to fame and fortune. Why don't you phone Lime Grove and tell them we need two more days? Look, Lawrence, you can tell them it is all my fault; I don't give a damn as long as the film is as responsible as we can make it.'

'All right,' conceded Lawrence, 'we'll work an extra day and I'll telephone them.'

'Good man; you won't regret it.'

After supper that evening I repaired to my room and began writing the Naval Brigade sequences. Just after 10 pm there was a knock on my door. It was the long gangling figure of Lawrence: 'Look, Kenneth, I've been thinking – we *must* return to London tomorrow.'

I jumped up and down and called him every indecent name that I could think of. And then the BBC made its weighty priggishness evident: 'Don't you dare speak to me like that!'

'I *am* fucking speaking to you like that!'

Full marks to Lawrence, bearing in mind that he had a six-foot arm reach: he didn't attempt to punch my head. But Lawrence was always a BBC gentleman – though new to it; that I will concede. He stalked down the corridor with me in Celtic pursuit: 'You're a bloody coward, Clark!'

No, it was not an auspicious beginning to my documentary career.

I talked things over with Ernie Christie. Of course Ernie had experienced worse conflicts than this one. He had trained himself to stand back and let the tussle continue – unless someone fingered his camera.

'All right, Ernie; do one thing for me will you? Give that Clark a message from me. Tell him that I'm staying in Ladysmith for two days – without a camera – on simple principle; I'll make my own way back to Britain!'

And I did that; I watched the huffy departure the next morning and then with my hands in my pockets I walked the length of historic Ladysmith, musing about what was right in this world and what was wrong. I must admit that I felt that I was doing the right thing, even though the vast marching army of conventional behaviour was certainly not in step with me. I felt that rare glow of contentment.

There is one last thing I want to recount about that visit to Ladysmith. At that time the South African Government had arrived at an awkward decision. Many of the isolated bodies of British soldiers from the Anglo-Boer War were to be dug up from the places where they 'fell' and were to be reinterred in central cemeteries. I was and am sorry about this; the uncomfortable face of bureaucracy. I was present as remains were exposed. There were still shreds of khaki and the badges and buttons and coins that had been in the dead soldiers' pockets were sometimes in mint condition. In many cases the officials all knew precisely who the dead men were: their names, numbers and regiments. I was given three of those coins. I have them in front of me now. There is a British shilling, with Queen Victoria's head on and dated 1899, which had belonged to Private McGrath of the Royal Fusiliers who was buried at Pom Pom Bridge. And there is a penny dated 1898 and a half-crown dated 1899 from the grave of an 'Unknown Soldier' who was also buried at Pom Pom Bridge. Both of these soldiers had been killed on the northern side of the Tugela River, while fighting up Pieter's Hill on the very eve of the Relief of Ladysmith. I have a photograph – an original print – of these poor victims advancing against the Dutch farmers (the Afrikaners) of South Africa. I keep these ghostly coin relics in the same frame as the photograph. Whether I should have taken possession of these coins again I don't know. But I treasure them and I remember the soldiers with respectful affection, just as I remember the Boer soldiers.

I returned to Britain and waited in an uneasy mood of curiosity about the film. I didn't receive any communication from Lawrence Gordon Clark. However, he was in possession of many Anglo Boer War-drawings and photographs belonging to me. In that style of film such graphics (illustrations) have to be 'fed' – edited – into what we had filmed and I also knew that Lawrence would have to call on me, in due course, to speak the voice over for those implanted graphics. But months went by and I heard not a word. Well, I thought: 'Let him get on with it.' I was not ignorant of professional discourtesy; though not as familiar with that unfortunate human trait as I am today.

Now, in those days my eldest son, David, was a young actor

and he was doing very well. Today he has chosen to spend most of his time as an affluent antique-dealer (which choice I have no disagreement with). But in those early days he found himself acting in a BBC television play and, one day sitting in Television Centre's restaurant, he was joined by a group of BBC men and one of them said: 'What about your Dad's film!?'

'What about it?' asked my son.

'A lot of it is out of focus and unusable.'

David telephoned me with this news. I leapt with rage at the fact that I had to learn of an alleged catastrophe in this manner. For the first time since my return to Britain I picked up a phone and asked for Lawrence Gordon Clark. His secretary, whom I knew, informed me that he was not available, so I gave her an earful and asked her to pass on the message.

Soon after that I received a letter from David Attenborough informing me that the film was assembled, that it was excellent, and that Lawrence wanted me to see it. No doubt I had also written to David Attenborough pouring out my anger at being ignored in this high-handed manner. Well, I turned up at Lime Grove and sat in a viewing theatre with Lawrence and his secretary and the film began. I was very impressed with the beginning and not only because of the dramatic success of the 'In Liverpool football ground' opening. But shortly, in my very strong opinion, the dramatic continuity and tension began to weaken and finally I felt painfully dissatisfied. Of course, having been completely ignored for months, I accepted that there was little will to consult with me, so I mentally fell back on philosophy: 'This isn't my real job. As an actor I have appeared in many lousy films. So, this is just another one.'

The lights came up and I quietly reached for my overcoat and began to remove myself. Lawrence asked: 'What do you think of it, Kenneth?'

Quietly (which is not my normal style) I said cruelly but truthfully: 'I am not going to sue anybody. But you will have to take my name away from it.'

'What is wrong with it?'

'It is bloody boring!'

And then I got noisier. Lawrence's secretary blurted out:

'Don't speak to Lawrence like that!' I felt that she was close to tears; and I do respond warmly to love and loyalty. However, I pushed on with some strongly expressed feeling: 'That film has some of my blood on it and the blood of others! It could have been better if we'd shown more guts in Africa and it still could be better now.'

'In which way?'

'Are you actually asking me – at last – Lawrence? Well, it needs punctuating and it needs dramatic paragraphing with the graphics we have available.'

I remember going on at considerable length, about building up the mounting tension on the eve of Ladysmith's relief. Of the British cavalry – illustrations of prancing and finally charging horses were available. Of the 'greyhounds straining at the slips'. Yes, Henry the Fifth and all of that! There was nothing wrong with our British tommies. There was plenty wrong with our bloody British money-power-hungry politicians.

'Thank you,' I said to Lawrence, 'for asking my opinion.' And I left!

I believe that David Attenborough instructed Lawrence to carry out my wishes on the film. It was done and after seeing this second version I said: 'Thank you, Lawrence. It is an excellent film.' I was serious and my thank you to him was sincerely meant. Lawrence Gordon Clark had brought valuable elements to the story. I received another letter from David Attenborough in which he emphasized that the second version (though he had liked the first) was infinitely better. And Huw Wheldon gave the thumbs up encouragement.

I had immediately returned to my acting profession and I continued to chortle along that yellow brick road; but at Huw Wheldon's insistence there was still some contact between myself and an executive department of the BBC at a place called Kensington House and it was there that I suffered, for the first time, the inhibitions that emanate from middle management. These pricks of irritation were of a minor nature. My hovering place at Kensington House was very unusual. I had been picked out of the air by two of the top brass: the managing director, Huw Wheldon, and the head of BBC Two,

David Attenborough. I hadn't been weaned by the documentary department at all. And it vaguely began to dawn on me that the BBC operates – to a large extent – on the satisfaction that heads of departments derive from their protégés.

The patronage game. I was totally open and blindly trusting, or as the French have instructed us: naive.

I loved Huw Wheldon's slogan: 'The Pursuit of Excellence' and I really believed that 'Excellence' was the blood that coursed down the corridors of BBC power. I *know* that Huw Wheldon meant what he said and I know that David Attenborough believed in it passionately, but that was not the driving force of the machinery that rattled on below them. That machinery was driven by, generally, lesser mortals and their fuel was 'political' self-advancement. How do you manoeuvre matters towards your own self-promotion? Egos were bobbing up and down all over the place and suddenly here was me, an outsider, who had landed in their midst with a completed film, plonked into the department at the behest of those Above. And – disconcertment upon disconcertment – the film was different to anything made before. It was the innovatory film to end all innovatory films! No one had carried on in front of the camera like that before! Mark you, people smiled; I think that I was seen as 'a bit of a boy' and hadn't I got friends and admirers in very high places?

The only conflict that I had at Kensington house at that time was over the title of the film. Since the film was now completed, the title was the only vulnerable morsel exposed. During the following years I learnt that BBC executives commonly express themselves by changing even heartfelt titles.

When the relieving forces entered Ladysmith, one man, a Christian chaplain, ran around obsessively asking those who had suffered the siege: 'What was it like?' He accosted a sergeant in the King's Royal Rifle Corps and the non-commissioned officer recounted some of his adventures, paused, thought carefully and summed up: 'I think we did the Widow proud.' The 'Widow' was the Queen. I wanted the film called: *The Widow's Warriors*. I think that it was Mr Aubrey Singer, then head of documentaries and later to sit in Huw Wheldon's honoured chair as managing director, who changed the title to *Soldiers of the Widow*. But Aubrey smiled at me so I ceased the fight.

As the day of transmission of *Soldiers of the Widow* approached I became concerned – but only for myself as a *performer*. My professional performance was once again to be publicly judged and survival depended upon such judgements to some extent. Of all of the television critics in those days I admired Stanley Reynolds of the *Guardian* most. And so did my friend O'Toole. Now that he was in the money, O'Toole would give twelve-month subscriptions to the *Guardian* as Christmas presents together with the advice: 'Read Stanley Reynolds'. The programme went out – I don't remember looking at it – and the next morning I bought a *Guardian* and in a state of dread carried it to a deserted public garden in Canonbury Square. Only a week ago I walked through that garden and eyed that seat I sat upon all of those many years ago. I shakily turned the pages of the newspaper and found Stanley Reynolds. He wrote something about a new dimension of art coming to the documentary field. I sat there, deeply moved. I had spoken up, loud and clear, for the poor bloody soldiers: both Boer and British. I had been allowed to say it in front of a fair slice of the British nation. And Stanley Reynolds was stating unequivocally that I had pulled it off.

To me, sitting on that seat, it all suddenly seemed awesome. Sitting there, it also began to dawn on me that I could, perhaps, go on speaking up for those who were often ignored or suppressed. I could perhaps redress a few balances. And above all – and very publicly – examine the very *causes,* the *roots* of the terrible contemporary conflicts that were often being so shallowly and ignorantly judged by public opinion. Most of my life I have known the vital importance of understanding the historical *cause* of tragedies before anyone can begin to fairly judge. On that seat in Canonbury Square it also became clear that I was on the edge of terminating my life as an actor and that I might be moving into the biggest pulpit ever devised so far – television.

SEVENTEEN

Three years and more have gone by since I wrote the above last words. It is now the 27th of December 1988. Other professional duties have monopolized my life – almost entirely my curious film-making enterprises – and the truth is that this is the first day, with a clear three weeks ahead, when I can again pick up my dog-eared manuscript.

I have spent two of those three years in India making a film for the Indian Government on the life of their first Prime Minister, Jawaharlal Nehru. (It should have taken no more than eight months, but India has a horrible skill at wasting time, and money, energy and, indeed, life itself.) Initially I had been asked to make the film by Pandit Nehru's distinguished daughter, Prime Minister Indira Gandhi, but more about that anon. And then I have spent a good part of the remaining last year writing and filming, mainly in South Africa.

At the moment, I am sitting in the excellent public library of Faenza, which is about thirty miles south of Bologna in Northern Italy. I have sat here, in the Biblioteca Comunale, writing about other matters, from the past. And I have come here to visit my friend Chiara Peretti over the Christmas holiday, until the 15th of January 1989 when we are both due to return to India to begin another film; this one about the astounding Doctor Ambedkar – an Untouchable who led the Untouchables of India towards a degree of freedom. Sadly the Indian Government is not too keen for me to do it; but we are planning to soldier on.

So I have sat here and have fatalistically wondered whether the foregoing words could have interested you readers.

Well, that strange old film *Soldiers of the Widow* did

radically change the course of my life. Huw Wheldon held on to me, keeping my head above water and telling me, enthusiastically, that I could swim. And true to the unusual pattern of my life I then knew that I *could* swim! First, some perceptive altruistic human beings (Evelyn Ward, Tyrone Guthrie, Roy Boulting and now Huw Wheldon and the critic Stanley Reynolds) had seen some spark in me (which I could not easily recognize for myself) and had pushed me into the arena. Then, having exhibited the spark, I have been impressed with myself and have suffered no humble, wilting doubts! Of course, pursuing such very personal dreams – detached from any academic strictures – my light has had little to do with 'how things are normally done'. It has been inevitable that everything about me is idiosyncratic – and particularly noticeable in my work: how I walk, how I talk and how I think. Very subjective; very personal. Well-meaning advisers – good friends – are ever advising me to conform to a more acceptable conventional style and of course I listen carefully and sometimes (but not often) adjust myself a twinkle. But not much. No one can please everyone; not even good Jesus Himself. One thing I know for certain, I promise you, like me or loath me, I am unshiftably *true* to myself. But if some authoritative person comes along in the future and says: 'Conform or I will pull your fingernails out!' I will reply: 'I conform!' Fortunately in our British society no such physical threat has been forthcoming. I have had several lesser threats within Britain's television world. Or rather not threats, but secret instructions have been issued which amount to: 'Do not employ him!' This order has emerged from the British Broadcasting Corporation (after Huw Wheldon retired) from ATV (during Lord Grade's time) and latterly from Channel Four. But these are the discreet methods of the British System and less horrific to me than the physical torture chamber. Get seriously out of the Establishment Line – though you may be telling a truth (indeed *particularly* if you are telling a truth!) – and you will have trouble paying your household bills. However, in my case, I have been very fortunate in having been offered several international escape routes. When the British going has got very bumpy, offers of employment have come from the United States of America, Australia, Canada, New Zealand, India and South Africa. But I have regretted the thought of emigration; sermons are best delivered from one's own patch – or from one's own pulpit. I am hesitant to be a missionary amongst, say, the Zulus or the Americans; they *may* have a better spiritual code of conduct than ours. Different, certainly; but 'better', I don't know.

And then, fortunately, some home-grown leader of principle emerges. Rare, but the miracle is persistent. Of course these leaders are under daily assault and often they sadly succumb. Today, now in 1989, I only know of one in the whole of our vast British television structure: David Elstein of Thames Television. I hate to expose him further in this manner; but I have to state that I admire him. And that statement from me can do him no good in certain powerful eyes!

After *Soldiers of the Widow* had been displayed, Huw Wheldon spoke to me in his deep-carpeted office somewhere on top of the British Broadcasting Corporation's Television Centre. He asked me to stay with the BBC and also asked me what I wanted to do next. Now, full of the confidence which he had pushed me into, I replied: 'A series of, say, twelve films about the rise and fall of the British Empire.' Huw eyed me with that beloved mixture of humour and truth: 'Don't you find that a shade portentous, Kenneth?'

'No,' I replied.

Huw there and then suggested that I should embark on 'two or three' aspects of our British imperial past 'to begin with'. I explained that I would *personify* the different aspects. That I would choose individuals from our British history who would, through their lives, represent the various epochs and so there would be no difficulty in communicating our British saga in this *ad hoc* approach. I pointed out to the great BBC leader that if I ploughed on in this manner and if I eventually completed twelve lives and if the BBC then chose to transmit them, eventually, in chronological order, the evolvement of our astounding Empire would be told.

I think that I suggested a life of Cecil Rhodes first; then

maybe 'Clive of India' and perhaps the splendid Gladstone. These were my off the cuff thoughts in response to Huw's suggestion. I have since made a filmed life of Cecil Rhodes and of Robert Clive but neither of them for the BBC.

Huw Wheldon then asked me to meet two of his BBC people whom he wanted to support my ideas and ability. One of them was Richard Cawston (who is linked in my mind with trumpet voluntaries about our British royal family) and the other one's name I think was Christopher Rawlings. However, Huw described this second BBC servant to me with his customary positive enthusiasm: 'He's a good chap! Bit stiff, but you'll like him. He's a New Zealander.'

In this last statement Huw was wrong and his error perhaps cost me dear.

For this momentous meeting, Huw asked me to visit his office before the others arrived and he primed me with more information about the bureaucratic structure of the BBC – adding I remember: 'But of course I am not without some influence here myself . . .' He was managing director.

'Just tell them, Kenneth, what you've told me.'

I remember the scene vividly: Richard Cawston smiling and nodding like an uncle and the other chap in his dark suit with suitable tie, sitting upright, and not smiling so much. So what? Stiffness does not necessarily mean harm. And in my heart I held on to the fact that he was a healthy out-of-doors New Zealander. How this life is snared with dangers!

Well the meeting ended. I had given my spiel with relish. As the two BBC men departed, Huw held on to me: 'No, no, Kenneth; I must talk to you.'

Huw was pleased with me: 'They liked you, Kenneth! Now I will arrange for Christopher Rawlings (the stiff New Zealander) to have lunch with you. I want him to produce your work.'

The truth is that I had suffered – even financially – over the making of Soldiers of the Widow and I had also learnt that the apparently honourable principles of BBC middle-management could often politely and mysteriously find an artist, such as I, expendable when it suited their personal interests. But I was still naively under the impression that the gigantic puritan rules of Lord Reith (the founder of the BBC) still basically pertained. Of course Huw Weldon was deeply concerned about the enormous responsibility the BBC carried; his slogan 'The Pursuit of Excellence' underlined that. But Huw was one of God's Democrats; he was no dictator and therefore his undoubted prayer for every employee's sense of responsibility was open to abuse. It was a different ethical spirit amongst the poets and philosophers and entertainers around Broadcasting House at Portland Place where the old miracle of British sound radio emanated from.

Therefore I approached the lunch with Christopher Rawlings, 'the stiff New Zealander' with a smidgen of trepidation. I took the precaution of taking my television agent along with me, so that he would be a witness to all that was said. But it didn't help that awful meeting. There was our host certainly stiff and rather aloof.

'Do you want wine?' he asked icily.

'Why not? I replied.

I immediately knew that I must attack the situation with warm Celtic 'hutzpa'. This means that all of the stops are pulled out. It even means that, in an emergency, even an audacious creep is called for. I thought of the high-flying All Blacks (the fearsome New Zealand rugby variety). Huw had given me the vital clue; the gap in the defence line: 'He is a New Zealander.'

'What a great opportunity we have,' I launched off with, 'to make a series of films on the History of the British Empire! And for the British Broadcasting Corporation! We are truly privileged!' But I was still confronted with this unrelenting poface. Ah well! – nothing ventured: 'Look, the English tend to be stiff and unimaginative. You are a New Zealander, I am a Welshman; what great things we can achieve! Never before have the Welsh and the All Blacks played on the same side!'

He was even stiffer and more unfriendly. I now admit that I had crept pretty low. Where was even the thin smile that he managed when Huw Wheldon was present? At last he reacted: 'What makes you think that I am a New Zealander? I'm English!' and by God he looked it!

Well I began to know that I was beaten. I didn't dare look at my agent as the full horror of that BBC producer confronted me. I threw my last despairing card in front of him: 'Are you keen to do this series?'

'Frankly, no! I have ideas of my own.'

I stood up: 'Let's thank Mr Rawlings for the soup and piss off,' I said.

And we walked out. Was that a dignified exit? That man, whose name until recently I have successfully erased from the tablets of my memory, produced a series of films about Darwin's life. It was an extravagant conceit and I thought that it was well done. But many actors – good ones – scattered the screen and therefore historical veracity in the eyes of some viewers, perhaps unfairly, was a little imperilled.

A silent invisible wave of opposition unrelentingly confronted me at the BBC. Three times I walked away from these priggish cuckoos and three times Huw Wheldon urged me to stick it out. But he did not overrule them. I finally wrote a plain letter to Huw, stating that I understood that he couldn't disrupt or rather alienate his permanent machinery. He had to live with them. I also stated that I now knew that the significant BBC Club was not the one that I paid my subscription to (subsidized drink, etc.). Huw replied that within the Corporation they held to a warning: 'It's very cold outside.' Of course every independent artist knows the truth about *that*. All truly independent spirits must experience the uncomfortable cost; often physical shortages.

There was some outside interest in the fact that this actor (me) had walked out of the BBC's documentary department and I was interviewed on the subject. I think that it was *The Times* that put a piece on its front page headlined (with an explanation by me): 'Who does he think he is?' That was it in a nutshell. There seemed to be no other possible reason. I had made an adventurous, simple film. Indeed it was a unique style. Just one person expressing his heartfelt knowledge on the precise historical locations. One writer, one communicator; very inexpensive. The breadth and freedom of radio. I could do anything under the sun that I knew and cared about!

But great responsibility and therefore power. Aye, there's the rub! Those cuckoos at Kensington House resented the self-sufficient power. And an actor holding it too! Hadn't their positions as producers and so on always given them the authority to instruct the actor and actress how to do his or her job? Now, with me telling my stories, such importance over me was difficult. And believe me, egos generally overrode the innovatory quality of the product. But I didn't go into all of the above with the journalists. Probably I was not as well-informed as I am today. So my explanation about my exits from the BBC was summed up by my statement: 'It was as if they had fixed a placard around my neck on which was inscribed: "Who does he think he is?" '

Even at that distant period, looking back at the slings and arrows of my personal fortune, I was stoical if not fatalistic. It was not the first time that an attractive carrot had been held out before me and then had been snatched away. Back to the Thespians! On with the motley again. I had got a whiff of that great television pulpit in which I could effectively preach what was within my knowledge. But that's life; here today and gone tomorrow. And even then I had spotted the inevitable grave.

I have always been basically simple-minded. Huw Weldon had brought me into this new wondrous field. He was the BBC at its best and the BBC as a whole had rejected me very positively and that was that. Even Huw had given up. He shook his head and said, curiously: 'They have vomited you up three times.'

EIGHTEEN

Patrick McGoohan, one of the most remarkable personalities to have hit the world's television screens and, as long as there are flickering figures to be seen, immortalized by his revolutionary series *The Prisoner*, telephoned me: 'Kenneth, will you make your documentary films for me? I saw the first one.'

I suppose Mr McGoohan had read my BBC story in the press.

'When shall I meet you and what time?' I replied.

'Tomorrow morning at 9 am in my office at Metro Goldwyn Mayer's studio in Elstree.' I have never forgotten that '9 am'. Not easy to get there by that hour if you have stopped driving a car as I had done.

'I will be there, God willing,' I replied to Patrick.

Patrick McGoohan is no ordinary mortal. With perhaps Douglas Fairbanks Senior and Peter O'Toole he is the most dynamic personality that I have ever witnessed on the screen. Explosive! The Edmund Kean syndrome. I have long believed that he has woefully, perhaps not consciously, smothered his own great potential. He is tall and he is handsome to boot. I remember once saying to him, when Steve McQueen was at his starry eminence: 'You could be a bigger name – influence – than him'. He swung on me: 'Never! My daughter has a large portrait of McQueen in her room. Young people would never think of me in that way.'

'What way?' I wondered but didn't ask. I simply said: 'But that's not true.'

Patrick is an extremely private man and he may not even approve of what I am writing. But there are aspects of him which I admire very much and indeed I have never – through thick and thin – lost an affection for him. Is manic the right word? But I have never seen him light-hearted. Always searchingly serious. Occasionally the flicker of a smile.

At 9 am he was waiting for me: 'Kenneth, you must understand that every word you utter in this room is being recorded and every move you make is recorded by several cameras.'

I grinned and cast my eyes jerkily along the walls. Nothing that I could see. What was I to believe? As with the nature of God, I keep my mind open. Patrick continued in this piercing vein. Many emotions could be conjured by that man; but never boredom.

Soon, he got down to the nitty gritty, which was an expression which he favoured; at least at that time. Yes, he would produce *The Rise and Fall of the British Empire*! But what would I start with?

'Cecil Rhodes,' I replied.

'How much?'

I gave a very vague estimate.

'Done!' and he held out his hand. I shook it.

'When can you leave for Africa?'

I pointed out that I hadn't written the script yet, but I hazarded a date.

'You'll need some initial expenses!' he rapped out – in that unique tone that is (no doubt) his seal of plain truth. And a reasonable cheque was thrust at me. Well, already it was better than those snide people at the BBC. I was now dealing with a fellow artist who was bent on action.

'How will you travel to Africa? Fly?'

'No, ship,' I replied.

'Why ship?'

'I can gather my thoughts together. I value ship travel.'

Patrick gave me one of those famous penetrating looks: 'Well, book your passage. Get first class.

'Oh no,' I replied, 'that's unnecessary.'

He looked sceptically at me: 'Well, please yourself. Have the bill sent to me.'

The truth is: manna had been falling all over me. Mr

Donald Baverstock – famed for his work at the BBC culminating in *That Was the Week that Was* had also telephoned me
at about the same time that Patrick McGoohan had: 'Kenneth,
I want to talk to you. I'm setting up Yorkshire Television.'

'Yes, I know.'

'Can you call round tomorrow morning?'

'Not till twelve midday. I have an appointment at Elstree at
9 am.'

'Midday it is then.'

And he gave me Yorkshire Television's address in London at
Portland Place, opposite Broadcasting House.

Mr Baverstock received me with open enthusiasm. Of
course, he is also a Welshman and I was warmed by the Celtic
spirit. He hurried me around the nearly constructed offices.
And then, sitting me down: 'Do you want to make this series
of films about the rise and fall of the British Empire?'

'Yes.'

'Do them for us. We'll pay you . . .' and he mentioned a
sum that was more money than I had ever hoped for.

'I can't accept, Donald. I've just shaken hands with Patrick
McGoohan to do them.'

'The whole series?.'

'Well, just Cecil Rhodes to begin with.'

'I'm offering you three years' work, Kenneth.'

'But I can't, Donald; I've shaken hands with him.'

'But you haven't signed a contract!'

'I've accepted a cheque.'

Donald Baverstock didn't push me further, but he did a
very good-hearted act which I have ever since appreciated; he
walked with me to the Oxford Circus underground station,
where I embarked on a train to inform my agent Dennis
Selinger of my morning's adventures! Of course, I have since
wondered what would have been my professional fate if I had
been free to work for Donald Baverstock.

I went to the Union Castle shipping offices in Bond Street
and a managing officer recognized me: 'Going to travel with
us again, Mr Griffith?'

'Yes, sir; to Cape Town.'

I gave him a date and emphasized that I wanted a single cabin, second class.

'There are no single cabins second class, Mr Griffith. You would have to share.'

'Oh! But I *have* to be alone. I have to do some research and writing on the voyage.'

'Then it will *have* to be first class.'

'Oh, very well,' I said reluctantly.

'Bath or shower, Mr Griffith?'

'Is there a difference in cost? 'Very little; a bath is a shade more expensive.'

'A bath please.'

'Well, that's fine: first class, bath and, of course, on the port side!'

Yes, I had heard of the élitist slogan 'POSH' – 'port out; starboard home'.

When I explained the story to Patrick McGoohan he gave me the wry variety of his smiles.

'And I think, Kenneth, you *must* take your wife and young son with you.' (By this time I had met the actress, Carole Hagar, while doing a television play together, and we had got married and we already had our son, Jonathan.) The BBC wouldn't have thought of or paid for that. Is it a small wonder that I prefer fellow-artists to bureaucrats?

Who was to direct the film? For many, many years I had taken an unusual interest in how films were physically structured and of course I was aware of the importance of mood and atmosphere in telling a story; indeed it was instinctive in me. I hardly ever worked on a film, as an actor, when I did not become friendly with the editor and I would spend many hours with him (it was always a 'him') in his cutting-room. This is probably unusual amongst actors. But I was not ambitious to become a director. And in any case, as I have often felt, my cup runs over – certainly in making my own films. I usually choose the subject; I inevitably become at least a part producer; I am the researcher, the writer and the entire cast! Yes, I was looking for a director.

On television I had seen a documentary film directed by Mr

Antony Thomas. I usually recognize outstanding talent when I see it. Mr Thomas's work was very fine, so I arranged to meet him. He was a young, handsome, softly spoken man; perceptive and yet quietly distant. There was a careful, charming facade around him, but as the years have passed by, we have developed an open friendship and I have been given access to his constant vein of humour. I asked him if he would direct the Cecil Rhodes film and he assented. I arranged for Antony to meet Patrick and everything was happily agreed.

It turned out that Antony had South African connections and that he had a strong sympathy for the Black Africans. Therefore he was emotionally committed to the script which I had by then written. Relevantly, the Rhodes script is the only one that I have ever written which is an indictment of the chief protagonist.

On our way to South Africa we stopped briefly at Las Palmas, and I took the opportunity to buy a copy of *The Times*. I read with more than a little interest that the BBC was about to embark on a series about the rise and fall of the British Empire. Of course, the idea was not an unfamiliar one to me, and I could not resist sending a telegram to Huw Wheldon, in which I repeated the words he had spoken to me back in his office in London: 'Dear Huw, don't you find *this* a shade portentous?!' I wouldn't have minded quite so much if the series had not turned out to be such a major television disaster.

When Carole, our young son Jonathan and I reached magnificent Cape Town, I saw Patrick McGoohan moving through the crowd at the dockside. Always alone, always mysterious. Patrick oversaw the basic production arrangements with us in Pretoria, in the Transvaal, where we set up our film production office. There we used the facilities of Mr Felix Meyburgh, a well-known South African film maker. Today, so many years later, we are close friends. Also I met a young assistant cameraman, Mr Grenville Middleton, who has one of those hearts that is said to be of gold. But more significant in terms of film making he carried in him a great enthusiasm. I said to young Grenville: 'If you tell me that you can photograph the Rhodes film, the job is yours; if you tell me that you have any doubts, the job is not yours.'

Grenville replied: 'I'll prove that I can do it on the negative.' And so Grenville was our lighting cameraman and operator – with the agreement of Patrick and Antony of course. Our crew finally amounted to six Whites (Patrick not included because he returned to Britain and thence to the United States of America) and two Black men. We bought a Volkswagen 'combie' and the adventure began.

We filmed in Cape Town and my vivid memories are of the Rhodes statue in the middle of the surely incomparable Botanical Gardens. There is the 'Colossus of Africa' pointing, to my ignorant eyes, directly at the Antarctic and underneath is the slogan: 'Your Hinterland is there'. Of course he is in fact pointing northward towards Rhodesia (now Zimbabwe). The coastline at this part of the southern tip of Africa is so convoluted that others have made a similar mistake, with probably dire results. One of the Cape bays is called False Bay; well it gives you an idea . . .

Clearly Antony was directing the film with great sense and imagination. We were a very happy and contented lot.

Rhodes' bedroom was untouched since his death. What psychological tales were revealed! By the side of his bed was a photograph of the ancient Matabele woman who had helped Rhodes to terminate the Matabele Rebellion of 1896. Was it the *only* photograph in the room? The only one that I can remember. Time after time over these many years I have had these great privileges pushed under my nose. To make films about significant people and then be allowed to ruminate amongst their intimate relics. I never cease to wonder at my good fortune. And, of course, how it helps the quality of my work and the quality of the work of my colleagues. Sometimes I am prepared to believe that the Spirit World lends me a breath of enlightenment. After all, if any places are haunted, I visit them continuously.

I remember sitting in Rhodes' very private library. At that time the treasure-house was not gainfully arranged. Particularly I remember the hundreds of specially prepared volumes of the lives and works of the Roman emperors, which he had commissioned to be translated and printed, jumbled all over the place. Again it was a direct reminder of the spirit of that terrible man; of his commercial-imperial time. I think he saw himself as an emperor.

We went to the imposing Rhodes Memorial; halfway up the beautiful mountain. Here we filmed, symbolically, the sparkling exchange between Cecil Rhodes and Gordon of Khartoum.

Rhodes (I paraphrase from memory): 'Is it true that the Empress of China offered you a roomful of treasure?'

Gordon: 'Yes.'

Rhodes: 'And you refused?'

Gordon: 'Yes.'

Rhodes: 'Then you're a damn fool! Nothing can be achieved without wealth!'

And me, subjectively: 'I am glad to report that Gordon declined to agree.'

Antony arranged this so that as I walked and 'made an entrance' from behind each pillar, I was either Rhodes or Gordon. Not easy, but we did it. While we were working on this scene, a tall middle-aged man clambered up towards us. I took it upon myself to ask him if he would remain still and quiet for a few minutes. The man kindly acquiesced and when we had finished our work thanked him and introduced myself.

'Well!' he said, 'My name is Griffiths! Ernest Griffiths!'

That of course is the name of my beloved grandfather. The man was an American, and he continued: 'I am a Rhodes Scholar; that is why I am here. To pay my respects.'

Again it seemed to be a circle in life. The Rhodes Scholar had heard my implied criticism of his famous benefactor and indirectly he was reminding me of the virtuous side of Rhodes; and then, to me, a man with the name of Ernest Griffiths *must* be significant.

And while we were up there at the Rhodes Memorial another middle-aged man appeared accompanied by two younger men. It was a medically historic event. The older man was the recipient of the first heart transplant ever; which disturbing operation had been performed by a young South African, Professor Christian Barnard. And this was the first outing for the famous patient. I talked for a few minutes with the happy man while his two male nurses hovered close by. I sensed that the extension of life for some human beings – even for a brief period – can be intensely cherished.

I remember returning to our smart hotel one evening and, as we sat down to richly dine, I asked where our two Black colleagues were. Well by the rule that then pertained (originally instigated by our *British* colonial policy) they were prohibited from eating with us. I stalked out of the dining-room to find them and there they were hanging around the kitchen area. They were in a subdued, angry mood. No, it wasn't that they had been denied the dining-room; they knew that that was impossible. What had bitterly humiliated them was that they were not allowed to use 'our' china plates. They were condemned to paper plates. I stormed back into the crowded dining-room and noisily created a scene. I remember my colleagues tried to quieten me. At least I had the grace to desert my meal; I shut myself in my darkened room and glowered emotionally. There was a knock on the door; it was the hotel's manager: 'What can I do? It is the law of this country.'

'Is it the law that my Black African colleagues must eat off paper?'

'It is the rule of the hotel, sir.'

'Then I will leave your bloody hotel.'

The manager somewhat appeased me by promising to give my friends china plates and proper cutlery and a reasonable place to eat. I did not move to another hotel.

Today, under a Nationalist South African Government, such rules have been done away with – except in a few reactionary areas of the country, which reaction is pointedly opposed by the present largely Afrikaner government. Today my Black fellow-workers sit with me at South African hotel tables and eat off identical plates to mine.

What sickens me today is the mass hypocrisy of the so-called liberal world outside of that hard-pressed country, now that they have discovered the easy 'whipping-boy' of South

Africa. The South Africans today – both Black and White – have the biggest cultural conflict predicament on the face of this earth and the White Government is struggling daily to solve the probably unsolvable – short of their own cultural annihilation. Recently I have visited Lusaka in Zambia at the invitation of the African National Congress there; I found them mendacious, inefficient and degenerate. And the President of Zambia, Kaunda, had just won another election with a majority of 95.5 per cent of the vote! So it was advertised. In Lusaka I asked: 'Who are the opposition?'

Lips came close to my ear: 'They're in jail.'

And the other one-party dictator, Prime Minister/President Mugabe of Zimbabwe has murdered a significant part of his political tribal opposition. Ask Mr Joshua Nkhomo – except that he wouldn't now dare to tell you. Apart from – perhaps – Botswana there is not one honest democratic Black African state on the whole enormous continent. And the reason for Botswana's possible exception is that the country has only one *basic* tribe.

South Africa, like every other human organization, has imperfections. And their problems are vaster than anything that we in Europe and America and elsewhere have to face. But the shallow Western do-gooders of today generally make me angry at their unctuous hypocrisy. They usually see themselves as decent people and warm themselves at their self-image. But that can only be born out of their facile shallowness and blind ignorance of the reality. I will not be associated with their noisy bandwagon. Is this apparent hatred of White South Africa born out of our European guilt of sometime slave-ownership and old colonial conquest? One matter is certain: we have thrown out all sense of fair play towards the struggling government of that country. They should be helped, not hit.

And then our film crew went up to Rhodesia, as it then was. On the tremendous boulder in which Cecil Rhodes has a chiselled tomb I found a hole carefully drilled into the hard stone. I enquired and was furtively told that African freedom fighters had done it and then had packed the hole with an explosive to blow the remains of Rhodes' body to where-I-don't-know but the charge had failed to function. Was that the first stirrings of Mugabe's or Nkhomo's lot? All around us were the mysterious Matopa Hills.

While in Salisbury (as it then was called) I was invited to an amateur production of *Stop the World I Want to Get Off*. I rather dreaded the prospect, but feeling that old Thespian obligation, I attended. First, I was pleasantly astonished at the beautiful modern theatre and then at the very high standard of the production. After the performance, in a state of gratitude, I congratulated the producer and he invited me to have lunch with him the next day at a Hotel in Salisbury. And while we were having that lunch I made one of those interesting, hidden, discoveries about myself. Before that meal I would have assured anyone that putting my actor's career behind me didn't trouble me one small tap: 'I have a new job and am happy about it!' While delicately taking my soup I heard my host say: 'Have you heard about the play *Baron Corvo* which has just opened in London?' (Yes I had; indeed I had been urged by the playwright, Mr Peter Luke, and by the impresario, Bernard Miles, now the late Lord Miles, to undertake the principal role) – so I perceptibly froze. But worse was to follow as my well-meaning friend continued: 'And the fantastic success of the actor playing the leading part?'

I managed to croak: 'Who is that?'

His brow furrowed as he struggled to remember: 'Ah, eh, ah! Alec . . .'

'Guinness?' I prompted with a dry throat.

'No! McCowen!' he blurted triumphantly. I had difficulty in putting my soup-laden spoon back in the plate. I had probably become pale through my African tan. Certainly I was in a state of shock. I think that I momentarily wondered what the hell I was doing in central Africa when I could have been triumphing in the West End of London. But that Thespian loss quickly evaporated as I got on with my Rhodes saga. You can't have *everything*! But of course the experience emphasized or exposed how much I missed that second oldest profession – or rather how deep was my curiosity as to how far I could have stretched myself 'on the boards' – if I had remained on them.

Part of our Cecil Rhodes story was inevitably the wicked Jameson Raid of late 1896. The Raid was a Rhodes financed jaunt into the independent republic of the Transvaal. It was a despicable enterprise by us British, which was meant to over-throw a peaceful country with what was virtually Rhodes' private army. And it was inspired, above everything else, because the biggest gold deposit that this world has ever known ran underneath the city of Johannesburg. This inter-national crime was led by Leander Star Jameson, Rhodes' chief lieutenant and friend, who at one time had been a respectable doctor of medicine.

The place from which they began their nefarious invasion was Pitsani on the border of Botswana (then called Bechuanaland) and Transvaal. An isolated place to this day. We based ourselves at a lonely store run, I seem to recall, by an Asian family. A largish military shell acted as a door stop: 'Yes, found nearby; one from Doctor Jameson's guns.' Quite unaffectedly, a nearby kopje (hill) was referred to as Jameson's Kopje. There are still bits of this world where hardly any-thing has changed for a long long time. I felt the old happenings of that wild bit of Africa acutely. I would like to return.

Yes, I am glad to inform you that the Jameson Raid was a deserved British disaster. The Boers very efficiently humili-ated them. But two or three years later the national army of Britain returned to assault the Transvaal officially: the Second Anglo-Boer War (1899–1902). And on that occasion it took more than Rhodes' brigands; it took about 450,000 imperial troops and nearly three years.

And we filmed in President Paul Kruger's house in Pretoria. Kruger was the long-standing leader of the Transvaal and his home is reverently kept as it was at the turn of the century, to this very day. For me, with my deep interest in the great drama of South Africa, this home of President and Mrs Kruger is a place of never failing interest. It is full of treasures of those epic times. The homely behaviour of the two old Afrikaners, against the cataclysmic explosion of British military imperialism.

Because we were filming at the Kruger House, a young Afrikaner, Louis Changuion, who worked for the nearby Boom Street Museum, was deputed to help us. To this day he is a candidate for being my best friend. He is now an author and a distinguished Professor of History at the all Black University of the North. But have I heard that White students are now being allowed in?

Louis and I have influenced each other. I suppose in those days of his youth I urged him to soften his conservative Afrikaner stance a little or perhaps I should write: liberalize it a little. But Louis Changuion and I want the same fortune for South Africa: the preservation of *each* People's culture and achievement, with *each* cultural talent helping the other. To mix them all up in one state-dominated structure would not be less than a degenerating nightmare.

The last sentence is entirely my own, not Louis'. Of course I am only sixty-seven years old; I can still learn – indeed I am learning – new aspects of everything! I can still have my mind changed again, Louis.

We did most of the editing of our Rhodes film in Pretoria. And while Carole and Jonathan were there – for some months – we stayed in the home of our cameraman and his wife: Grenville and Juliet Middleton; yes Grenville had proven his skill 'on the negative'. For my family and me it was an idyllic time. On Sundays Carole, Jonathan and I would drive in our combie in all directions of the compass into the Transvaal countryside. We would see a pretty place and would then scan the 365 degrees for the farmhouse (there was always one) and we would approach the owners to ask permission to picnic on their land. Not only would they always smilingly say 'yes', but we quickly learnt that they would always insist that we partook of additional hospitality: tea, coffee or something more intoxicating, and cake.

Those days were another of my experiences which have drawn me emotionally into the Afrikaner people. The so-called 'English speakers' of South Africa are often startled to hear me express love for the Afrikaners. The 'English' will often tell me that the Afrikaners are difficult to get on with. 'Well,' I remind them, 'we British mustn't forget that we have harried and killed them during a large part of their history, culminating in being responsible for the deaths of a large proportion of their women and children over nearly a three-year period (26,000 at a conservative estimate) and they are a very small nation. This during the Second Anglo-Boer War. And in spite of all of that, if you express a knowledge of their trials and a sympathy for their long suffering, they will embrace you.' I have yet to meet an exception to this Afrikaner rule.

I have a Boer friend (Afrikaner tends to be too soft for him) who tells me about a hardline uncle of his, whom he implies would eat me if he met me. Gustaf Opperman (that is my friend's name) doesn't want to see me (a rooinek – a Britisher) eaten alive, so he refuses to take me to his uncle's farm. One of my prime wishes during what remains of my life is to confront this remarkable uncle. There would be difficulties, I acknowledge, because I am told uncle refuses to pollute his speaking powers with one word of English. But – and this I *know* - if *anyone* was to attempt me harm, Gustaf Opperman would give him one across the ear or somewhere. That is the Boer. For many reasons I want to have them as my friends. Be very wary, Reader, I beg, of accepting the stereotyped endless image, thrown around the world, of the brutal Afrikaner policeman. Of course there are Afrikaner 'hard cases', but so are there Welsh ones and Black ones that would make our hair stand on end! But we rarely hear of *them*, do we?

Anyway it was a happy time for Carole and myself and little Jonathan (who is at this moment looming above).

NINETEEN

Before leaving Britain to make this Cecil Rhodes film, Patrick McGoohan had been, as you have already read, extremely solicitous towards me. He had finally asked: 'Is there anything else, Kenneth, that you are anxious to do?

Well there was. I had got to know quite a number of British veterans of the Second Anglo-Boer War. I used to visit them at the Royal Hospital, Chelsea, where some of them resided as Chelsea Pensioners. The Royal Hospital was inspired by that splendid lady of easy virtue, Nell Gwynne, who used her influence over King Charles I of Britain to achieve the magnificent home. Also there was a British South African Veterans' Association, I think it was called, who kept tabs on many of the old soldiers. Sometimes I was a guest at their meetings. And therefore I had a dream-idea: I wanted to film the old gentlemen before they became extinct. I wanted to film their memories of the last of Queen Victoria's major wars. And so I told Patrick and he replied: 'Do it' and he provided me with some money. I promptly got a first-class small film team together and we travelled from the south of Britain to the north interviewing the ancient warriors in their homes.

I selected the men carefully so that between them they covered every facet of the terrible war: its coming, the journey to South Africa, the set-battles, the sieges, the guerrilla war and the coming of peace. In their private homes the soldiers pinned onto their jackets the medals of long ago. What an experience that was for me! I had already studied the war extensively; I knew what I was talking about (well, not as much as I know today, but I was well informed) and above all, I ardently cared. That is the secret of communicating and of encouraging others to communicate: to care. I would sit in humble rooms between Southampton and Newcastle and listen to these men shuffle through their memories to tell me of frightening events when they fought and often suffered great pain for what they believed to be the honour of Britain – and, of course, for other reasons.

The stories and shadows of Victorian truths poured out of the soldiers; I think that I garnered about seven hours' screen-time of them. At the Chelsea Hospital the men who had fought in South Africa put their red coats on for our filming and they wore their medals. While talking to one of the warriors I noticed a medal placed *before* the Boer War emblems.

'What is that medal for, sir?'

'Relief of Khartoum, sir!'

And so, being in South Africa filming a life of Cecil Rhodes, my mind crept towards the *Boer* veterans and my good crew – and distant Patrick McGoohan – agreed that I should film *them*. And so we began our trek around the Republican countryside interviewing the old 'outstryders' as the Afrikaners call them. Again what a privilege that was for me! Again the standards that the Afrikaners lived by came from that old-time tradition that we in Britain have tragically left behind us. At one farm in the Transvaal the Boer fighter described his youthful war adventures with the physical grace of a fine dancer. After the long interview was over we were entertained in the farmhouse by his family with a substantial spread of food, and then simply but ceremoniously a silver spoon was presented to us; a gift to visitors. It was actually given to our lady film editor, who had accompanied us into the countryside. The whole experience was truly one of the highlights of my life.

Felix Meyburgh, whose film services we were using in Pretoria, saw some of our rushes (prints of the Rhodes filming that we had done). He was greatly impressed by the style of our story telling.

'Will you make a film for me, Kenneth?'

'Yes, if Patrick McGoohan agrees. After all, he brought me out here.'

In Pretoria, Patrick and I had formed an unwritten partnership. I telegraphed Patrick in Hollywood.

'Yes,' he replied, 'half profits for me.'

And Felix was delighted: 'What subject will you choose?'

'I would like to make a film in praise of the Black rubbish collectors of Pretoria.'

Felix was now astonished; I suspected that he had wanted another historical saga.

'Why do you want to do the rubbish collectors?'

'Well, in the first place they are great athletes and splendid entertainers and probably they are the best rubbish collectors in the world.'

Felix was still doubtful, from the expression on his face.

'Felix,' I said, 'because you see them every day, you don't really recognize how remarkable they are.' I think I explained the example of G. K. Chesterton's postman who was not observed because he was present almost every day.

Felix is not a man lightly to say no to any adventure, so the simple deal was struck. I would research and write a script and direct and Felix himself would be the cameraman. Oh, and Felix would also handle the sound-recording; he is a man of multiple talents.

I put my project before the Pretoria civic authorities and they willingly agreed.

'Any help that we can give you, Mr Griffith?'

'May I travel for one week on the rubbish truck, observing the various happenings and then film those happenings the following week?'

'Certainly, Mr Griffith.'

And so I was allotted to a rubbish truck.

The team comprised a White Afrikaner driver, a supervising Black man who wore a khaki peaked cap with an oval brass badge, on which was inscribed 'Boss Boy Number One' and twenty-odd Black rubbish collectors. They mainly belonged to the Shangaan tribe, which tribe comes from up Mozambique way. Oh, and 'Boss Boy Number One' had a whistle through which he loudly and insistently issued instructions. I coveted that cap with its badge; I was promised one by Pretoria's cleansing department and I never got it! They *owe* me that cap and badge!

A great joy for my rubbish collecting colleagues was to leave one of their chums behind. Then they would urge the driver to accelerate and then as the tardy-one charged down the street in pursuit, with the huge bin on a shoulder, he would unbelievably accelerate his pace, gain ground on the truck and with an impressive flick of his shoulder, send the loaded bin through the air into the yawning receptacle at the rear and then it was comparatively easy for the man to leap aboard.

And so the daily adventures were constructed. The streets of Pretoria at that time of the year – September, October – were magically coloured by thousands of jacaranda trees and the pavements were thick with their lilac-coloured blossom. Again I did the initial editing of the film in Pretoria with the help of Mrs Connie Meyburgh.

When the time came to return to Britain a difficulty loomed: Patrick McGoohan had, as far as we were concerned, disappeared into the multifarious corridors of Los Angeles. We could achieve no contact with him whatsoever – by telephone or telegram. And Felix Meyburgh was owed money for the use of his facilities. Over financial matters I have the mind of a Welsh peasant. You pay what you owe or you are in serious trouble. And no frills. I am frightened of the significance of money. I suppose that it comes from my early poverty and near-puritan upbringing.

Anyway I addressed happy-go-lucky Felix: 'I must return to Britain; I propose that you hold on to *all* of the Rhodes film and when you are paid, forward everything to me in Britain.'

'No,' replied Felix, 'I can't do that to you! It is *your* film.'

But I left Pretoria, with Carole and Jonathan, by train for Cape Town, where we would catch the ship that would carry us back to Southampton and we went without the film. I can be stoically relaxed about such matters; so long as I *believe* that I have done the right thing. I sent a last telegram to Patrick informing him of what I had done. Shortly afterwards, Felix was paid and all of our hard film work miraculously arrived in Cape Town in time to be loaded onto our ship.

In London I quickly took the Cecil Rhodes film to Huw Wheldon. Very speedily he replied: 'We *must* buy it!' and through Patrick McGoohan the BBC did. Huw asked: 'Have you got anything else?'

'A film in praise of the Black rubbish collectors of Pretoria. It is called *Keep Pretoria Clean!*' (On each side of the rubbish trucks this legend appears; on one side in English, on the other in Afrikaans.)

Huw looked at it and said: 'Kenneth, it is a brilliant film.' This remark of his has always warmed me. I had conceived the simple idea; I had researched it; I had written it and directed it. And Huw was the man who had masterminded the great television series: *Monitor*. And of course – credit where credit is due – Felix Meyburgh was the entire technical crew. The BBC also bought that film.

'Anything else?' pursued Huw.

'Well,' I uncertainly replied, 'I have about twelve hours' screen-time of old soldiers who fought in the Anglo-Boer War.'

Of course Huw Wheldon considered me to be an eccentric friend, so he took the above news with fascinated equanimity. He appointed a producer to view it all and to report. And so I was asked to transform the raw material of the interviews into four forty-minute (was it?) films which were to be shown on BBC television over consecutive weeks.

Now I had not filmed the Boer War veterans with any plan of making a film or films. I had been told that the British South African Veterans' Association was about to disband because of disappearing membership through old age. I enquired if there was to be any 'standing down' ceremony. 'No,' I was told, 'we will simply "close the books".' I then asked that if the BBC and myself were prepared to help, could there not be a fitting ceremony so that we (the BBC) could film it and use the result to open our Anglo-Boer War film series? And this was agreed to and that the ceremony would take place in the Royal Hospital at a specific time and on such a date.

The Royal Hospital and the Veterans' Association made a splendid job of the arrangements; indeed they did not call on us outsiders further. We (the BBC film crew) arrived early on the morning of the occasion and began to light, for filming purposes, the noble chamber and then it began to dawn on me that the ceremony was going to be grander than I had visualized. No harm in that. There were going to be generals and their wives present!

The BBC cameraman snatched a shot of me gazing very intently – some would say too intently – but I become deeply involved in human drama and I was not unconscious of the fact that I had concocted this last act of that old, terrible imperial adventure.

The governor-or-whoever was in full pompous sway when the BBC director mumbled some words at him in the far distance. The words were: 'Excuse me sir, would you mind doing that again.'

The Military Importance stood in a state of explosive disbelief. Finally: 'Do *what* again!?'

'Make your entrance again; we have to film you from an alternative angle.'

'I have never heard such impertinence in my life!'

I did not join in the distant altercation; I remained where I was and kept my head down like a wise soldier.

The governor continued: 'I will do it *once* more, but under no circumstances will you interrupt me again!' And they all trooped back into the anteroom.

And so the ceremony flowed on. Finally Colonel Lang of the Argyll and Sutherland Highlanders and President of the South African War Veterans' Association – who had even fought at the Battle of Magersfontein in 1899 – made his statement, by initially quoting a letter which he had addressed to Sir Michael Adeane, who was some sort of side-kick to the English Queen: 'Her Majesty the Queen is our gracious Patron. We ask you to convey to Her Majesty our humble duty and to inform her that owing to old age and physical infirmities we are obliged to stand down our Association in its 70th year . . . Please assure Her Majesty that the oath of allegiance we gave to Her Majesty Queen Victoria has remained constant to her successors to the present day.'

Colonel Lang then read out an astonishing (to me) reply. It did not come from 'Her Majesty' and not even from Adeane, but, presumably, from one of Adeane's helpers: 'Dear Colonel Lang, Sir Michael Adeane has passed on to me your letter of the 16th October, which I have submitted to Her Majesty. The Queen particularly asked me to thank you for your loyal messages. Yours sincerely, Tryon.'

I sat and fumed at the arrogant insensitivity of that wretched so-called Royal Family; though I must register the overwhelming improvement that Prince Charles is manifesting in the teeth of what many contemporary vulgarians would wish him to be. I suspect that Charles would have dropped a personal note to Lang and company or even called at the Royal Hospital himself. Though, quite incidentally, I have heard a distant whisper that I personally might be nearer to the *true* Prince of Wales than he; but no fear – I don't want the job. Got troubles of my own.

In our completed film I was then seen walking eastward and past Buckingham Palace and, as luck would have it, at that very time, a Guards band and company of soldiers came marching by in their red uniforms and I took the opportunity to address the camera: 'I understand Tryon is the assistant to Sir Michael Adeane, secretary to her Majesty the Queen. And his miserable reply from Buckingham Palace, I presume, is the very last royal response to the warriors of the Empire, upon which the sun never set.'

All of the six films were transmitted (which included *Rhodes* and *Keep Pretoria Clean!*). They were all received by the Press and public, generally, enthusiastically – except in the case of a journal which was sent to me from Rhodesia. A longish piece had been written by a son (?) of G. K. Chesterton who, so it appeared, was a bit Rightish, politically. As far as I can recall – and I recall it vividly! – he (me) 'should live in the sewers with the rats; but come to think of it, the sewers are far too good for him . . .' What a press notice! Well, you win one; you lose one!

TWENTY

O f course, all through this period of my life I continued to act in films and on television. In fact I was incredibly busy. The pieces ranged from Tolstoy to six Feydeau farces (in which I had the honour of alternating husband and lover in succeeding plays with Mr Alfred Marks). As far as I recall both Tolstoy and the Feydeau romps won American 'Emmies' – whatever that may signify.

A strange thing happened to me in London a few months ago. I was lolling in front of my television set watching some drama (of a somewhat more muted style than in my day) and I said to myself, as I contemplated the actors: 'What a strange way of earning a living.' I sat bolt upright and thought: 'But *I* used to do *that*! Perhaps as much as anybody else in Britain.' Quite often members of the public will come up to me and ask: 'But when will we see you *act* in a play again, Mr Griffith?'

During that welter of television acting, I was engaged on one of those BBC 'classic' series: an adaptation of Thomas Mann's *Buddenbrooks*, directed by Mr Michael Imison, a highly intelligent and sensitive man, who, for some mysterious reason, the Corporation eventually got rid of. They can often do that: drive out their best and retain their worst. Also acting in *Buddenbrooks* was Mr David Swift and he and I immediately became friends. David, I believe, had trained to be a lawyer; he had become a successful businessman, but longed to give all of that up in order to devote his energy to creative work. He also had a great sense of fun and we had much to talk about. David was enthusiastically interested in my own documentary film efforts and their boundless potential.

One day I was walking up the Charing Cross Road when I met him. This, incidentally, is a classic location for two actors to meet. David asked: 'What film are you making now?'

'Oh, I'm truly finished in that direction; I'm back on the acting lark.'

'Why?' demanded David.

'Well, I'm finished at the BBC.'

'Why don't you make films for commercial television? Within the past week people have talked to me about your work at both Thames and ATV [Sir Lew Grade's company].'

David was opening a professional door for me and the sunlight peeked through; there in the Charing Cross Road.

'Would you like me to introduce you to them?' he urged.

'Yes please, David.'

'Which would you prefer?'

'I don't mind. They're both about equidistant,' was my quaint reply.

David lost no time. The next day he organized a lunch for Charles Denton, himself and me. Mr Denton was then deputy head of ATV's documentary department and over that happy luncheon table, Charles said to me: 'Would you like to work for us?'

'Yes, indeed.'

'Well, you don't want to be kept hanging about, do you? If we can agree on terms, it's a deal.'

I asked David if he would arrange a contract for me and the next day it was done. Oh, and Charles Denton asked me: 'What subject would you like to tackle?'

'A life of the Irish patriot, Michael Collins,' I replied.

'Fine,' said Charles. And so I launched myself into big trouble; and me all pale cheeks and delighted innocence.

My feelings for Ireland stretched back to my childhood when I first heard of Mr Flynn having 'the roof of his house burnt over his head'. As my life moved along I garnered the appalling story of England's behaviour on the island of Ireland and as it dawned on me, that in certain respects, my country, Wales, had joined England in their endless exploitation and brutality, I felt a personal shame. Wales' involvement was personified for me by David Lloyd George and I have grown to detest his name. Welsh cunning ('The Wizard') is not good enough.

Strangely, Harold, my father, served in Ireland as a very young British soldier. During the First World War he had volunteered to be slaughtered in France, but before he could be despatched, my grandfather (Ernest, who brought me up) heard about it and reported that his son was under sixteen years old and Harold was given two weeks in the 'glass house' for lying and was then sent to Ireland with the Yeomanry. I remember my father telling me that the Irish people were very kind to him, but that one evening he went to see a play in a village hall and as he sat there in his khaki uniform he became aware that the drama on the stage was about poor starving Irish people being cruelly misused by British 'police'. I remember him telling me that he began to feel very uncomfortable. Of course my poor father knew little about what evils the British have perpetrated in Ireland, as I fear few British soldiers know today. In actual fact my father was inadvertently assisting the often bestial behaviour of the British 'Black and Tans' and their élitist colleagues of the 'Auxiliaries', who then carried out the role of today's Special Air Service (SAS). What a day for rejoicing it will be when we finally remove the British Union flag from the island of Ireland!

And by this time, Peter O'Toole had come to live with Doria and me, and my Irish acquaintances multiplied and my knowledge of personal Irish feelings increased.

I have always felt at home with Irish people, as I have always felt warmed by Jewish company. It has something to do with the deep level of imagination and emotion at which they both exist. Of course between the Welsh and the Irish there is also the Celtic bond.

An English joke about us is that Welshmen are Irishmen who couldn't swim; I welcome the suggested connection. There *is* a notable difference in character between the Welsh and the Irish, but I have wondered if this is because we Welsh have been caught in the black net of Puritan Nonconformism and that the Irish (as against the Anglo-Scottish Irish) are given weekly forgiveness of their sins through Roman Catholic confession. *I* will carry my guilt with me to the grave. However, beneath our disparate religious arrangements, we both are the ancient folk of the islands who were philosophizing together, long before the Roman and the German and the Norman turned up to breed the famous English mongrel. Not that I dislike the English! As a matter of fact I enjoy living in London; indeed I call myself a Welsh Cockney. Yes, a cockney; if the wind is blowing stiffly east-south-east.

But I am on the side of Irish Republicanism and if ever they need me, they have only got to ask. That is as long as I believe the request is morally viable. I'm not a car-bomb man. But if the Prime Minister ever feels the need to punish me for my loyalty to the Irish people, I would regard it as the greatest honour to sense a touch of Mr Bobby Sands' brave light on me. Or, of course, the light of any of his fellow martyrs. And none of us would be too far away from another Celt: William Ewart Gladstone. Does the Prime Minister know anything about Britain's record in Ireland? Is the creed of 'my country; right or wrong' sufficient? The terrible patriots; the outraged people of Ireland are an inevitability.

I chose Michael Collins because he was the finest of 'the outraged people' that I could think of. I seem to operate on spontaneous instinct, which pops out of my accumulated experience, and of course includes my nonstop talking and listening and – oh precious gift! – reading. I do not scheme; I am no Machiavelli. Could it be a 'still small voice'? What a comfort that would be! But I am an agnostic.

Michael Collins was an Irishman of tremendous courage (one of an endless Irish queue); a man of the highest principles, and uncommonly handsome. He was one of the sun's heroes. So my instinct drove me, unerringly, to Michael Collins as the perfect personification of Ireland's seven-hundred-year-old dream of complete independence from the physical and spiritual brutality of England.

Through a friend it was arranged that I should meet a Roman Catholic priest who was close to the men who had fought with the Irish Republican Army, under Michael Collins' leadership. The priest was introduced to me without much explanation, as Monsignor Jerry Newman. Now, I knew nothing about 'ranks' in the Roman Catholic hierarchy and for whatever reason I was a little overchallenging in my exchanges with this Christian Irishman; my language was not the best. But Jerry Newman rode it with ease. He took me out to a very good supper at the seaside, just outside of Dublin. We had a drop to drink and I decided that he was a very good chap.

At the end of the evening Jerry said to me: 'We ought to continue our discussion tomorrow. If you are free, come and have a bit of lunch where I live, and I'll have a close friend of Mick Collins' there to meet you. I live at a teaching college.' He gave me directions on how to get to Maynooth, and added: 'But anyone here in Dublin will tell you.'

I had imagined one of those lonely priests – like a captain on a ship at sea – perhaps with a dour housekeeper, and I actually imagined my new friend preparing a bit of something personally over a gas ring. But as my car drove into a great Gothic complex, which is the very centre of Roman Catholic power in all of Ireland, I began rapidly to readjust my expectation. At the central entrance of the main building I enquired of the man supervising that post: 'Where do I find Monsignor Jerry (I think I should have said Jeremiah) Newman? I have an appointment with him.'

'He's waiting for you, sir,' and I was whisked upstairs.

Jeremiah Newman stood in his fine atmospheric apartment with a gentle-faced man, surmounted with a mass of white hair.

'Hello, Kenneth, this is Sean Kavanagh who was a close friend of Michael Collins and he is most anxious to help you in any way he can.'

Sean Kavanagh was to become a close friend of mine and now that he is gone – like all of the Old Patriots – I miss him very much. He was a fighting agent for Collins and a train-raider.

Jerry said: 'We must go; I mustn't keep my colleagues waiting,' and we chased after him down the stairs. He stalked ahead of us like a virile White Rabbit and suddenly we were in a vast dining-room with very lengthy refectory tables stretching away, and as we entered the massed priests rose. Monsignor Jeremiah's ritual was brief and peremptory; I sat on one side of him, Sean on the other. The food and the wine were first class. The very last time I spoke to my chum was in the city of Limerick, where he reigned as Bishop.

And so I was well launched into the best of Republican circles. I should have emphasized that I had already researched my subject and written the script, which, as far as I was concerned, anyone was free to see. It had been applauded by the Old Republican Guard who had fought through that great Irish Saga and, it would appear, the contemporary ranks of active Republicans also nodded approval. One evening I was in a crowded Dublin bar, having a glass of that smooth Guinness, when a stranger passing swiftly by, touched my arm and said: 'Thank you.' I barely caught a glimpse. Around me there was silence and then someone whispered: 'You know who *that* was?'

Of course, in any urban guerrilla warfare situation, the sense of unorthodox military death is tingling. I have willowed past it elsewhere: in the black townships of South Africa, in Iran during the Ayatollah's time, and on the West Bank of 'Greater Israel'. Even in London my telephone has passed on to me death threats. I've had them on the streets of Harlem in New York City too. But in Dublin it was a message of reassurance from 'a passing party'.

Antony Thomas was again the director and Grenville Middleton was again in charge of the magic camera. How fortunate I was – or rather the film was – in having the creative skill of these two men. For many years now I have been discouraged from being allowed *even* to look at the Michael Collins film, but recently a BBC film crew visited my house in London to interview me on another subject. The producer talked to me about *Hang Up Your Brightest Colours* (the title of the Collins film) and I said to him: 'Ah, but you haven't *seen* it.'

'Oh yes I have,' he replied, 'I saw it yesterday.'

'Where?'

'On our "Steenbeck" (a film editing machine). You mean *you* haven't got a copy?' he asked.

'No, I have been, say, formidably discouraged.'

'Would you like ours? It's a poor quality print.'

'Yes, please.'

And within a day or so it was delivered to my house.

Now, the interesting thing about this event is that I have all of the necessary equipment to look at the film in my comfortable sitting-room and I hadn't viewed it for many years; but I could not bring myself to slip the cassette into the aperture and push the switch, for three weeks. I was afraid that there would be some content in the film – after all it had been suppressed in Britain and disallowed from being sold overseas, in the United States of America in particular – which I could no longer agree with. And then, one afternoon, the house was empty and I quickly shoved it on and sat staring at it for the hour and a half. I was transfixed. I agreed with every delivery and at my totally uninhibited style of telling my truth. And I was deeply impressed by Antony Thomas' great skill in, as it were, dancing with the tempo and theme of the great story and deeply impressed by Grenville Middleton's fine photography. The quality of the sound and everything was commendable. Alone in the house, I shouted: 'Bravo.'

Again my memories of those filming days are multiple. On the edge of Dublin is Kilmainham Jail; the site of such appalling anti-Irish atrocities by us British and yet enshrouded to this very day (I presume it hasn't changed recently) with a penetrating Celtic aura. We filmed within those dreadful tall stone walls for days on end. The curious angles of dark inner chambers. There was something of Norman-English practicality about them; the implacable English masters are still in the offing. Immovable ghosts in the Celtic Republic. And beyond? There are the cells and the execution yard for ultimate solution of what England has called 'The Irish Problem'. Come to think of it, the Collins film begins with an image of youngish me, coming over a green hill in County Cork: 'An Irish friend said to me, "There is no such thing as an Irish problem; only an *English* problem!" Well this film is about that old English problem,' and I was past the camera. So, you see, it was fists and wallop from the first bell sounding.

One of the enormous advantages of working intimately on my sort of film is what one can discover and learn from the historical protagonists themselves. I was to make a film about Napoleon and I learnt so much from that man. On the island of Saint Helena, where we British finally imprisoned him, Napoleon spoke one of his arias, refuting the accusations made against his ideas for a European Common Market, and so on. And observers of his seismic verbal attack have recorded that the giant of a man suddenly stopped – you could have heard an eagle's wings – and then he said: 'It's only the *truth* that hurts.' And that is why the British Establishment suppressed the Michael Collins film. No other. On the subject of Ireland – as far as Britain is concerned – the truth is inadmissible. That is why the synchronized images of Sinn Fein spokesmen are disallowed in Britain. Think on it, fellow country people. And rustle your feathers, as a warning to your political leaders.

The execution yard of Kilmainham Jail is the precise spot where almost all of Ireland, inevitably, became a Republic via the ambiguous 'Irish Free State'. At Easter Time in the year 1916, a gathering of Irish idealists from every walk of life quixotically occupied Dublin's General Post Office, together with a few other central buildings and defended them with rifles, when British soldiers attacked. It proved to be no more than a bloody symbolical act and when those Irish leaders of the noble insurrection were incarcerated – at the end of six days – in this Kilmainham Jail, it was but a short time before we British shot them in that yard. They were not only the butcher, the baker and the candlestick maker; they were also – and were led by – the teacher, the lawyer and the fighting philosophers.

Ireland's poet, W B. Yeats, wrote a bit of his unique gossamer about the dead men who had just breathed a new life into Ireland: 'A terrible beauty is born'.

And down in Bailn'Blaugh (Valley of the Flowers), where Michael Collins was shot dead, I finally emerge from an ancient cottage, quoting the words of another Irishman, George Bernard Shaw: 'I will not demean myself by snivelling over the death of Michael. What better end could he have than dying for Ireland? Killed by another Irishman [it happened during Ireland's Civil War], a damn fool but one who thought that he was doing it for Ireland. So, my dear Miss Collins [he was writing to the great leader's sister] tear up your mourning, and hang up your brightest colours in his honour!'

Yes, I had enjoyed that quiet enviable emotion of having said something worth saying and saying it pretty well as I had planned; nothing more. Well, let me dig as deep as I can into my recollection. I was astonished, as I have always been, at the fact that the gift of opportunity had presented itself for me. And I then suffered that powerful instinct *not* to waste the gift, and unerringly, I went for the big, desperately needed issue – *why* we British should finally remove the last vestige of our sometime imperial presence from the small island of Ireland; I mean our unwanted Union Jack flag and its authority.

I had presumed that when British people saw and heard the story of Michael Collins' life on their television screens they would ask themselves and each other one or two healthy British questions: 'Is this story about Ireland correct?' and 'If it is correct, then shouldn't we apologize to the Irish Nation and, with dignity, withdraw to our own island?'

I was told the date of transmission and as it drew close I was informed by Mr Charles Denton that 'there is a bit of a problem; transmission is delayed'. Now I always, again instinctively, hold my fire. I always hope that the enemy will retreat and that there will be no war. Only when an offence is confirmed will I fight. I remember that phony peace over the Michael Collins film. I can only presume that whoever was instigating the stoppage – at a *very high level* – hoped that I and my film would silently fade away like the morning dew. I remember suffering a dread that this silence was all that would happen. Please remember again how isolated and innocent I was. I still believed that the morality of my grandfather, Ernest Griffiths, and the morality of his undoubted hero, William Ewart Gladstone, pertained in my British land! Can you believe it!? But, I need not have despaired. Britain is not dead and finished. The Press (I mean of course the enlightened Press) got wind of it: that something was being suppressed secretly in the undefined Establishment, and they began to blow the gaff.

I was informed, I think that it was by the late Mr Robert Heller, the then head of Sir Lew Grade's documentary film

That is me, sitting on the lap of my great-grandfather, Edmund. On the left is my grandfather, Ernest, and on the right my father, Harold.

At Penally, with Tenby in the background, when I was about nine years old. I am holding Daisy, my greyhound.

My grandparents Emily and Ernest Griffiths, who brought me up.

The Shop at Sly Corner: my first film role after the war,
and the first film role ever for Diana Dors.

With Peter Sellers in *Only Two Can Play.*

With my
closest
actor friend,
Peter O'Toole,
thirty years
ago.

Communicating with Silvio Narizzano, director of the Granada
television production of *War and Peace*. On the right is my
fellow Thespian, Nicol Williamson.

With my children: David, Eva, Jonathan, Polly and Huw.

My first chosen film team, in Botswana - filming a life of
Cecil Rhodes. To the left of the camera is Antony Thomas and on the
extreme right Grenville Middleton.

On the island
of Aix, while
filming *The Man
on the Rock*.

With Chief Minister Buthelezi, speaking for his ancestor, King Cetewayo,
in a film remembering the British-Zulu War of 1879.

With Prime Minister Indira Gandhi at her home in Delhi.

In a rain-forest in West Africa, while making the Roger Casement film, *Heart of Darkness*. Here, I have been caught unawares, considering the script I had written in Europe. And *below*, the death threat I received from my fellow Protestants of the north-eastern part of Ireland.

X X X X
POWYS

A VIDEO OF YOUR RAVINGS ABOUT IRELAND HAS BEEN SENT TO :

Mc _ _ _ _ _ ,
c/o H & W.
WELDERS CLUB,
BALLYMACARRET,
BELFAST.

IF YOU OPENLY SUPPORT SINN FEIN & PROVISIONAL IRA YOU MUST TAKE THE CONSEQUENCE REMEMBER! EDDIE FULLERTON THOUGHT HE WAS SAFE

W HUNTER

Receiving a BAFTA 'life-time award', and using (or misusing) the occasion to talk about the deterioration of British television and about Perfidious Albion in Ireland.

With my latter-day patron, Geraint Stanley Jones.

With Roy Boulting, Chris Lawrence and Chiara Peretti.

department, that Members of the British Parliament were requesting to view the Michael Collins film. And that Conservatives were seeing it separately from Socialists; whether Liberals were involved I don't know. (Perhaps their failure to appear was a clear sign of the very end of that once great Liberal ideal. Let me remind you that there was a time when Gladstone, without question, would have been the *first* into that viewing theatre. He would have sat in the front row and dead centre and I am confident of the Grand Old Man's approval at the end.)

Sir, as he then was, Lew Grade gave a grand viewing at ATV House, close to Marble Arch, for the many Tory Members who turned up. And there was an excellent (as you can imagine) luncheon provided. And – surprise – I was invited to the grub afterwards. It was the only time, till very recently, that I have had the opportunity to sit down and chat to massed Conservatives. I recall them to be pleasant and affable and in my jolly corner of the assembly was my brief boss, Sir Lew Grade himself. And at that moment someone came up to me and said: 'The Press is downstairs, Mr Griffith, and they want to see you.' Was the dark door opening? As I excused myself, Sir Lew whispered to me, urgently: 'Be careful what you say, son!' What does that request mean, I briefly asked myself as I hurried downstairs. And there they were – perhaps the *true* gentlemen of the Press (I recall no ladies) – sort of huddled in the main doorway. I said: 'I am angry with the bloody Independent Broadcasting Authority. I consider them to be cowardly bastards hiding behind my friend, Sir Lew Grade.' And Hallelujah, they printed it verbatim! Was that being careful about what I said? It depends whose side you're on.

You see, what had happened is this (though at that juncture of the powerful proceedings, I didn't know as much as I was to learn later): the Independent Broadcasting Authority (now the Independent Television Commission), being responsible for everything that is shown on Britain's commercial television, had to view any serious programme that was related to Ireland and so they were duly shown the Michael Collins film. Now they realized what a dangerous challenge the programme was to our contemporary policy in the Six Counties of Ulster; the film exposed some of the foul British roots and directly implied that we had no moral or ethical reason to be in the North-East. We British have had *expedient* reasons for being there and upholding our authority there, but that is a totally different matter; indeed the antithesis of the former.

I believe that the IBA officer in charge of the operation of suppression was a Mr Bernard Sendel. I have often wondered who might have been the influences above him; but I don't know. And I presumed that Mr Sendel had given Sir Lew Grade a telephone call and had asked him *not* to offer the Collins film to the IBA for viewing and thereby save the IBA from being *seen* to be guilty of political censorship. But later I learnt that Mr Sendel didn't telephone Sir Lew Grade about the matter; he visited him personally.

Now here's another rub. The IBA is/was all powerful to the commercial television companies, of which Sir Lew's ATV was one of the biggest. The renewal of their 'licence to print money' as one shrewd, influential man put it, was in the hands of the IBA. Suffice it to state that Sir Lew Grade didn't argue with Mr Bernard Sendel of the IBA. *Hang Up Your Brightest Colours: The Life and Death of Michael Collins* was not offered and so viewers throughout the English speaking world were prevented from seeing it and judging British behaviour in Ireland for themselves. But now, as I wrote above, questions were very properly being asked. And I was learning a few facts of our inner British way of life.

After the Tory Members of Parliament had seen the film, it was the turn of the Socialists and Sir Lew Grade addressed me personally: 'Son (and I was already getting on in years) if *I* promise not to attend the viewing of the Collins film, for the Socialists, will *you* promise not to attend?

'But, sir, it's your viewing theatre; if you tell me not to go, of course I won't.'

'No, no! I wouldn't *tell* you not to go. I'm simply asking for a gentleman's agreement.'

'I won't go, Sir Lew.'

On that day of the Socialist viewing, I sat in an office at

ATV House reading a book; research one might call it. There was a knock on the door.

'Come in.'

And there before me were most of the leaders of Britain's Socialist Party led by Michael Foot. What did I feel like? Mr Foot spoke: 'We don't know what to say to you, Mr Griffith. It is perhaps the most moving and powerful political film that I have ever seen. We don't know what we can do, but we plan to have a discussion about it and I will be in touch with you.'

I remember the smiling, enthusiastic faces and they shook hands with me and were gone. I have always believed that young Neil Kinnock was amongst them. But for me it was a traumatic experience and I am simply left with the above vivid impression. I really was becoming, it seemed to me, a successful Nonconformist preacher. Yes, Michael Foot did write to me.

Of course they could not do anything to get the film transmitted, but I now knew that I was supported by Englishmen, Welshmen and Scotsmen, as well as Irishmen, in my efforts to help the emancipation of the whole island of Ireland. Perhaps I had even increased their knowledge and feelings for the subject and they were political leaders of a very large proportion of the British people. I felt that I had already achieved more than my human share of satisfaction in this strange human journey.

Now where could I go from here? I thought about the sympathy that the United States of America had for Ireland and I went to see Mr Robert Heller (the head of ATV's documentary department). Mr Heller was a North American and I think that he was a refugee from Senator McCarthy's reign of persecution. He was a very quiet, private man. I felt a little in awe of him; but the barrier between a more intimate friendship was more a tired shyness than anything else. It has suddenly occurred to me that he would have been very pleased with the film that I was eventually responsible for: *The Most Valuable Englishman Ever: A Life of Thomas Paine*. Robert is dead now; but I want you to know, Robert (and you, Charles Denton), that probably I could not have got as far as Tom Paine if you hadn't helped me on my way.

Robert Heller said to me: 'Kenneth, if you go to this

address in New York City, you can collect a print of the Michael Collins film. In the States you can do what you like with it (he had a fair idea of what I intended to do), but before you return to Britain, you must replace the print in that New York office.' Well, that is what I did. And I first organized a viewing of the film at the United Nations Headquarters in New York. I simply wanted to publicize what Britain was up to in its suppression of the film. Of course I would much have preferred that the British Establishment had had the bright courage to broadcast the film as originally scheduled, but since they were guilty of cowardly subterfuge, I would take what counter-measures I could.

For the first time I had to begin to contemplate the reality of the United Nations. I approached those multiple synthetic flags naively believing that in the fine structure behind them were hundreds of men and women: white, black, brown and yellow, all eagerly anxious to put the world's wrongs to right. What I found, and have personally had confirmed since, is that the place is teeming with miserable humanity, only desperate to advance their own usually miserable nations forward materially, and often, I fear, their even more miserable personal self-interests forward materially. However, I showed the film and I was given sensitive help by a young Irish diplomat who wrote good poetry.

And then I ploughed on to Washington and the Irish community there and the Senators in their great Chambers of Government. As I passed into the foyer of the airport I was greeted by a deputation of Irish Republican activists. Of course in that patriotic brand of company it is impolite to ask any immediate personal questions; but the gathering seemed to be equally divided between Roman Catholic priests and Irishmen having a breather from active service in the northeastern part of the Old Country. The leader of the concerted group was the famous Irish–American firebrand, Father Sean McManus. And very soon I was to meet another impressive Irish–American, who looked, and acted, to me remarkably like Patrick McGoohan: Mr Fred Burns O'Brien. Before we left that foyer and after being warmly embraced by my fellow Celts, I felt compelled to make a statement, particularly to the secular section: 'Friends, I have reservations about *some* of your methods.'

And an enormous man replied: 'Be that as it may, Mr Griffith; where do you want your bags carried?' and he picked them up, very easily.

The actual viewing of the Michael Collins film was in the Senate Building and it was quite an emotional affair; after it was over, a lady in the audience unpinned her Celtic brooch and gave it to me.

My private mission, once I was in Washington, was organized by Fred O'Brien. He was clearly very well known in the political centre and with him I talked to Senator Eugene McCarthy, who had just run for the Presidency; with Mr O'Brien I was given easy access to Mr Edward Kennedy's quarters – and not quite so easy access to the offices of Mr Tip O'Neal, who was the Speaker of the House of Representatives. I wasn't creating a revolution, but, on the other hand, I was not allowing the British system of suppressing truths about their behaviour in Ireland to pass unnoticed. And that was all I could hope for. Once I had done my utmost for what I believed was right, I felt a decent degree of peace.

Out of many curious experiences I had on that journey in the United States, one experience sticks out beyond the others. I was with a group of these Irish patriots when I began to talk about the hard-working virtues of my friend, Fred O'Brien. There was a telling pause and then: 'Ah, Ken, Fred's a member of the FBI.'

'What! Are you sure?'

'Yes, Ken.'

'Does he suspect that you know?'

'Yes, Ken. We've informed him. We're pretty good at spotting such chaps.' (I received a strong impression the 'such chaps' were usually British.)

'And what will happen now?'

'Oh, we'll leave things as they are. Fred understands. And he's a hard worker. And he's a true Irish patriot at heart.' And I sat there trying to unravel this apparent James Bond world, when suddenly the Irishman added, perhaps to himself? 'And better the devil you know . . .'

I also showed the Collins film in Boston to a packed audience. And my Sicilian–American friend, Mr Joseph de Cola, arranged for a senior man at the American Broadcasting Company, Mr Av Westin, to view it. That was interesting. I had never seen a top American television executive in action before; he came hurrying down a corridor, closely followed by a small group of aides. In he went to look at my film and inside the viewing theatre I could hear the bloody telephone continuously interrupting the proceedings. Suddenly someone came out and yelled: 'Av says "cut the phone",' and the human powerhouse didn't emerge for an hour and a half. When he did he told me that he was 'impressed' and he invited me to have a meal with him and his Irish wife in their very private home on the south-west side of Central Park.

Back in Britain I strayed very briefly into the epicentre of the British Establishment; no, I don't mean Buckingham Palace (that can never happen), but into Number Ten, Downing Street. Mr Harold Wilson was Prime Minister. After receiving the invitation I, uneasily, telephoned the residence and asked why I had been invited.

'Oh, he is very interested in your work.'

On the appointed day, I headed off for Downing Street early. As I grow older I set off for all places of rendezvous more and more early. I discovered that it was easier to say to a taxi-driver: 'Paddington Station' than 'Ten Downing Street'. After a while I added: 'Look, I'm going to be monstrously early; would you drive me up The Mall and then round and round Queen Victoria's Memorial, in front of Buckingham Palace, for at least fifteen minutes?'

'Certainly, sir,' said my representative of far and away the most superior taxi service on the face of our earth.

Of course, I was not the only guest. The astounding moment inside the place was when Mr David Steel (distinguished Liberal) and Mr Neil Kinnock, both laughing, rather hustled two Irishmen towards me: Mr Gerry Fitt (as he then was), a leader of the Irish in the House of Commons, and a leader of the Scottish–Irish Unionists in that House of Government, whose name has slipped away. Either the Liberal or the Socialist (I cannot now recall) said to me: 'Mr Griffith, please tell these two Irishmen why you made the Michael Collins film.'

Well! Can you imagine what this sometime actor now turned film storyteller felt? This was some stage, with the British Prime Minister breathing not too far away! 'Fair play', as Huw Wheldon, like a good Welshman, used to say. I didn't hesitate for a moment. I paid my respects to both and then turned to the Scottish–Irish Protestant.

'Do you know, sir, that I was brought up a Protestant?'

'I understand so.'

'Well, the only reason that I made myself responsible for the making of that film was to present sufficient evidence that if only we Protestants could bring ourselves to look at, primarily, English behaviour in Ireland over the past seven hundred and fifty years – not the myths and legends, but the hardest facts, statistics and dates – we Protestants could only come to the conclusion that we are in *far better company* with Mr Fitt and his people than, sadly, what this house has represented in the past and, even more sadly, what it apparently still represents today. We British must look to a leader who will apologize to you Irish Protestants for having *used* you, and then apologize to Mr Fitt's people for having *misused* them. And if you two gentlemen continue to suffer a compulsion to fight – which I would regret deeply – commonsense dictates that you Irish must combine forces and fight this country Britain together; the cause of *all* of your respective troubles.' That is what I recall saying, more or less, and there are the distinguished witnesses still alive and well. Mr Fitt stared at me and the Protestant said: 'I hear your point, Mr Griffith, and Mr Fitt and I must make arrangements to see your film again.'

I heard no more, but a year or so later, while being entertained by Mr Merlyn Rees at the Northern Ireland Office, I met and talked to Gerry Fitt again. He was a bit shaken; I believe that there had been some attempt on his life – by my fellow Protestants.

TWENTY-ONE

My inability to cope with my domestic life ravaged on. Somewhere around this period of my life I found myself acting in a BBC radio play and my spirit was very low, brought down by some emotional trauma. The director of the drama – who was a singularly kindly man – noting my misery (though private feelings would never intrude into a performance) tried very hard to cheer me up in a local pub and his generous efforts culminated in urging me to go to the theatre with him. I replied: 'Thank you very much, but I don't enjoy going to the theatre when I'm happy and I certainly wouldn't when I'm miserable.' But he persisted: 'It's not a play; it's American Black people singing and dancing.' I remember that this remark disturbed my despondency: 'Well, all right; as long as you will forgive me if I have to leave the theatre at any moment.'

The show was called *Black Nativity*. It was the story of Jesus's birth told by Black Gospel jazz singers and two Black dancers. The company was led by Professor Alex Bradford and Miss Marion Williams. Well, I sat there uneasily and the singing and the vitality and the high cultural skill exploded in front of me. I didn't know about gospel jazz. At the end of the performance I was feeling even elated. I am, even when friends are performing, reluctant to visit backstage; I feel a strong sense of intrusion. But on this occasion I felt such a positive gratitude that I was compelled to try and say thank you. I debated with myself how best I could do this and concluded that I should ask if I could meet Alex Bradford.

Alex, who was the master musician, is an astounding character. He was a very specific, strict disciplinarian – as far as the music went. In his tightly self-contained style he was nevertheless sympathetic to his flock. I was told, as far as I remember, that he was the pastor of the Abyssinian Church in Newark, New Jersey. I was also told that he was the inspiration of other, more famous Black American singers such as Muddy Waters. Alex Bradford was a deeply complicated man who controlled himself, formidably, but – again, so I was told – if he broke, it would be wise to keep well away from his range. He and I immediately became friends and I was duly lifted out of my despair.

Marion Williams, in my opinion, is not less than a great singer. She would walk on to the stage alone and sing a Christmas carol that I have heard and sung most of my life, 'O Come All Ye Faithful', and you would have to realize that in fact you had *never* heard it before – not its deep, full implications. I must have heard Marion sing it one hundred times and never did it fail to bring tears to my eyes.

Alex Bradford and I would go out together; he was a man who clearly had passed through a hot fire and therefore he had a worldly wise wisdom – if he would allow you to tap it. Sometimes we would go together to that great actors' club, The Buckstone, tucked behind His Majesty's Theatre, behind the Haymarket. One night we both got a bit maudlin via wine drinking and I made the astounding pronouncement (which I would never make today): 'You know, Alex, sometimes I wish I was Black.' My friend wavered a gaze at me and replied: 'You know, dear Kenneth, sometimes I wish that I was White.'

I attended performances of *Black Nativity* night after night and endlessly insisted that friends, particularly those who were fine artists themselves, must accompany me: Peter Sellers, Peter O'Toole, Huw Wheldon and many others. I remember Huw Wheldon saying to me afterwards: 'My father was obsessed with Chaliapin; I never understood the depth of his feelings until tonight.'

Whenever I have worked in the United States of America I have made what effort time allowed to find these two outstanding musicians, but always failed. A few weeks ago, in Italy, I was scanning a newspaper and saw a photograph of Marion Williams with President Clinton in the White House and I was relieved and delighted to know that someone else had obviously recognized her genius.

In the *Black Nativity* company was a tall, lean, young woman named Madeline Bell, who had an undoubtedly unique voice which usually shook up the show by its unexpected quality. When I sat in Alex's dressing-room after the show was over, Madeline would invariably look in to say goodnight, to which he would reply: 'Goodnight, Daughter.' I, in my ignorance, even presumed that this might be their relationship. Africans and people of African origins – and three hundred years absence from the darkest of all continents makes little difference – think and act from a decidedly different point of view to us of the European culture. My fascinated confusion about Alex's and Madeline's relationship was the beginning of a two-year journey through the Black maze for me. With all of its ups and downs there was never a boring moment; very up and very down but always pulsating with adventure.

One evening, as usual, I was watching *Black Nativity* and Madeline Bell didn't appear. I was very disconcerted and I was surprised by my feelings. When I went round to Alex's dressing-room after the performance I asked where she was. 'She's ill, in her hotel, the Regent Palace.'

I then declared to my friend: 'I think Miss Bell is the most beautiful woman I have ever seen.' The beholder suffers a highly complicated process in recognizing beauty.

Her illness was brief and soon she was again in Alex's dressing-room. 'Goodnight Alex; goodnight, Mr Griffith.'

'Goodnight, Daughter. Oh! Mr Griffith thinks you are the most beautiful woman he has ever seen.' This was delivered in a factual, unsmiling tone. Professor Alex Bradford constantly called a spade a spade without a flicker of doubt. There was barely a moment before Madeline murmured 'Oh', and left the room.

Soon after this mildly alarming event I informed Madeline Bell: 'I have some days free and if you wish I would very much like to show you around London.'

'I would like that very much.'

I called for Madeline at her hotel and we walked down the Haymarket in London. In those far-off days it was an unusual sight to see a White man with a Black woman; I definitely felt an unease; quietly, Madeline took my arm and never again did I experience that uncomfortable emotion. How long were we together? Two years? We travelled far and wide; on public transport in Britain and elsewhere, and never once did anyone say or do anything to hurt us. I was surprised at this; indeed, people, both Black and White, were always kind to us. And initially we were the most innocent of friends.

At this time I had the good fortune to become associated with the outstanding director Silvio Narizzano; five plays for him in one year, I recall. My first job with him was playing Napoleon Bonaparte in an adaptation of Tolstoy's novel *War and Peace*. During the dress rehearsal, with me accoutred as the Emperor himself, I was handed a telegram. It came from Madeline and read something like: 'Have taken an apartment for us in Venice' (*Black Nativity* was then touring Italy). Well, between representing Napoleon and receiving this message, I was barely coping; the cup was near to running over. However, I moved positively; wearing the great man's uniform – and undoubtedly resembling him – I hurried to the receptionist in the foyer with my urgent reply. While I was giving instructions for its immediate despatch I became aware of a physical tussle between two uniformed commissionaires and a third man. Evetually the apparent intruder broke away and from the marble hall turned an intensive gaze on me. Slowly he advanced on me – the Emperor – with two Granada guards just behind him, tensely poised to pounce. I stood transfixed by the burning eyes that came closer and closer, all thoughts of Madeline Bell dismissed, temporarily, from my head.

The man suddenly spoke: 'My God, what a coincidence! You're Napoleon!' I think that I managed to nod my head slightly in confirmation. 'What a coincidence! You know who I am?' I think I managed a perceptible but silent shake. 'I am the Duke of Wellington!' and the Granada guards jumped on His Grace, the claimed adversary of myself-the-Emperor on the battelfield of Waterloo.

Dear Reader, this adventure happened as I have related it. I won't pull your leg in this book. I am not clear about what happened afterwards except that our drama of *War and Peace* sailed along finely and won one of those 'Emmies' mentioned above, as we were wont to do during those better days, when Granada *et al* were concerned with social responsibility and quality as much as they were with profit-making. The decline of British television is a very serious matter for the British State, and the commercial Tories must carry the awful responsibility.

I didn't join Madeline in Venice – professional obligations prevented that – but I did in Genoa, where the company was playing. And so I was committed to living within a totally different culture. I was the odd one out and I happily tried to understand and adjust myself to their way of thinking and feeling. Naive do-gooders readily assume that it is all a simple matter of colour and perhaps acknowledge a slightly different physical shape, but the significant difference – the uncomfortable reality – is inside the head: the thought processes and God knows what else. I am in no way judging which of the vast ethnic groups is 'superior' – that would be presumptuous nonsense – but we are all entitled to a preference (in the teeth of racist laws); for instance, 'You know, Alex, sometimes I wish I was Black,' and vice versa.

This chapter of the book is not exactly an afterthought; the truth is I half-funked writing it, for several reasons, but now, in March 1994, I (with Chiara) am once again perched on the southern tip of Africa at Knysna. One of the reasons that I am here, at this particular time, is to be present, during April, when the elections by both Black and White take place. As far as I know, during the whole history of our world, there has never been such a mutual test of different cultures; totally different human beings, attempting to live – politically – as equal human beings. Of course this state of affairs has been thrust on South Africa by a self-righteous, largely hypocritical, world outside, that had previously decimated if not annihilated their own indigenous racial problems – in Australia, New Zealand, Canada, the United States of America, and so on. For what my opinion is worth, I cannot remotely see it working unless the Black Africans and the White Africans are going to allow each other to freely exercise their respective cultural gifts. The people of European extraction (together with certain Asian countries) have a talent for producing sophisticated technology and a talent for accumulating a disciplined wealth, together with the democracy that emanated from Greece. All of this, it appears to me, is alien to the Black African. Yes, they talk about democracy, but from one end of this continent to the other that talk has only been a means to a dictatorial end. Of course, we Europeans have had our monstrous aberrations during this century, but the people have finally insisted on the free and disciplined rule of democracy re-emerging. Never amongst Black Africans. But if they don't want it, why should they have to have it? Well, there are a lot of Europeans here in South Africa who have built a highly sophisticated, clean, well-oiled infrastructure and those Europeans are aware how it was built and what qualities it will take to keep it running, leave alone improve it. The outside world that has created this astounding situation seems smugly pleased with itself and also seems near oblivious of what will probably happen. But most White South Africans that I have met on this visit are determined to do their best to make the unique event work. They confess that they have no alternative except to flee elsewhere and the Afrikaner, in particular, has a deep love and commitment to this land. All of this comes to my mind when thinking of my personal two years in the Black world.

I remember the great warmth and lavish hospitality of our West Indian friends; and how much I enjoyed the highly entertaining food. And the free expression of the joy of living.

I was now travelling around Europe with the *Black Nativity* company. On the long train journeys they would sing, wonderfully well, hour after hour, and they would laugh continuously. I remember my friends singing one song that Ray Charles had recorded which well-nigh hypnotised me. I have never heard it since; it had a refrain: 'Down the avenue . . .' Knowing that I liked it they would repeat it very often. I sat for hours, quietly absorbed, like Alice in Wonderland.

There was a nightclub in Rome named Bricktops which was run by a redheaded Black lady who, herself, was a formidable entertainer. After the *Black Nativity* performance we would all repair there and during the cabaret period the hostess would call upon us (well, not me!) to also entertain and everybody did their party-piece. Even the two fine dancers would sing humorous songs. I remember Madeline singing – devastatingly – 'My Funny Valentine' and it seemed to be directed at me. I felt like Mickey Rooney when Judy Garland performed in his presence. Maybe I fantasized about giving a turn myself; maybe a purple passage from Shakespeare or a poem, but, probably fortunately, I refrained.

Madeline and I stayed in a simple, pleasant hotel in the middle of Rome. One day I was surprised to be told that a Mr John Dexter wished to see me; I cannot now recall whether there was any preamble to this visit or how he had unearthed me. And though I was already consciously detaching myself from the British Theatre, I did know that he was a successful stage director. We met in the small foyer of our hotel. Mr Dexter, who immediately greeted me as if we were old friends, asked me if I knew that Britain was forming a National Theatre, with Sir Laurence Olivier, himself, and one other person as a triumvirate of directors.

'Yes, I have heard.'

'Sir Laurence wants to know why you won't work with him?'

This question, out of the blue, astonished me. I replied that I have never said that I would not work with the very famous man: 'Indeed, as far as I know, I have never been asked.' However, I did confess and reminded John Dexter that I had expressed on television my own grim reservations about the, to me, blind adulation that was being poured over him. I think I said what I had to say on the BBC programme *Late Night Lineup*. The subject was 'The Modern Actor' and there were only two participants: myself and the distinguished theatre critic, Mr Michael Billington. All of this took place just after Sir Laurence had played Othello. Yes, I was naughty and unfavourably compared Olivier with the American Black actress, Miss Claudia McNeil, who was at that time acting in

James Baldwin's play *The Amen Corner*. I felt that a sense of proportion (usually an impossible hope in our weak world) should be expressed and I also felt that Sir Laurence's shoulders were broad enough.

Having heard all of that, John Dexter ploughed on: 'Well, Sir Laurence – and I – want you to be a founder member of the British National Theatre.' At this point Madeline joined us and she heard some of the complimentary remarks that John was making about my ability as an actor. Surprisingly Madeleine knew very little about my professional doings and status – though we had gone to see me in a film in Rome where they had dubbed my voice into Italian and had given me a ridiculous squeaky voice – and so I turned to her and said: 'So you see, I'm good too!'

To which she replied: 'What do you want, a cookie?'

Looking back across my life – a disturbing occupation – I now realize that that episode in Rome was a very significant moment in my fortunes. That was the moment when my fate had to be decided. I still have unexpected and astonishing dreams about my turning away from British theatre. What is it about my instinctive and aggressive feelings towards many things? Most of all – after the fear of having my fingernails pulled out – I dread the power of the Establishment and its capacity to annihilate the individual's ability to flash lightning, and now, via John Dexter, I was being invited to return, or rather enter, the New Fold.

I didn't say 'no thank you'. My brain spontaneously went 'click click'; I immediately knew what I had to say and I said it. When the Royal Court Theatre successfully launched its 'kitchen sink' regime, the Establishment actors, the Knights, hastened to Sloane Square and adroitly mounted that bandwagon – with one exception: Sir Donald Wolfit. Now, I am not criticizing them for doing so, but I was concerned about Wolfit's fate; yes, I was personally concerned. It seemed to me that the big traditionalist who could certainly illuminate a great text, was being excluded from almost everything. They were changing times. I even wondered, sympathetically, about his financial position. Actors must work to live. My reply was a question to John Dexter: 'Has Sir Donald Wolfit been invited to be a founder member?'

'I don't think so.'

'Well, I tell you what: if Sir Donald is invited, then I think that I would like to join; if not, I think I will carry on elsewhere.'

Like my attitude or not, that was the conversation. In due course, John Dexter reported back to me: 'Sir Laurence says that under no circumstances will he appear on the same stage with Sir Donald Wolfit.' And I stuck to my idiosyncratic guns, renouncing the chance to play Richard the Third (though didn't Sir Laurence collar that for himself?) and all of that. And so, in my dreams, I am occasionally as sick as a dog with deep unease. I concentrated on making my radical films. We can't have everything we want in this life, can we?

One day in Rome the great Marion Williams asked me if I knew where the Vatican was. 'Would you take me there, Kenneth?' Of course, Marion was a serious Christian, but, I suspect, a long call from Roman Catholicism. Off we went and inside the great church we approached, for me, perhaps the greatest of all human creative achievements: Michelangelo's *Pieta*. I presumed that Marion had received little in the way of a classical education; rightly or wrongly I suspected that Marion might never have heard of the Italian Immortal. I deliberately lagged behind. In those days the *Pieta* stood free and unprotected in the body of the church. (In the meantime, a force for evil has damaged it and now, I have been told, it is protected.) So Marion had to pass it; what would she do? She came level and froze on the spot. I stood behind her left shoulder. She stared and stared. After a very long wait she turned her head to the right, anxiously looking for me, then to her left, and said: 'Oh Kenneth, isn't it wonderful what men can do when they put their minds to it?' Those words I will remember while I am alive. Marion Williams knew Michelangelo the moment she saw him. And I have little doubt that she would have walked past so many of those offerings that our Tate Gallery regularly displays; not, probably, with the ridicule which I express, but with injured mystification.

Outside the Vatican it was a special day; Pope John the 23rd was visiting the city. I stood peering at the grand ceremony, and His Holiness in the midst of his cavalcade of long, black Mercedes Benz (so I thought) motor cars. I couldn't resist bawling: 'Where's your donkey?' The crowd understood my point and I was in a little hazard from the devotees, but I escaped physical injury. Today I felt I shouldn't have said it; he was a decent old man who good humouredly preserved his common touch. Little doubt that he too had pondered the same question, without my public prompting.

Madeline wanted to be a pop-star. I felt that she had a higher potential. But one must follow one's own hope. She wanted me to attend her television performances; it was an agony for me. Once I stood in the studio when she was preceded by a group of young male performers. I was shocked at their (to me) wonky ineptitude; I have never been impressed by loud energy and nothing else. I recognized what had inspired them: they were copying a Black recording which I was then familiar with. I felt embarrassed and sorry for them because they were trying their utmost. As the singer finished and came down from the stage I was impelled to speak a professional lie to comfort: 'Well done, son.' It was Mick Jagger. Well, to some extent I have had to eat my opinion. You can't ignore the reality of millionaires.

My final humiliation was attending a *Ready, Steady, Go* Christmas party with Madeline. Everybody – except me – was jumping up and down to the sound of the raucous noise. The event was being televised. As I stood there, shocked and incongruous, I noticed a hand-held camera approaching in my direction and so I slid behind a piece of scenery which was propped against a wall. Of course the lively cameraman had noticed my attempt at concealment and poked his machine in my direction. I believe the odd situation was transmitted throughout Britain.

Yes, Madeleine and I failed in our Black–White bridge-building enterprise. I fear that we were a microcosm of what will happen to the New South Africa.

TWENTY-TWO

By this date my appalling domestic sub-plot had extended into a third divorce, leaving behind me this time, not only Carole and Jonathan but our twins: Polly and Huw. I do not feel that it is for me, here, to try to analyse my rhythmic failures in this marital direction, more than I have stated earlier in this book. Except perhaps to confess that I have always got on better in the company of men than with women. I suspect that it requires a formidable exterior social discipline to make a successful marriage possible. Or, perhaps, the union of a man and a woman who both want to give rather than take. Rare! And for my part I was landed with this private dogged compulsion to survive and make some creative statement – at almost any cost. I moved in with a woman named Margret Kopala in her spinster pad in the Portobello Road, one of London's famed streets of antique shops.

Margret was, in many ways, an ideal friend and partner for me in my chaotic existence. She was a script editor in the BBC's drama department. At that time, wedged between my own documentary films I was still performing high-kicks in television plays, and I met her while working on a series called *Perils of Pendragon*, in which she was performing her literary duties and I was playing the central role of a typical Welsh character with pretensions to run a Welsh Mafia in his village. My partner and nephew in the series was Mr John Clive, one of those rare human beings who will remain quietly patient and loyal to the end of one's days.

Anyway, my relationship with Margret Kopala seemed to be perfect for my condition of man. She presented a strong facade which undoubtedly carried some considerable depth.

She was undoubtedly intelligent and held academic qualifications (which certainly is not the same thing). She took an interest in my work and earnestly began to put that work – for the first time – into efficient order. And she proceeded to look after me. I began to be happy and easier in my mind. However, as you may easily guess, our life together wasn't without its problems. I now had to support Carole and our three children and our main asset, our fine house in Canonbury, London, was given to Carole. The truth is that there was very little money, week by week, for me to survive on. However, I somehow scraped together enough to pay my own way in terms of basic subsistence. And Margret gave me a sense of happy security.

I would visit Carole and the children on Sundays and then I would suffer a well-justified price for my irregular arrangement. During the evening I would dread to leave them. It was an agony for Carole, me, and I suspect, most of all, for Jonathan, who never murmured a complaint. And when I returned to Margret in the Portobello Road, usually at about 11 pm, there was never anything except cheerful words called out to me: 'Have you had a good day, love? Have you eaten?' I felt that I had truly found my haven at last. Though I was never unaware of the trail of misery that I had left behind me.

On one of those journeys from Canonbury to the Portobello Road, rather late at night, I was sitting in a carefully selected 'No Smoking' carriage of the London underground train service, when two Hell's Angels clattered in wearing their uniform of black leather, decorated with various silver-coloured threatening images and with the customary blasphemous silver Christian crosses in their ears: they were both smoking and continued to smoke.

There must have been another twelve passengers in that carriage. The transit between Canonbury and Notting Hill Gate was a limbo place for me and I felt very tired.

'Oh no!' I audibly said as I pulled myself onto my no longer young feet and prepared myself to confront these two representatives of the famous 1960s.

This is what I felt (and still feel). Because I could observe the inner strength of Britain disintegrate so fast, led by Carnaby

Street and the pop world, if I allowed the shame of it all to pass without opposition, I would clearly be an accessory of that shame and would deserve to live in the approaching filth. And so I stood before the two smoking Hell's Angels and asked them to conform to the 'No Smoking' sign. I tempered my request with a soft-padded untruth: 'Excuse me, friends, but unhappily I have contracted lung cancer through smoking and I have to travel in a non-smoker.'

Both of the men stared up at my swaying figure. One, his eyes on mine, flicked out his cigarette and the other simply said: 'Fuck off' and continued to puff. *Now* what do you do? There were a dozen witnesses to this vitally important (in terms of Britain's future) scene, and being apparently English, they pretended that nothing untoward was happening. But ears were closely attuned and the tension was like invisible inflammable gas.

'Ah!' I said to the remaining smoker. 'Your friend heard what I said, but I don't think that you did.'

And I repeated the lie: 'I have contracted lung cancer through smoking and I *have* to travel in a non-smoker.'

'Then move to the other end of the fucking carriage.'

Now what do you do? It's 'High Noon' time. And I moved to my guns with the threatening glint: 'Put out that cigarette immediately, or I'll pull this Emergency Lever.'

'Fuck off!!' he spat at me.

And I pulled the '£100 Fine' lever very firmly. The effect, I promise you, is spectacular. My remembered impression is of flashes of fire, blue smoke (both outside the carriage of course) and a shudderingly attained halt. And everyone looks at you (even the English!) pretty openly and directly. Just as if you'd won the pools. In the distance were men's voices: 'Hello! Where's the trouble?

'Here!' I bellowed, startling, even more, the preferred Anglo-Saxon silence. The disbelieving Hell's Angel quickly threw away his cigarette and braced himself to lie. Into the carriage puffed the driver and train guard: 'What's the trouble?'

And from their excited demeanour, such an event had never happened to them before. I said: 'These two men were smoking and I politely asked them to desist. This man put his cigarette out, but this one refused.'

'Who's smoking?' was his last shot.

Fortunately one of the other passengers intervened: 'Yes, he *was* smoking.'

What would be the official judgement? What does 'Improper Use' signify? The fine was of a monstrous size bearing in mind my straitened circumstances.

'Right!' said the guard, addressing the black-leathered men, 'You two get out at the next station!' and then turning to me: 'I'm sorry about this, sir, I don't see what else I can do.'

'That's fine sir,' said I, 'and thank you.'

The guard stayed with us all till we reached the next station, where the two threateners departed from us like black lambs. So, in spite of my anxious and uneasy state, I was reassured that I and Britain were not quite finished.

ATV, through the good offices of Robert Heller and Charles Denton, asked me what film I would like to make for them next. I am unlikely to know what might have been said by Sir Lew Grade about me around this juncture of the proceedings; he was to say to me later that the Michael Collins film had given him more sleepless nights than anything had ever done before. But fairly or unfairly I took that with a liberal pinch of salt. Later, while I was involved in preparing a legal action against ATV over the suppression of the Collins film, I was presented with a letter written by Robert Heller to Lew Grade. Robert Heller wrote that I was 'unpredictable' (in actual fact I am totally predictable) and rather dangerously implied, very clearly, that I could not be bought. Bear in mind that Robert quite approved of me. That letter contains one of the most precious comments about myself that I have ever heard. Even though I am not blindingly clear whether the compliment is justified or not. Every person has their price, so it is said.

Anyway, the enquiry was made and I replied: 'A film about the last six years of Napoleon's life, which he spent, almost entirely as a prisoner of the British, on their small colonial island of Saint Helena, deeply south in the Atlantic Ocean.'

And without a moment's demur the project was given the green light. It was all most satisfactory; I had given this extraordinary story a considerable amount of thought, while the BBC of Kensington House had kept me insensitively hanging about.

I got down to serious research and thought. Now, I saw this film as an exercise for me in objectivity, a quaint obsession of 'democratic television': the idealistic but inhuman theory that one must not lean towards one side or the other. I foolishly thought that the story of the most energetic man on earth, being confined to a small island in the South Atlantic Ocean, could stand up alone on its bare essential facts. No *human* embellishments. I quickly found that I couldn't do it; or if I could, I would much rather change my profession and perhaps learn the high skill of stonemasoning.

What a man Napoleon was! Of course he did some naughty things, as you and I have done; but his vision of good order was perhaps without equal in this world's human experience except for, perhaps, a collective thought in the Athens of Pericles or the Rome of Julius Caesar or perhaps . . . and I almost wrote 'during the brief time of the British Empire'.

I gave the script to Antony Thomas, hoping and praying that he would direct it. I think that I read it to him, and I received the impression that I had trapped him in his chair. Anyway, at the end of the fantastic saga which I was relating, Antony, looking harassed and confused, politely hurried from the room. He said something about being worried about the military aspect of Napoleon; but there is always a lot more to Antony Thomas than meets the eye or ear.

Antony and I have, very sadly for me, never worked together again; though when he has embarked on his feature film work for the cinema he has always approached me to be an actor for him. Unfortunately this has never come to pass. And when he was being persecuted by Arabian kings and such English characters as Lord Carrington, over his outstanding and timely film *Death of a Princess*, he publicly reminded me that it was I, during our earliest professional relationship, who had urged him 'to stand up and say who he was'; a valuable slogan that I, in my turn, had learnt from Mr Lindsay Anderson, the notable film director. Antony and I remain mutually valued friends.

It is a truism to state that we humans only *fully* realize a value when we have lost it. Now what was I to do? Of course there were plenty of directors who would have liked to direct a film about Napoleon, shot in France, at sea on a warship and, fabulously, on that mysterious island of Saint Helena. But the *right* talent, and someone who could handle the very unusual relationship that must survive and flourish on such a project . . . Imagine an ambitious director's predicament? *I* have chosen a subject because it interests me. I have researched and written the script of the subject as I see it; the subject is distilled through *my* evolving enthusiasm. And finally, I am present the whole while during the reconnaissance of the locations because I will have more historical knowledge of what once took place there than anyone else who would be working on the film. And finally, I would be closely present throughout the filming because I would be there in front of the camera, communicating the entire story. At best the relationship should be a trusting dance. But that is the ideal.

Well, Fortune smiled – but as every thinking human being knows, Fortune has her own secret thoughts which she *never* allows to be reflected on her facial muscles. John Pilger, the distinguished radical journalist, informed me (no doubt through my friend and then partner, Mr David Swift) that there was a youngish chap from Australia who made films and had come over to the Big Pond of Europe to try his luck, but, having met with rejection everywhere, was on the point of returning miserably to the Antipodes. And so I met Michel Pearce for the first time. My feelings were very mixed. He was tall and strongly built and he had a pleasant face, though at that time wearing a woebegone and worried expression. But on the other hand he also looked like a bit of a hippy and perhaps tending towards the flower-people cult. Not that Michel had a flower on him; but I'm sure you – and he – know what I mean.

I explained to Mr Pearce that I, perhaps, embarked on only *one* of my films per year – no more – and that as far as the film-cum-television industry was concerned I kept myself strictly to myself and therefore didn't know what was going on elsewhere.

I explained that I was on the edge of beginning a film about Napoleon and so wouldn't be thinking about anything else for a long while. Of course there was no remote possibility of this rather 'way-out' (as they used to say) unhappy Australian (he was in fact born around Liverpool, which was quite fashionable at the time) directing the extremely difficult Napoleon film.

Under sympathetic questioning from me, he made it clear that he had done everything possible to get himself launched as a film maker in Britain. He had shown two films (which even in our interview he held in a *very* hippy bag, which for some reason I always referred to later as his 'shepherd's bag') to anyone who would look, and under increasing cross-examination from me, he said: 'Yes, Mr Aubrey Singer has seen them, but has advised me to return to Australia.'

'Well,' said I, 'the best I can do is to look at your films and think.'

And nice Michel Pearce left his work with me, saying: 'I'll have to collect them on Friday because I'm skint and must get back to Aussie.'

I went down to our viewing theatre and looked at the first of the two films that came to the projectionist's hand. Michel Pearce had made it entirely on his own – script, photography, sound, editing, everything. It was a trade unionist's nightmare. On the other hand it was a beautiful film. The story was shot in a remote Polynesian island that was inhabited, almost entirely, by beautiful women, children and old people, because all of the men in their prime had gone to Fiji or somewhere, to earn a commercial living. I learnt afterwards that Michel had filmed the whole thing within two weeks because a government boat had dropped him off and would pick him up at the end of those two weeks and wouldn't return to that island again for six months. I was enormously impressed by the 'hippy's' outstanding professional talent. But of course there was still no evidence (for me) that he could direct a controlled dramatic saga such as *The Man on the Rock*, which is what I had determined to call the Napoleon film.

On the following Friday Michel Pearce reappeared in the office and I wholeheartedly congratulated him on the film.

'Did you look at the other one?' he properly asked.

'Ah! I've been so hectically busy . . .'

'Well, I've got to take it now, because I'm off.'

'Hold on,' says I, feeling guilty, 'let's see if the viewing theatre is available.'

It was, and I sat down with Michel to look at his other film. It was called *The Money Game* and it had been written by an Australian visionary and cartoonist named Bruce Petty. The story was set in a large international stadium where a great sporting conflict was about to happen. The camera moved through the various smoke-filled dressing-rooms where the sports journalists interviewed the competitors as they were being massaged and cajoled by their seconds, handlers and so on. The competitors were Labour, Third World, International Business, Banker and Politician; that was it, as far as I remember. Confidence was exuded by all of them, except Third World who, strangely enough, was an Oriental; surely he should have been a Latin American or, more obviously, an African? Anyway, he was rather silent (not too good at the English language?) and a shade over-awed. They were then called into the huge stadium, which was packed and controlled by even mounted police. In came the contestants, projecting their varied characters as they responded to the cheers and boos – the normal animal roar.

In the very centre of the great arena was a Heath Robinson contraption. It was a mass of improvised wheels, pulleys and levers, and the contest began as the men manipulated the astounding machinery. I think that it was Labour (represented by a typical loudmouthed lazy-but-greedy British worker) who crashed into an initial lead. But one saw the shrewd eye of International Business and then everyone went into rational materialistic action and all for their separate self-interested reasons. I sat there in the viewing theatre, suffering that extremely rare synthesis of hilarity and being educated. Suddenly, for the first time in my life, international financial 'How's your Father' became crystal clear. I watched International Business deftly throw a switch and out sprang a boxing glove on the end of a long spring, plonk into the Third World's face. It was exciting

and very funny. The poor Oriental! He was subliminally transformed into a shattered Vietnamese face (that is why he was an
Oriental!) and nothing was funny anymore. Only very clear. Of
course, International Business came out the clear winner, and he
was very magnanimous in his overwhelming victory. He stated
to the excited Press (there was a lot of blood aboard): 'They *all*
did extremely well. And I would like to put in a particular word
of praise for the Third World; he's a dark horse, he played well,
and I'll have to watch him very carefully in the future!' It's
many years since I saw that film, so forgive me, lads, if I'm not
word perfect.

As the lights came up in the viewing theatre, I turned, rather
eagerly, to Hippy Pearce.

'Mr Pearce, would you like to direct this film about
Napoleon?'

'I expect so.' And he did.

Eventually Maggie Kopala and I embarked on the ship and we
set sail. It was a very pleasant voyage and we were especially
spoilt. However, I went down with a small fever and retired to
bed. Maggie, as always during our first years together, was very
attentive and I remember suffering pleasantly. She urged me to
eat fruit and our pleasant steward arrived with a fine selection,
together with a large linen serviette; it was that sort of journey.

The wide circled ocean had a speck on it and though the sky
was clear and blue, above that speck, was a waft of white cloud.
Saint Helena! It was impossible for me to see any aspect of the
place except through Napoleon's eyes. That is what he saw as
the great sailing fortress, His Majesty's Ship *Northumberland*,
of Nelson's fleet, spied its place of destination.

A long-boat, manned by islanders, came out to collect us
and as we reached the stone jetty, where a large proportion of
the island's population (which totalled some five thousand
souls) was waiting to see us, a high-hanging rope was slung out
and we used that to guide ourselves from the heaving sea onto
stony land. Hazardous; and *everyone* landing has to perform it!

Perhaps, if I were given the natural choice, I would prefer to
see Saint Helena again more than anywhere that I have visited;

no, it isn't Venice or Dubrovnik, but it is so redolent of dramatic history and it is almost untouched. No tourists and little reason to 'improve' and thereby ruin – in one respect. We had arranged to rent a house up on Longwood Plain, very close to Napoleon's sometime abode. Before going to bed that night I made my way by intermittent moonlight and peered through the wind-bent fir trees at the pulsating prison-house; that is what it was.

When the rest of our film crew finally arrived at Saint Helena from Ascension, where they had been stranded for four weeks, we were ready to begin our Napoleonic saga. As a matter of fact, the filming didn't get off to a good start. On the evening before our first shooting day, I studied our approaching arduous task and retired to my bed early, while most of our team decided that a party was called for and they returned from Jamestown very late and very boisterous. I said nothing that night, but on the morrow, when I sensed hangovers and I felt that the morning's work was suffering, I got angry, and a division was driven between us.

I had one quiet, *very* hard-working, unshiftable ally on our team: our electrician, Mr Derrick Boulter. Now, Derrick is no ordinary electrician; he is also the managing director of one of Britain's biggest film and television lighting firms and certainly one of the best. He, like myself, had come up the hard way and on unadorned merit. I had persuaded him to take a sabbatical from his chair of authority at his business place in London and return to the other dignity of controlling our electrical problems 'in the field'. I was lucky that he came. He is a quiet reserved man and as we worked – and it was often *very* hard work, man-handling heavy equipment across high and dangerous cliffs – Derrick was always to be seen in the thick of the hard labour and not, necessarily, carrying only lights. It is also interesting to me that Derrick Boulter derived more pleasure out of the historical magic of Saint Helena than anyone else on our crew, with the exception of myself. We shared our amazement about the island recently. And just a few months ago the television company, HTV, were recording a television programme about my life and in the audience I discovered Derrick.

But we got going with *The Man on the Rock*. The journey

through the story was deeply disturbing and yet exhilarating for me. Napoleon was dumped into Longwood House with a small entourage of his Court who had volunteered to go into exile with him; he remained on the island for about six years and like everything else in his life, he made the maximum use of his time that prevailing circumstances allowed. The oligarchs of Europe, led by Britain (and represented on the island by the English Governor, Hudson Lowe) were neurotically fearful that the Giant of Europe would escape from his isolated rock and sort them all out once again. Britain stationed regiments of soldiers on Saint Helena to keep a few thousand eyes on him and British men-of-war patrolled the ocean around him. Napoleon said: 'They must have all gone mad to imagine that anyone could escape from this place.' But Russia, Austria and France also were going to risk nothing; they each sent emissaries to live on Saint Helena – to make sure.

Napoleon therefore decided that his time would be best spent inscribing his philosophic statements for the defence of his policies, to be presented at the bar of historical judgement, in the future. He dictated and dictated. Of course, it was a large part of my job in the film, as Napoleon's advocate (which I found I could not avoid being), to present the heart of these arguments, and this set us a problem of effective communication to our potential mass television audience. The passages were lengthy and obviously of a serious nature. And, of course, they had all been delivered within the confined rooms of Longwood House. Michel and I were both conscious that this was our biggest potential problem in the whole film.

I believe that if I approve of the director or have chosen him (or her) that director should be the final arbiter. However, Michel seems to have no insecurities in that direction and he has always urged me to speak about any thoughts or ideas I may have: 'Sometimes they have been very useful to me,' he has said. And so I began to talk to him about these momentous passages: 'I see them Michel, as two separate arias. Perhaps the first has a more domestic context about it than the second. Therefore why don't we divide them into those two parts; the first *inside* the house, where they were *all* spoken; and with the second aria we should take artistic licence and speak it from the cruel cliffs and heights of Saint Helena, into the teeth of the South Atlantic Ocean.' And this is what we did.

The first aria we filmed as Napoleon swept through the house, from one end to the other. Someone had asked the Emperor why there were not more memorials erected to his great achievements?

'What!?' he must have barked. 'What are the new roads of Europe and the harbours of France, but memorials to my wishes? What about France's new educational system, which is already preparing the generations of the future?' He spoke about his universal Napoleonic Code of Conduct. I remember I especially noted a small but vitally important matter: Napoleon's insistence that the citizen's access to all museums and art galleries must be free of any charge. At the time Britain was debating that point of principle and I wasn't above urging Napoleon in, to rebuke that unattractive form of Toryism.

And then the second high-flying aria: 'Will they accuse me of *wanting* war!?' High on the volcanic crests above the seething sea, and me, with collar pulled high, pointing north north east at *them*, the European oligarchs. Michel and Grenville did superbly well; some of the shots in this film are comparable with the best that I have ever seen in any film anywhere. And at the end of this outdoor aria, we recorded those memorable and important words of Napoleon: 'It is only the *truth* that hurts.' How often that sentiment has come back to comfort me in the intervening years.

Under the second-class tyranny of Governor Hudson Lowe, one by one, Napoleon's people began to break and even leave the island; but there was no breaking the Emperor himself. Hudson-Lowe gave orders that Napoleon must not go outside of his quarters unless he was accompanied by a British officer. So Napoleon ceased going out. Then Hudson-Lowe gave orders that, in that case, a British officer must enter Longwood House and see Bonaparte, with his own eyes, every day. Napoleon drew a line across the front door and informed the British Governor that the first of the British officers who crossed it, he would kill – personally. No one put Napoleon to the test.

The nearest the Emperor came to even confessing weakness was when he became terminally ill and noting Count Monthelon's sad countenance, suddenly said to him: 'Do you think that I do not have *my* bad moments, when I consider what I once was and what I am now?'

Napoleon at that time was lying on his portable military camp bed which he had once slept in on the eve of the Battle of Austerlitz.

As we left Saint Helena to return to Europe I was informed that about half the population of the island – perhaps two thousand five hundred people – were on the ancient stone jetty to wish us farewell. Two ropes ran along the long exit for us to make our way to the island boat that would carry us to the waiting ship. The island people were on each side of these ropes and they are not a demonstrative people; they simply looked at us. Most of them I knew and I found myself continuously crossing the rope barriers to assure friends that I had every intention – God willing – to return some day. Gilbert Martineau, the French consul and historian, was there: handsome and immaculately tailored; I think that he carried a walking stick.

'Tell me, Kenneth, why didn't you complete Napoleon's statement when you were quoting him, up on the cliff top? You know very well that he added: "One day, even a British historian will speak on my behalf."' I looked as steadily as I could manage at the French Consul, as he continued: 'Well, Kenneth, I would like you to know that today I have sent a cable to my Government in Paris, assuring them that at last, Napoleon's prophecy has been fulfilled.'

We had not finished the film. We began our story with Napoleon's defeat at the Battle of Waterloo and it was to end with the Emperor's remains being reinterred in the spectacular tomb at Les Invalides in Paris. Big problems still lay ahead of us and amongst them was Napoleon's journey aboard British warships from the coast of France, via Plymouth, England, to Saint Helena. I wanted to film this on a modern British warship at sea. And so I communicated with our Admiralty in London but they were not helpful. Perhaps I telephoned for an appointment – I don't remember – but they certainly put me off. I had not *fully* digested Cecil Rhodes' advice to me: 'Do it on the personal.'

I remember that naval voice on the telephone: 'Ah, Mr Griffith, I'm afraid our ships are a bit thin on the ocean these days; but we'll do our best. We'll let you know.'

Now, film making is so expensive that one must have a firm schedule. A film crew is hired and workless days are dangerous for survival. Of course, I didn't just try that telephone call once; but always that negative voice. Come to think of it, it reminds me of India. Well, not nearly as bad as *that*, but . . .

Well, what now? France. That seemed the big one! Off Michel Pearce and I went – without a command of the language between us. And the first of many surprises about that fine country hit me. We British are raised from our cradles to believe that 'the Froggies' are impossible to deal with. But immediately Michel and I met the French authorities they speedily put themselves out to help us in any way possible. And they never once asked to see my script. For all they knew it was yet another British libel-cum-slander on Napoleon's life. However – and it is many years ago, so she must forgive me for being hazy about the matter – before leaving London I had visited Madame Brigitte Oudiette-Marger, who was France's Cultural Attaché in our country, and perhaps her integrity and charm had eased our way. Whatever, our path was cleared for us. I can recall only one minor hiccup, when Michel and I wanted urgently to look around the Elysée Palace, in Paris. The official in charge who, to me, was a classic Parisian, was more swarthy than a Britisher might be; he had longish black hair, wore a well-cut dark suit, with a broader white stripe than an Englishman might select, and he chain-smoked. He was very encouraging to us, but complained that we couldn't enter *then*.

'But,' I explained, 'we have very little time in Paris before we must return to Britain and collect our film crew and equipment.'

'Monsieur, the *President* is in the building *now*! You may go in when he is *not* here.'

'But, Monsieur,' I fought on, 'this film is in praise of Napoleon's great achievements; nothing like it will have ever been seen in Britain before! And America!'

'But Monsieur Griffith – President de *Gaulle* is *in* there!'

'President de Gaulle would be delighted with this film. I am sure that he would do *anything* to help us make it.'

Don't imagine, reader, that the above was the total sum of our friendly debate. It went on, urgently, for, say, a quarter of an hour. My French friend's point of view was more than reasonable, and though he has probably forgotten me (or might he still be recounting the stubborn persuasion of that British film maker, long ago, as an explanation of our difficult Island character?) I remember him with affection. Anyway, suddenly he took an enormous pull on his Gauloise and waving his spare arm in the air despairingly wailed: 'Go in, Monsieur Griffith; for God's sake, go in!'

And no, I'm sorry to report that we didn't catch even a glimpse of General de Gaulle.

For the rest, we were given the run of the French Parliament Building: the National Assembly; of the Elysée Palace and of Malmaison, the nearest thing to a home that Napoleon had – all of them literally packed with treasures. We followed the spirit of Napoleon from specific location to specific location. High on the podium from which he rallied the new concepts and led France out of its reign of Civil Terror. And, as always in our films, only his very words were repeated. And repeated from his innermost sanctums. Yes, there would be officials in the vicinities, but they went on with their own activities and would only turn to us if we required assistance.

At Malmaison the senior curator set about removing the brass rails that separated visitors from the national treasures, so that we could film unencumbered. On our last day in Malmaison, and the time was about midnight, I approached the curator with the good news that we had finished our work and thanked him profusely. Anyone who helps one of my films is looked on by me as one who has helped a child of mine. The curator said that it had all been a pleasure for him, and anyway, the extra time that he had spent in Malmaison had helped him to do some useful extra work. He then, at that very late hour, asked if there was *anything* else that he could do for us.

'No, sir,' I replied, 'you have made our work so profitable;

I only hope that you will approve of the finished film.'

'So you have no more problems, Monsieur Griffith?'

'Ah! I didn't say that! But my only problems now are in Britain.'

'What problems in Britain?' And I humorously told him about my struggles with the British Admiralty.

Now it may seem incredible, but this is what happened. There in Malmaison, the distinguished French curator pondered my British problem.

'How long do you want to film on a warship at sea?'

'About four days.'

'Soon?'

'As soon as possible.'

'Well, I have some influence and I think that I might be able to arrange for you to do your work on a *French* warship.'

I stood there looking at the man and it was quite clear that he was very serious and totally confident.

'Ah, sir, that is so good of you, but there is one insurmountable snag; we would have to fly a White Ensign (British Royal Navy flag) to demonstrate that she was a British warship.'

Again, in the same almost matter-of-fact spirit the curator replied: 'I don't think that that would prove a problem. We have access to a White Ensign; the French Navy would fly it for your film – briefly and discreetly.'

'Thank you, sir,' I rounded off, joyously, 'I think that you have just solved my problem; but I won't have to put you or the French Navy to any trouble. And again thank you!'

Back in Britain I hastened to a telephone and spoke to that naval officer. He was politely impatient with me: 'Mr Griffith, I told you we would inform you when this enterprise *might* be possible.'

'Yes, sir, but I *must* have a word with you; we might be on the edge of a diplomatic difficulty.'

'What do you mean, "diplomatic difficulty"?'

'Well, sir, we have just returned from filming in France where they have been extraordinarily helpful, and they, having enquired about how the film was progressing – well, the French have offered me the use of one of *their* warships.'

The silence at the Admiralty end was profound – except for naval breathing. And then, with fine critical timing (though I write it myself), rather like a Mohammed Ali *coup de grâce*, I added: 'And they plan to hoist a White Ensign, to help us out.'

I swear that the breathing became even harsh in Whitehall. Finally: 'Mr Griffith, may I come back to you on this one?'

Seven and a half minutes later my telephone rang: 'Mr Griffith, Commander so-and-so here. When would you want to do this filming?'

'This week, sir.'

'If you could be at Pier Number so-and-so, Plymouth, by 4.30 am on this Thursday, a boat will pick you all up and take you aboard HMS so-and-so. She is on NATO exercises. Good luck.'

'Thank you, sir.'

At 4 am on the Thursday, we all stood with our film gear on that dark pre-dawn jetty. Within a few minutes a Royal Naval boat slid towards us out of the wavy gloom and we were heartily taken aboard. And then high above us was a grey spotless British warship. Rope ladders were lowered over her side and up we went, trying desperately to hide – well, my terror – and to appear as if I performed that sort of feat every day.

The voyage around the North Sea on a British warship was a flash of revelation for me. Having emerged from a crumbling second-rate Britain, I was suddenly back in a floating bit of our Island Home that was as efficient and positive as we have ever been. Nelson himself would not have been displeased. The shock to me, the layman, was extreme. Here were a group of British men who appeared to be conscious that they owed their State some service and they were happily carrying it through with precision. I was given a cabin to myself for work and sleep. I was able to spend time both with the officers and the men. There seemed to be an excellent balance between both. Discipline was taken for granted, yet an affection seemed to run between the commissioned and the non-commissioned. Those four days at sea with the British Royal Navy were, perhaps, the most satisfactory and reassuring of my post-war life. I tried to convey this feeling of gratitude that I had to the ship's company.

You see, I have always been an anti-imperialist (but during my usually bitter two years in India I learnt to admire certain aspects of my ancestors who were the British Raj) but to observe Britain decline from running a quarter of the earth's surface to our topmost national fame in Carnaby Street and our usually appalling pop world, was more than I could bear with equanimity. And here on this ship was the proof that our British courage and sense of responsibility was not dead. Dormant perhaps; but with this undisturbed naval cell, breathing healthily. And, when needed, and against all odds, it sprang to brief brave life over the Falklands Emergency. I was deeply moved – and proud – to be aboard that ship.

And we had our laughs on the warship too! My hair is very thin and fine and if there is the slightest breeze, it wafts all over the place, and so I always issue one rule – the only one I think, apart from members of our team not moving unexpectedly in my eyeline when I am 'performing' – that all synchronized pieces should be spoken with the strumpet wind *behind* me. I have always argued that this is not entirely a matter of vanity; that hair in the air looks ugly and is a distraction when seen on the screen. On this particular occasion I was studying and relaxing in my cabin when I was called up aloft to do the next piece, which was on a gun platform. Everything was, as usual, most carefully set up; the team was ready to film. Michel Pearce was consulting with me about the choreography (the movements of the camera and myself) when I realized that not only was I being asked to speak into a wind, but on top of that our warship was speeding along at a remarkable number of knots, which made the force on my face not unlike that of a gale. I stopped:

'Michel, how the hell can I do this, slap into a hurricane?' (a typical Griffith exaggeration).

There was a subdued altercation and the young naval attendant intervened: 'Is there anything I can do? What's the problem, sir?'

I explained the difficulty: my hair, not vanity and all of that: 'You see, the trouble is, as you have witnessed, it takes a long while to set up, creatively, a scene like this and now it means that the whole thing has to be turned round; we'll lose an hour.'

Imperturbably, the young naval officer listened to this mumbo-jumbo of our film-making process.

'Ah ha,' he said, 'I think we *might* be able to help,' and he spoke quietly into his walkie-talkie. Almost immediately the fine warship changed her course and with a great curve through the northern ocean, sped in the opposite direction – which suited my hair fine. I looked at Michel and he looked at me and then I turned to the Royal Navy: 'Would you please thank the Captain very much.'

And what privileges we were given! The idea was that we told the story of Napoleon's journey aboard HMS *Bellerophon* to England and then on HMS *Northumberland*, heavily escorted, to Saint Helena, aboard a very modern man-of-war. It is part of our unique style, to bridge the many years, by even flaunting our contemporary setting. There is always our creative battle to persuade the television viewer that what they are seeing is hard, dramatic *fact*. This is not your dramatized historical fiction. And this modern warship helped to sell this new concept in telling true historical stories. Of course this involved some professional sleight-of-hand; as all works of art involve carefully thought-out techniques. Having done everything possible to urge the viewer that I was *not* acting; that I was telling them the bare-faced *truth* of what happened, I then proceeded to act! To *become* Napoleon, with his voice and his gestures, and in the background, as we ploughed through dark green, deep sea, was radar equipment, and God and NATO know what else!

The Royal Navy also allowed us to make use of a helicopter which was on the ship. Grenville Middleton, with his camera, went up with the pilot and filmed our ship cutting firmly through the great water, from a distance. Closer and closer to the warship comes the image and, over it all, I am speaking about the ominous journey of HMS *Northumberland* southward. The warship begins to fill the screen and a single figure can be seen leaning forward on the tip of the prow and now it can be *recognized* as Napoleon – or rather me by proxy – before the shot zooms up and away. I state here, categorically, that I cannot recall seeing a more effective and disturbing piece of cinematography in my life.

Does he exaggerate? you may properly wonder. Shouldn't the film perhaps have won some sort of award? Well, in the first instance, as I have said, I have always expressed a personal desire that nothing I ever do should be put forward for competition; I have always – since a child – felt that such an idea, to me, is obnoxious. But may I submit a more positive claim for the film's quality?

I have been for many years an ardent admirer of Mr Stanley Kubrick's work. As far as I am concerned he happens to be the most important film maker that I have ever known. He chooses subjects which are not less than fearful prophecies (e.g. *2001: A Space Odyssey* and *The Clockwork Orange*) and then he films them magnificently. Well, out of the blue I was given a message from him, by courtesy of his distinguished designer, Mr Kenneth Adams, which message stated that Mr Kubrick watched my work and admired it. Well eventually I was invited to dine with this very private film maker and, as I entered our host's apartment, Stanley Kubrick seemed to appear from behind the door and he immediately confronted me. He said that for many years he had wanted to make a film about Napoleon and he told me of the astounding extent of his research and the boggling sum of money that it had cost.

'How much, Mr Griffith, did *your* film cost?'

I replied that I tried very hard to keep away from the business side of things, apart from ever urging my colleagues and myself to work hard. I ventured an approximate figure – which would have amounted to part of a big feature film's telephone bill. Mr Kubrick then said to me: 'Mr Griffith, in your film, you have accomplished everything that I had hoped to achieve.'

Again this was one of the remarks of immense value to me that has helped to keep me afloat when the going has got rough.

So was that sequence in *The Man on the Rock* as good as Barbra Streisand hitting a top note on top of the Statue of Liberty? Yes!

The Man on the Rock was generally well received and was shown across the United States of America, where, in California particularly I seem to recall, it was greeted with rapture.

TWENTY-THREE

B ack in Britain I felt that I should not allow the suppression of the Michael Collins film, *Hang Up Your Brightest Colours*, to pass without my doing *everything* I possibly could do, to object and stir up the shady scandal. I would not be a party to yet another nefarious act, by Britain against Ireland, without howling my outrage.

It seemed to me that I should turn to the law of Britain and ask two questions. First: was the Independent Broadcasting Authority's – personified by Mr Bernard Sendel – action, in asking Sir Lew Grade *not* to offer the film to them, illegal. Surely any act of suppression of facts should be open? Or did the IBA's action come within the orbit of the Official Secrets Act? I didn't think so. And second: where was my share of the overseas sales? Our company (David Swift and myself) were entitled to about fifty per cent, I think, and the film was being asked for in the United States of America and elsewhere. And, ethics and idealism apart, I *needed* my share. In those days I was always fighting to survive financially. Remember I had several dependants to support (and in all fairness to my domestic instability, those multiple dependants always came first. Not once, in all of those many later years have I failed even by one week) and I was often left disturbingly short of funds to pay for even my simple way of life.

Well, David Swift and I, together with our company's solicitor, Mr Tom Crawley, and with his very enlightened Law Clerk, Mr Eric Hillier, in attendance, visited a distinguished Queen's Counsel, who had his knowledgeable side-kick with him. What took place is of enormous significance to the integrity of Britain. Not less. So I hope that someone will read these words carefully and will decide what exactly they can do about it. There were six witnesses of the event and as far as I know, they are all alive.

The Queen's Counsel asked me how well off I was. I replied that I, personally, had virtually no money. I confessed that I owned a large library, but that this was my livelihood: it was all for research. The Queen's Counsel then informed me that the Grade Organization (who, having carried the can for the IBA was the *only* target for my accusations) had already assembled an extremely experienced legal team against me. 'Though they have only just started, something like £30,000 has already been incurred' – words to that effect.

The Queen's Counsel continued: 'Now your contract with ATV has clearly been breached by them. But, Mr Griffith, in spite of that, I must tell you that there are three judges [in Britain] who will find against you because you have spoken up for the Irish Republican cause. There are certainly three of these judges – possibly four.'

After the shocking interview, the four of us stood amongst the leafless trees of Lincoln's Inn, with the sun penetrating. I have thought that it was not unlike the aftermath of a funeral; all of us in our dark suits. David, then and there, said: 'Ken, I must get out of this; I can't afford to put my family's welfare in jeopardy.'

Now, *my* family's welfare didn't for one second come into my calculations. And by all means judge me for that. I replied to my partner: 'David, I fully understand your point of view. I have very deep feelings about this matter. Why should you? Now I have to tell you all that I have suddenly developed a pain in my tummy,' and I touched a place on the bottom left-hand side. It was clearly a manifestation of fear, of dread. 'I confess that I am frightened. But I can't withdraw from this action – come what may – because I have a deep wish to make a film on the life of Thomas Paine [it was the first time *ever* that I had mentioned this potential project to anyone] and *if* I withdraw from this action which, amongst other matters, is in defence of the natural rights of Irish people, for fear of financial ruin, I *cannot* make that Tom Paine film. I would have lost my validity to speak for him.'

And so I continued the action against ATV alone. I undertook to conduct our claim against ATV and indirectly of the IBA, without further assistance from the Queen's Counsel.

Sir Lew Grade had asked me to visit him at his headquarters in ATV House, near Marble Arch, and David Swift came with me. Sir Lew is famous for his enormous cigars and he offered me one.

I said: 'I don't smoke, sir, but I would like to own one.' And today it is framed, together with the flag of the old hoped-for Irish Republic, and underneath is a printed legend: *A Present from Lew Grade*.

Sir Lew said to me (and David Swift is my witness): 'Son, ever since Patrick McGoohan left me, I've been looking for a man with balls, and in you, I've found him!' And then the great showman proceeded to impersonate me (my style in full flood), up and down his office. I am sure that neither David nor I will ever forget it. 'Now son,' he continued, 'I'm about to start filming a spectacular life of Moses and I want you to act in it. Now I *have* to be straight with you: Moses is cast! Charlton Heston.' Fleetingly I caught sight of myself wearing a big white beard. 'But Aaron! That's for you *and* Aaron does *all* the talking!'

David told me afterwards that while listening in some awe, he was anxiously wondering if Sir Lew was inclined to offer *him* a part; even a much lesser role would have sufficed. But the threat of international stardom was focused sharply on me and no one else. I decided to keep absolutely silent on the subject of Aaron and to hang back from the highly remunerative bait. I suppose that it was this instinct of mine that fulfilled Robert Heller's old prophecy that I couldn't be bought . . . The part of Aaron was eventually played by that fine actor, Anthony Quayle.

I must confess that I was disappointed in Sir Lew Grade (whom I still rather like; anyway he's a damned sight better value for us entertainers than the financial manipulators who are taking over the declining hopes of British television) in that he didn't choose to exploit my 'balls' and finance me to go forward, even in spite of the fact that I stuck to my Irish guns. Indeed, I had some romantic hope that he would support me *because* I stuck with those guns – though they were being (necessarily) aimed at him. But sadly, he didn't. He was to drop me like that famous hot potato.

However, Sir Lew was not finally finished with me as a potentially troublesome fish. One day I was rehearsing a television play (I was still acting in the dramas, endlessly) when an assistant director interrupted my histrionics: 'Pst! Ken, a phone call . . .'

'Come on!' I said. 'Take a number.'

'It's Sir Lew Grade,' and his voice was definitely quaking. The director intervened with authority!

'Take it, Ken!' After all this was nearly God.

Sir Lew came to the point: 'Son, I'm in *trouble*, I want you to help me out and leave for Italy *immediately*!'

'What's the trouble, Sir Lew?' I asked – not a little nervous myself.

'Son, I've got involved in a co-production with RAI Television (at that time Italy's television monopoly) and the scripts have just arrived and they are a load of incomprehensible, poetic nonsense. I want you to take over the whole project for me.'

'Sir Lew, do you know where I am at the moment?'

'Where?'

'I'm in a BBC rehearsal room. I'm an actor, rehearsing a television play.' Sir Lew dismissed this information and remonstrated: 'Son! I'm in *trouble*!'

Yes, I really still like Sir Lew.

'But, sir, *you* know I can't walk out of a play! But in one week I will have finished recording in the studio and then I have a whole week free before I start again on location. I'll help you during that free week.'

'Great!' said the Mogul. 'These terrible scripts are on the way to your home *now*!'

And so, a week after from that conversation I was aboard an Al Italia aircraft, bound for Rome – and travelling first-class. Now my best friends in the Eternal City, led by Signor Tonino Caputo, the distinguished painter, are pleased to call themselves Communists; though even then, it seemed to mean, in Italy, little more than decent easy-going liberal souls. Therefore, while enjoying the luxury of riches, I took the precaution of wearing a black Marks and Spencer pullover with *holes* in both elbows. The Italian arrangements had all been made for me at ATV. Charles Denton had gone on ahead and I would be met at Rome Airport by someone from RAI, who would escort me to Charles at our hotel. And that evening I was to have a meeting with the directors of RAI and then, on the following morning, I was to meet them again, together with a Very Important Person; it will soon become clear why I cannot mention him by name. Suffice to write that he was the boss of RAI.

Of course I had left London in an unavoidable rush. I had just finished recording my drama and had plundered my way through the enormous pile of Italian scripts – ostensibly about the Mafia – which Sir Lew had very efficiently delivered to my home as stipulated. Sir Lew was absolutely right in his assessment of this material: it consisted of meaningless, portentous, pseudo-poetical-academic drivel. Over this matter, I had no difference of opinion with the Governor. But I like to be thoroughly prepared before I discuss any professional matters with anyone and as we approached Italy I was not genned up to discuss the Mafia with a group of influential Italians . . . Yes, I was uneasy.

Now I knew a *few* things about the Sicilian Brotherhood and I am *never* short of opinions about *anything*. A German friend of mine – in the television game – having heard (international television is a tightly compressed matter with more ears to the ground than Red Indians have ever dreamt of) that I was being nudged towards RAI, had telephoned me in London from Bavaria: 'Kenneth, I must warn you! We [very powerful people] planned to do a series, two years ago, about the Mafia. We sent a production manager to Sicily and as he entered Palermo Airport he was approached by two strangers. One of them asked "Herr . . .?" "Yes." "We have a present for you," and the Sicilian reached inside his jacket and pulled out an envelope: "Open it!" Our man did so and it was a return ticket to Munich. And that was wisely the end of our ambitious project.'

Yes, I was armed with the factual warning. But I also always carry with me a built-in faith about the power of simple Truth. I hope that that doesn't sound priggish; the quality was thrust on me by my Grandfather. Of course, it has not always worked. Above all, in India, Truth is almost invariably to be misused. Speak the truth in India and it will be regarded as an opportunity to stick a knife in your back. And my personal experience has been similar, but not as sly, in certain Black African states I have visited. Perhaps therein lies a *cause* of the Third World. Anyway, I was imbued with this spirit of truth; the power of it.

I was thinking along these lines: Sicily is perhaps the most invaded, walked-over bit of land on the face of our planet. It is understandable that the Sicilians should, for centuries past, form themselves into groups for self-protection – The Brotherhood. Also, realistically, one should digest the fact (and I am a lover of Garibaldi) that the further you go south in Italy, the more prevalent is Arab blood. And, liberally forgive me for stating my truth again, but Arabs are *very* different from Northern Italians, whom I can hear at this moment, outside of a window close to my left ear. These voices are clear to me as they resound off the Guilian Alps which tower half a mile beyond.

I thought that I could somehow disarm – pacify – the Mafia if I were to ask the leadership – the Capi dei Capi, the Godfathers – to tell *their* side of the story! I have this terrible trust that I, personally, will be protected by my irrational faith. I suppose that Mr Terry Waite carried this invisible conviction; a sort of halo, before he left London for the last time. (It is now August, 1989.) Incidentally, just before Mr Waite disappeared, I came face to face with him in the Strand in London. We clearly eyed each other; I now suffer a frustration that I lacked the spontaneity to speak to him.

While in this frame of mind, and in that first-class aircraft cabin, a smartly dressed Italian unexpectedly leaned over me and spoke excellent English with a pleasant intonation: 'Excuse me, Mr Griffith, but I am travelling with my son, who goes to school in England, and he would very much like your autograph.'

'Certainly; that's no problem', and I wrote the piece.

'Thank you, Mr Griffith.'

And as he left me I called back: 'Signor, perhaps you could help me,' and I urged him to sit in the empty seat at my side. 'Signor, I have been anxious to speak to an Italian – a man of the world – who speaks English. I have been landed with a difficult job and with no time for preparation . . .' And I told him the whole story of my mission: of the board of directors of RAI television I was to meet that evening and of the VIP I was to meet at 11 am the next morning. My Italian listener stared at me with a blank fixed expression. I continued with my theory of offering the Mafia leadership a friendly opportunity to speak for themselves and I ended with the vital question: 'What should I do, sir, to approach a top man of the Mafia to discuss this possibility?'

I was now aware that there was a peculiarly potent silence in the first-class cabin of the Al Italia aircraft. And was not my new friend peculiarly slumped very low in his seat? He spoke in a whisper: 'Signor Griffith, you want to meet a *top* man in the Mafia?'

'Yes.'

'And tomorrow morning you meet . . .' (mentioning the VIP). But then he frowningly searched his thoughts! 'Well *maybe* one or two senators . . . but you will be, tomorrow morning, at the very top.'

The meeting that evening went well. Lots of laughs and bonhomie. My argument to them was that if I had anything to do with the Mafia project, the series would have to tell the *whole* truth: not only about the vices, but also about any virtues that there might be. Or perhaps I mean that I cannot see the validity of such a series if we failed to communicate what was the psychological *cause* of Mafia atrocities. It is more than a cliché to consider the injustices of the Treaty of Versailles when judging Adolf Hitler and his degenerate Nazis.

But the next morning was very different with the VIP. And the directors who had laughed with me the evening before were more subdued in his presence. His office was magnificent; it was Italian style at its best. Also present was a woman interpreter and she was brilliantly clever. I had been assured that the VIP could speak English, but he chose not to utter one word. Everything that passed between us went via the fine subtle lady. And I felt confident that she was communicating every nuance of what I wanted to say.

I observed two similar features of the VIP, as I spoke: his head, in clear profile against a window, perceptively quivered continuously and an immaculately shod foot, which hung from a crossed leg under the table, also continuously jerked. Yes, there was high tension there all right. We broke up the meeting for a sip of best Italian coffee and no doubt a cake. I took the opportunity to corner our interpreter and congratulate her. And she immediately pounced and said (I had never known till then what *sotto voce* really meant): 'Mr Griffith, what you have suggested is wonderful, but it is *absolutely out of the question*. They will *never* allow it! Even the little criticisms of the Mafia that were in the scripts originally, have been removed.'

The meeting resumed and the VIP made his statement – through my lady interpreter friend: 'Mr Griffith, thank you for coming to Italy and giving us your ideas. We all admire your film work very much. But it is impossible that our scripts should be fundamentally altered. They have been written by distinguished Italian academics and we value their work. Of course, by all means we would welcome you here to comment on what already exists and perhaps adjust.'

There was a silence that carried finality and so I replied: 'Gentlemen, Sir Lew Grade asked me to bring my skill to this series about the Mafia, so that they could be made acceptable to British and American audiences. I am absolutely clear what I must do if I am to be associated with this series.' And I even went so far as to recount the telephone warning that I had received from Munich in Germany and when I had finished the bit about the menacers at Palermo Airport, I added that 'of course I myself would have no intention of leaving Palermo and returning to Britain' and at that promise the VIP's head seemed to shake even more violently – though minutely, you understand. And I finished my peroration with: 'Fortunately, for me, I have other projects in my head, so I thank you sir, gentlemen, for your generous hospitality and I will now return to Britain.'

The VIP said: 'I am very sorry, Mr Griffith, that you have

decided to leave us. Maybe there is another subject that we can do together.'

'Ah!' said I, 'I have longed to make a film on the life of one of my heroes: Guiseppe Garibaldi.'

'Ah,' said the VIP, 'unfortunately we have just completed a life of Garibaldi!' And I momentarily suspected that RAI's life of the Liberator must have been as innocuous as the Independent Broadcasting Authority, in Britain, had wished my Michael Collins film had been. The Mafia – in one form or another – is everywhere (not so bad as it is in Sicily and India, but it is everywhere). What is this element in human society? It is always the preservation of the Establishment's self-inter-est. It applies to the Government and it applies to the British Trade Union Movement. And I hope that I can assure you, Reader, that in both of those cases justice can speedily go out of the window if natural justice crosses their wishes. Yes, even in Britain!

I breathed in a great draught of fresh Roman air by visiting my friend Tonino Caputo. He showed me around his new workplace. It was not a simple self-indulgent artist's study. It was a concept where other fine artists and craftsmen created side by side. Tonino urged me to examine the finesse of other people's work. Would that RAI television could touch Tonino Caputo's ethics. Then RAI would be lifting the Italian nation upward; instead of that, it is dragging it downward with a general programme vulgarity that I have not viewed else-where, not even in the United States of America! What any national television service is, so is its national character becoming! Let the British Government digest this fact quickly. There has been no character-forming influence in this world remotely comparable to television. The laws of the market-place must not pertain – without creative, cultural, ethical restraint. I'm warning you! But who is to follow John the Baptist this time?

Back in Britain I wrote Sir Lew Grade a letter without ben-efit of typewriter. I gave him a run-down of what had occurred in Italy and stated that, while I rejected the job, I was also urg-ing him to withdraw his capital as quickly as possible; I really advised him not to touch the RAI project with a barge-pole. But Sir Lew replied that he was sorry that I wouldn't stay in Rome and fight; that he couldn't withdraw from his association with the Italians because he had already invested a large sum of money. That was the last word I received from Sir Lew Grade for nearly five years. And I was sorry about that. Not only could he have helped me with my well-meant radical projects, but, perhaps – who knows? – I could have saved him from going down with the *Titanic* . . .

TWENTY-FOUR

Mr Jeremy Isaacs was then Programme Controller of Thames Television and they were the next of the big wedge companies to take me on. In those days it was a more friendly – though little doubt more wasteful – atmosphere. One appeared in the Documentary Department and the treatment was friendly and informal. Mr Jolyon Wimhurst, the pleasant head of the section, said to me: 'Ken, you always make films about big, powerful people; why don't you make a film for us about a little man?'

I looked at him soberly; I have long believed that *every* person who has reached the age of ten years has a universal story to tell, but that area should be the job of conventional investigative films. My forte is to tell about universal sagas of political significance (as Stanley Kubrick recognized). I should stick to these world-disturbing issues. However, I asked Mr Wimhurst: 'Who do you suggest is a little man?' and his reply was immediate and staggered me: 'Grimaldi', he said.

Now for anyone who has divorced her or himself from every remote aspect of the British Theatre, I must explain that Grimaldi was, as far as we know, the greatest clown that we British have ever had. I asked, disbelievingly: 'Are you suggesting that Grimaldi was "a little man"? He was a giant amongst men!'

Of course, here was the outraged actor speaking. Mr Wimhurst replied: 'You know what I mean. He wasn't a great soldier or a great politician.'

'Yes, I know what you mean. Let me think it over.'

And the next day I strolled in (you can't do that any more, and more's the pity).

'I can't tell the story of Grimaldi's life because he was a spectacular acrobat and I am too old to learn to walk the high-wire. *But* I have been a classical actor, who has played Shylock, Hamlet, Oberon, and Iago and the greatest theatre man of my time, Tyrone Guthrie, rates me high, so I *am* equipped to tell the life of our presumed greatest classical actor, Edmund Kean, and I would like to do that.'

'Good,' said Mr Wimhurst, and I was committed.

Incidentally, I once found a series of water-coloured drawings of different clown expressions; I suspected that they might be associated with Grimaldi, so I gave the old link to Peter O'Toole. If you are privileged enough to visit him you may see them hanging on the wall of his studio.

Grimaldi would have had respect for Kean; and Kean for Grimaldi, because they were both shooting stars. Kean is *the* catalyst for the seismic actor. I will dare to inscribe that if you were able to ask, say, Laurence Olivier, Peter O'Toole, Albert Finney or Anthony Hopkins, who was their romantic inspiration, I am fairly certain that it would be Edmund Kean. More mundane but talented actors would go for David Garrick. A certain sort of artist has a secret thrust to walk on water or piss over the moon and Edmund Kean was one of them and he, perhaps, *did* walk on water and *did* piss over the moon . . . The elimination of those histrionic ambitions must, for the time being, be laid at Mr Peter Hall's door.

Edmund Kean was perfect for my parable of the theatre. During the twenty-four hours which I spent moving from the idea of Grimaldi to the decision for Kean, I had to resolve what the universal value of his life-story could be. Not difficult! The story should be about every artist who ever dreamed a vision and who had fought to achieve it. Kean, with his blood, sweat and tears, could speak for us all.

I would like to briefly mention the shades of great artists who are unknown. I have long believed that human beings with the talents of divine Mozart and Shakespeare and Michelangelo have passed through this world unfulfilled and unrecognized. Of course there are those talented youths – some I knew – destroyed by war, but beyond them are the victims of discouragement. They were never encouraged to open their mouths or to take up their pencils or to consider the uses of a brush. Edmund Kean opened his mouth and immediately began to suffer the whole gamut that the artist is heir to: rejection, adulation, wealth and abject poverty.

For seven years Kean strolled about Britain, often with his ailing small son on his shoulders, and accompanied by his poor wife, Mary, and earning their grub by barnstorming. Suddenly, he was thrown onto the stage of Drury Lane Theatre because of some messy emergency and the few people who were in the auditorium ran out into the street and dragged passers by into the theatre to view the phenomenon on the stage. Kean was playing Shylock in a play that Shakespeare originally and rightly called: *The Jew of Venice*.

Was it the poet Coleridge who described such a performance by Kean as 'watching Shakespeare by flashes of lightning'? What have the instigators of that concrete mausoleum and a similar one called The Barbican, in the City of London, done to our great British histrionic potential!? I say: 'Damn them! Damn them! Damn them all!'

Kean was a terrible lad, both on and off the boards. I have often wondered how the public could expect to have a giant of an artist on the boards but a polite curate off it. The artist and the private person are indivisible. Peter O'Toole has been naughty, but (and this is going to sadden him) he has never been *quite* as naughty as Edmund Kean.

A theatre critic, writing about Kean, impulsively threw his prose away and wrote (I quote from memory):

> Whate'er thine errors, Kean,
> What e'er thy shame;
> Thou art the sun's bright child!'

When the populace began to cheer him to the rafters, the artist, Kean, was unimpressed: 'Why should I take note of them? When only a little time ago they laughed at me or ignored me while I was giving the same performance?' It is the misfortune of the truly great player that he has to create with the public present. The painter doesn't have to suffer the layperson's presence, nor the composer, nor the writer. And I totally reject the insulting definitions of 'artist' and 'artiste'. Sitting here amid the Italian Alps I listen to classical music from Austria: Vienna, Bayreuth and Salzburg and at the end of too many performances there is hysterical cheering. It seems to me like a ritual mutual masturbation. Strangely, I found much the same unbalanced support for particular ballet dancers in Moscow a few months ago. It seems often like some upper middle class indulging in a safe, and respectable orgy. You can also see it going on at Wimbledon while young men and women explode with ego as they hit a ball over a net – or fail to. Or at a pop concert. Edmund Kean was never very impressed by that sort of public wanking.

While Kean acted, so it is said, not only did people 'pass out with shock' in the audience, but so did some fellow players on the stage. Anyway, Edmund Kean is the great mythical ideal. And, as a remarkable friend of mine, Richard Huggett, said to me, upon hearing that my televised Raskolnikov in Dostoyevski's *Crime and Punishment* had not been recorded: 'Ah! Lost on the Desert Air!' However, the point that I want to make about Great Kean is that he has something over Michelangelo or Mozart: the 'flashes of lightning' are 'lost on the desert air'. Not a bad place to disappear into.

I had an experience along these lines once. A splendid man of the theatre, Colin George (who has spent too much time in the Australian theatre for my good), once asked me to play Shylock in Shakespeare's *The Jew of Venice* at the Ludlow Festival. Now, at that time, I had recently seen my chum, O'Toole, play the part at Stratford-upon-Avon and I had been deeply impressed with his Shylock; there were characteristics in *his* performance which I felt that I could never escape plagiarising. And if an artist hasn't got a compulsion to be unique and the best, he may as well go home and give *all* of his time to his postal history collection. So I refused the job. But Colin George persisted and after three refusals I undertook the challenge. It proved to be one of the happiest experiences of my life. The play was performed in the magnificent ruin of

Ludlow Castle, the company was a delightful credit to our profession and, of course, the Shropshire countryside is beautiful. My dread that I should in any way be influenced by O'Toole's performance was unfounded. I discovered, finally, there in Ludlow, that if an actor grasps what the character (in this case Shylock) uniquely means to him – or her – the characterization is, and remains, unique. You cannot stray away from *your own* unique, unbroken truth. Of course you can cheat and do anything for effect but then you have broken faith with your assumed character.

Now, in every performance on the stage, almost every player strives for that impossible perfection. And on this one night I just about got it. Doria happened to be in the audience and she knew. Afterwards she said to me: 'If only O'Toole had seen you do that tonight!' (All three of us had once lived together and there is a special bond!)

I remember the stars were very bright and because of my performance I felt exhilarated. I truthfully replied: 'That would have been nice; but the truth is it doesn't really matter. *I* know that I did it.'

I think that Kean died at the age of 39, worn out by playing every card in the human pack. Just before he went, a poor young actor walked out to his house at Richmond, London, close to the River Thames. He knocked on the door and Kean's housekeeper asked: 'Yes, what do you want?'

'I want to see Mr Kean.'

'I'm sorry, Mr Kean doesn't see anybody.'

'Please, ma'am, tell Mr Kean that I'm a young actor and that I have *walked* from London to see him.'

The housekeeper was good enough to report the message to the shattered recluse and she returned: 'Mr Kean says you may come in.'

The greatest of all tragedians looked at the young man: 'Yes, cockie; what d'you want?'

'Please, Mr Kean, what do I require to be a great actor?'

'D'you know how to *starve*, cockie?'

'Is that *all*, Mr Kean?'

'That's all, cockie.'

I have been told that Laurence Olivier (who died last week) called people 'cockie'. I presume that it was an unspecified tribute to our great predecessor.

My two invaluable colleagues, Antony Thomas and Michel Pearce were not available to direct *The Sun's Bright Child: A Life of Edmund Kean* and so the uneasy search began to find another director. I saw a film directed by a young actor named David Munro and I thought that it displayed an unusual theatrical talent and that was what Kean required. And David agreed to direct it.

I think that we captured the period (beginning of the nineteenth century) well. I tend to tell my stories in strict chronological sequence. And so there we were hustling amongst the dark august shadows of Covent Garden and, of course, that was before most of the ghosts had been driven away by the popularizing of the area; though perhaps with the proliferation of the young buskers, they may be creeping back again. I hope so.

And then we were out in the wild English country where Kean and his family suffered those first seven dreadful years – high on the Yorkshire moors. And it was here that David Munro and I had a tentative (on my part) but very interesting disagreement about our unusual style of communicating. Kean has been reported – during those cruel years – to have walked and walked 'with his hands deep in his pockets, cursing his rejection' by the Great British Theatre. David wanted me to be filmed walking over those moors, with my hands 'deep in my pockets', which would be 'covered' by my voice-over telling the story. And I asked my director a curious and revealing question: 'David, you don't think that I'm supposed to *be* Edmund Kean, do you?' I felt that we were treading on critical ground; perhaps the ground of the conventional fictional cinema film or television drama. I play a sleight-of-hand: now you see me, now you don't. Avoid obvious acting. Persuade your audience that this is the simple truth. Not fictional theatre.

I have never deeply *analysed* what we do in these films. To some extent I have talked to my colleagues – particularly the three directors, Antony Thomas, Michel Pearce and then David Munro – but only informally for an hour or so and have rather left it for them to recognize the task of dramatizing the historical truth without allowing the viewers to suspect unadulterated acting. If that happened, I believed – and I still believe – that we would lose our unique power to persuade. Also David wanted me to go mad with grief – as Kean did – when he digests the appalling truth that his beloved son is dead. I was torn between my instinctive doubt that it would be bad for our film if I was perceived to be acting 'naked and unashamed' as it were. You see, it's all right, so I have argued with myself, if this nutter, Kenneth Griffith, with his obsessive study of history, coolly tells the camera that so-and-so once entered 'this very room' and then we metamorphose to the same storyteller, performing what the historical character actually said, and what actually took place, as against an unexpected piece of introduced acting. It's the transition from narration to historical quotes that is critical for our survival. On the other hand I didn't want to inhibit the creativity of David Munro's vision. Those were the horns that I briefly hung on, up there on the moors. But, having put my point of view, I did what David asked – and acted my head off.

What was the result? After David Swift saw the finished film, he was full of praise for it, but when I pressed him he said: 'There was only one moment when I thought you'd lost it: when Kean went mad. But you pulled it back.' When I have watched that film with other people I have anxiously glanced at them to see if they accept the scene as documentary fact.

Until now, it has only been in the United States of America that I have been urged to talk about my curious work. Harvard University, outside of Boston City, has taken an interest. It has been said there that my films are a totally new form of communication; that they are *not* documentaries, neither are they drama as it is generally understood. I have been invited to speak about the matter at the Carpenter Center, which is the creative section of that great university. It is true that I was once asked to deliver a *Guardian* Lecture at the

London Film Festival, where they showed two of my films. But the emphasis there – or rather my commission – was for me to talk about censorship in British television, particularly towards Ireland, and *not* about the creative door that I had stumbled on, pushed by Huw Wheldon. A pity because so much else could be done; I am anxious to share and I know the secrets!

We didn't have Grenville Middleton photographing *The Sun's Bright Child*; instead we had Thames' top man, Mr Mike Fash, and his sound partner, Mr Sandy Macrea. Both of them did fine work which helped us to achieve the period atmosphere.

Edmund Kean became the phenomenon that supported the very existence of Drury Lane Theatre and this fact thrust at me one of those towering problems that always crop up in all of our films. This particularly cruel challenge was that I had to appear briefly on the Drury Lane stage – as Kean – playing Shylock, Macbeth and Richard the Third!

'It is unfair!' I cried. We had the Drury Lane stage for *one* day. There was no time for *any* rehearsal and my three costumes were heavy pieces, made for films. I had already played Shylock but none of the other roles. But somehow we pulled it off.

The end of our film was inside the church in the middle of Richmond, just outside of London. There I reminded the viewers that no one now knew where Edmund Kean was born 'and no one knew exactly, until recently, where precisely he was buried; somewhere within the precincts of this Richmond Church'. And then I called: 'Mr O'Toole' (and the player walked out from a vestry) 'shall we two actors have the privilege of laying Edmund Kean's tombstone?' And together we did that. O'Toole has seven words in the film and they are the very last words: 'Mind your fingers, Kenneth; mind your fingers!' as the fine Welsh slate falls into position. The legend on it cuts deep: *The Sun's Bright Child, Edmund Kean* and the date of his death, I think. Yes, go and have a look for yourself; particularly if you are a Thespian.

During our researches we were surprised that there was no known burial place for Kean in Richmond Church. But an old verger said that when he was a boy, another old churchman had pointed out to him the unmarked place and when the blank flagstone was lifted, there was the great man's small coffin. Kean was not a big man in physical stature; only in spirit. I think of that sequence, at the end of the Kean film, as a consummation devoutly to be wished for.

I remember exactly what O'Toole said as we walked away from the church: 'Thank you, Griffith, for asking me.'

'Who else?' I thought to myself.

TWENTY-FIVE

Friendly Thames Television asked me what film I would like to do next. I said: 'Baden Powell in the Siege of Mafeking', and the then head of their documentary programmes, Mr Ian Martin, said: 'Good idea.' Life for the likes of me was easier in those days.

Perhaps I have always been at my happiest in the Republic of South Africa. I discussed this fact with my friend, Chiara Peretti, a few days ago – we were travelling through north-eastern Italy on a most beautiful morning – and Chiara shares with me this nostalgia for the southern portion of the African continent. Maybe it has something to do with the southern hemisphere; maybe it has something to do with the South Pole. Well, Chiara is a visionary, and who knows?

I have studied South Africa's history from the time the Europeans first arrived: the Portuguese, the Dutch, the British and the Huguenots, primarily. Before that, writing was unknown in that part of the world. There were tribal legends: and anthropologists continue to puzzle. There were monumental invasions of black-skinned people from the far north of Africa and the indigenous brown people, the Hottentots, having little ascendancy, began to disappear. The present-day Black people are best comprehended in the Zulus and Xhosas. And so every part of the great country has its immediate dramatic evolvement for me and my interest is great.

Of course, there in South Africa is the biggest clash of stupendously different cultures on the face of this earth. Unless one has observed the vastness of difference in inner motives, between Black African and White African, it is rash to judge the present situation (1989). I have compassion for both cultural groups. But recently, the highly principled White anti-apartheid activist, Mr Peter Hain, challenged me: 'You wouldn't *prefer* to live in P. W. Botha's South Africa to Mugabe's Zimbabwe, would you?' I didn't reply because it was not an apt time or place; I was interviewing him in his home and I wanted the interview to continue. But the truth is I would much prefer to live south of the Limpopo River than north of it. I feel more at ease amongst my own cultural standards – for all of their sometimes cruel difficulties. Recently I entered Zambia at Lusaka and the immigration official kept fingering through my perfectly proper British Passport.

'What's wrong?' I asked.

'Problems. Come!'

And off we went to an office where this Zambian pulled out his wallet and began counting his money. I was not rescued from miserable corruption until an African National Congress official, who was the worse for alchohol, whispered in his ear. I don't want it. I don't want to live in the Third World! And I am fed up with *all* of the blame being pointed at White South Africa.

Baden-Powell had been sent to South Africa because war was coming between the Boers and us British. We were determined to control the newly discovered gold that lay under Johannesburg and we were attacking for other imperial reasons. I was, and am, inevitably on the Republican Boer side and it was meant to be strictly a White man's war; that was mutually understood by both Boer and Briton. And the whole project in my mind was meant to be a relatively jolly holiday for me. The possibility for this jolly time lay in the astonishing personality of Baden-Powell. He was an unorthodox colonel of the 13th Hussars and at the time of his orders to depart for Mafeking, he was on leave in London; his regiment was serving in India.

I was actually being filmed, high up on the plinth of Nelson's Column (a good imperial image with all of those huge lions) when Mr Silvio Narizzano, the distinguished director, called me down and informed me that our innocent film had just been blacked by the Association of Cinematograph,

Television and Allied Technicians; they were ordering our crew (again Mike Fash and a Thames film crew) not to depart for South Africa. In those dangerous trade union days you did not cross the ACTT, and worse than any tyranny from their headquarters was the Thames Shop; that is the ACTT people working within the Thames Television Company. They were not less than vicious and vindictive. It was a touch of your Marxist totalitarian spirit or the Mafia for that matter. But nothing is perfect. Perhaps today there exists the uncomfortable threat of Corporate Business. Certainly a new whip is cracking.

Anyway, Baden-Powell in the Siege of Mafeking was being cancelled. Why? It was said to be an anti-apartheid action. Hypocrisy up to the very hilt I would suggest. Or if there was a moment of considered sincerity, it was as thin as Dylan Thomas' razor.

Give me credit where it's due! I was quick-witted in Trafalgar Square. As the enormity of the miserableness of the ACTT struck me, I said: 'Keep the cameras and sound running – all the way back to Jeremy Isaacs' office.' And this was done, even in the lift going up – where all the creatives live. We ran our camera into Mr Isaacs' office where Mr Ian Martin was also present.

'I don't want to take my loot for nothing,' I said, 'I've had one film suppressed by the Independent Broadcasting Authority, which rightly or wrongly I equate with the political Right, and now I've had another film prohibited by the ACTT, which rightly or wrongly I equate with the political Left. I think, sir, you ought to allow me now to make a film investigating what elements in our British society dictate to the British people what they may be allowed to see on television or not to see.' (The truth is I had nipped into Jeremy Isaacs' office as soon as we had arrived back at Thames from Trafalgar Square and had asked him if we could plough in with the camera going. I was cheeky but not that cheeky.)

Jeremy Isaacs spoke, with the camera peering at him, about the ideal that freedom in television should be expanding but that he suspected that it was contracting (this was truly a prophetic comment): 'Go ahead and make your investigative film.'

I stood up and bowing first to Ian Martin and then to Jeremy, said: 'Thank you, sir! Thank you, sir!' and I made a well-ordered exit.

Jeremy Isaacs called me back: 'What do you mean "sir"!? You've never called me "sir" in your life!'

And so we set out on our investigative film. From a creative point of view, it was much easier than my usual style of carefully scripted factual story-telling; this film was to be primarily 'talking heads' of the relevant people.

First we invaded Mr Morley Safer's inner American sanctum in London and with Mr Safer we had a considerable professional communicator. I had gone to him to speak about the suppression of the Michael Collins film because Mr Safer had been, probably, the first American reporter to be censured – at Presidential (Johnson) level – for reporting horrible facts about the war in Vietnam. But, there is a written constitutional divide between the definition of 'censure' (reprimand) and 'censor' (suppress). The first is welcome in a democracy; the second is not. Mr Safer roamed far and wide for us in his dissertation, comparing his hard experience over Vietnam and then my treatment over Ireland. And then he enlarged on the reality of our social/political structure: 'But that is the British way of doing things. How could *Sir* Lew Grade, knighted by Her Majesty herself, oppose the wishes of one of her Majesty's Ministers?'

And that is the unattractive trap for all of us Brits. Accept one of these royal baubles and you are, inevitably, deep in the Establishment's pocket. Say 'yes' enough and you can even become a Lord! Not that I blame Sir Lew Grade; he is not a political guy; he has always been a showman, banging a big drum and a peer's coronet is very good big publicity. And Britain needs more of them – showmen I mean.

Mr Safer also pointed out that the United States had a written Constitution (which Britain hasn't got) and that in that Constitution there is a Fifth Amendment.

'What's that?' I innocently asked. When Mr Safer strove to

reply, one of his friends who saw the finished film later delightedly said: 'Morley had a little difficulty in quoting it.' But Morley did well enough: 'Basically, it is the public's right to know.' And so I picked, out of the air, the title of our film; it was called: *The Public's Right to Know*.

We then transported our cameras to the Bristol Old Vic, to where my dancing partner (a not-so-soft shoe shuffle), Mr Peter O'Toole, had returned briefly, after having staggered the international film world for some years. I asked O'Toole, as an Irishman, to explain to me why Michael Collins was so loved, and he repeated what I wrote about 'The Big Fellow' earlier in this book. I then asked O'Toole why the British were so frightened of Michael Collins, to the extent that they were suppressing his life's story, so many many years after his death? O'Toole replied: 'Jesus! They were terrified of him when he was alive. They are ten times more terrified of him now that he has been resurrected.' An apt reply.

And then we progressed towards the beautiful home of the writer and sometime musician, Mr Benny Green, because Benny, as the then television critic of *The Jewish Chronicle*, had objected, at the time of the suppression, to not being allowed to review the film. Many journalists (and I thank them again!) had aired the political scandal, but the only *critic* who objected, at the time, was Benny Green. Of course, Jewish people are acutely attuned to such a dangerous change in the democratic wind. I had never met Benny Green before; today he is one of those treasured friends whom you are glad to have around, even if you don't see them for years, because their caring perception gives one comfort. The ones you can count on.

Benny spoke to me in parables and they are in the film. He touched fleetingly on the Jewish experience: 'The Jews are the Southern Irish of Russia.' The mutual pogroms; no less. He examined the curious sense of proportion that the British have over censorship: 'Show a tit or an arse on television and the Whitehouses are up in outraged arms; remove a historical human fact from the television screens and – nothing!' And he continued: I don't know whether it is part of a fiendish plot or just British inefficiency, but nobody has been *told* that the film has been suppressed; it has been shuffled out of the way.'

And then on to Dr Cathcart, who at one time had been one of the judging officers at the IBA (who had suppressed the Collins film). And it was from him that I learnt an honest fact about our British method to annihilate the Michael Collins film. He told me that his boss, Mr Bernard Sendel, had asked him to accompany him on a visit to Sir Lew Grade for the purpose of deviating the virtual destruction of the film away from the IBA onto Sir Lew's bonny shoulders. Until I received that information I had presumed that the questionable work had been done by Mr Sendel either by letter or over the telephone. Of course I was ever naive and only then realized that the Irish matter-in-hand was much too delicate to be handled by post or telephone.

The doctor also told me that he disapproved of the secrecy exercised over the matter: that if the IBA was going to suppress the film they should have announced that fact publicly. 'Indeed,' said the doctor, 'the failure on the part of the IBA to do this was one of the reasons for my resignation.' And incidentally, when I first established that I was going to take legal action against Sir Lew Grade, the IBA, getting wind of my intention, hastily placed a very small statement in the press, that the responsibility for the prohibition of the film was now theirs! I presume that this belated confession was meant to give themselves some validity in court; whether it was before a prejudiced British judge or not. Dr Cathcart emphasized to me that my quarrel should be with British law and not with the IBA. Of course I retaliated forcibly with the argument that I detested the apparent willing creatures of any misplaced law – or the vagueness that seemed to pass for a law in our constitutionless system – as much as the law itself. But the doctor was very nervous: he was a Protestant from Dublin and he didn't like being associated with the lousy business at all. And he had resigned from the IBA. What more could he do? But all of those years ago, I refrained in the film from mentioning what his Christian denomination was, or from whence he came. At that time, when the Collins film was a *cause célèbre*, some Republican activist could easily have misread the shady issue and might have done the decent doctor some harm. And he knew it, and yet had the undoubted courage to talk to me in front of a camera.

And then I was doing that hopping through the traffic of Fleet Street on my way to meet young David Brasil, the Irish journalist. As he talked to me, we had carefully angled the camera so that a Protestant (Unionist) death threat could be seen pinned up on the wall behind him. Today, I have one of my own, and mine is carefully framed. David is a deeply committed Republican, as any self-respecting Irish Irishperson should be. He quietly expostulated his astonishment that the British authorities should make such a song and dance about events that had taken place in Ireland so long ago. Of course David Brasil had his Irish tongue in his Irish cheek for every moment of the interview. I thoroughly enjoyed the bland expression on his boyish face. He knew – better than I when I chose to make the film – that if the historical rotten British roots in Ireland were exposed, they would reflect as vividly as ever on our actions in the north-east of Ireland today. David Brasil knew as well as Peter O'Toole what the resurrection of Michael Collins could mean. And we all knew that the British Government would cotton on. What I hadn't bargained for was that the British authority would have the bare-faced cheek to suppress the film. Full marks to them as a repressive government against Ireland, which they have been for something over seven hundred years.

David Brasil *had* bargained for it. Nothing, as far as he was concerned could be 'beyond the pale' as far as British behaviour on the island of Ireland went. He reached for his journalistic file and pulled out a piece that he had written and published about me when I was actually, relatively innocently, making the film. And in his article he prophesied that since the British had never dared to tell the truth about their behaviour in Ireland, he very much doubted that they would allow me to film a truth and *transmit* it on *this* occasion. An old Irish head on young shoulders. David Brasil and I became friends and he used to call on me regularly. But I haven't seen him for some long time, which I regard as a serious loss in my life.

We interviewed Mr (now Lord) William Deedes, sometime
Tory Minister for Northern Ireland and sometime editor of the
British newspaper, the *Telegraph*. Now Mr Deedes' reactions
to certain statements that I made in his presence were worthy
of a film to themselves; I mean silent, visual reactions; I have
known no one to touch him with the use of eyebrows and we
certainly showed them on the screen while I was talking. They
were eloquent.

Mr William Deedes was very fair with me. He is the sort of
Tory I can like. I hope that he is what they mean when they
say 'a gentleman'. He never lost his sense of humour with me.
Could I write that perhaps – and I mean *perhaps* – he felt a
slice above me? Anyway, I tested his patience and his patience
was not found wanting. Mr Deedes, in trying to explain to me
why the Michael Collins film could not be shown on British
television, said something to the effect: 'If mothers or wives or
sweethearts of British soldiers serving in Northern Ireland
[like most Britishers he was careless about such nomencla-
ture] were to see your film, they might begin to doubt that
their sons, husbands or lovers should be serving there.'

I replied, truthfully: 'But that is *why* I made the film!'

And at that confession Mr Deedes's eyebrows were not less
than wonderful, as he sternly, but without malice, said: 'You
have just committed treason and you jolly well know that
you've committed treason!'

It is quite a thing to be accused of treason on television and
by a 'Northern' Ireland Secretary to boot! Now, I am not as
solidly packed with knowledge of William Shakespeare as I
should be, but this afternoon, in an Alpine meadow I was
reading the True Master's 'First Part of the Contention'; and
King Henry the Sixth says:

> What stronger breastplate than a heart untainted?
> Thrice is he armed that hath his quarrel just;
> And he but naked, though locked up in steel,
> Whose conscience with injustice is corrupted.

Anyway Mr Deedes' repeated strictures didn't perturb me much. And in supervising the editing of the film I was insistent that the threat to me of the Tower of London was broadcast.

And so between that distinguished assortment I concluded my case against the British policy to suppress the Michael Collins film.

But that was not the end of *The Public's Right to Know*; we ploughed on to examine the no-less sinister machinations of the political Left who wave their shallow, hypocritical, masturbating activities on behalf of the South African anti-apartheid movement. Those adjectives are, of course, mine. *My* opinion. And, of course, they don't carry the *whole* truth I *know*. What worries me about them – the Left liberals – is the enjoyment, the self-satisfaction, derived from being a do-gooder, without the hard study that is necessary to understand even the beginning of the whole three-dimensional truth. And the Marxist concept seldom helps a clear vision for anybody. The equality of human kind! Sounds tremendous! And it is reassuring, for some people, to follow the party line. Of course, now that the party itself is disintegrating at an unbelievable rate, that prop must be gone or going. The prop of unreality is splitting into many sad pieces. Somewhere in the back of Karl Marx's head was the gist of an ideal – but the battle of ideals is that they are always in immediate conflict with the reality of the human condition. So along come the terrible executives of that smidgen of Communist idealism – I mean Lenin and Stalin and the whole bloody company – and in the name of equality they begin to butcher on a monumental scale. And perhaps even worse than the millions of corpses, sacrificed for the Red Star and the Hammer and Sickle, are the greater millions of annihilated spirits.

Be that as it may; first we went along to the Association of Cinematograph, Television and Allied Technicians headquarters in Soho Square, to interview Mr Alan Sapper, the General Secretary of the Union. Mr Sapper, as always, was affable towards me. I learnt while visiting him that my idea of a trade union was embarrassingly simplistic. I also quickly learnt that our arrest from proceeding to South Africa was not even an inscribed straightforward rule. The machinations of the Thames Shop and God knows what other envious and shriller Marxist voices were at work; some of them pecking painfully even at Mr Sapper. I soon began to realize that the union was not preoccupied with the needs of its membership, but rather the personal ambitions of its multiple executives. I began to suffer even a protective instinct towards Mr Sapper.

My film crew (all members of the ACTT) were bitterly disappointed at not being allowed to film in South Africa a famous adventure in Baden-Powell's life. But no union official that I ever met was in the least bit concerned about the membership feelings; they were only concerned about their own political leanings, which did tend to veer towards the Great Virtues of Moscow. I was a little surprised that the legislators and executives of the ACTT didn't make bigger efforts to ingratiate themselves with the membership, who must, in some manner, vote them into the chairs of power. But that they didn't seem to do. I don't think that anyone would argue with me that if the entire membership of the ACTT had been asked if they would like to go to South Africa to work, they would overwhelmingly have replied: 'Yes!'

There was one lady in a position of power at the ACTT at that time who had worked assiduously against our going and therefore we urgently wanted to interview her to try to understand her stance. She actually turned up at the Thames Television building in the Euston Road, London, but then refused to be interviewed. Mr Mike Fash, closely followed by Mr Sandy Macrea clutching his sound equipment *chased* her, with her squealing: 'No!' and me rather shouting questions at her. Mike and Sandy were not pleased about their lost opportunity and had no compunction about playing hide and seek with her. The last glimpse I had of the mysterious lady was of her hiding under a table with Mr Fash's lens poking towards her. I then gave up, overcome with paroxysms of laughter, I'm afraid.

When I met Mr Alan Sapper I immediately said that I wanted to tell him all of the questions that I had in my head *before* the interview began. I planned no surprise questions.

The film crew, which now included my support and comfort (but not *always*) Grenville Middleton, were setting up the cameras in the General Secretary's office and so Mr Sapper and I climbed the stairs to a small room where I went over the ground that I wanted to cover about our being blacked. The General Secretary thanked me for my courtesy. To no one else did I give my questions before and Mr Sapper didn't ask for them. But I now recognized that his position was ticklish – to say the least – surrounded as he was by a band of colleagues-cum-conspirators, and he not unlike Julius Caesar in the Capitol. And Mr Sapper displayed courage in facing up to me – and the camera – on this issue; unlike his under-the-table-hiding colleague.

Well, once settled in his General Secretary's seat, a full side-board of social refreshment behind him, Mr Sapper gave the anti-apartheid spiel with fine rhetorical style. He said that his Black brothers and sisters in South Africa had requested the ACTT to boycott all filming in South Africa except news items (news items could be helpfully detrimental to the White Government of South Africa) and that the ACTT had decided that this request must be carried out. I, also, was in a ticklish situation; I had just had one film blacked by the ACTT, and I knew that they would consider blacking this one and if that happened to me, I would begin to look even more eccentric in the eyes of my television peers – leave alone the public. And so I refrained from stirring the Marxist pot by telling Mr Sapper that I had some Black South African friends who were going to be very disappointed that we weren't going to film in South Africa. From the very outset I had insisted to the Thames Television Management (my employers) that while filming in the Republic we must employ at least one Black film technician (and there are many in South Africa) at a full European rate of pay, and Thames, being a decent company, agreed with alacrity. This was long before the ACTT even thought of giving us trouble. But the bitter truth is that the anti-apartheid movement, leave alone Nelson Mandela's African National Congress, rarely give a damn for the simple welfare of the mass of Black South Africans. What they do care about is that a Black culture, as against the present European–African culture, prevails, and that power will be achieved by the likes of Oliver Tambo. Thereby the inevitable Black, tribally dominated (Xhosa) totalitarian State will appear and all of the territory south of the Limpopo River will inevitably begin to slide into the Third World, where the rest of the African continent rests. Looking at Tambo and his degenerate 'Government in Exile' recently, in Lusaka, confirmed these worst fears of mine.

Many Whites have made great sacrifices in order to achieve the impossible of unifying the Blacks of South Africa and the Whites in some sort of happy minestrone soup. Brave people, sometime friends of mine: Huw Lewin, journalist, who 'did' – was it? – seven years in Pretoria Central Jail, and Albie Sachs, lawyer, who after periods in jail, has had his body shattered. But my bitter belief is that their dream is never going to happen this side of evolution. Neither Black Africa nor White Africa can allow it. And it has very little to do with colour; colour is only the flag of centuries of very different evolving cultures. Indeed different states of evolutionary minds.

Mr Sapper also mentioned two other countries from which comrades had appealed to the ACTT for non-cooperation in filming: Portugal (Salazar still ruled) and Greece (where 'the Colonels' were in charge). Of course, at that time, it was impossible for the masses of the left-wing Communist world to appeal to the ACTT. But Alan Sapper concentrated his impassioned attacks on South Africa.

Film in a ciné camera doesn't run for ever and when we had to change reels in Mr Sapper's office, he asked me how I felt the interview was going. 'Excellent!', I replied; and so it was.

'Would any of you like refreshment?' asked the General Secretary.

'Well . . .' said Grenville, with an encouraging intonation from behind his camera.

Mr Sapper turned round to his big sideboard to do the honours and his eyes promptly froze on a fine bottle inscribed 'Portuguese Sherry'. Now, you may recall from the above that Salazar's Portugal was one of the three countries that were to be boycotted. Mr Sapper turned to me: 'Is this bottle of Portuguese sherry in the frame?' (That is, was it within the frame of our moving picture, which would be seen on the nation's television screens?) I, like the good professional that I can be, kept a firm control of myself and casually (perhaps a wee bit *too* casual) asked Grenville: 'Was that bottle of Portuguese sherry *seen* over Mr Sapper's shoulder during his interview?'

And Grenville '*went*'; there was no comprehensible reply as Mr Middleton endeavoured to peer through his viewfinder; only a choking sound and the camera quivered. Finally we got a reply from our distinguished cameraman: 'Yes, I'm afraid it is *clearly* seen.'

Well, that reply might have been even a morsel sadistic; but we *all* had keenly looked forward to that aborted visit to the Republic of South Africa.

'Ah,' said Mr Sapper, with that masterful self-control and iron pragmatism that is required to lead you to the highest chair, 'then we'll have to do the interview again!'

And we did *and* the General Secretary personally handed around the refreshments. I have always liked Alan Sapper, much as I have always liked Lew Grade, though neither is going to thank me for linking their names in any way.

And then an astounding thing happened. The governing committee (or whatever the jargon is) of the ACTT blacked Mr Sapper's interview. They simply announced that we were *not* to use it in our film. And that was that! In those wretched days you didn't cross certain British unions or you might find yourself unemployed. The only difference between certain areas of the British Trade Union Movement and the Italian Mafia was that our British lot didn't kill you – though I met a few in the Thames Shop who would have had no compunction to do so, if they had felt that they could have got away with it.

It wasn't the fear of exposing the Portuguese sherry, lying deep in the heart of the ACTT, that had rung alarm bells. I doubt whether this aspect of the boycott situation had reached the collective ears of the ACTT Committee; it was some darker, more treacherous fear that had rattled them and it is not for me here to probe further into theoretical machinations. But we made the best of it. Indeed we made the very *most* of it. As I strode through a poorer part of London to interview the Black African representative of the African National Congress, I recited the above story and concluded that I considered it was cowardly of the ACTT to leave this hard-pressed African entirely alone to explain our prohibition to film in South Africa and the *other* action in censoring Mr Alan Sapper, their own General Secretary. And they, the ACTT, who had, rightly, complained (not too forcibly!) about right-wing censorship, when the Independent Broadcasting Authority had suppressed the Michael Collins film! Benny Green, while I was interviewing him, had said something to me (yes, it's in the completed film) which is simple yet profound, I often have cause to pull it out of my memory; Benny said: 'The truth is indispensable.'

And he's bloody right! Be good, sweet maid, and let who will be clever.

In Mr John Hatzeweh's humble room, with a picture of a Black African head in the shape of a boycotted Outspan orange being squeezed by a white hand for its juice, I asked whether the African National Congress could see any virtue, or anything wrong, about us Brits making an innocent film about one of our imperial adventures seventy or so years ago: and, at the same time, pointing out that Thames Television was even anxious to employ one or two old Black colleagues of mine, at full European rates of pay. And *that* must have been some sort of a breakthrough. But it was fruitless: Mr Hatzeweh was a nice, simple, well-meaning man, but he had no power even to begin considering reason, leave alone take action on it. I doubt from bitter personal experience of Tambo and company in Lusaka, whether his ANC bosses, back in Africa, were capable of any clear decision themselves. Between the ACTT and the ANC it was all a typical Marxist uneasy mess.

So with some sorrow we left lonely John Hatzeweh and progressed to the Royal Court Theatre in posher Sloane Square, where Mr Athol Fugard's play *Sizwe Bansi is Dead* was rehearsing. Mr Fugard, remembering me from the time when Mr Robin Midgely had asked me to play in his television production of Fugard's *Bloodknot*, had readily agreed to be interviewed. Perhaps he had also learnt of my visit to the Department of Information and of my probing at BOSS (South African Security) in Pretoria, to secure his release from house arrest or whatever. Athol Fugard was in the auditorium of the Royal Court, and we interviewed him as, perhaps, the most effective fighter against human injustices in South Africa. Mr Fugard, of course, is far too intelligent and creative to follow any prescribed creed. He is left with his own puzzling conscience. He can see the uneasy torment of the Whites of South Africa as well as of the Blacks. More than that, I would not dare to comment about.

Athol Fugard said to me, with a camera by my side, looking at him, that he deeply regretted that the ACTT had prevented our film crew from journeying to South Africa.

'Opportunities would have crossed your paths which could have helped [human understanding].' He appealed to any British playwrights who were prohibiting their work to be produced in South Africa, to lift their boycott: 'Not only can we suffer from physical rickets, but mental rickets also [if deprived of new ideas].' And then Athol made a terrible but revelatory statement about the African National Congress and the anti-apartheid movement (though he didn't specify any movement), which I believe is of the greatest importance for us all to consider. He said: 'When I am with people who advocate the boycott of South Africa, I often feel that I am in the company of those who hate the system more than they love the victims of it.'

Leaving Sloane Square I would normally – in my own lifestyle – travel by underground train and this I did for the ending of our film: *The Public's Right to Know*. And as I was filmed entering the underground station there were two buskers playing on a banjo and a ukulele respectively, and as I was passing them, by an extraordinary coincidence, they happened to be playing 'Sarais Marais', the Afrikaner National Song! I gave them a grateful contribution and said (to round things off nicely): 'Up the Republic!' A camera

followed me down to the platform, with me chatting away
about how you, the British people have been disallowed from
seeing these two films; a life of the Irishman, Michael Collins
and the adventures of the founder of the Scout and Guide
Movement, Baden-Powell, in the famous siege of Mafeking in
South Africa. And as I squeezed through the sliding doors of
that underground train (and by arrangement with London
Transport) I got caught in those doors as they shut! And with
me, mouth open, shouting: 'Ouch!' we freeze frame (the
moving picture halted into still life) and up come our credits.

Now what would happen? We had exposed a few home
truths about several Sacred Cows (if they will forgive the
expression): Sir (soon to be Lord) Lew Grade; the Independent
Broadcasting Authority; the Association of Cinematograph
Television and Allied Technicians and the anti-apartheid and
African National Congress caboodle. Would those who command allow *this* film to be transmitted? Mr Peter O'Toole,
who had been raised in Irish horseracing circles, had put the
question bluntly in the film itself: 'Are you going to get the treble?' Fortunately for me, *and* the public's right to know, only
one of the above judges of what we should or should not see
and hear on television had the public duty of declaring their
wishes: the IBA.

They were surprising and peculiar times for me. I was
astonished to learn that officers of the IBA were going to view
our film, *The Public's Right to Know*, in one of Thames' own
viewing theatres in the Euston Road and I was allowed to
attend. I suppose that I had asked if I may, so that I could
answer any objections that might be put. Amongst the IBA
officers present was my favourite (of those that I had met), Mr
David Glencross, who is now, in 1993, their Chief Executive;
or rather the CE of the Independent Television Commission.
He has always struck me as a gentle sensitive man of a liberal
nature. I do hope that in expressing this opinion I am not
doing him any harm amongst his peers! I have long felt that he
should be on my side in these ethical judgements. Perhaps he
was in spirit, but those rules were the rules . . .

When the lights came up at the end of the viewing, I can

remember the silence that prevailed. I looked to my right at the IBA officials, who seemed to be looking at their shoes.

'Well,' I asked, 'what do you think?'

It was probably Mr Glencross who replied: 'Bit hard on us, Kenneth.'

'What is?' I enquired, and David mentioned something in the film that was so slight in my opinion that it seemed meaningless.

'What happens now?' I persisted.

'We'll have to consult.'

'How long before I'll know?'

'Within this week.'

Almost immediately – I mean the next day – I was given the green light. Of course the IBA knew that the Press was breathing down my neck, wondering if I was going to get that treble.

The Public's Right to Know was enthusiastically received – generally. It was something of a sensation within the television business. No one, before, had made a film investigating our own British Television Establishment. After the Michael Collins film *Hang Up Your Brightest Colours* had been suppressed, one or two television producers had murmured to me, perhaps with a shadow of guilt: 'We could have made a film like that but didn't because we *knew* they wouldn't show it.' Well now we had made a film 'like that' and it *had* been shown!

I think that it was about this time that Mr Aled Vaughan, of Harlech Television (HTV – based in Cardiff and Bristol) came to see me in London, to ask if there was anything that I would now like to do for HTV. I remember eyeing him very carefully. I was presuming that as a Celtic patriot he would not have liked the suppression of the Michael Collins film at all. So I replied: 'One of the major objections to the Michael Collins film *Hang Up Your Brightest Colours* – expressed by Tories and the IBA – was that my ability to tell stories on television could not be balanced by anyone else, to put the Protestant–Unionist point of view. I had remonstrated that Ian Paisley and Enoch Powell were pretty good salesmen.

'Therefore, Aled, I would like to make another film explaining the Irish Republican point of view, but one in which I do not visually appear at all.'

'How would you do that, Kenneth?'

'I now know and have the trust of several influential Irish patriots. I would like to meet a number of survivors of the Easter Rebellion and of the Anglo-Irish War, in Dublin, and I would like to film them, interspersed with historically correct English quotations about Ireland.'

Obviously that statement hadn't come off the top of my head in that Soho office; I had been musing about it for some time, while wondering how I could try again to inform the British people about our depredations in Ireland and thereby try to persuade them to tell the British Government to change its policy towards my Irish cousins. And that is the spirit of democracy, isn't it? Aled Vaughan more or less said yes there and then.

I had met a young Irish American from Chicago named Timothy O'Grady and he had been most supportive over my Irish sentiments; he was a committed Republican and he was also proving to be a valued friend. I was instrumental in bringing him in to our company, Tempest Productions. Now I took him with me to Ireland to make our arrangements for this second Irish film.

The format quickly fell into its simple pattern. We made arrangements with a fine group of elderly Irish people who had all been involved in the famous rising of 1916 and in the Anglo-Irish War which followed. There was Maira Comerford, who had been secretary to de Valera and who remained an unshiftable Republican rallying point till her death. There was cheerful Doctor Brighid Thornton, who had keenly carried a large hand-gun in her apron pocket in 1916; Martin Walton, now the biggest music publisher in Ireland, but who then, in those shadowed Celtic days, had personally shot – at very close range – a British secret agent; Sean Kavanagh, my friend from the Michael Collins film days; General Joseph Sweeney, who had actually fought in the Dublin Post Office; David Neligan, a double secret agent, whose machinations would have shocked James Bond; John O'Sullivan, another of Michael Collins' men and therefore a Freestater in the Civil War as against Eamon de Valera's Republicans; Sean Huston, a typical Dubliner, who had changed sides in the Irish Civil War and so was still in fear of his life; and last, but never least, Commandant General Thomas Barry, who had virtually run County Cork for the Republicans.

The point that I intended to make in the film was to present these pillars of contemporary respectability and responsibility to the laws and customs of their Irish State, but who had all been what some people please to call terrorists in their youth. But, at the time of filming, they would happily adorn any quiet tea party. Their behaviour would be gentle and exemplary; their great National work was well nigh over. The only fly that remained in their ointment was the north-east of their country: the six British occupied counties of Ulster. And over that – this last remaining British tragedy inflicted on their island – they were offering nothing but generosity and welcoming friendship to those Protestant Unionists. The consensus was: 'How valuable the hard-working Protestants of the Six Counties would be in a United Ireland.' They all ardently prayed for that; it didn't happen during their time on earth because today they are all dead.

I was hurrying to finish our filming of Curious Journey – as I called the film – in Ireland, because for all of this while, the burdensome legal process between myself and Sir Lew Grade's ATV had been trundling on, organized for me by my legal advisers: Mr Thomas Crawley and Mr Eric Hillier in London. And the time had virtually arrived for me to enter a British Court of Law to personally prosecute my sometime boss, Sir Lew Grade, and the Independent Broadcasting Authority, presumably, since they had recently and belatedly publicly confessed their responsibility. My feelings at that time were in a right pickle. I was deeply involved in this second Irish film. My emotions were with my Irish friends. I had given no thought to the ritual or process of law; however, I knew that my legal advisers would guide me on how to behave in court. I was simply fatalistic about the whole thing. I knew what I had done and why I had done it; I believed that the IBA had behaved illegally and certainly unethically in asking Lew Grade not to offer *Hang Up Your Brightest Colours* to them and also, because of the suppression, I was losing 'an opportunity for professional advancement', and where was my financial share of the overseas sales of the film? Yes, I knew what I wanted to say; I knew how to talk, and I would say it.

And then, on the very verge of the precipice, which I was determined to try to jump over, I received a telephone call from Mr Crawley. He has a laconic English voice, which in times of emergency is just as well: 'Kenneth; some good news: Grade has broken. He wants to settle out of court. He has offered to pay all costs and expenses and to pay you £5,000 in compensation. Of course, I immediately informed his representative that this offer to you was derisory.' I cut in: 'My dear Tom, before you talk any more about derision, I have to inform you that the pain in my stomach has suddenly ceased.'

But Mr Crawley was the professional in charge and he pressed Sir Lew's people and I received considerably more money. However, my then partner, David Swift, suggested that I put half of it into Tempest Film Productions and this I did; so I didn't emerge a rich man, but certainly a relieved one.

Yes, ATV and the IBA had kept the details of their behaviour out of the Law Courts and out of the newspapers. But I felt that enough was enough. I could not see any way how, at that time, the film could be shown. So let's call it a day. It was widely known that the film had been suppressed and *that* publicity in itself was a service to Ireland. I hope that Bobby Sands and his Band of Brothers knew about it because my poor spirit yearns to touch their noble courage. I know that this act on the part of the British Establishment has helped, a little, to stiffen Irish Republican resistance to the British on their island, and I am very proud of that fact. An incidental happy ending of the story is that I bought a new home in Islington in London. And part of the cost came from my compensation for loss of overseas sales; so, in due course I gave the house a name. Above the front door it is painted: 'Michael Collins House'. Isn't it at least quaint: 'The Big Fellow' as the

Irish have ever called him, chipped in a fair contribution for my home? We Celts are given to whimsy and quite often, as I approach that front door, particularly after I have been away in foreign parts for long periods, I *do* murmur: 'Thank you, Michael.' Oh! the Irish have a tremendous sense of humour!

But what of *Curious Journey*? This title carried for me a private hidden meaning. For me the film was the curious journey of a Welsh Protestant Brit, to visit his Irish Catholic Republican brothers and sisters, in total support and sympathy. Well, the film had, so I was told, been sucked into the Welsh cutting rooms of HTV in Cardiff. It was not under my control and I got on with other work. But once again, as with the Michael Collins film, an inordinate and inexplicable silence extended itself. I never *want* to interfere. Just a simple: 'Please God, let it all be reasonably well and good.' And in this case a misty hope that HTV would send for me soon to speak the voice overs. However, no call came. And so I telephoned Aled Vaughan and he told me that there had 'been problems, but all would be sorted out'. Yes, after my experience in the suppression of the Michael Collins film I was feeling uneasy, but refrained from pushing it. Women are not the only humans with intuition. And then the plot thickened; Aled visited me again and said very little except: 'They [at HTV] have failed to put the film together so that it makes any sense. If I have everything sent up to London, will you edit it?'

'Yes!' I replied with alacrity. I was surprised that I was not being asked to edit the film in Cardiff, but again I did not want to probe in case I unearthed a difficulty or an unpleasantness that I didn't need to know about.

Yes, the film that arrived was incomprehensible, but I could see no difficulty and with the help of my friend and distinguished film editor, Mr Max Benedict, we efficiently put it together and I was very pleased with the result. Aled Vaughan saw it and was impressed and *Curious Journey* was shipped back to Cardiff.

What a mystery! Another long silence and then an invitation to meet the Managing Director of HTV in his London Office in Baker Street! Not too far from Lord (was he a peer of the realm by this time?) Grade's office either. Was this to be a recurring nightmare? Was I once again to be loved for my balls? But to tell you the truth, I rather enjoy these adventures. For me, it is as if I have been invited for a pow-wow in Geronimo's wigwam.

The Managing Director, after the social niceties were over, asked me if I would like to own *Curious Journey* entirely myself; 'for a small token payment'? I sat there looking at the businessman while the unbelievable offer flashed through my mind. No, they weren't going to televise it to the nation!

'Small token payment?'

I asked, 'Do you mean like a peppercorn?'

'For one penny (or was it a shilling?) Mr Griffith, you can own *Curious Journey* outright; on condition (I listened very carefully) our logo and our name, HTV, is removed completely from the film.'

I looked at David Swift and he said: 'May we give you our answer tomorrow?'

'Certainly,' said the Managing Director and David and I left Baker Street with our eyes dazzled as we wondered if there was any hidden catch. After all, the film had cost many thousands of pounds to make . . . A penny!

Well, there was a fundamental catch, of course. If HTV would not offer *Curious Journey* to the Independent Broadcasting Authority for transmission, for whatever reason, then it was highly unlikely that any of the other commercial television companies would. What was the reason for our Mysterious British Centre shuffling an Irish theme away this time? And how was it done? That is the question that we should all ask and understand. I knew that questions by me to HTV would be pointless. I could have asked good Aled Vaughan, but in doing so I might have placed him in a cruel position and that I did not wish to do. Perhaps, indeed probably, he had been asked to keep silent on the matter and I knew him well enough to know that he would not relish saying 'No comment' to me. Perhaps, and again probably, he had got himself into enough trouble by allowing me to make the film.

TWENTY-SIX

About this time of my travail through this vale of tears – together with a few laughs – I received messages from the great American Broadcasting Corporation in New York. First it was from my chum Joseph De Cola, who was a producer for that company, and then from high up; from Av Westin, the man who had viewed the Michael Collins film during my pirate expedition to the then near-useless United Nations and then on to Washington. Mr Westin and his colleagues wanted to know if I would make a film for them, in my style of course, about the American War of Independence from Britain. The bicentenary year (1976) was imminent and this film was to be ABC's serious contribution to the celebrations. I thought briefly about the offer and replied that if I would be allowed to write and make a film about what had *caused* the American War of Independence, I would be happy to do it. And the deal was concluded by David Swift. I was to be paid more money than I had ever earned before, but again, a large proportion of it was given to Tempest Film Productions, so again I escaped any measure of financial security. But what of it? I felt in those younger days that all was challenge and adventure and I was growing up a bit. I was beginning to learn some of the facts of this life. Particularly important was this constant need to reconcile the idealism that was wafted by philosophic dreaming to the reality of our human condition.

What could have been the thinking of those giants of commercial television in the United States of America that they had asked *me*, a Brit, to speak about their world-shattering national birth on its two hundredth anniversary? They had seen my work and they had recognized that it was unique and that it had an essential veracity that a vast, expensive conventional dramatization could not have. And did they also note that the Michael Collins film *Hang Up Your Brightest Colours* was formidably critical of Britain? Did they presume that I was congenitally anti-British? And therefore would be unshiftably on the side of the thirteen American Colonies and rigidly against Britain? If those thoughts were mooted just off Broadway, the executives were making a miscalculation. I knew from my general knowledge of American history what aspect of the Revolution most interested me and I began to dig into my research by scouring the bookshops of London and New York.

I was given an American director and so the seeds of shortfall for the film – in my opinion – were sown from the outset. The director's name was William Peters and I remember that on his desk was an upright container which held an extraordinary number of *always* finely sharpened pencils.

I shared the apartment of my friend Joseph De Cola and it was a happy time. Jo is a real New Yorker and he has a firm place in that deadly jungle of American commercial television. What is impressive about such men is that they retain – or rather can have – an unshiftable social and ethical integrity; I mean in that environment where the dollar would appear to be the only true God. And a terrifying God at that! Morley Safer also belonged to Joseph De Cola's breed. Jo and I lived on One Hundred and First Street, off Broadway, and our two separate routines ran along easily. Jo, because of his varied duties, followed a more rigid professional pattern than myself. I was more of a roamer studying and writing. As Jo speedily prepared his breakfast I would lounge in the big kitchen and chat away on various chosen subjects. Jo tended to be monosyllabic at that hour of the morning. One breakfast time I tried to provoke him into a discussion, by giving a dissertation on President Richard Nixon (who had just been hammered from grace).

'What has Mr Nixon done that other American Presidents haven't done?' I demanded.

From Jo (while cooking): 'Ah ha.'

'Have they not all used bugging devices?'

'Um.'

'The only thing that was different about Nixon was that his political operation was exposed.'

'Ha ha!'

Jo is a liberal spirit; surely I could provoke him into some sort of argument!

'What shocks me, Jo, is all of this self-righteousness on the part of Americans. It seems to me that America has sacrificed Nixon, but as far as I can see no American has the slightest intention of changing his or her own ways. Generally they will go on behaving exactly as they did before – just like Richard Nixon.'

'Um. Well, see you in the office, Ken,' and off he went; across the hall, into his bedroom, back to the hall and the front door slammed.

I leisurely finished my breakfast, musing over the self-control and philosophic patience of Joseph De Cola, and then I made my way out of the kitchen, across a reception room, into the hall and there I momentarily froze; out of the corner of my right eye I saw a man in a dark suit (such attire was unknown to Jo), leaning against the inside of the closed front door. I turned and it was Richard Nixon smiling at me and he was holding out a hand of greeting! As I took a step or so closer through the pale gloom I realized that it was a life-sized photograph and that along the bottom there was a hand-written inscription: 'To my valued friend, Joseph De Cola – Richard Nixon.'

I am going to digress. Soon after my films began to appear on British television, with credits such as 'Written and presented by Kenneth Griffith', I began to get letters from British publishers, inviting me to write a book. I usually replied that I was not equipped to write one; what I really meant was, that with my varied domestic responsibilities, I could not afford the time that would have to be spent writing a book. I had heard how little money the average writer was guaranteed for his labours. And then a young emissary, Anthony Whittome, from the publishing house of Hutchinson came to see me. Anthony Whittome is

everything a top-class literary editor should be. In my opinion it
is a singularly difficult job to do well. It is a delicate relationship
between the writer – who is often giving his creative blood – and
the representative of the publishers. A good literary editor must
be on the side of the writer, but at the same time, obviously, he
or she must also be answerable to the publisher.

Anthony Whittome and I immediately became friends and
we will always remain so. I will enlarge on this because
thereby I can convey much about the struggles of writing a
book as well as one can. When Anthony first approached me
it was clear that he hoped and cared very much that I would
have a go. I explained to him that though I had researched and
written the films which had impressed him, their *impact* was
achieved by how I *spoke* the words that I had written. I have
no false modesty whatsoever; I had for a long time believed
that what I wrote for myself was, generally, superior to the
scripts that I had received in the past, even from some distinguished writers. But this work of mine was born out of my
knowledge of how I could most effectively communicate
exactly what I wanted to say. The additional elaboration that
a book would entail – I had no vision of that being within my
ability. Anthony was *certain* that I could do it and he *cared*
that I should try. Here again was another vitally important
catalyst in my life who was telling me what I *could* do. First
there was Evelyn Ward at Tenby Grammar School telling me
that I was something special as an actor and very nearly pushing me physically onto a stage. Then Huw Wheldon telling me
that I could make films about my ideas and feelings and again
pushing me into it. And Roy Boulting. And now here was the
gentle young man assuring me that I could be an author.

Then I explained to him my financial problem in the ratio
of *having* to earn so much in such a period.

'Can I tell you how much money we could advance to you
for a book?'

I waited dismally and was immediately astonished at the
generosity of the offer.

'How many words?' I asked and I am still astonished at my
untutored shrewdness.

'Oh, about eighty or ninety thousand . . .'

'That's not much,' I thought to myself. Now, with more hard experience, I know that words are not quarried that easily.

'All right,' I said, 'I'll have a go.'

'Good,' said Anthony. 'What will you do?'

'The Siege and Relief of Ladysmith,' said I, like a card-sharper.

'Good,' repeated Anthony; and that is what I did. I titled it *Thank God We Kept the Flag Flying: The Siege and Relief of Ladysmith*. Of course I knew the saga backwards; I had trodden the ghost-ridden ground; I had made the film and my library, which was all around us, contained every published work on the subject and much that was not published.

I wrote the book in Margret Kopala's sometime spinster pad in the Portobello Road while I was acting my head off at the same time in this or that piece of television drama. On one day I scribbled some four and a half thousand words and then fell off the chair in exhaustion! Maggie calculated that I wrote the history book in about three months, if one excluded my other work.

What has all of this got to do with Joseph De Cola's apartment? Just at that very time the book was published in Britain and it received disturbingly good reviews. One of them stated that I was 'a revisionist'. I hastened to my *Oxford Dictionary* to discover what the word meant. 'Oh! Yes, I *am* a revisionist all right! Ask the IBA and company.' Another comment was that I was 'one of the New British Historians' and the short-list given included Miss Jan Morris, a historian whom I admire very much. My ego was polished, but I confessed to a couple of friends that to link me with Miss Morris in talent as a writer of history books was ridiculous; I couldn't be *that* good. And then a bundle of letters arrived from London, forwarded to Jo's apartment and halfway through reading them: 'Dear Mr Griffith . . .' it was a letter of admiration for my book, and it was signed 'Jan Morris (Miss)'. I was deeply moved.

Now, on the evening of the arrival of that letter I was due

to have supper with a lady (she won't approve of that word!) film editor, who was something of a New York feminist. One of the virtues of this particular female persuasion is punctuality. Well, while I dolled myself up (roles can often be reversed in this modern situation) she preached her creed and while doing so she coincidentally criticized my cherished Miss Jan Morris: 'That . . . has done our movement endless harm; declaring that she enjoyed men opening doors for her and offering chairs to her . . .' And much else that was more unkind and cruel was said.

I didn't give a hint that I was angry. I simply excused myself and going to my bedroom I then returned and placed Jan Morris's generous letter under her nose. I took a leaf out of Michael Collins' record and I never saw the lady film editor again. Synchronicity is the word, I believe; it happens to me endlessly.

What else about my life on One Hundred and First Street with Jo? Well, just where I got off my bus from downtown work was a 'Cakemaster' shop. These establishments put every scrap of their all-American creativity into the most outrageous cake concoctions: chocolate, vanilla, jam, cream; you name it and there it is, in super-abundance. Cakemasters are my immature idea of Paradise. *And* directly opposite, on the other side of the road, was a pornographic-movie house, to which I was also deeply addicted. That is life for you; or an aspect of it. I could have got off that bus, evening after evening, like an innocent abroad, if those two establishments hadn't been planted there, long before I arrived from the old world. And I fell from potential innocence evening after evening. And I had one ever-lurking obsession: that one day I would go into the Cakemasters and buy my favourite enormous chocolate fantasy and then cross the road and eat it in the pornographic-movie house. Of course, I discussed this dual temptation that I daily suffered with my friend Jo, but there was little that he could do to strengthen my willpower. No, I never ate the chocolate cake while gazing up at the more than silver screen. Jo came over from New York recently and visited me: 'I've got some bad news for you, Ken.'

'What?'

'They've *both* gone: Cakemasters and the blue-movie house.'

'Both!' And I sat down.

I was asked by ABC most courteously, what I would feel if the telling of the American Revolutionary story was shared between myself and the outstanding American actor, Mr Lee J. Cobb? I would, as arranged, write it all and I would tell the British side of things while Mr Cobb would speak for America. It was a novel idea and why not? The famous actor was sent my script; he agreed and was contracted.

Mr William Peters was pleased with the script. 'I think we've got it beat!' were his words. To tell you the truth, I was relieved to hear it. I was well aware that I had not written the conventional American fairy-tale about little George Washington owning up about his stupid action in cutting down that cherry tree. I explained the deep *cause* of the American Revolution as a pressing lust of New England businessmen for increased profits (and what's changed; and what's wrong with it anyway?); indeed of any limitations being placed upon the colonialist's inexorable human push westward into Indian Country; and finally some pretty formidable envious bitterness against well-nigh everybody – but against England in particular – up in old Boston, Massachusetts. Of course there was also the very relevant: 'No taxation, without representation!' and 'Give me liberty or give me death!' – which I remember taking with a tiny pinch of salt. But praise be! William Peters was not arguing.

I recall that the above happy consummation was on a Friday evening and Mr Peters departed for his fine Long Island home. Jauntily I rejoined him in that same office on the Monday morning and he was already behind his desk, glumly shaking his head, with my script before him: 'I don't know what we're going to do about this, Kenneth—'

'About what?'

'Your script; it just won't do—'

To cut a long row very short, I recall shouting and jumping up and down in front of him, while he, infuriatingly, lay back in his adjustable chair with his hands behind his head and his rather long legs stretched out over his office desk. Indeed the contemporary cliché 'laid back' could have been invented in that office on that morning. I actually heard him say: 'I'll consult with—' and named some academic acquaintance of his.

'We'll try and put it right.'

I telephoned David Swift in London and warned him about the red light, that was suddenly blinking very fast in America.

'Come home,' said David.

'I need the bloody dollars,' (how often has that been heard?) I replied.

The script was 'put right' by William Peters and his academic chum. I walked straight to the Boss's office.

'Sit down, Kenneth,' said Av Westin. 'Got a problem?'

'Mr Westin,' I said, 'my script has been changed and in my opinion it is now as dead as the dodo.'

Av looked at me and without hesitation asked a series of remarkably relevant questions: 'Too many new historical characters introduced?'

'Yes.'

'Conventional opinions introduced?'

'Yes.'

'Toning down on provocation? Playing safe?'

'Yes.'

Mr Westin, with his easy manner, born out of endless bitter experiences, looked lightly at me. You can believe me, I was Celtic tense.

'Mr Westin, I'm here in your office for only *one* reason. I have enough experience to know that you would have an awkward time persuading Mr Peters that I am right and that he is wrong. I don't know what happened to change his mind over that bloody weekend on Long Island or elsewhere. All I am here to do, is to put it on the record that no one in this organization must ever ask the question: "Why didn't Griffith do for *us* what he has often done for his own British?" Mr Peters, with these boring adjustments, additions, and other amendments, has killed that hope dead.'

I think that Av said something like: 'I'll look into it.'

But I never heard another word.

Our American film crew repaired to the intriguing city of Boston, where we were to start our work. An eve-of-filming meeting was held in Mr Peters' hotel room and it was there that I met my fellow Thespian, Mr Lee J. Cobb for the first time. William Peters did most of the talking; I, uncharacteristicly, retained a strained but philosophical silence; I had accepted the fact that our film was doomed to be second rate and Mr Cobb was silently aloof. When the organizational chat was finished, Mr Cobb spoke: 'Mr Griffith, will you have some supper with me?'

'Yes, sir!', I replied, anxious to leave the meeting room.

We were still moving down the hotel corridor when Mr Cobb boomed: 'What happened to your script, Mr Griffith!?'

And I told him the whole tale.

'Exactly what I suspected, Mr Griffith. Pity. Damn good script it was.'

But we both ploughed on with our jobs, doing our respective best.

I remember it – in spite of the doomed film – as a happy time. Massachusetts is beautiful and historically on fire. I had never seen the Green at Lexington before and many other world-changing sites. I still dream of the potato clam chowder at the Oyster House in Boston (I pray that it hasn't gone, like the Cakemasters and the blue-movie house on One Hundred and First and Broadway) And Lee and I were friends. I remember walking through the streets of Boston with him and asking him what the 'J' in Lee J. Cobb stood for.

'I had a premonition you were going to ask me that. My real name is Lee Jacob; I'm Jewish. When I first went to Hollywood I was advised to Anglicize it.'

I called my script, with a touch of irony, *Give Me Liberty*, but Mr Peters and company changed that to: *Suddenly an Eagle*, which must give you some idea of the chasm that lay between us. I had no influence over the film whatsoever, so it was entered for the 'prestigious' Peabody Award (more upmarket, as they said over there, than the Emmy Award); a vulgar yen for success, which I would have vetoed if I could have. Eventually I received a telegram from the ABC in America informing me that *Suddenly an Eagle* had won the Peabody Award as being the best documentary during Bicentenary Year. I, no doubt ungraciously, replied that if *Suddenly an Eagle* had won the Peabody Award it didn't say much for the Peabody Award.

When I got back to Britain, an unexpected invitation cropped up; I was asked by the BBC if I would quickly make a film for *them* about the American War of Independence.

'Yes,' I replied, feeling that I could redeem my sense of aesthetics by using my original script. 'And here is the script!'

But my bicentenary year was fatalistically marked; we were under-financed for the wide-ranging project and, again, none of my old know-how team were present. It was a curious experience retreading the same ground in Massachusetts, Virginia and Philadelphia. But it was not a happy time and in my double failure to live up to my creative expectations, I know that I was frustrated and behaved badly. I can cope with most setbacks, except if my work is falling short of what I think that it should be.

The BBC version went out under the original title: *Give Me Liberty* – or did it? I think it did . . .

TWENTY-SEVEN

When I returned to Britain my friend and colleague at the British Broadcasting Corporation in Cardiff, Mr John Hefin, invited me to Wales. And in his encouragement he was firmly backed by the then Managing Director, Mr Geraint Stanley Jones. They jointly asked me if I would like to make my historical documentary films for them in Cardiff. Of course, as with all of Wales' major programmes, they would be networked throughout Britain.

We discussed the idea over a supper in Cardiff. I think that initially I was wary. I was uneasy at the potential loss of my well-tried colleagues and I was a little worried that I might be limited to Welsh subjects. But Geraint and John wanted our relationship to happen and readily agreed that Michel Pearce could direct our productions if he wanted to. And they both listened sympathetically to my argument that the Welsh element in whatever we might do must be our Welsh *spirit* and, not necessarily, a Welsh story. Looking back now, years later, I can recognize that I was slow in digesting the dimension of what was being offered to me: I was being invited back home and, in general, it was the most human, decent atmosphere that I had ever encountered in the world of television, apart from my relationship with Huw Wheldon. In actual fact, though I have been slow to recognize it, I was on the verge of the best creative period of my life.

It was I who suggested a Welsh subject for us to kick off with (of course it was understood that the ball would be oval shaped). I reminded my colleagues that 'next year, 1979, will be the centenary of the British–Zulu War, when Welshmen (24th Regiment; the South Wales Borderers) suffered shockingly and then redeemed themselves militarily and without parallel in the annals of British imperial history at Rorke's Drift, in Zululand. It certainly shouldn't, however, be a film in praise of war or even in praise of winning more Victoria Crosses than have ever been won, in a single action, before or since.' And the film was on. John Hefin would produce; Russ Walker, our sensitive cameraman; and Mr Edward Doull would be in charge of sound. And then there was Michel Pearce and myself.

As always, I had already cast around in my head for the broadest issues involved in that disgusting war. I can truthfully state that the specific stories that I tell are rather like historical objects that are thrown into the middle of a still lake and the concentric circles emanating widely across the water are the most important matters. Encompassing the centre of this Zulu War story is the arrogant, shallow-rooted cynicism of Disraeli's Toryism, in conflict with the unearthly, though often practical, idealism of Gladstone and his Liberal banner. (Again I must ask how our contemporary Liberals could be so unutterably stupid as to throw away that simple noble flag?) And our war story of 1879 – another of the great rings on the water – was an examination of two of the vastest and most divergent cultures in this world: the European (at its nearly worst) and the Black African (at its nearly best). Not theory, like I scribble here, but this is what was actually *said* and *done* on this piece of grand English ground or on this piece of sun-baked land in Southern Africa. Seen through my eyes of course – it must be confessed. But the last time I met with the present paramount Chief of the Zulus, Mangosuthu Buthelezi, about six months ago, he did me the honour of embracing me and saying: 'You have a great empathy for our people.' So my view of things can't be far off the mark or jaundiced.

We filmed an architectural definition of British imperialism in the ancient magnificence of the Guildhall in the City of London. I have often filmed there and I have always been received with the greatest kindness and courtesy. How could I dislike England when, in the very heart of that country, they are at *pains* to help and make us feel at home? First, I contact Mr John Lucioni, who is a sort of major-domo, and with a name like Lucioni, I must emphasize that England has never produced finer stock. He speeds through his diary: 'Well, Mr Griffith, you can't come on the fifteenth because the Queen is here . . . on the eighteenth the King of —— How about the twentieth and twenty-first?'

I emphasize this relationship with the Guildhall of London because my film efforts would be so much the poorer if that bulwark of Britain hadn't helped me so unstintingly. Occasionally, those conservatively suited Lords of the City will stroll into our working area, smiling affably: 'May I ask what you're up to, sir?'

'A film about Robert Clive [or Thomas Paine or Jawaharlal Nehru, etc.] sir.'

'How very interesting. How's it going?'

'Fine, sir.'

'Good. Good!' as he strolls away.

Again I have experienced that mystic impression that more Roman Patricians remained in England than we appreciate. These gentlemen don't seem particularly concerned whether my point of view coincides with their own; they are a bit above that sort of thing. After all, we fortunately live in a democracy, don't we? Generally, I have grown to like British gentlemen over the years.

And suddenly, from the massive stone memorabilia in London, we are startled by the colours and hot, hot sun of Natal in Africa. The words of Disraeli are arrogantly repeated beneath a Zulu-held sunshade and in reply are the firm but friendly words of the old Zulu King, Cetewayo: great feathers, leopard skin, battle axe and shield.

As I approached Africa on that occasion, I mused about my normal practice to speak for *all* of the historical characters in my various stories. But now, high in the air, the 'still small' adviser whispered: 'Don't speak for the Black Africans – the Zulus.' Then who better than Buthelezi, with his world renown as a statesmanlike spokesman for the Zulu nation? And he agreed to speak the words that his ancestor had spoken in the year 1879. And could he nominate other Zulus to speak for the other historical Zulu statements?

'My cabinet will!'

More than even Mrs Thatcher might dare to say!

An appointment for us to film the patrician Zulus a week hence was arranged. We were to meet in the tribal capital of Ulundi.

As our two-car cavalcade motored through Zululand on that given day, I addressed our film unit – which included one lady, Ms Beth Price, who repeated several times as she gazed apprehensively at Africa: 'Oh! I much prefer Cardiff!' (This, incidentally, is the authentic voice of Wales at its strongest).

'Look, lads,' I warned, 'we have got to face the possibility that Chief Minister Buthelezi and his colleagues will not be ready for us.' Of course a lost day's filming on such a production as ours would be a serious matter. 'But let's be philosophical; we are doing our best and what an interesting day it will be for us, whatever happens.' But how I had underrated our Zulu friends. By the time that we turned up – early – for our appointment, the chosen members of the Zulu Cabinet were already there, waiting, with the typewritten words that they had been asked to learn and speak, bound into covers. They were all immaculately dressed in European clothes and they also had with them an extra man who turned out to be their drama adviser. There in Ulundi, surrounded by pulsating Africa, we Brits were beginning to look relatively shabby. And then a large black shiny chauffeur-driven Mercedes-Benz appeared and out stepped Buthelezi himself, dressed in a finely cut safari suit and with a silk neck scarf.

Having paid our respects, I asked the Chief if he had been able to learn by heart the historical words of his ancestor, King Cetewayo.

'I have done my best, Mr Griffith.'

Chief Buthelezi was so friendly that I tentatively asked him: 'Would it have been correct, sir, for me to have asked you to wear traditional costume?'

'Perfectly correct, Mr Griffith. Would you like us all to do that?'

'Yes please, sir.'

Chief Buthelezi spoke to his Cabinet colleagues in the Zulu

language and then to me: 'It will take us about half an hour, Mr Griffith.'

And they all left us – we musing on many things. In 1879 their forefathers had killed many of our Welsh forefathers and we had killed many of theirs, right where we now stood in Zululand.

After something over half an hour the big shiny car reappeared and out stepped the Chief Minister in all of his terrifying magnificence – tempered though by horn-rimmed spectacles and socks. My confidence grew and asked: 'Sir, would it be possible to film these pieces against a bundu (wild bushland) background?'

'Why not, Mr Griffith? There it is.' And he gestured with a knobkerry (battle club) down the short road where the Zululand bushes grew.

Chief Buthelezi sat on a low Zulu stool, surrounded by his colleagues similarly attired in their traditional war gear.

'Sir,' I said, 'do you know that I have been a professional actor for most of my life?'

'Yes; I understand so, Mr Griffith.'

'Then, sir, would it be of any help to you if I were to read the words that you have to speak?'

'Indeed it would help me, Mr Griffith.'

And so I quietly and firmly spoke King Cetewayo's famous warning of 1879 to the threatening British authorities at Pietermaritzburg in Natal culminating in: 'Go and tell the white man that he is ruler *there* and that I am ruler *here*!'

Buthelezi said: 'And again please.'

'And again please.'

About six times I repeated the eve-of-war statement. Again, it was for me, one of those many astounding events in my life that makes me wonder by what mysterious tricks of fate and complicated permutations had brought me there. Chief Buthelezi said: 'I think that I am ready now.'

I quickly and politely warned him to remove his socks and glasses; Michel Pearce told Russ Walker to roll the camera and we learnt that Buthelezi was word perfect and so were all of the other Zulu 'actors'.

All of this time in the middle background, the white South African official, who performed the duty of Private Secretary to Chief Minister Buthelezi of Kwa Zulu, hovered. I did not know exactly what his function was or whether he was also a liaison with the South African Government; but to me he was a significant symbol as we repeated these old challenges to White authority. I weighed up in my mind whether I dared be a bit cheeky and deciding that I would, I leaned down close to Buthelezi's right ear and murmured: 'Of course, sir, these words of demarcation that King Cetewayo spoke one hundred years ago are not irrelevant to the situation today.' And I flicked an eye towards the White official still pacing up and down.

Buthelezi turned and looked very directly into my eyes: 'Mr Griffith! *Why* do you think that I am doing this?'

After the Zulu victory over – largely – the South Wales Borderers at the Battle of Isandlwana, the Zulus had sung a hymn of military praise to their king, Cetewayo. The words are extant and one of the Warrior Cabinet Members had undertaken to sing it for our film. Before commencing he explained to me that Zulus, unlike Europeans, do not all repeat the same tune; each singer improvises according to his own spontaneous inspiration. And then he sang for us in his magnificent voice, about the White soldiers invading Zululand and of their crushing defeat, ending with: 'When will they dare to come again?' Well, we British had dared, with our heavy field guns and our massed fire power . . .

Before leaving Britain we had filmed at the old military headquarters of the South Wales Borderers, which regiment is now incorporated into the Royal Regiment of Wales. And as I prepared to tell of the Welsh departure for Zululand, soldiers were loading army trucks in the background. I enquired, and was told that they were bound for north-eastern Ireland. A hundred years earlier the regiment had been ordered to fight a dishonourable war and now they were embarking on something similar. What makes me angry is that these soldiers of the past and now of the present are so ill-informed about *why* they have to kill Zulus or Irishmen. And these days the ethics and morality are blinded by contradictory legal and political mud. Ignorance of the moral law is no excuse. At Nuremberg we anxiously executed German soldiers because they had carried out the orders of their political masters. And yet, within my own close experience, two films which fairly and truthfully put the Irish tragedy before the British people were suppressed because, as William Deedes eloquently put it: 'If wives, mothers and sweethearts saw your film, they might not want their husbands, sons or boyfriends to go there.' I presume that if I had been able to inform my compatriots of the South Wales Borderers in 1878 of the perfidious mentality of Benjamin Disraeli and his morally unacceptable Tory face, I'd have been suppressed into the Tower of London. And how are our soldiers to judge the morality of their shootings if the Government disallow those British soldiers or their mums from hearing what the Irish Republicans have to say on television – even if they are elected Members of the British Parliament? We British would have to go back a long way (in peace time) to find our country so undermined by the totalitarian mentality, as under Margaret Thatcher's régime. Anyway, the modern soldiers of the Royal Regiment of Wales were busily loading in the background of our film, without any comment from me. But I was glad that they were there for any perceptive viewer to put two and two together.

While working on the horrifying battlefield of Isandlwana, where almost the whole British Force was annihilated, I was approached by a young Zulu boy who was wearing a long raggedy coat. My first thought was 'the Artful Dodger'; and indeed this young man had an old head on his small shoulders. In good English he asked me: 'Are you interested in the battle that was fought here in 1879?'

'Yes,' I replied. 'Do you see that group of people down there? I belong to them. We are making a film about the British Zulu War.' And the two of us had a serious conversation about the one-hundred-year-old conflict. I was astonished at the depth of the young boy's knowledge and that he was communicating his opinions in a foreign language – English.

'Do you know why,' he asked, 'the Basuto People [another

famous tribe who lived in Basutoland – today's Lesotho]
fought for the British against us Zulus?'

Well, that is a very complex matter; historically complicated between Black and Black and Black and White. But I
gave my opinion and the young Zulu said: 'Yes, that is what I
have thought.'

'My name is Kenneth Griffith; what is yours?'

'My name is Chelmsford Ntanzi,' and we shook hands.

'Chelmsford!' I said. 'That was the name of the British
General commanding our army here!'

'That is why my father gave me that name.'

I gazed at the Zulu boy; around us was the great empty valley which those hundred years ago had soaked up so much
Zulu and British blood.

'That's a jolly impressive name you've got: Chelmsford
Ntanzi.'

At the end of our hillside meeting I said: 'Tomorrow I hope
to meet your Paramount Chief, Mangosuthu Buthelezi. Please,
Chelmsford, write down your name and postal address' and
this he did; it was a Mission School.

'Now I can't *promise* anything, but if I have the opportunity, I will tell the Chief about you. I suspect that he will be
interested.' And as I said farewell to Mangosuthu Buthelezi,
after he had finished his filming stint, and we were walking
together towards his car, I told him about this encounter. The
Chief Minister stopped and listened intently and when I had
finished, said: 'And now, Mr Griffith, I presume that you are
going to give me Chelmsford Ntanzi's address?'

'Yes sir.'

Indeed it was already between finger and thumb.

'Thank you Mr Griffith. I shall communicate with his
school and ask for a report about him.'

And Chelmsford was given a job on that hypnotic battlefield and with a salary. Who arranged it, I can only guess.

Our film was made with a relatively small budget. The
Twenty-Fourth Regiment was represented by a single bell tent
with a little Welsh flag drooping from the top of it. But what
it lacked in finance, it made up for in human talent and sheer

bloody endeavour; much credit must go to Michel Pearce who was using a sow's ear to produce a truly outstanding silk purse. Well, there was no money for an Elimak (the carriage that moves on rails and carries the camera for tracking shots – and can make a considerable difference to the polish of our films) and I am not sure that we possessed an expensive lens that we usually like to have.

But we did have our share of luck. We were travelling over extremely rough Zululand country to an historical site called, to this day, 'Fugitive's Drift'. When the British Line at the battle of Isandlwana broke and the Zulu warriors literally began to cut up the British soldiers; a few of them managed to escape in the direction of the Buffalo River. Two of them, Lieutenants Coghill and Melville had been ordered to get away and save that near religious symbol of a British Regiment, the Queen's Colour – which is a flag. They reached the river, closely pursued by blood-thirsty Zulu warriors, but in mid-current, the precious emblem was swept away. Well, it didn't make much difference; the two officers were slaughtered high up on the far bank and there, today, stands a lonely stone cross, commemorating their fearful end. All around is naked mamba-ridden Africa. A couple of weeks later the British were able to send out a patrol to search for the bodies, but, perhaps, more importantly, the Queen's Colour. They found it further down the Buffalo River and today you can view its disintegrating remains hanging from a wall of Brecon Cathedral.

Along that road from the Natal side of the Buffalo River we bumped into a fierce African heat while being guided by our 'White Zulu', Mr George Bunting. George had been born and raised in Zululand and therefore was entitled to that appellation. Mr Bunting would chat away endlessly to the Zulus, with me interposing regularly: 'What are you talking about, George?'

As we ground along we met a White man and George demanded that we stopped: 'A friend of mine! Haven't seen him for a long time!'

Of course, I clambered out too and was introduced; the man was an Afrikaner and I stood there as the two men spoke in the Boer language. Well it was interesting but bloody hot and time was precious and my BBC colleagues who had remained in the cars were clearly wilting. I opened my mouth to tell Mr Bunting that we must move on when I clearly heard in the babble of Afrikaans, the farmer say: 'Queen's Colour'.

'What was that about the Queen's Colour?' I asked quickly.

'Oh,' said George, 'a few weeks ago a big film company came here to photograph the loss of the Queen's Colour in the Buffalo River. They had a specially made copy of the flag with them and when the two actors jumped into the river on their horses, *they* lost *their* Queen's Colour in the Buffalo current, just like Coghill and Melville did a hundred years ago.'

'Well?' said I.

'Well,' explained George, 'our friend here and his son, fish in the river and they know where to look. The film company searched for that flag for three days, but they couldn't find it. After they were gone, his son went into the river and found it.'

'Where is it now?' I asked mistily.

'Hanging from a rafter in his farmhouse down the road.'

I knew about that film; it was called *Zulu Dawn* and I had been asked to act in it, but as usual, I was not available to do so.

When we returned from Fugitive's Drift later that day, I stopped off at the isolated Boer farmhouse and gazed up at the finely made Queen's Colour, hanging across an old roof beam. It was not a wealthy farm. In South Africa today there are poor White people; poorer than some Black people. But that sort of fact is of less than little interest to those liberals outside of the territory who wish to supplant the White way of doing things with the Black way of doing things, which of course, might be irrelevant . . . But there *are* soup kitchens for poor Afrikaners in Johannesburg, which are run by the ultra Nationalist Afrikaner, Mr Terreblanche. Think on the implications of that!

'Mamba-ridden Africa' did some reader mutter? Well, just as I arrived at the hard-pressed farmhouse, the father and son killed 'the biggest black mamba [one nip and you can bypass the hospital] that I have ever seen!' – and that from the *old* man. The snake was a giant and they had accosted its lethal presence in the chicken shed.

But the Queen's Colour! As I gazed upward I heard the old Boer say: 'Would you write on BBC paper that you have *seen* this flag in my house? Then I can ask more money for it.'

'How much do you want?' I enquired, without a tremor of excitement.

'Make me an offer,' came the immediate reply. And I mentioned a carefully judged figure.

'Done!' said the farmer in his own language. The Afrikaner is astute, but is usually a man of his word. The transaction was not unlike the Portobello Road on a sunny Saturday morning. Today, the Queen's Colour hangs high on a wall of 'Michael Collins House' in London, and quite close to Lord Grade's large cigar. Two trophies from my life's endless struggle. Oh! We used the Queen's Colour in *our* film and it gave us proper 'production value'.

With us in South Africa was our BBC producer and now my chum, John Hefin, and I began to realize that he was, perhaps, for me, the most valuable television producer that I had ever come across. And no one has improved on him since. He is quiet, unobtrusive, makes me laugh and is splendid at smoothing my choppy water. He is also brilliantly charming. Later in my life he was going to reinforce this budding opinion I had of him.

The 'Beecher's Brook' of this film was the Battle of Isandlwana. It was a long sequence about a vast Zulu army attacking a substantial British Force. There was much information and frightful drama to be communicated. And there was only me and a bell tent. So I got to thinking. Hadn't the director of the epic, *Zulu Dawn*, Mr Douglas Hickox, and some of his associates come to my house in London to ask my advice about a few Zulu matters? And hadn't they asked me to act in the saga? Well, they had big Zulu/British battle scenes in *their* film; maybe, out of love for me, they *might* let us possess a few off cuts from their film editing room. *And* wasn't the editor, Mr Malcolm Cooke, an old friend of mine? I talked to Michel Pearce and to John Hefin about the wild long-shot idea of mine – but it is usually my long-shots that come off.

We learnt that *Zulu Dawn* had created a scandal in South

Africa by the film makers leaving before they had paid all their bills. I was also told that hundreds of Zulus who had been employed as extras to represent the Zulu Army, had also become dissatisfied by a shortage of food; but that they had speedily solved *their* problem by killing the trek oxen and eating them. This was unfortunate for *Zulu Dawn* in two ways: first, these oxen were meant to work in moving stores, and second, they were meant to be photographed. And so, for various reasons, all 'responsible' people connected with *Zulu Dawn* had disappeared into the thinner air of Africa. However, some friend of mine whispered into an ear and gave me an address in a rich area on the edge of Durban. And we arrived at the mysterious house to be confronted with unblinking observation cameras and finally a flat, disembodied voice, denying all connection with the film. Having travelled a long way, we *saw* no breathing human. However, on our eventual return to Britain, I learnt that Mr Douglas Hickox, the director, and Mr Malcolm Cooke, the film editor, were putting *Zulu Dawn* together in Paris. And I telephoned the cutting room and told them of my wild hope.

'Dear boy,' said Douglas, 'come over to Paris immediately! We'll have a marvellous time! Of course, you can have whatever you want for your film!'

Well, I took that surge of kindness with an enormous pinch of salt and also, sadly, I was unable to go myself, so off went Michel on his own. Suffice it to write that Michel came back dripping with treasures. His disbelief in what happened has never truly left him: 'They said to me "help yourself to what you want," and Mr Hickox added, "Anything for dear Kenneth!"'

I never *properly* thanked Douglas Hickox and he's dead now. This material helped our film enormously. Of course we printed a credit: 'By courtesy of the makers of *Zulu Dawn*' and so it was good advance publicity for *their* film. But like Mr Lucioni and his colleagues at the Guildhall in London, it is upon such personal goodwill that our film efforts have often shone with an unusual lustre.

Towards the end of the filming we entered Brecon Cathedral where a military religious service was in progress and our camera tracked along the faces of the young soldiers in their Sunday-best uniforms. The faces are White, White, White, Black, White, White. The image is not meant to 'say' anything and yet, I am always disturbed emotionally when I see it.

After the ghastly disaster at Isandlwana, there was only one British military post between the slaughterfield and the small towns of the British Colony of Natal, and that place was Rorke's Drift, held by one company of the South Wales Borderers. There were about one hundred fit men and twenty-odd men who were sick, housed in a small stone hospital, attached to a Mission Station. The soldiers waited in terrible trepidation. Would the Zulu Impis (regiments) come? Soldiers were posted on the kopjes around; particularly to the east where, only seven miles away, towered the mountain called Isandlwana. Suddenly one of those lookout men turned and shouted at his comrades below him: 'Here they come! Black as hell and thick as grass'.

Not long after the film was transmitted in Britain, I returned to Southern Africa to work, and I was invited to the University of the North to speak to the students about the skills of communication, through television in particular. This beautiful university is for Black students only, though the faculty is both Black and White. It is generally accepted that the University of the North has been, and probably still is, a significant breeding place for African National Congress ideals; indeed just before I arrived there to speak, the Black students had burnt down their remarkably comprehensive library. Anyway, it was in this rather touchy young Black atmosphere that I had decided to talk about the reasons for making and the techniques employed in making *Black as Hell; Thick as Grass*. I was expecting trouble, but I was determined to hide nothing and the threat came like the whizz of an assegai: 'Why did you call it *Black* as Hell!?' But when I told them the truth about the frightened White soldier when he saw the impi appear over the hill crest, they roared with laughter and all was apparently well.

TWENTY-EIGHT

I think that it was about this time that Mr Robin Midgeley directed, for the stage, the very last play that Mr Terence Rattigan wrote. It was called *Cause Célèbre* and it was based upon a historical murder trial during the early 1930s. A woman was on trial for the death of her husband. Ms Glynis Johns played the tragic lady and before the play opened at His Majesty's Theatre in the Haymarket, London, Mr Midgeley asked me to play her defence counsel, a famous eccentric Irishman.

I felt then, as indeed I feel now, that I had virtually retired from the stage. I had developed this new career of writing and making my own films and this I had managed to do with a continuous sigh of relief. There was no Guthrie any more; I regarded the 'institutional theatres' (The National and The Royal Shakespeare) as too aridly clinical for my taste – and I am trying to be as polite as possible. I had long left the treacherous race, having turned my back again and again on significant opportunities to stretch myself, particularly as a classical actor. *And* I was frightened of appearing on a stage. Why suffer fear in such an inhuman setting? It had to be worth it if one was in the company of Edmund Kean or Tyrone Guthrie; but I didn't see Mr Peter Hall or any of his inheritors quite in that vivid, breathing light.

I was left with two uneasy regrets, which I still have. I miss my fellow Thespians; I feel that I have deserted them – and I anxiously *did* desert them for my own peace of mind. The second regret is wondering how far I could have gone if I had stuck to my guns in the theatre. However, after I have finished my one thousand five hundred words each day, for this book,

I quietly meander through the alpine village of Valbruna, wishing the occasional friend *buona sera*, and carrying a cushion and a *Complete Works of Shakespeare*. I walk between the great trees and across a wooden bridge over a mountain stream, to a paradisiacal meadow and there I do not only wonder at the genius of God and Shakespeare, but I also ponder whether I should try very hard to play Shylock again or . . .

Robin Midgeley is one of my favourite humans. And I accepted the challenge of playing O'Connor, I think his name was. Robin took me up to Leicester to watch the pre-London performance and in particular the part I was to take over. It was a nightmare for me. I sat there, in the packed theatre, watching the performance of the actor in whose shoes (not literally – he was much bigger than me) I would soon be. His moves on the stage, his intonations, all of that. I sat there to the point of wanting to vomit with fear.

'I've got to get out of this theatre, Robin!'

'What's the matter?' he asked, laughing.

But we left. The psychology you must work out for yourself. I don't want to dwell on it.

O'Connor was an exceedingly difficult role, but my fellow players were a great pleasure and support for me; I remain particularly devoted to one of them, Mr Bernard Archard, to this day. Even though Bernard had to speak to me firmly on one occasion about 'treading' on one of his lines. O'Connor was such a tenacious bully in the courtroom that verbal impatience was liable to happen. But we actors tend to be more civilized than, say, politicians and so all was immediately resolved with amity. Perhaps from Bernard's complaint onward, there was henceforward *too* pregnant a silence before I then said whatever it was I had to say.

Robin Midgeley reassured my elastic nerves that there was nothing for me to be alarmed about: 'Dear boy, we have *five* public dress rehearsals before the first night.'

Now I had so decisively cut myself off from the theatre that I didn't even know what he was talking about.

'Public dress rehearsals – what are they?'

'Oh, rehearsals into which the public are allowed.'

'Do you mean that while the public is watching, I can call out to you in the auditorium: "Look, Robin, I don't like this bloody piece of furniture!"'

'Oh, no, Ken, you can't do that.'

'Then I bloody well don't see the difference between such a performance and a first night!'

Ms Glynis Johns was obviously ill during those rehearsals and hers was an arduous part of the play. I said to Robin Midgeley, rather hopefully, I must confess: 'We're *not* going to open you know; it is out of the question.' And then, immediately before the first of those euphemistically named 'public dress rehearsals', Glynis walked onto the stage and gave an immaculate performance and contrived to do so night after night. I did tell her that I loved her a bit; to which she replied: 'Yes I know.'

And so there were two 'first nights'; the factual one and then another, presumably for the critics, a few days later. I had to open the play with a short, sharp interrogation, on a sort of small spotlit platform, slung somewhere in the darkness. A living nightmare for me, but it came and went like all else and, as it happened, with success. Yes, we were a success. I can't quote any Press comments because if there are any surviving in 'Michael Collins House', I am, as usual, a long distance away; but one written by Mr Michael Billington of the *Guardian* pleased my ambiguous position in the profession. He wrote: 'It is not so much a return to the stage as a take-over bid.' And I want Mr Billington to know that it helped.

Another manifestation of my terror of performing a stage play, is that I never invite anyone to a first night. It is bad enough having those strangers out there, watching me walk the high-wire without a net, leave alone loved ones. I suspect that they will turn up because of whispered 'good lucks' and then the kindly habit of sending you telegrams, which are traditionally stuck up around one's mirror. Of course, if the evening has gone well, I am glad to have chums around in the warm aftermath of terrible tension.

One evening, after a performance, several people had come round to see me and were all happily chatting when through the door came Peter O'Toole. All of his entrances are effective and this one I will remember as long as the old brain will function. He quietly said: 'Will everyone please leave the dressing-room for a few minutes; I have to speak to Griffith.'

When they had all departed like lambs, O'Toole put his hands on my shoulders and peered down at me: 'Griffith, you *know* that you are a *great* actor, don't you?'

Forgive me for quoting this, but those words from that actor, are enormously significant to me. Tyrone Guthrie once said something similar; my only regret is that Edmund Kean didn't have even the opportunity.

Oh yes, I miss my Thespian mates. One night I went somewhat astray in the courtroom and very discreetly but firmly, Mr Patrick Barr, who was playing the judge, put me back on the rails. Placed high up in his judicial chair, I believe he always had the entire play before him, for the very purpose of such an emergency. In the wings I would say, 'Thank you, Patrick,' and he would reply, 'That's all right, dear boy.' Not unlike being a soldier, under fire, night after night. In my Edmund Kean film I remark subjectively that 'players are brave people'; that they cover their various fears and get on with the job that they have chosen to do.

And yet another demonstration of the agony I suffer on the boards is that I demanded the near-impossible when I agreed to be in *Cause Célèbre*; I made it conditional that I had 'a three-month get-out clause'. That meant that I could leave the play after it had run for twelve weeks. Of course, that was partly so that I could return to making my own films. But one night, after the performance, two distinguished film makers, Mr Euan Lloyd, the producer, and Mr Andrew McLaglan, the American director, came into my dressing-room. They told me that they were going to make a film epic in Africa, about mercenaries fighting in the recent Congo War and that they wanted me to act in it. They wanted me to play the mercenary who was in charge of the medics, and that he was a self-proclaimed homosexual and openly 'camp-gay' about it. The immediate problem, Euan Lloyd explained to me, was that I would have to leave for Africa two weeks *before* my theatre contract terminated. Would I agree to Euan trying to buy me out of this contract? I confessed how fearful I was of each and every performance and wished Euan Lloyd every bit of luck in his endeavour.

Then Euan Lloyd reeled off the other actors that he had already put under contract: 'Roger Moore, Richard Harris, Richard Burton' and, at the latter's name I stopped him: 'Ah, Euan, Mr Burton and I have known each other for years and for some reason unknown to me, Mr Burton has always rejected me.'

'What do you mean, Kenneth?'

'Twice, after I had been cast in a film, and Richard Burton had arrived on the scene – the last time being in the film *Where Eagles Dare* – the producers have had to explain to me that Mr Burton wanted someone else to play the part that I had accepted, but was not yet contracted for.'

'Oh, no!' said Euan, 'that is not the case now. Indeed Richard asked who was going to play Witty (the ticklish character that Euan and Andrew wanted me to play) and when I told him that we were going to try to get you he replied: "Good, he won't be afraid to do it."'

Euan Lloyd's film was called *The Wild Geese* and it was inspired by Colonel 'Mad' Michael Hoare's mercenary exploits in the Congo (now Zaire) horror. Indeed we had Colonel Hoare with us, as our military adviser, and several of his staff who had fought with him 'up North' worked on the film as advisers and extras. Euan had begun his preplanning of the film by assuming that we could make it in the Congo itself, but quickly disillusionment swept over him. Corruption and murderous African propensities were so open that he was forced steadily southward and compelled to make the film at a place in the rough African bush called Tshipese. And what a strange world that was! How many human souls were we – three hundred? And the crane camera. And the daily run of our own aircraft down to Johannesburg. But, it was *not* tough at base; Tshipese had hot natural springs and around them was built a 'luxury' camp, for the more adventurous tourist. We lived in these well-appointed buildings in reasonable comfort.

Out of this goodly number of film makers my closest friend quickly became Colonel Hoare. For all of his fame for hair-raising daring-do, he was a softly spoken intellectual and an unswerving realist to boot. He sincerely believed that the best service that he could perform for South Africa was to try to hold the disease (as he saw it) of Communism – and in particular Black African Communism – from moving any further southward. From what I have observed of the Black variety of Communism, it is virtually nothing more than another incompetent system of cruel exploitation through totalitarian power.

Michael Hoare, who is undoubtedly a steely pragmatist, has mused, in my presence, whether the day might come when European civilization in the Republic of South Africa might have to move south and hold a defensive line along the Vaal River or even the Orange River against everything that Black Africa has to offer – rather like the Israelis have been forced, through regular treacherous Arab attacks, to hold the defensive line of the north–south Jordan River, which is why they are on the wretched West Bank. A similar situation: having to hold a cruel line in order to preserve civilization – as *we* Westerners know it.

Michael Hoare is also a very well-read man. 'How strange,' I have thought to myself, 'that I should find a patch of intellectual peace with this, even notorious man of action.' But, getting to the heart of the matter, we are not so dissimilar; it is simply that his special talents have run in different directions to mine. I would not be unhappy being equated with Mad Mike Hoare. He told me that he was a professional accountant and that the survival of his mercenaries in the Congo was due to his ignoring conventional military formulas and, astoundingly, applying common sense; which, as my grandfather used to remind me, is the rarest species of sense. And in 'ignoring conventional military formulas and applying common sense', he was doing no less than emulating Wolfe, Clive, Nelson and Napoleon.

When Michael Hoare suffered his abortive attack – not so long ago – on the Seychelles Islands and was put on trial in South Africa, he wrote me a letter in which he stated that if he was allowed to tell the truth 'they' could not put him in prison, or words to that effect. I was not surprised to learn this; I had presumed that no such armed assault could be arranged without a degree of undercover South African acquiescence and I wrote to him stating that, therefore, I was not unduly worried about his comfort. However, South Africa put Mike Hoare into notorious Pretoria Central Jail. And still I imagined my friend to be segregated inside in some well-appointed suite. But Euan Lloyd managed to inveigle himself into the prison and he saw Michael Hoare. Euan has told me that conditions did not look at all comfortable for our mutual friend.

Years later I was in the Transvaal village of Irene, which is between Johannesburg and Pretoria, and I saw a newspaper billboard: 'Mad Mike Hoare Released'. I explained to the shopkeeper that 'Colonel Hoare is a friend of mine; could I please have the poster?' and it was willingly given to me. I sent it to Michael at his home, care of Tulio Monetto, his chief aide.

Mr Roger Moore had his fiftieth birthday at Tshipese. I don't think that this light-hearted actor is going to mind me remarking on his age. Anyway he is astoundingly well-preserved; he is Peter Pan. Rather like Cary Grant; but Mr Grant was shyer about advancing time than Roger. Some news agency once sent a cable with the question: 'How old Cary Grant?'

To which the debonair wit replied: 'Old Cary Grant fine. How you?'

Euan Lloyd, who, when very young, was the best publicity director that the Rank Film Organization ever had, threw a fantastic party for Roger in the middle of the African bush. It was an astonishing setting. Trees and bushes were cut and swept away at the foot of a wild stone kopje, where a platform had been constructed and on which a band played jolly music. But I was not happy that evening, in spite of the champagne and lobster. Not *all* of our three hundred film people could be invited and that made my puritan Welsh soul uneasy, and the Press was present. Well it was, partly, a film publicity job and publicity is essentially part of the great film game. Anyway, a woman journalist from Johannesburg asked me, in the line of her duty, what I thought of the junketing and in my down-cast mood I was not complimentary. What I said was very good copy; today I still shudder at its potential. And Euan was my friend and so was Roger and the birthday party was well meant and in the context of the big film business, very proper. The lady journalist didn't quote my sour remarks. When I was next in Johannesburg I telephoned her and thanked her. She said: 'I thought that you might regret what you said, so I decided to put it aside.' Now, there are those who would say that she was not being a good journalist. But I think of her with favour and admire her very much.

Richard Burton was pleasant enough towards me, but he had his new wife with him and they kept themselves to themselves, so I didn't see much of him. One day a few actors and I were discussing the cause of the Iron Curtain between the USSR and the West; I was searching my memory as to whether it was H. G. Wells or Bernard Shaw who had questioned Lenin about murdered kulaks. From a little distance – and without joining us – Richard called out the historical fact. He was a highly intelligent man who had chosen, or been forced for psychological reasons, to hide his inner warm virtues under a distant prickly bushel.

A number of scenes in *The Wild Geese* were filmed around a vast baobab tree; the trunk was the size of a very large room. Our goodly number had just finished eating lunch and were resting, in our camouflaged uniforms, before restarting the day's work. There was an unusual silence and I was with one group of men reading in the warm shade of the giant tree. I became aware of Richard Burton deliberately walking towards me across an open patch of ground. I looked up as he virtually stood over me: 'Kenneth, when I was a young actor, I was in awe of your talent,' and he turned and began to walk away, stopped and turned again, 'and, of course, I still am.'

The actor next to me said: 'What was all that about?'

I said nothing, but have often puzzled what it was all about. I might hazard a guess.

Some time later, Welsh actors and actresses congregated in a theatre in St Martin's Lane one evening, and amongst other entertainments gave a performance of Dylan Thomas' *Under*

Milk Wood; indeed we had all assembled to raise money for the poet's memorial in Westminster Abbey. Richard Burton, clearly very ill – and he died not long afterwards – travelled from Switzerland, where he lived, to perform 'the Speaker'. It was the last time I saw him and he looked vulnerable and was smiling and was probably exposing his true nature. The fists were down.

I said to him: 'When you were having a very bad time, I had a strong inclination to write to you.'

His smile was open and warm: 'Oh, Kenneth, I wish you had; it was a very bad time.'

In the story of *The Wild Geese*, Witty, the character that I played, had to be killed by the Simbas while fighting a brave, camp, rear-guard action (if you understand me). We were near enough to Mozambique to require decent paramilitary protection and this comprised a White major and quite a few extremely big Black soldiers-cum-police. And it was these latter lads who had to transform themselves into Simbas and finally flay me to death with their great knives – pangas. Before this scene was shot the White officer carefully and emphatically talked to his Black men in a lingo I didn't understand.

'Excuse me, sir, but what are you saying to these men?'

'Oh,' he replied, 'I'm explaining to them that this is only *pretend*. They are not long out of their tribal homeland and they don't clearly understand what is happening.' I listened to these words aghast. I made a quick calculation to make sure that Euan – the film – would still require my acting services *after* my bloody death.

'Please, Andrew,' (addressing our director) 'make sure these big men understand that this is only acting.'

The Black soldiers had been particularly interested in me from the beginning; they had noted my metamorphosis into Witty and now, grinning broadly, they were making suggestive gay gestures in my direction. I felt that I was in some sort of peril. With only partial relief I noted that their big steel pangas were then being exchanged for big wooden ones. I made a last appeal to their Colonel to explain that it was only bioscope-acting and fatalistically placed myself into the care of Thespis and suffered the drubbing that followed, as the excited camera turned. I emerged black and blue and the shrieks from Witty in *The Wild Geese* are only partly simulated. Could those big Black men have been sympathetic to the African National Congress? The sinister thought has only occurred to me now.

The Wild Geese was a great success and many people in widely dispersed corners of the world recognize me as Witty, the brave, gay mercenary. And more than once I have had to explain to admirers that I have five children. Euan Lloyd is an exemplary film-producer; everything is preplanned with precise exactitude. I remember seeing, several times, members of the production staff hurrying into two cars and disappearing here, there or anywhere into the bush; some problem was stirring and they were the hatchet people.

Back in London, Euan and his wife Ingeborg invited me to their home for supper and I questioned my host about his painstaking efficiency: 'Euan, I have received the impression that if I had delayed your filming by one day, for whatever reason, those hatchet men of yours would have bundled me into a car – and before they shot me, out in the bush beyond Tshipese, you would have said: 'Kenneth, I'm very fond of you, but I have to do this; the rules are the rules.'

I have stood with him talking, while a vast scene is being prepared by a few hundred people, when suddenly Euan has said: 'Oh, excuse me,' and has dashed away to pick up a morsel of paper, in case, presumably, it blew into the shot.

I went to the royal first night in my dinner-jacket and parading across from the Odeon, Leicester Square, was an anti-apartheid demonstration. I felt a strong inclination to go across to them and tell them how Euan Lloyd had tried and tried to make the film in various Black African States, but had failed because of the degeneracy of these states. I suspect that Euan had refused to deal with the Black Africans for two reasons: his financial budget could not meet their bribery demands and, secondly, he is a Welsh puritan, like me, and he wouldn't wish to get involved in such standards. But I thought better of my instinct and I didn't cross the road.

TWENTY-NINE

I wanted to make a film about an inspiring Christian leader and Thames Television employed me to make what I wished.

The year before, a producer at Thames, Ms Margery Baker, had won a much-coveted Italian award for a Christmas television production and since this had brought kudos to the company, she had been asked: 'What would you like to do next?' She had replied: 'The Journey of the Magi', and her wish was granted. Immediately problems arose (all of this I was told later; I was in no way present) because on closer examination of the New Testament almost nothing is known about the Three Wise Men – the Magi. But apparently the budget had been found and it had been placed in the Thames computer (again this was simply information given to me) and money is difficult to get out of a computer! Treatments (résumés) of the Magi story had been produced and were not acceptable. And at this juncture of the problem, my name was mentioned for the first time: Mr Ian Martin, with whom I had worked on *The Public's Right to Know*, was head of the relevant department, and during an emergency meeting he had said: 'Kenneth Griffith is around and he makes idiosyncratic films; perhaps we should ask him.'

'Kenneth, are you at all interested in the Magi?'

I thereupon replied: 'Dear Ian, only a fool wouldn't be interested.'

'Would you like to make a film about them?'

Now I knew next to nothing, but I did have the nous to reply: 'But very little is known about them. How long must the film be?'

'Fifty minutes or so,' replied Ian, and added: 'Think about it.'

The options, the possibilities of an idea usually come to me very speedily. Recently, a lady I have long been devoted to, Ms Nancy Banks-Smith, of the *Guardian* newspaper, wrote: 'By some oversight Kenneth Griffith has not yet done a film about that notorious underdog Jesus Christ and one can only regret it for one would have greatly enjoyed his performance in the lead.'

Well, dear Ms Nancy, it was not entirely an 'oversight' – a bungle I will confess to . . .

With Ian Martin breathing down my neck, I peered and peered at the possibilities and this is what popped out: the Magi were one of the sub-groups of the Medes, who had appeared from Central Asia and had settled on the great Iranian plateau. And the Magi specialized in astronomy and astrology; they became the most famous wise men throughout the Western world and the Middle East, if not elsewhere. Wizards! 'Now,' my wily brain (soon to come badly unstuck) told me 'in entering Israel they – the Magi – would have almost certainly entered the Holy Land from the north-east, over the Golan Heights. And therefore on their journey, following that miraculous star to the birthplace of Jesus at Bethlehem, they would have passed through most of the specific locations of His ministry. Was this not a daring opportunity to quote Christ's words en route to His birth?

'Yes,' I said to Ian Martin, 'I'll have a go!' And the dire die was cast! Yes, Ms Nancy, I've sort of done it. You and I must sit down together and look at it, though the only part I will enjoy is your company. Why am I *so* devoted to Nancy Banks-Smith? She once gave me the best press-notice that perhaps any Thespian has ever received – O'Toole and Kean have good reason to be envious; she wrote, in the *Guardian*: 'Set fire to his socks and he could play *Gone With the Wind* single-handed'!

Troubles confronted me, and were building up like a seismic hurricane. But, I confess it, I thrived on the prospect. I wrote the script, confining my New Testament quotes entirely to Saint Matthew, who is the only Holy Scribe who mentions the Three Wise Men. And I felt that the film must begin at fabulous Persepolis: this I reasoned was essential to communicate to the viewer the sheer size and magnificence of the culture of which they were such a famous and integral part. Unhappily, though I did not then fully realize how potentially unhappy it was, the Ayatollah Khomeini had already arrived in Iran and was beginning to kick his murderous tyranny into top gear.

At that period the obnoxious Iranian fundamentalists had already partly burnt the British Embassy but hadn't yet taken over the American Embassy. It was beginning to dawn on me that Khomeini was more tyrannical than the Shah's outfit, but how much more, no one – then – really knew. My first job was to persuade my producer not to travel with me on the reconnaissance: 'We'll sail together down the Euphrates!' she'd said. But I didn't foresee the immediate work ahead quite like that . . . I also took the precaution of arranging to stay at the British Archaeological Institute in Teheran; I sensed that I would be less obvious there than at the International Hotel, where all journalists were confined and under close observation. And so off I went on a flight of Iran Airways.

As I arrived at the British Archaeological Institute (a fine looking period building in the suburbs of Teheran), I found a young man actually padlocking the wrought-iron gates. With a frantic air he swung round and stared at me as I pulled my luggage from the taxi: 'What do you want?' he challenged.

'Oh, my name is Griffith. I'm staying here.'

'No, you're bloody well not,' he replied. 'I'm the last, and I'm leaving *now*!'

Well, he was hardly well-mannered, but I could see that he was unnerved.

'Where should I stay?' I asked.

'International is the only hope,' and he was gone.

This International Hotel was fairly packed with journalists from most qualified corners of the world. I am a poor drinker and tend to keep myself to myself and I also tend to put my faith in dealing strictly off the top of the pack. And so I walked to the hotel desk – having secured a room – and asked for directions to the British Embassy. I was advised not to walk but to take a taxi. The streets were astoundingly crowded; cars, including my vehicle, progressed by snatched inches from the traffic that pressed close all around. The sound of car horns was deafening and the place was plastered with lurid posters devoted to Islamic human hatred. The United States of America was the focus of this Muslim vindictiveness and was referred to everywhere as 'the Great Satan'. I found this description very difficult to equate with the human friendliness that I have always experienced in America over many years. But it began to dawn on me, even from the general aspect of the people, that they were collectively unbalanced. Well, the demeanour was far from what one was accustomed to see in Britain – apart from some football matches! Again and again, as I travel about this world, I am forced to the frightening conclusion that the Third World and all of the other sub-divisions of the material losers are in trouble because of what their culture *is*; not because of what other 'exploiters' do to them. This is frightening because all cultures (ways of thinking and behaving) are *deeply* engraved and are born out of ethnic evolvement. Human beings vary vastly around the world and all of the handouts that the First World – the developed countries – give or lend to the Third World, will not change the Third World's basic behaviour hardly one iota. Until the liberal instinct faces up to this reality, the world will continue to edge down a sentimental but hopeless road.

It wasn't until my taxi jolted two inches by two inches into the British Compound that I learnt, by the fire-blackened front, that our bit of territory in that aching city had been attacked. There was no serviceable front entrance to the embassy. I uneasily walked round the right flank into a fine ornamental garden and there, striding thoughtfully towards me, were two English ladies (I can spot an English lady at fifty yards). One of them saw me: 'Good God! What are you doing here?'

'I've come to Iran to prepare a film.'

'Ah.'

'I didn't know that you'd been burnt down.'

'Oh yes.'

'Were you here at the time?'

'Yes.'

'My! Were you frightened?'

'Oh, no! This is the third – no, I lie, the *fourth* embassy I have had burnt over my head.'

And then rather jollily: 'Who do you want to see?'

'The Ambassador, please.'

'Come with us; we'll show you how to get in.' And they took me through a back door.

Persepolis and the ancient remnant of Passegarde are some eight hundred miles south of Teheran and when His Excellency – I think it was him – heard, he said: 'Dear Mr Griffith, I don't wish to be pessimistic, but don't you understand that every European and American, south of here, has *fled*. There are, I understand, two or three rather foolhardy journalists at Qum, some two hundred miles from here, hoping to see the Ayatollah Khomeini, but apart from them . . .'

'Oh, sir, my mission is so innocent; I feel I can't come to any harm.'

'I am forced to say, Mr Griffith, that I think you are embarking upon a somewhat lunatic venture.'

I flew to Shiraz, the nearest modern city to Persepolis, on an Iranian aircraft and apart from the colourful human passengers (I am sure that I also recall goats) no one gainsaid me; I just phased my way southward. At Shiraz airport I became aware that people were staring at me; later that day I considered that I looked different to everyone else facially; that I might just as well have been a Black man. This realization surprised me.

A taxi took me to the only feasible hotel for a foreigner in the whole city. It was a vast, magnificent and half-lit place; certainly shades of the Shah. It was ghostly, but I was weary and simply went to my given room; except it wasn't any old room, it was an ostentatious suite. I began to settle in, but the heat was so burdensome that I tried to adjust the air-conditioning; nothing happened and I returned to the hotel desk.

Around me everywhere was empty, except for towering dark marble spaces; I noted a couple of distant figures moving – servants? It was eerie. Not a guest except me – or so it appeared – in the great hotel. The man behind the desk said: 'I think, sir you must speak to the manager; he has just returned from jogging.'

The manager, slightly breathless and wearing a smart track suit and looking all of twenty-seven years, smilingly asked me if he could help.

'Ah!' he said, and lowering his voice, 'You see, sir, it's the revolution. We have no spare parts. It's awful, I know, but we are helpless.' It could easily have been an Eton education.

I was abject for him: 'Oh, I'm so sorry; please don't worry. I understand.' And I returned to my sweat-suite luxury.

It was quite early the next morning that a servant knocked on my door and entered: 'Excuse me sir, but the manager would like to see you in his office as soon as you can get there.'

Was this a touch of menace in the already oblique atmosphere? I hurried down the great staircase. The manager's office was spacious, but devoid of everything except essentials *and* Islamic slogans stuck on the walls; I could see outlines where pictures had recently hung and I *knew* that they had been of the Shah and his consort. The young man, now immaculately attired in a suit, rose from behind his expensive desk and offered me a seat and coffee. I thought to myself: 'He looks as if he should be at the fashionable end of the South of France.'

Again he lowered his bright, sophisticated voice: 'Mr Griffith, would you mind telling me what exactly you plan to do in Shiraz?'

And I told him about the film and that I wanted to look at Persepolis, where I planned to begin my story.

'Mr Griffith, I have to tell you that we don't know, here in this hotel, what is going to happen from day to day.' He looked at me very closely: 'The truth is, we are expecting the Revolutionary Guards here at any moment.' I now realized that in no way was the young man a threat to me; but he was concerned for my safety as well as his own.

'Have you made any plans?' he asked.

'Yes, I thought I would visit the Governor of this area, Mr Cosroe.'

'Ah!' said the manager, 'you must be very careful. Mr Cosroe is no longer the Governor; he was, but no more. You could be going to the worst possible man if you want help.'

'Well, in that case, I'll go and see the Revolutionary Guard.'

'Mr Griffith, I don't think you truly understand. Everyone – except the Revolutionary Guards themselves of course – is trying very hard to keep out of their way. It's *dangerous* Mr Griffith.'

'Oh,' I repeated as I had in the British Embassy, 'my mission is innocent.'

What I didn't realize at the time was that there were far more innocent people than myself – the Bahai for instance – who were already being lined up by the fundamentalist Muslims of Iran, there in Shiraz, for most brutal slaughter.

'Well?' pressed the young man.

'Can you nominate a driver who would take me to the Revolutionary Committee's headquarters and who speaks a little English?'

'Maybe; I know a driver who has worked for the Americans in the oilfields, and he knows everything. And he's tough.'

This driver took me on and I had no alternative but to take him on. We did a deal which covered several days.

'Will you take me to the Revolutionary Headquarters?'

'Sure, get in.' He had a strong American–Iranian accent. He drove me to a luxurious mansion, which had young men outside it in battle-fatigues and carrying what I took to be M16 rifles which appeared to be bigger than themselves, and without more ado my driver swung his car through the high ornamental gates while the young Revolutionary Guards screamed at us in Farsee – a language which, needless to write, I do not understand.

'Stop!' I yelled at my aggressive driver.

He half turned: 'Ah – they're all shit!' as he continued.

'Stop!' I repeated. 'They're *aiming* at us!' And he stopped.

'Tell them I have come to visit their boss man, and that I'm important.'

Well they chatted away and he turned to me: 'The Committee is not here any more.'

'Do you know where?'

'Yes.'

'Please take me.'

This time it was a building that looked like a town hall and here again were the youngsters with the big rifles. My nerveless driver told them that I wanted to speak to the Revolutionary Committee. I was led into a room and was painstakingly searched. Something was said to me which clearly meant 'Wait!' Eventually I was escorted through labyrinthine ways and into a large room in which, around an enormous table, were, perhaps, thirty men. On the table papers were strewn and several maps. At the far end of the oblong table were two older, more sophisticated men who were in charge. I soon gathered – though I no longer remember how – that they were 'doctors' but doctors of what I never learnt. I do remember, vividly, that one of them wore a white polo-necked pullover under his well-cut grey suit. I was told to wait and I stood there observing the unusual scene as they debated away in Farsee. Revolutionary Guards stood on each side of me and it did cross my mind that I *looked* as if I was a prisoner. And scant respect was shown because the Committee ignored me. I saw that much furniture and things were roughly piled up at one end of the room.

One of the doctors finally turned to me, and indeed they all suddenly stared at me.

'I'm very sorry,' I said, 'but, unhappily, I don't speak Farsee; only English.'

'I speak English,' said the gentleman in the polo-necked shirt.

'What do you want?'

And I proceeded to tell him the now old tale. But I laced it up with Welsh cunning: 'I want to make a film about the three wise Iranians who went in search of the child Ysau [as Muslims call Jesus].' And I ruthlessly pushed in, for full measure: 'I'm not a Christian; but I feel that this world – particularly our Western world – is in desperate need of ethical and spiritual elements. I would like to begin the journey of these wise Iranians at Persepolis. I am here to ask for permission to film and to look at the remains of the famous city.'

No cock crowed as I rejected Christianity; after all, I claim to be an agnostic (that is by my definition: I don't know what exactly God is). Mark you, I didn't emphasize how much I admire and appreciate Christ (so perhaps I should have got *one* crow). I felt that I had done pretty well.

And so did the doctor; he said: 'Have a seat, Mr Griffith,' and one of the guards ran and placed a chair for me. Everything that I said was interpreted into their language either by the two doctors or there were one or two other members of the Committee who seemed to have a smattering of English. I wasn't frightened in the least. Again I thought to myself, with considerable satisfaction, what pickles I get into. It was like being James Bond in a harmless – so I believed – sort of way. I smiled around the table, as Charlie Chaplin might have done in a similar predicament, which smiling was received with very mixed reactions; the truth is some of the men didn't smile back at all. I noted this hard fact. But I was in good form and, as is my wont, chatted away lengthily in reply to all of their questions. I was making headway; the other doctor asked: 'You like a cup of tea, Mr Griffith?'

'Thank you, sir!'

And at a snap of a thumb and finger, another guard raced off and after a few minutes returned carrying what could have been a fine baroque silver tray with a porcelain cup and saucer – and the tea.

Now, as any thinking person knows, disaster is usually arcane and unpredictable. I sat there, at the height of my confidence, and picked up the cup and saucer to have a sip. Well, since my prolonged military hospitalization during the war and nearly perfect recovery, my hands nevertheless shake whenever I am tired or excited or under any – even mild – stress. Two doctors have told me on different occasions that there is nothing wrong with me physically and both have stated that this little problem is all in my head. But, sitting there in Shiraz, with the entire Revolutionary Committee staring at me – albeit *some* of them smiling – the loud rattle of my attempt to replace cup back onto saucer had a devastating effect on them all. Every expression, from sympathetic to unsympathetic seemed to thunder: 'What is he frightened of!?' And that *did* make my shaking hands worse; I spilt a little tea.

One of the doctors curtly said: 'You will have to see the new Governor,' and I was escorted to another room where two large men in European suits and ties offered me a seat. I had asked the Revolutionary Committee for some written permission or pass for me to visit Persepolis and for permission to film at a later date, but no one would give me anything of that nature. And now, having told the Governor my well-rehearsed story, he and his side-kick were affable, but again refused to give me anything written. I began to recognize that everyone that I was meeting were more fearful than I was. But of what? Soon the whole world would know.

'Written permission is unnecessary, Mr Griffith. You are free to visit Persepolis. Would you like us to provide you with protection?'

Ah, ha, I thought to myself, but said: 'Oh no, sir. I have a good Iranian driver. We have become friends and he keeps an eye on me.'

'Good.'

My rough and ready driver and I got on together very well in our independent ways. On our journey to Persepolis he stopped at a somewhat primitive eating-house (I carried my neat hotel sandwiches) and he sat there puffing away on a large hookah. As we drew close to the awesome city our car passed a vast, enclosed area of magnificently apparelled tents and marquees; this was where the recent Shah had held his ostentatious international party for the Toffs of the World.

The ruins of Persepolis are difficult for me to describe; they are of such antiquity and yet so vivid and redolent of sophisticated *and* barbaric times. Get out of line there, from the ancient bosses' point of view, and everything could be chopped off. And yet so widely divorced from the shoddy tyranny of

Iran today – when still things are chopped off; Ancient Persepolis is conservative grandeur at its grandest. Could one hear the distant sounds? Yes! And I was especially privileged; there were no half-baked rich tourists or portentous archaeologists; only funny-peculiar me (the husky driver kipped in the car). Was I the last of the pseudos to dawdle around the stupendous images? Quite possibly, yes. I was going to direct this Magi piece, so I eyed the white shapes with a professional eye and was overwhelmed with the superabundance.

And then on to Passegarde and the solitary tomb in the wide uninhabited valley – or so it seemed. The centuries had ravaged, but unlike Osymandias, there seemed no acknowledgement of defeat. Just ageing implacable arrogance.

That evening, back in Shiraz, I decided to walk around the city on my own. Everywhere people stared at me; it was clear to them that I was an alien and all aliens had supposedly fled. I went into a small bookshop which was crowded with men; I received the impression that it had Communist leanings. Again, the men were not overly friendly. I bought some postcards, speaking English. As I came out onto the street, three of the youngest of the men approached me and one of them, who spoke reasonable English, questioned me about what I was doing in Shiraz and I told him. I suspect that I felt a shade of unease. Then the young man said that they were soldiers – he was a paratrooper – and would I return with them to their quarters? By now it was night-time, but I agreed. I suppose that as I enter the other world I will say to myself: 'Well, if you don't go in, you won't *know*, will you.' As the four of us walked through the crowded streets I looked behind me: backtracking it's called; but with the talk going on, I was soon totally lost.

We arrived at a series of large buildings which seemed to be populated entirely by young men. A sort of informal barracks? My new acquaintances led me up open stairways and before entering through a door they removed their shoes; I did the same. Inside, the room was carpeted and there were plenty of cushions. And at this point I began to relax, because it was clear that all three of them wanted to make me feel at home.

They quickly prepared coffee and produced sweetmeats and apologized for the inadequacy of their hospitality. Islam at its best. What can I write? I had feared them a little and here they were showering me with human affection.

And yet, within some months, if our friendship had become known to the Khomeini hierarchy, what would have been done to them? And after the careless and massive bloodletting of the obscene war with wretched Iraq, are any of them now alive?

They asked me many questions about the West and eventually one of them asked me what was the truth about the relationship between men and women 'in your part of the world'? He explained that no contact between young men and women was allowed in Iran before marriage and that, he emphasized, made their lives very difficult. 'Do you think that I could write to a girl in Britain?' I told them about my daughter Eva and, giving her address in London, I said that I was sure that she would like to receive a letter from him. A long while afterwards Eva told me that they had corresponded, but then his letter-writing stopped.

I had taken the precaution of telling my friends an untruth as we had left the bookshop. I had said that I mustn't be late in getting back to my hotel, because I was expecting a message from their Foreign Ministry in Teheran. It was a shrewd warning shot fired into the night air. The three soldiers escorted me back on the long walk to my hotel. Somehow I remember our parting with sweet sorrow.

Before leaving Shiraz I had the good fortune of wandering through the essential bazaar. Foreign suckers – the tourists – had disappeared and so I was a rare item. Nevertheless, it still took me ninety minutes to purchase a fine carpet at what I sensed was a good (and so did the vendor, I suspect) price. That carpet is now in my library on the fourth floor of my house in Islington. Like very many possessions in that house it reminds me, forcibly, of an event. It is another visible punctuation in the journey of my life.

I had a valuable thought a few days ago while walking with Chiara and three other ladies, in the foothills of the wild

Romagnian Appenines. Well, it now seems to me that we do this and that in our lives and thereby store up memories and these memories are stashed away in our human computers and we virtually feed on them up to the point of mortality. What happens at the last hiccup I really don't know. However, we all *share* our store of memories with other humans and thereby influence them. It is as far as I can get to the concept of immortality. Memories are the *only* stones that we have to build with. I think that my grandfather, Ernest Griffiths, had a concept of the mysticism of his craft.

I made my way over those eight hundred miles back to Teheran and into the International Hotel and there, to my mild astonishment, found myself to be a journalist's celebrity. In their own properly inquisitive style the media lads – I saw no girls – had discovered where I had been and they were receiving no information from the distant south. Quick as a living reflex, two young chaps employed by Reuters were at my bedroom door. I saw them to be slightly public school snide, though pleasant enough. I am reasonably certain that they had privately agreed that I was a nutcase – and I am not gainsaying that diagnosis. And surely we all agree that nutcases are often the most valuable elements in our human societies? Anyway they questioned me with that minute air of superior doubt: 'Are you *sure* that there was a Revolutionary Committee in Shiraz? We've not heard of one that far south.'

'Yes, I'm sure.' And I gave them the whole spiel.

'What do you propose to do now?' enquired one of them.

'Go to the Foreign Ministry here in Teheran,' I replied.

'Oh,' said the other one, 'what a bit of luck! Tomorrow morning at 11 am, the Foreign Minister, Ibrahim Yazdi, is holding his very first Press conference; go to the Ministry and ask him.'

It has suddenly occurred to me that perhaps these two Herberts from Reuters were feeling a bit off centre because I, the layman, had ventured forth to where they, perhaps, should have ventured forth, instead of lurking in the synthetic safety of the International Hotel. On the other hand they may simply have been wiser.

My new Teheran driver battled his way to the Foreign Ministry the next morning. I was inefficiently equipped; I had a Thames Television identity card, but I had failed to stick a photograph of myself in it. I fear that this oversight was due to my instinctive belief that I don't need such trivia; that I can talk my way into any joint. And sometimes I fail and then I need the boring card. However, on this occasion, having instructed my driver to wait 'for a long time', I entered the Foreign Ministry through a seething mass of insipiently hysterical revolutionaries and I importantly flashed my Thames Card with an impatient: 'Thames Television, Britain! Minister Yazdi's conference!' I was frisked and another of those ubiquitous khaki-clad youngsters with a tall gun, hustled me into a lift and without more ado I was shovelled into a palatial chamber where Yazdi himself was at the centre of a line of men, behind an endless and beautiful table. And facing him were perhaps a hundred journalists with their pencils and paper, still cameras and movie cameras. Quickly I realized that the Muslim world predominated. But also, there they were, the two British Reuter men, leaning – as only a young Englishman not long 'down' from Oxbridge can lean. I gave them a cheeky wave and they both stiffened. Again I suspected that they might have been half having me on. Yes, they gave me genuine information about the press conference, but would I ever gain access?

The whole scene was electric for me. The Arab gentlemen of the Middle Eastern Press and television asking apparently obsequious and ingratiating questions, and Yazdi all teeth and very trimmed beard, holding forth. And those two Brits – looking, in this gathering, uncommonly white – standing back from it all, but keeping a curious eye on me. Not for a second did I really feel that they were friends of mine. The Raj will always be alive and well! We British don't need to *own* the bloody countries! But contrary to some half-baked Indian opinions in New Delhi, I am *not* Raj material. I identify myself too readily with *all* of the poor human sods for that! No, I am a fighting underdog or nothing.

I was impressed by the demeanour of Foreign Minister

Yazdi. He didn't stop smiling. What miscalculations I can be guilty of! Of course I now realize that no one present – certainly not the Reuter boys, leave alone the Arab creeps – was going to ask him why he and his Islamic mates were butchering so many innocent (in the eyes of God, as against the great Ayatollah) men, women and children. It was a curious medieval gathering, strongly flavoured with a brutal interpretation of whatever Mohammed stood for, and mixed up with a sparkling array of Japanese-made equipment.

Yazdi spoke in Farsee and it was not until he gave an especially large flash of teeth and springing to his feet said, 'Finish,' did I understand a word. I was told that the man had spent twelve years in the United States of America.

As the Foreign Minister left, he turned to his right, followed by his advisers and heavies. He rather sped down his side of the table and for me it was now or never. Instinctive decision. I sped down *my* side of the table, dodging the massed journalists. At the bottom I met him and saying: 'Sir' I recklessly reached into the inner pocket of my jacket. And so did the heavies, towards hidden holsters . . . But I was the first to draw, fortunately for me, and I pulled out an envelope. Yazdi had frozen in his tracks: 'What do you want?' he asked me.

'Sir,' I said, 'everything that I want is in that letter. May I stay inside this building until you have read it? I am in no hurry.' Yazdi eyed me and barked: 'Follow me!' and I marched out of the grand chamber with the men who counted. As I marched I flung a smile back at Reuters, whom I hoped were craning their necks.

Inside another vast palace room I was told to wait and I sat on a gold brocaded settee with a Revolutionary Guard close by. Also in the area were several Iranian women, acting as secretaries it seemed. These women were typical of that time: one would be dressed in the height of contemporary conservative fashion, well-cut silk dresses and high heels, and next to her, a woman in the chadar – the hideous all-black, all-encompassing shroud, that is now compulsory for all, so I am told. And these 'sisters' carried on with their business as if there was no division between them. I was intrigued by this phenomenon.

I waited for hours, but of course, I was not bored. Groups of men arrived and were escorted to the distant golden doors through which Yazdi had disappeared. One of the lady secretaries explained to me that the Foreign Minister was, at that moment, appointing ambassadors. Eventually, a tall, handsome man with silver hair came through those impressive doors and walked straight over to me: 'My name is Zanousie, Mr Griffith. What exactly do you want?'

In the letter which I had given to Yazdi I had enlarged on my reasons for wanting to film in Iran. I had stated that I was perturbed by the sinking spiritual values in Britain and wanted to make a contribution in lifting them up by relating the story of the three wise Iranians travelling so far to confirm the significance of the prophet Ysau's birth. It was a mixture of truth and contrived pleading. And I now repeated the well-worn story to Zanousie. And for full measure – already knowing of a local abhorrence to Christianity – I slipped in the reminder that I was an agnostic.

'Ah, Mr Griffith, I think that you are aiming too high in approaching our Foreign Minister to give you permission to film at Persepolis. Anyway, it would only be passed into my hands.'

'Well, sir,' I rejoined hastily, 'I don't mind if the permission comes from you.'

'We'll see,' he said, and as he departed: 'Please wait.'

One of the ladies explained to me that Mr Zanousie was the head of internal security. Wow!

Eventually those distant golden doors burst open and towards me thundered black-suited Mr Yazdi, followed by the head of internal security and all of the heavy brigade. Yazdi was *waving* my letter as he shouted: 'I have read your letter, Mr Griffith, and I could not agree with you more about the degeneracy of your country!' (That's a bit over the top, I thought.) 'I could not have put it better myself!' And then coming very close to my nose he growled (and I do not exaggerate): 'But I do not think that *this* is the time for *my* country to lift *your* country out of the mud!' (Come on, I thought, I never wrote that.) And then turning away from me, he barked: 'Get him out of here!'

Well that did it for me. The old short fuse that became a by-word in the more ridiculous parts of Delhi, instantaneously fizzed: 'Sir!' I now yelled (and the big-chested men froze as well as Yazdi), 'I'm not talking about oil and power! I'm only concerned about the human spirit!'

Yazdi seemed to dance: 'Get him out!'

And the young men with their unwieldy guns removed me without further discussion.

Some weeks ago I stood with my old friend and sometime literary editor, Anthony Whittome and one of his clients, the distinguished Iranian historian, Mr Amir Taheri, who informed me that Yazdi was now 'on the run', being hunted by whatever faction now holds the terrible power in Iran and that Zanousie was 'long ago executed'. I suppose that I had veered fairly close to having the fingernails pulled out; but I then hadn't realized the real hazard . . . As I was expelled through the main doors of the Foreign Ministry I noticed a red stain on my suit. Well, they had drawn a drop or two of blood, which I now think of as very much to my Welsh credit.

I believe there were those at the British Embassy who doubted that Islam would let me out of the country, but I got to Teheran's airport and apart from uncouth official Middle Eastern manners (Israel always excepted) and one miserable effort to take my Shiraz carpet from me (which tussle I won), I winged my way to the birthplace of our concept of fair play – Greece. Here my carpet was held at the airport for thirty-six hours till I re-embarked for Tel Aviv. I used the day in Athens well; climbed to and mused at the Parthenon.

At Tel Aviv airport the Israeli official perused my passport: 'Sir, do you expect to visit any Arab country?'

'Maybe; why do you ask?'

'If you do, I won't stamp your passport; I'll give you a separate paper.'

I looked at the civilized Jewish citizen:

'Mark my *passport*, please – *three* times.' Bang, bang, bang, he went.

'Thank you and good day.'

Why does human decency when it is present seem to affect

the very air? I proceeded to travel around Israel with my old friend, David Phillips, visiting the historical sites of Jesus Christ's known life and to write the script.

Arriving at Heathrow Airport, London, I wheeled my luggage towards the sometime-Asian officer: 'What is that?' he asked, pointing at my Shiraz carpet.

'Oh,' said I, confidently, 'that is a carpet I bought deep in the Ayatollah Khomeini's bloody country, Iran. Perhaps you've read about my tribulations? However, I got it out and through Greece and through Israel and now I'm home!'

'Let me see the carpet.' And so I laboriously undid the thin ropes. The uniformed bureaucrat peered: 'I will have to charge you for it.'

'Oh, come on!' I moaned wearily.

'The rules are the rules.' Truly a voice from New Delhi; hoist with our own bureaucratic petard, I now know. But I must be fair; he added: 'I will charge you as little as possible . . .'

THIRTY

Now what? The film had received a rotten blow: no grand opening at Persepolis. Well, a change of tune was called for! I decided that a sort of comedy was the best alternative because of the emergency: I would open the Magi saga by reconstructing my dismal arrival back in London and by briefly relating my woebegone tale to a ciné camera as I pushed my trolley with the carpet on it towards a taxi, and giving the cry 'On to the British Museum!'

My idea was to film the opening story – about the power and pelf of Persian power in the most relevant galleries of the British Museum. We Brits can improvise miraculously – as the Falklands War was to prove. Well, on that Magi enterprise, the old Hearts of Oak spirit was to be crushingly challenged. Again and again. There was a murderous hand on the whole enterprise from beginning to end. They do crop up once in a while. This one could have been the curse of the Ayatollah.

Of course the Middle Eastern sections of our national museum have some wonderful images and I decided to throw the ball about very freely. I thought that we could conjure anything out of anything. I roped in the huge Egyptian face, the Elgin Marbles and monstrous men-animals from Babylon, I think. Not unlike the mismatch of another Griffith, David Wark, in *Birth of a Nation*. Everything, including me, was beautifully photographed because I had Grenville Middleton at the camera. The British Museum staff were unobtrusively helpful.

As I have already recalled, the Thames Television ACTT Shop was a truly sinister organization. The committee had

long since moved beyond workers' rights to a vindictive grasping war with the Thames management to plunder and
manipulate for self-interest wherever possible. Every inch forward had to be bargained for. And once again I had foolishly
imagined that we all on the same side. The enemy was
within. First I had to fight for Grenville (who was of course a
member of the ACTT – but *not* a member of the wretched
Thames Shop). It was acknowledged that Thames' best
cameramen (including Mike Fash) were engaged elsewhere
and I argued – indeed rightly insisted – that the film now desperately needed fine photography. But they rejected Grenville
because he was an outsider. They wanted to promote their
own; rather like the Mafia. The quality of the film to them
was quite irrelevant. I must accept one of their relative
novices. In desperation, and innocence, I went to see Mr Alan
Sapper, my old chum, the General Secretary of the ACTT and
pleaded with him on behalf of Grenville Middleton getting the
job. I pointed out all of the human arguments, even including
Grenville's availability and the needs – like everyone else – of
his wife and three daughters. Then I made a blunder. I said:
'And he is a superb photographer.'

Mr Sapper jumped on that one: 'Ah, Kenneth; I've heard
that *merit* argument before!'

It was said as if I had been caught stealing or had been
exposed as a liar. To this day I am still unravelling this open
statement. But I stuck to an ultimatum and eventually got
Grenville. And that was very fortunate; otherwise the film
would have got into even deeper trouble than it did.

But the Grenville problem was only one of endless gremlins.
I had asked if Michel Pearce could direct the piece, but this
was refused. What conspiracies went on behind my back and
were unreported to me, I know not. And so it was agreed
that I should direct the film; though I would of necessity be in
front of the camera

I decided to take my actress daughter, Eva Griffith, with
me because she is a devout Christian and had never visited
the Holy Land. I would pay her air fare and accommodation
and she would look after my very varied wardrobe and keep

my spirit in good order. Of course she received no salary.

I was informed excitedly that we would all be travelling first-class to Israel. Our entire film-crew. Now I am always obsessive about my film budgets. I want to keep the costs as low as possible while making no concessions to any drop in quality.

'I'm not travelling first-class,' I announced.

Finally I was told: 'You *must*; it is an ACTT ruling.'

Again my ultimatum won the day and Eva and I travelled cabin class. 'I' being the researcher, the writer, the director and the entire cast, while the rest winged their ways with more leg room. Of course, all of this made me an awkward uncompromising customer and already there were whispers against me, which eventually became loud. One was below the belt: that I insisted upon travelling 'cabin' because I wouldn't buy a first-class ticket for Eva. Well, I can't afford to pay first-class for anyone; but that was not my basic reason. I come from a different world.

However, on the El Al flight to Israel I got a sort of come-uppance. I am, as I have related, a poor drinker of alcohol, but, when flying, I have got into the habit of drinking champagne. It is part of my organization to help pass away the only boring mode of transport that I know of. Somewhere over Europe and heading south-eastward, a stewardess asked me what I would like to drink.

'Champagne, please.'

'We don't have champagne.'

'What!?'

The chief stewardess was brought, who was rather like a pleasant Jewish Mama.

'What!?' I repeated, 'You mean to inform me that El Al, on an international flight, doesn't carry champagne!?'

'Sir, we carry it but it's only for first-class passengers.'

'What!?' became an essential word in my argument.

The fine woman finally stared at me and lowering her voice said: 'I'll *give* you some champagne; I can't charge you for it.'

'That's all right,' I said; and Eva and I enjoyed the stuff. Sadly and somehow surprisingly, none of the other passengers followed me up and demanded their (free) champagne. I also wryly thought of my film colleagues having it virtually thrust upon them. There is a moral buried here somewhere.

Of course, apart from Grenville, I didn't have any of my old, no-doubt long-suffering film crew with me. And I became much put out that the Thames unit insisted upon sticking to the rigid union working hours. It is only now, sitting here in Faenza's Biblioteca Comunale that I begin to feel that I have – perhaps – pushed my Protestant work ethic too far into the teeth of these contemporary times. But it was like my encounter with the Hell's Angels; if you don't fight it, are you not part of it? And there may be victories: now, in London's underground train service, there is no smoking allowed at all; and today Thames ACTT Shop has disappeared with the excellent company itself.

But what memories of the film making? The overwhelming experience was the impact that Saint Matthew made on this agnostic. I am deeply interested in human character; and in recounting the words and actions of Jesus Christ, Matthew presents an astoundingly unique man who was unswervingly consistent in character. Even his idiosyncracies were consistent. I presume that if a writer of great fiction (Dostoyevsky for instance) sets out to invent a human character, he must ponder and ponder the specific characteristics and must then, as he writes about the adventures of his creation, make sure that the invention is unbrokenly true – under all circumstances. All that I can write is that Matthew's account of Jesus is of a total, unique and inspiring human being. Jesus warms me and makes me laugh.

To represent the Magi we hired three Mercedes-Benz motor cars and they were all white. After careful thought I had decided that the Magi could have entered the Holy Land (Israel) from the north, following that magic star. And we had a helicopter! So, from the ground and from the air we followed the three white cars. Over the bitterly fought-for Golan Heights, down along the western shore of the Sea of Galilee and passing the Man's working patch, towards Bethlehem, where the celestial star stopped to mark His birthplace.

We filmed all of this from the air with complete co-operation from the Israeli authorities. Nevertheless and understandably, there was one security proviso: the military authorities must look at and pass all of this aerial film mater-ial before we could take it back to Britain. And that in itself was a revelatory experience. Two Israeli military security offi-cers viewed our helicopter shots, which were quite lengthy. They informally invited me to look at it with them and we sat in a small viewing theatre at their headquarters in Jerusalem. First they expressed their regret that I was being put to this trouble 'but the Golan Heights and our Eastern Border can be sensitive areas'. The film ran and ran punctuated by 'OK, OK,' from one of the officers. Down the border we travelled; it was fascinating for me to watch. 'OK, OK,' and then sud-denly 'Stop!' to the projectionist. 'Run that last section again, please.' The two officers peered closely at the image on the screen. 'And again, please. Again,' and the two of them had a quiet chat in Hebrew. At the end of their confab they turned to me and said: 'That's all right, Mr Griffith; nothing for us to worry about.'

I do like the Israelis; they are hard working, alarmingly efficient and as liberal and considerate as possible even under their endless war conditions.

At that time the ancient temple called Korazim was unren-ovated. The ruin stood amid the flowers and trees. It was spirit-ridden rather than ghost-ridden. Isolated. We saw no one in that heavenly place except an old Arab guardian who ever offered me coffee. In the evenings a sort of rock rabbit hopped and flitted about. It was here that we filmed the deeply intense passages, such as the words Christ spoke after His crucifixion. Close by, amongst the tall grasses, was where I recited 'the lilies of the field'.

In the synagogue at Capernaum we filmed about the faith of the Roman Centurion and of how Jesus turned to his disci-ples and spoke the astounding prophecy that his future followers would come from the Goyim.

And not far away we went to the Mount. And there, on the historical site, I spoke the indelible revolutionary sermon. It was all arrive-there-and-do-it. No alternative to the inspiration of the moment. Yes, I needed Michel Pearce. I would have a quiet chat with Grenville. But we both had our hands full with our respective specialities. I decided to film the spiritual rules of the human game as if Jesus was completely surrounded by listeners. On the elevated rock He spoke as He turned the 365 degrees again and again. Grenville's camera would pick up the movement from this position and then this and then this. And back in London, during the editing period, we would dissolve from one camera position into another, into another, as the sermon continued. That was the idea. But disasters were being prepared for us back home.

At Bethlehem we filmed at night, deep into the golden rock where the site of the nativity is located. The head of the Greek Orthodox Church in that place supervised our access. He was a lean, highly strung and affable man. After our work was over he happily, and somehow vitally, entertained us in his large bare living-room in the precincts of the Church of the Nativity. He chain-smoked and gave us whisky to drink as I remember it.

Down in that claustrophobic area which is focused as the beginning of physical Christianity, our camera lights made this small centre uncomfortably warm and around the intense illumination was shadowy darkness. High above us, in the church itself, littered with icons and antique brass, an apparently mad priest belonging to an alternative sect howled and screamed abuse at our Greek Orthodox benefactor. I climbed up the stone staircase and caught shadowy glimpses of the violent altercation. Our priest friend tried to calm his adversary but to no avail. I asked what the conflict was about and I was told that the deranged priest was discontented about the sharing of our fee for filming. The Christian churches have lost sight of the very simple instruction. They seem incapable of seeing the wood for the trees or rather the cross for their own arrogance.

We wanted to film by the River Jordan at the place where it is believed that John the Baptist blessed Jesus with water and where the dove descended. This request was not easy to achieve. It was at the front line of two nations at war: there, across the running water, was the Kingdom of Jordan. And our camera dangerously reflected the hot sun. However a small patrol of Israeli soldiers was arranged and the young officer in charge focused his binoculars on Jordanian soldiers and showed me. I saw them move and I saw something glint: 'Is that a gun?'

'No,' said our officer, 'that is *his* binoculars; he is looking at you.'

Along the bank of the River Jordan were the various Christian churches, all of them now deserted and bullet scarred; the site of Jesus' baptism is now no-man's-land. The young officer, whose first name was Israel I think, stooped down and fingered a glass phial out of the mud and handed it to me. It contained holy Jordan water which a church would once have sold to the pilgrims. I asked the charming young man to write on it and he inscribed 'From Israel'. Yes, we did our filming there.

Eva and I stayed in a ranch complex high up on the hills above the western shore of Galilee, which is run by a Jewish family who came from Chicago. It was a most pleasant time. We derived some of the quiet happiness that the whole countryside generates. There is a good, easy-going restaurant at the centre of the ranch which turned out to be a favourite haunt of people from embassies in Tel Aviv. One evening Eva and I entered and there was a party from the British Embassy. They were all very happy and bright and one or two of them recognized me and began to good-humouredly chide: 'Oh my God! What are *you* doing here? Not going to give *us* any trouble, are you?'

I took up the challenge, but wanting to get on with my supper, I suddenly bellowed: 'When are you lot going to move to Jerusalem, where you should be!?'

That was the end of the exchange. I wish that diplomats could play a straighter, braver game and stand firmer on the uncomfortable moral ground.

We lived in little cottages. One late afternoon I found a black snake catching the last rays of the sun on my veranda; it hastened away as I appeared. My friend, David Phillips, asked for a description and said: 'It's harmless.' My last memory of that visit to Israel was standing with Eva in the garden of the ranch, looking down on the sea of Galilee on which the moon had cast a bright pathway. I am ever quietly challenging my daughter's faith (only to try to discover my own). Of course I go gingerly: 'You see, Eva, my trouble is that I have difficulty in believing that Jesus walked on that water and didn't sink.'

She promptly replied: 'Well, Daddy, I believe that He was the Son of God and therefore walking on that water was the least of His problems.'

There's no answer to that. I hope that if certain distinguished 'advanced' British clergymen read my daughter's reply, they will have sufficient grace to blush.

Back in London chaos reigned. The permanent staff of commercial television had gone on strike and the poor bloody film was doomed to be edited and everything in two instead of ten weeks with precious little proper back-up from anyone. The film editor was in a tizz. The programme was scheduled. I did two desperate things: I wrote to a Mr Brian Cowgill, who was then the boss of the whole Thames outfit, appealing to him to withdraw the film from the date of transmission; he, predictably, lacked the basic good manners to reply. Such men rarely have respect for the artists. The second action I took was to ask Michel Pearce to help me. I paid him to advise me. But his position was next to impossible. The conspiracy against my efforts to redeem the film intensified almost to the point of an open explosion. But not quite; my adversaries didn't operate in that way. Michel, having looked at the film, mumbled about it being 'fine'. I wasn't completely convinced.

It was transmitted as Thames had arranged. It began in a cloud of inexplicable muck on the print. Both Grenville and I desperately telephoned Thames for an explanation. We both received the same answer: 'Someone forgot to clean the tape.' Whether this was a last act of mysterious viciousness or gross incompetence, I don't know.

Two reactions to the film stick in my mind. Mr Clive James, the newspaper columnist, was in the habit of regularly attempting to destroy the careers of people who appeared on television. But he had always, as far as I can remember, been reservedly supportive of me. The last piece about one of my programmes read: 'He is compulsive viewing; but so is a cobra,' which was about the nicest that he ever wrote about anyone – unless (I have noticed) the performer happened to be an attractive woman. Well, in those days I used to write a column for the BBC's *Radio Times* about their programmes for the approaching week that had impressed me most – or something like that. And on one particular week I had just read a piece by Clive James which set out to ruin and destroy a BBC series called *Connection* and in particular the programme's presenter, Mr James Burke. This piece of writing – I cannot call it criticism – was unbelievably cruel. Mr James uses ridicule to destroy people. And so I wrote about this unhappy man from Australia. I didn't know him personally or Mr Burke. Also on *Parkinson*, the excellent television interview programme, I spoke about James, whom, I regret to remember, Mr Parkinson defended. Well, having delivered my broadsides as effectively as I could, it did cross my mind how would Clive James react when my next programme emerged, which was to be the Magi film. I wondered whether he would give me credit for standing up to his bullying of other people or whether he would go for my throat. I needn't have pondered; it was headlined 'Saint Vitus Dance' and it was relentless ridicule. I did laugh at it and I felt that it could do me no harm; it was too obvious that it was prompted by a furtive hate or perhaps envy.

Years later I returned to Israel to make a film about the life of Israel's first Prime Minister, David Ben-Gurion. We were filming in an upstairs chamber of a sometime pasha's palace which is now a charming hotel called 'The American Colony'. I was re-enacting words spoken by the old King of Jordan, the present monarch's grandfather. For this I wore a heavy silk embroidered jacket which I had bought in India. Suddenly one of our film-crew broke my concentration: 'Hey Ken! Isn't that your old mate down there?' I peered below into the palm-treed courtyard: 'By God, yes! It's Clive James!' He was sprawling on a garden chair, drinking tea with another man who turned out to be the *Sunday Observer*'s Middle East correspondent. 'I'll be back, Michel,' as I hurled myself downstairs in the direction of Clive James. I dashed across the courtyard straight at him. He saw me and partly rose from his seat.

'Look, James,' I bellowed. 'Look what you've done to me!' I pointed at the silk jacket: 'I'm a bloody waiter in an Arab hotel!'

Well, the truth is we shook hands and he said: 'I concede that you've given me as bad a time as I've given you.'

Now, if we shook hands in Jerusalem, why am I raking the whole conflict up again? Yesterday I received a letter from Doria Griffith, my second wife, and I quote briefly from it: 'Your friend Clive James has been given two hours before the old year ends to destroy all the stars of the past decade . . .' So old Clive will never stop and I feel entitled to go for him again. And what does the television company or corporation that employed him think that they are doing? I always presumed that Clive James lusted after Mr Burke's job and mine. And he knew that the shortest and most dependable road to public success is to be scandalous. He is comparable to Page Three in the *Sun*. He has achieved his television exposure and to be charitable to him: to injure people seems to be his only apparent talent.

For what it is worth, the other notices that I saw seemed to be good. But the second reaction that I nurse came from the Programme Controller of BBC Wales: 'I have been reading and listening to the New Testament for most of my life and I have never heard it spoken as well.'

So we salvaged something worthwhile out of the effort and it was often a wonderful experience. I wish that it had been better. I haven't seen it since it was transmitted, but I'll have a look at it again when I return to London. Oh! I called the film *A Famous Journey*.

THIRTY-ONE

My two influential friends at BBC Wales, John Hefin and Geraint Stanley Jones, had listened carefully to my argument that we should make films of *universal* value; that we should not confine ourselves to Welsh *subjects*. What should be Welsh about them would be their Celtic spirit. As I have mentioned, I had long wished to be Thomas Paine's advocate. Thomas Paine, the artisan from East Anglia, who rose so high in human affairs that he held the American Revolution steady and then, having partly inspired the decent half of the French Revolution, stayed on through the eventual hell, begging Robespierre, Marat and Danton to apply themselves to *moral* issues! The man who wrote *Common Sense*, *The Rights of Man* and *The Age of Reason*. And John and Geraint agreed that I should make a film about Thomas Paine.

However, at this time I was – as usual – involved in numerous pickles. My relationship with Margret Kopala had painfully ended. Also a film had been made – not by me – which involved the lethal debate about our British role in north-eastern Ireland: I had been interviewed for it and had spoken my mind, which included, of course, the *Curious Journey* story – and this action on my part was brewing trouble for me. Also I had agreed to work, as an actor, on another film for Euan Lloyd, this time in India. It was a star-studded military adventure to be called *The Sea Wolves*. But BBC Wales arranged for me to have ample time to research and write my Tom Paine script while I fulfilled my contract for Euan.

I now feel obliged – reluctantly – to write something about my break-up with Ms Kopala. I have to do this because it changed my nature to some extent. Margret, with her intelligence and determination, had brought a degree of order and security to my life. Although I was financially wiped out (not that there was much to wipe out!), I felt happy and relaxed because I was being looked after – very efficiently. We lived in her small flat in the Portobello Road, and that whole ambience of antique dealers suited me very well. Though, when contemplating this episode of my life, I have constantly had the image of Michael Collins rebuking one of his followers who had been abusive to Eamon de Valera, because of his betrayal of Collins on the eve of the Irish Civil War: 'If you can't say anything good about him, then say nothing!' Injury can blind a person to virtues if we are not very careful.

I can hazard a guess – but it is only a guess – as to what went wrong. As usual I was totally absorbed by efforts to perfect my own work and since Margret was helping me I presumed that any success I was having was for us both. I gave some attention to her work, but in retrospect, not enough. However, she gave me confirmation of the permanence of our relationship and indeed we were together for (was it?) seven years. I have to accept the fact that I was ridiculously blind. My friend, Peter O'Toole, was the first to intervene and warn me. He visited us and after a while grabbed me into some privacy and fairly shook me: 'Griffith, what do you think you're doing!? I've never seen such hatred in a person's eyes! They change colour – to a milky blue – with hatred!'

Yes, I knew what he was driving at, but I couldn't accept that it was hatred and I laughed it off.

By this time the Women's Liberation Movement had completely encompassed Margret. I became very familiar with the unhappy jargon. But when I returned to London, having virtually escaped from Iran, we uneasily agreed to get married. It was not to be; she returned to her home in Western Canada and the less I write about it the better.

However, I was left deeply disturbed and I was never to be quite the same person again. I spotted in myself a breakdown, but it never quite came to that. I recognized the wafer divide between all of us 'normals' and those who go over the edge.

Good friends urged me to leave the house that we had both lived in together, in Islington, but I didn't want to. I didn't shout; indeed I was inordinately quiet. I remember sitting in the garden with a few friends and knowing that I was now *living* Chekhov. I did some weeping through some nights. Three separate friends, incredibly, offered to travel to Canada to see her on my behalf, but I discouraged this. Eventually I received a letter from her which included: 'I am seriously considering returning.' I was ecstatic; only in recent times have I peeped at the arrogance of it.

I then telephoned to Margret explaining that I was about to leave for North America: to speak to the Commissioners of Canadian Television; to speak at Harvard University and to record a lengthy television interview about my work. And then I had business meetings at both New York and Washington.

'Why don't you join me in Canada?'

'Yes.'

But she wouldn't attend my address to the Canadian Commissioners and several times she telephoned while I was speaking. And I began to realize that she was in a far worse state than myself. When I had finished my talk – which was about objectivity and subjectivity on television – a friend, Roy Faibish, rushed me to the apartment where Maggie and I were living and she was dangerously distraught. Later she wandered around the place, naked, muttering rapidly, 'Kenny, I love you! Kenny, I love you!' but any words from me were met with screams. My friend and I put her on an aircraft for her home in Edmonton. She wouldn't allow me to go with her.

I kept all of my engagements in the United States of America and performed them reasonably well. In Washington I stayed with Amanda and Anthony Holden and they helped to hold me together and in New York with Nikki and Steve Scheuer who did likewise. But on my return to London, and in spite of loving support from a number of friends, I slipped into a hazardous phase. I didn't seem to have a centre; I lived through several affairs with women and though they were good people, the only redeeming memory, in retrospect, was that the relationships were anarchically funny. The term that I used for myself during that period was 'abject'. I can only repeat: my centre had gone and, in certain ways, I was out of control.

I believe that I comprehend the psychological pattern. I believe that my mother's disappearing when I was six months old had an everlasting effect on me in my relationships – particularly with women. I believe that two elements have ruled me in this respect: a deep need for some female replacement and, having found her, my travelling bags were ever packed for a hasty retreat. At the very least I must leave before 'she' did! With Margret Kopala – irony upon irony, and for a number of reasons – I was persuaded to unpack those bags, or drop my guard, and, what I so deeply feared, 'she' went again!

Of course, I had sufficient balance left even then to digest that I had inflicted similar injuries on others. I remember thinking of Mark Twain's come-uppance. To assess and balance the respective damages is impossible and beyond the scope of this book. But abject I was and I apologize to those I have messed about.

Strangely I do not think that this emotional disaster affected any of my work at all. I acted in Euan's film as well as I could have before the blow was delivered. Of course many of the actors were old comrades and their company – particularly the kindness of Bernard Archard – was a happiness for me and, finally, I met Ms Chiara Peretti, who, to this day, is a special friend.

But this Indian experience is included in my book called: *The Discovery of Nehru* (Michael Joseph, 1989) and I will repeat no more here.

I had often wondered to myself when I would grow up; begin to behave like a mature man is supposed to behave. I believe that it began to happen then. There are things that I like about my metamorphosis and things that I don't like. But I hasten to underline that I have not entirely put away *all* childish things.

The team to make the Tom Paine film proved to be truly outstanding; most of them I had worked with previously. Michel Pearce was to direct it, Russ Walker was to light, photograph and operate it, Ted Doull was to be in charge of sound, and the editor was Chris Lawrence. Of course John Hefin would produce and travel with us in the field. Ms Beth Price would act as producer's assistant and we all hoped and prayed that she would find New York and other American cities comparable to Cardiff, though we all knew in our bones that this wasn't remotely possible. (You may recall that Ms Price found Africa a big let-down after her life in South Wales.) And giving the whole enterprise his protection against the beginning of snarls from BBC London was Geraint Stanley Jones.

We filmed at Thetford where Paine was born in the atmospheric back-water of East Anglia. I am prepared to believe that I can sense human spirits of the past; that is when a land has been relatively undisturbed. We filmed on the areas where Paine had operated as an excise officer and again we were capturing on film those specific hauntings and also, as I struggled with my problem of achieving clean-cut communication about the infinite nuances of a human life, I was reminded and reminded of the ingenuity of Michel's direction and of the very silent efforts of Russ Walker to bend and mould the light for maximum effect. Ted Doull, I am afraid, we took for granted, which is the usual fate of sound. We knew that it would be all right even if Ted said nothing. And we were all aware that Ted rarely delayed us with any technical problem, which is often how the sound man is judged. Perhaps it was only when I heard that high-powered television Mogul in New York mumble: 'How the hell do you achieve such a high consistency of sound?' did I fully appreciate what a high class professional we had. Fortunately I found the grace to report this New York comment back to Geraint in Cardiff.

Though this film, *The Most Valuable Englishman Ever*, is an outstanding work (I write as a member of the team) and was received by most of the Press and public with enthusiastic approbation, it was destined to do me considerable harm professionally. I then had two good friends in highish positions at the BBC and they acted as kindly moles on my behalf. Within a few days of the film's transmission they informed me that a formidable warning shot had been fired against me by, primarily, Mr Brian Wenham, the head of BBC2. This information was later – much later – painfully confirmed to me by my friends and colleagues at BBC Wales. This element in London successfully warned off Cardiff from using me in the future. I am philosophical. So be it!

Mr Jeremy Isaacs was setting up the new British television concept of Channel Four and he communicated that he wanted to talk to me. Timely! I went along with my then partner, Mr David Swift. With Jeremy, in his new office, was a man named Paul Bonner, whom I vaguely recalled as a person I had briefly met in Ireland while we were making the Michael Collins film. I wondered why he was sitting with Jeremy; I later learnt that he was the programme controller for the new channel; even later I was told that he was a chum of Lawrence Gordon Clarke, whom I had badly upset on my very first historical project *Soldiers of the Widow*. So you see, my life has been rather like Douglas Fairbanks Senior in one of his swashbuckling roles; and I like to see myself like that: surrounded by multiple assailants whom I successfully beat off. But at that interview with Jeremy, as usual, I knew nothing about anything except what stories I wanted to communicate and the confidence that I could make them. It appeared to be a merry meeting and Jeremy, the Boss, had invited me . . .

Jeremy kicked off most generously: 'Kenneth, we need you here *badly*!' Mr Bonner said nothing.

'Well Jeremy,' I replied, I have a little patch at BBC Wales and I have been responsible for two films there: *Black as Hell* and *The Most Valuable Englishman Ever* and we have a good team and I want to hang on there.'

To which Jeremy replied: 'Kenneth, loyalty is a wonderful thing; now what are you going to do for *us*?'

Well, I had already sensed a more detached attitude from John Hefin and Geraint Stanley Jones at BBC Cardiff and I had pondered the leverage that Mr Wenham and perhaps company had over the Principality, so I told Jeremy and I said that I wanted to make a film about the great Liberal, Gladstone, and a film about the equally great Afrikaner, Paul Kruger. I wanted – and still want – to communicate some truths about those remote puritans of South Africa in order to counter the endless slander and libel that the liberal world seems to derive so much pleasure in inflicting on them. Oh yes! The Afrikaners also have a point of view that is not without honour.

Anyway, Jeremy replied: 'Do Gladstone first; we don't want you getting into trouble at the very beginning! Anything else you have in mind?'

'Well, Jeremy,' I ventured, 'I have long wanted to make a series on a theme.' And before Lord Clark and Bronowsky and Alistair Cooke made their respective series, they were all sat down at Ealing Studios – so I am informed by various editors and projectionists there – to study my films, but I realize that the BBC under its present management, would find me far too outspoken . . .'

'What would you do, Kenneth?'

'A series of films about prisoners in the Tower of London; each one was a political prisoner, therefore all of them would be significant good stories. Show them in chronological order and you will demonstrate to the viewers – whether the State cut off their heads or not – how we have stumbled forward to our present stage of democracy.'

'Marvellous!' said Jeremy Isaacs. 'Would you agree to allow me to help you in choosing some of the subjects?'

'Of course, Jeremy; I would be very pleased.'

Not only was he boss man, but he is also perceptively intelligent – which has rarely been the same thing in my experience. As I left that office with David Swift, I addressed Jeremy: 'I came here very depressed about British television; I am leaving feeling very good. Thank you!'

I could have saved my precious enthusiasm; within a week Jeremy Isaacs spoke to David Swift (*never* to me): 'Please inform Kenneth that there is formidable opposition to his presence here. I am leaving for Israel at the end of this week to look at some archive material. I will look into this matter personally; but warn him to prepare for the worst.'

'The worst' was predictable; Jeremy Isaacs *did* come back and again to David Swift: 'Kenneth cannot work here.' That was as it was reported to me.

Come to think of it, I am not in the relatively comfortable predicament of Douglas Fairbanks Senior; he was face to face with his villainous enemies, mine were never to be *seen* and even if there were dozens of them within burgeoning Channel Four, they never – not one of them – confronted me eyeball to eyeball. I confess that I would have enjoyed that. But who were these unfriendly characters? What were they? And what did they so deeply resent in me? It couldn't have been the effect that the Tom Paine film had had even on the nation; it had received astonishing praise far and very wide. Distinguished political figures wrote to me apart from many hundreds of letters from general viewers. And this support culminated in an invitation to visit Mrs Indira Gandhi in her home in Delhi. I suppose the deep resentment against me at Channel Four *could* have been the very impact of this film. Resentment is born out of many varied causes; reaction always depends upon the calibre of the person, the quality of the person. Of course it can simply be mundane and political (which is much the same thing). A couple of days after *The Most Valuable Englishman Ever* was transmitted, I was a guest at a very grand party and the hostess asked: 'Kenneth, did you read your editorial in the *Telegraph* yesterday?'

'The *review* of the Paine film?' I clarified.

'No, Kenneth, the *editorial* was about you!'

The next morning I was in Fleet Street. Two big cockneys were behind the counter: 'Come for your editorial, Mr Griffith?'

'Yes,' and as the newspaper was handed to me, one of the lads said: 'Of course, *we* don't agree with this muck, Mr Griffith. Good luck to yer!'

Well I was doubly grateful for any support just then. My professional options were once again diminishing very fast. The editorial was a traditional and baroque refutation of my argument in the film that Tom was a candidate for being 'the most valuable Englishman ever'. It could have been written by Edmund Burke himself; which statement may please Mr Peregrine Worsthorne or Lord Deedes. It gave me great pleasure and, like old Clive James going berserk against me, made me laugh. You know where you are with James, and Worsthorne and Deedes – indeed I almost like them – but those creeps at Channel Four are another matter.

THIRTY-TWO

Once again it looked as if I was beaten in Britain but again I seemed to have multiple professional retreats throughout the English-speaking world. There had been various approaches to me to make my films in New Zealand, Australia, Canada and with options in the United States. America seemed the place: I went to New York and had discussions with the Columbia Broadcasting System, cable people, with representatives of Mr Ted Turner and with representatives of Public Television all of whom had invited me. Also at this time I accepted a contract with American commercial television advertising, which really amounted to preventing me from selling any product for a rival on American television. I think a firm called Procter and Gamble were involved. It was very curious to me; I have never accepted to perform in any television commercial, but I was quite happy to accept dollars *not* to do so.

However, again I felt uneasy at the prospect of leaving Britain, even though I would be paid much more money than I was accustomed to. My films were not *primarily* for entertainment. They were made first and foremost to inform; but they had to be as entertaining as I could make them to ensure that viewers with a serious propensity watched. And my stories were essentially radical. They carried themes which were humanistic. They were about historical events which focused on universal problems. Better that I made them about my *own* country's behaviour or misbehaviour; they would be none the less humanly universal for that. But the irony was that I was ever being edged out of the British nest and welcomed far far away. Even this very fact that my British films were admired overseas did not seem to make my life more welcoming at home; indeed the contrary seemed to be the case. Not even my commercial potential seemed to help me. I think that a British envy of independence was the ever recurring trouble for me in Britain. What are desperately needed for all high-flying makers of things – artists – are big impresarios: like Tyrone Guthrie, Korda, Huw Wheldon and – yes! – Lew Grade. We British tend to have little men in charge. The servant artists, the 'yes, sir; thank you sir' performers are relatively safe in contemporary Britain, because we are astoundingly short of employers with courage, principles and vision.

I was literally packing to depart for the United States of America when I received a message from Richard Attenborough who had just completed his famously effective life of Mahatma Gandhi. Richard said: 'For years I have wanted to make a film about the life of Thomas Paine, but had come to the conclusion that it was impossible. Oh! I've been in India . . .'

'Yes, I know, Richard.' And it flashed through my head that an average Chinaperson, in the streets of Peking (or whatever the place is called now) would know where Richard had been.

'Well,' continued the very remarkable man, 'on my return to Britain, I have been told that you have made a wonderful life of Paine; would you show it to me?'

'Of course, Richard.'

I arranged a viewing for my famous friend and ushered him into the theatre and I sat outside in the little foyer. Ninety minutes later he came out and I received the impression that he was drying his eyes: 'Marvellous, Kenneth. Marvellous! What are you going to do next?'

'Well, Richard, I'm going to work in America.'

As far as I can recall – and the film projectionist, Mr Andrew Young, was a witness – Richard, like a good Britisher, rather barked: 'How dare you!'

'Hold on!' I countered, 'I'm only going there because no one in British television will now employ me.'

'But,' argued Richard, with all of his considerable vehemence, 'you made that wonderful film for the BBC – go on working for them!'

'Ah, I don't think that you understand the changes that have taken place; the BBC is *not* the place that it was when your brother [Sir David Attenborough] and Huw Wheldon were running it. Now furtive men preside and there is no place for me.'

And I related what I had been told by my few BBC friends.

'Then Channel Four!'

'Ah,' I repeated, 'I really think you don't know what is truly going on.'

And I related the experience with Jeremy Isaacs, beginning with: 'We need you badly, Kenneth!' and culminating two weeks later with 'Kenneth can't work here.'

Sir Richard Attenborough stared at me intensely. Andrew Young stood at the door of his projection room and watched the unusual encounter. And then Richard, pointing a finger at me, said: 'I'm not telephoning Channel Four; I'm not writing to them! I'm going round NOW, to tell them what I think!' And he made a crashing exit through the swing doors and then immediately reappeared: 'I'll be in touch with you by tomorrow, Kenneth!'

When he had finally disappeared I turned to my friend Andrew: 'Hasn't Sir Richard got something to do with Channel Four?'

I know nothing about such matters; Andrew knows everything and he soberly replied: 'He's deputy chairman.'

And within a few days I was informed by that sinisterly enigmatic Channel Four that I would be allowed to work for them: 'What subject does he want to make for us?' Well again, no one spoke to *me*; again the improved news came through David Swift, as far as I can remember.

My old friend, Euan Lloyd, had recently visited my home in Islington and had spent a long while peering at my large library. When he came to the 'Asia' section, he gazed at the wodge of books about Robert Clive, 'Clive of India'.

'You know, Kenneth, for years I have hoped to make a film about Clive; people are beginning to forget who he was!' Euan mused sadly a little longer and then spontaneously: 'Kenneth, would you make one of *your* films, about Clive, for me? I know that they are seen on television throughout the English-speaking world. It will remind people who Clive was and we can use it to prepare for our big cinema film!' There was a moment of hesitancy from Euan. 'But where do you find two hundred battle elephants today?' which was quickly dispelled with: 'We'll find them! How much do you get paid to research and write?' I told him and there was a cheque in my pocket.

Well, my immediate answer to Channel Four's belated question was: 'Clive of India', and they paid me to research and write the script. I had the pleasure of returning Euan's cheque; he didn't mind that Channel Four was financing the production; all he wanted was the film to be made and seen.

You can't criticize me for wondering what words were demonstrated by Sir Richard Attenborough on my behalf at Channel Four, can you? A few home truths must have been communicated, mustn't they? But just as they avoided expressing their views to my face, so I restrained my curiosity and I didn't ask them any questions. It is a strong instinct I have: say nothing unless there is a good reason and preferably until there is a listening ear. Or until war is openly declared and wait for the whites of their eyes, or whatever is the equivalent in these days of potential nuclear conflict.

After this helpful, indeed life-saving, encounter with Richard Attenborough, I received an invitation, once or twice, to top-table film functions; once at the Guildhall in London. I could only surmise who had slipped my name onto the list. However, I was always out of Britain and was never able to attend. And around this time a distinguished Canadian Jew, Mr Roy Faibish, took me to a dinner given by the Royal Television Society, in London. Roy is a humorous man; he was fully aware that he was inviting a cat to sit amongst the most influential pigeons. He has that sort of sense of humour. It is inconceivable that anyone else would have invited me to such a gathering; that is, except for Huw Wheldon. (Huw at that time was ill; an illness which was to lead to his death.) Well, there they all were: the big Establishment winners! The nearest I have got (and I suspect will ever get) to writing a novel, is the title: *The Winners and the Losers*. The whole human arena of winning and losing intrigues me. Of course it depends what one means by winning and losing. Not far from where I am now scribbling away, Michelangelo wasn't too concerned about material comfort; nor was hard-pressed Mozart a big bankable commodity. And again, not very far from here, that mystic genius, Uccello, penned a letter to the Florentine tax people: 'I am old and cannot make a living. My wife is ill and I cannot work any more.' So what is a winner? But the television Moguls were present in force that evening.

It was a memorable and uneasy occasion for me. I sat with my naughty chum some little distance from the top table and I tended to crouch out of sight. Of course it was fascinating for me. The President spoke first. I believe that he was then Programme Controller at the BBC in Birmingham. He began by saying something to the effect: 'I have noticed Mr Kenneth Griffith is present' (there must have been one hundred and fifty top-brass there) 'and I have to say how much I admired his film on the life of Thomas Paine.'

To his left and facing me was Aubrey Singer an influence who, in his times, had prohibited my reappearance on BBC television. The second speaker referred to me in supportive terms. And finally, Jeremy Isaacs spoke. He kicked off resoundingly about the great potential of Channel Four and of British television in general. He spoke about freedom on television and courage . . . Jeremy Isaacs paused; it is difficult for me to describe the moment. Behind Jeremy's pundit/executive facade is a man – so I sense – of deep, complicated emotions. He unexpectedly said: 'I can feel Kenneth Griffith's eyes gimletting into me.' And this was in front of the whole hierarchy. Yes, my eyes *were* focusing on him very intently. I don't know, I cannot remember, whether my travelling bags were still packed to earn a living and speak a few words in America on that very day. I certainly had received no practical benediction from any of them. I sat there as still as that cobra that Clive James had remarked about. I think Roy Faibish laughed; he is an amused observer of even human tragedy. I said, wisely,

'Let's go!' and we departed. Roy Faibish also told me, at a later date, that he had attended a similar function – was it in Birmingham? – and Huw Wheldon had stated that by the year 2000, theses would be composed about my style (love it or hate it) of television communication. People were concurring and Roy told me that Huw then asked: 'Then why don't you help him?' Of course by that time Huw Wheldon was out of executive command at the BBC and shortly - afterwards I would suffer the devastating loss of his going.

Despite the fact that I had so much research material about Robert Clive in my library, I doubt whether he would have been included amongst my next twenty choices as a subject to film. Euan Lloyd had nudged me into it and I am always poised to break even my own pattern of thought, as long as it does not mean joining the ranks of convention.

India was beckoning and I didn't know then what treachery was lurking for me in that Other Darkish Continent. Mrs Indira Gandhi had viewed the Tom Paine film; I suspect that Ms Marie Seton, sometime film editor and lover of the celebrated Russian film director, Sergei Eisenstein, had sent it to her. Anyway I was invited to visit the leader of India at her home in Delhi.

Mrs Gandhi was a woman who made a disturbing impression on me. Her home, at Safdarjang Road in New Delhi, was a smallish, homely place. She made no pretensions to importance or power; she behaved simply as she was: intelligent, very perceptive and unintimidating (to me). She was a no-nonsense lady. She always wore variations of those beautiful Indian costumes. Sitting on a *chaise-longue*, she stated that, 'The Tom Paine film was perhaps the most moving and disturbing film that I have ever seen . . .' I had heard similar words about both the Michael Collins film and the Tom Paine film from other political leaders elsewhere. And they were all significant punctuations in my life. No matter how self-sufficient one might succeed in being; no matter how honestly self-critical one might try to be, such utterances as Mrs Gandhi made – and the few other political achievers – are clarifications about what I might have succeeded in doing. At least you know that you have influenced a few human beings, part of whose job is to influence millions and millions of other people.

I said to Mrs Gandhi that she must be well used to talking to people (like me) who suffered some difficulty in treating her as just another human being. Mrs Gandhi jumped on that remark with alacrity: 'Why is that, Mr Griffith? Clearly I am just another ordinary person.'

I replied: 'It is difficult to address you as an ordinary person when one knows that you lead six hundred million souls.'

'Six hundred and *seventy-three* million, Mr Griffith!'

Her correction of my too loose figure was a haunted reflex. She was deeply disturbed about India's exploding population. She told me that her surviving son, Rajiv, was also an admirer of my film work and that he wanted to meet me. I asked Rajiv Gandhi if he missed flying. (With the death of his brother Sanjay, in a flying accident, Rajiv had retired from being an airline pilot to help his mother.)

'I can't describe to you, Mr Griffith, how much. But with the death of my brother, I must now do all I can to help my mother – and India.'

The Prime Minister and Rajiv's wife, Menka, were present when he said that. Soon his mother was to be most treacherously murdered by her own Sikh guards who had, no doubt, sworn an oath to protect her. It was bestial. And Rajiv was elected to her political place to do his best to help India. For what my opinion is worth, I believe that he was honest and did his best. But the job of running India is as near to being impossible as one can imagine. It has to be understood that the disparate cultures, religions and ethnic groups of the Indian subcontinent had never been unified except by us British, and that of course was only achieved by a remarkably discreet force of imperial arms. What a role for the quiet airline pilot . . .

Before I parted from Mrs Indira Gandhi she said: 'Perhaps Mr, Griffith, you will consider making one of your films for India about the life of my father.'

This request was the most disquieting moment of my visit.

I knew very little about her father, Jawaharlal Nehru, the first prime minister of independent India. I sensed that he was a good man and I knew that he had spent a large proportion of his life battling to get rid of us British from India. I sensed a man in the shadow of the astounding Mahatma Gandhi. Nothing more did I know. And now here was his daughter, the inheritor of his dread role, asking me if I – a Britisher – would make a film, for India, about his life! Two things disturbed me: first that this Indian woman trusted this Welsh Britisher sufficiently to offer him the job, to make a film about the life of a man she revered so much. And secondly, I couldn't then see the *story* that I needed in order to make one of my films. I had long seen the obvious potential in a filmed life of Gandhi. But that was not what I was being invited to do. And Richard Attenborough had just done it – on a grand scale. So I made no comment, except what must have been articulated on my face.

When Euan Lloyd made *The Sea Wolves* in India he employed a distinguished Indian, Vice-Admiral Rusi Ghandhi, to advise him on how to do things on the subcontinent. Rusi and I became particular friends and I quickly recognized how shrewd Euan had been in appointing him. Now, being faced with my own production of *Clive of India*, I asked Rusi to look after our film unit. He had just become the chairman (was it?) of the India Shipping Company and therefore he was not available. But, he had a friend, a retired admiral, Satyindra Singh, who would be perfect for the job. It seems to me, in retrospect, that Satyindra Singh was not less than essential. I moved with him in New Delhi and sat by his side as he unravelled and coped with the indescribably destructive machine that is the Indian bureaucracy. Again I must remind the reader that I have written a book about this astounding experience and here it must suffice that most of it was an excruciating nightmare except that 'Saty' (pronounced by me 'Setty') extricated us from their snares and traps with almost total success.

Michel Pearce was the director and Grenville Middleton was the lighting cameraman and operator; so we had a first-class team.

A few experiences are essential for me to repeat in this book because they began to shift my nature somewhat. On the very first morning of filming we were at Humayun's Tomb, in Delhi, to achieve a grand image of the sheer size of the Mogul Empire. We set our camera up in the vast garden and while we waited for the inevitable sun to rise, I retreated to a distance where I could mull over what I had soon to say to the camera. As I mulled I noticed a curious phenomenon: I saw several separate Indian men, striding over the grass, dressed in grey flannel trousers, tweed sports coats, collar and tie and holding substantial walking-sticks, while they exercised their respective dogs. Now, writing as a Welshman, and much travelled, I have only seen English people behave like that. Suddenly one of these men was standing over me: 'Excuse me, but may I ask what you are doing?'

I jumped to my feet: 'Ah, sir, we are just about to begin making a film. There is the film crew,' and I pointed.

'Yes, I see; but what is your film about?'

'Robert Clive.'

'Ah! Clive of India!'

'Correct, sir.' And I felt that I should reassure: 'But I promise you that there will be no jingoistic nonsense in this film; there won't be much waving of the Union Jack here!'

The Indian stared at me firmly and held up a finger: 'Sir, I hope that you are going to be fair to the British Empire!'

I was being admonished.

'We must not forget that it was your people who unified this great sub-continent; that it was you who inaugurated our comprehensive transport system. And our bureaucracy.'

Putting aside the latter, I felt contrite: 'I take note of what you say, sir. I will be particularly careful not to be unfair to the British Empire.'

The Indian smiled happily: 'Well, good day to you sir!'

'And good day to you, sir!'

And off he strode. But he suddenly stopped; his eyes moved round to the great Mogul tomb: 'And,' his dark eyes now fixed on mine, 'you saved us from a terrible tyranny . . .' And I knew which religion he pursued.

All that I will reiterate here about those thirty days of filming are a few of the ghost groaning locations: what remains of
the ramparts of Arcot, where audacious Clive and his East
India Company lads stuck it out against enormous Muslim
hordes. And Plassey; now a lonely isolated area, where the old
high obelisk to commemorate our take-over of India is crumbling. And the city of Murshidabad: a desolate ruin which was
until young Clive arrived, far richer than the City of London
and the last hope of the Moguls.

The cobra turned up again in Murshidabad. As I walked
through the overgrown garden of the shattered harem with
one of the old ruler's direct descendants, he confessed that
the place was snake-ridden. I asked him if he suffered no
unease: 'Me! Of course not! I am from the direct line of the
Prophet. A cobra fell from there (he pointed to the high ver-
durous wall above us) around my shoulders, but it would
never bite *me*!'

I felt unease and was uncommonly wary. However, even I
became relatively blasé. I was sitting in a chair up against a
wall of the wrecked palace when I noticed a serpent approach;
I quietly stood up and allowed it to slither past before I resat
and continued my thoughts.

Clive of India is an illustration of how imperialism, and
particularly the British brand, was born: our British request
for trade; our competition for trade (in India particularly
against the French); our demand for trade; our wars for trade
and finally the necessity to annex for trade. Young Robert
Clive understood, broadly, the game that he had been tipped
into. Having broken the French power in Southern India, his
business bosses in Calcutta, the executives of the English East
India Company, asked him if he could militarily erase the last
French stronghold, then called Chandernagore, to the north.

He replied: 'I believe so. But I warn you. If I take
Chandernagore from the French you will not be able to stop
your advance there – even if you want to!'

The young man could see, in his mind's eye, what the consequences would be. The French presence in India was almost
a buffer between the British and Mogul power; at least the

French were an alternative distraction. Clive again won at Chandernagore and immediately the reality became clear even to the greedy business men of the English company. Clive moved his small army northward to that place called Plassey.

Today, in the back of beyond, in a straggling village is Plassey. You are far, far away from India's tourist routes. People there are very poor but it was here that the British Raj was born – the Brightest Jewel, or whatever it was. The site of the battle is introduced by a high, imposing obelisk, suitably and imperiously inscribed, but now, like most remnants of our imperial presence, it is fading in the intense heat. Oxen carts trundle past it and Indians have little to say about such ephemeral matters.

The loner, Clive, noting that his army would be heavily outnumbered by the Mogul leader, Siraj-ud-daula and his French allies, uncharacteristically hesitated on one side of the River Cossimbazar. Even more uncharacteristically, he called his senior officers together and asked their opinion about the deadly situation; seven advised against giving battle, two daredevils were for it. Clive pondered alone for about one hour, in a mango grove, and made up his mind. The British force crossed the river and prepared for victory. However, the French guns began to overwhelm the British and Clive was forced to withdraw into another grove; defeat seemed inevitable. At that juncture a monsoon storm broke. The short of it is that the British had covers for their artillery and the French didn't. When the rains ceased, Clive was able to blast the enemy into defeat and panic retreat – back to Murshidabad. And virtually the vast subcontinent of India was, inevitably, becoming British.

Incidentally, while we were filming on that disturbing plain, the monsoon rain exploded on us. My main memory of the event is of two formidable Indians fighting to hold me upright in the deep mud. Why the three of us were laughing I don't now understand.

Because of Euan Lloyd I became involved in this film *Clive of India*. As a rule, I choose a subject to demonstrate, through history, a vital cause of some contemporary conflict. Today, above everything, my priority is to demonstrate that we British are the deliberate creators of Ireland's endless tragedies. In the case of *Clive* I had quickly to understand *why* I was doing it. If one hasn't got a sound *reason* and fully comprehends it, the film will be relatively meaningless. Documentary film makers – or any film makers for that matter – often scratch around for some sensational subject and then make it simply because it is sensational. Not good enough; you must understand why and believe. *Clive* was a colourful illustration of the nature of imperialism. Robert Clive, at the age of forty-nine years, cut his throat. I hope that the film demonstrates that imperialism is a big mistake in the long run. Which again makes me think of the British civil and military presence in six of the counties of Ulster and the hell that we British are ultimately responsible for.

THIRTY-THREE

Emily Hobhouse was a great Englishwoman. She was the daughter of an Anglican vicar in the West of England. When the Anglo-Boer War broke out during October 1899, we British quickly discovered that we were not going to walk over the White farmers of South Africa (the Afrikaners of today). Well, it wasn't on the cards that the Great British Empire could be defeated, particularly with greedy, envious Europe looking on. So we instituted a conscienceless scorched earth policy: we began to burn down thousands of Boer farms and even towns, as we did in Ireland some seventy-five years ago; but in South Africa on a vaster scale. And then we carted off the women and children and very old men (males from twelve years to seventy-five or so were generally out on their horses fighting the invading British Imperial Armies). These Imperialists came from not only Britain but Australia, Canada and New Zealand; finally they totalled some four hundred and fifty thousand! We dumped the Boers into enormous tented towns on the veldt. Unhappily we, logically, called these places concentration camps. Was it Lord Halifax who surprisingly complained to Hermann Goering about the advent of the German camps and the Field Marshal ordered an *Encyclopaedia Britannica* and pointed out that we British had invented them?

Miss Hobhouse was the first Britisher who worried about what was happening to these uprooted people and decided to see for herself. She was not materially well-off but she raised her ship fare and a few hundred extra pounds with which she bought chocolate and soap and other innocent niceties to hand around. She started off as a Lady Bountiful. Arriving in Cape

Town she used her respectable family name and her innocent seductive charms to gain access to the very perimeter of the war area. She wheedled her way to Bloemfontein, the capital of the Orange Free State, which was losing the 'Free' bit at the military behest of us British and was being renamed, the Orange River Colony, and then made her way, with her chocolates, to the local concentration camp. What she saw transformed her: the uprooted Boer people were dying in astounding numbers. Miss Hobhouse disposed of her parasol and rolled up her Victorian sleeves and she began to create hell for the local British civil and military authorities. Her life's mission was under way.

The distinguished Afrikaner actress, Ms Hermien Dommisse, who had for some years followed the evolvement of my style of documentary film making, asked me if I would write her a script telling the story of Miss Hobhouse's life. It was to be financed by the South African Broadcasting Company. This I readily agreed to do. I find it extremely difficult to accept the dictates of any trade union (in this case my own well-meaning Equity) or, for that matter, my Government, if I believe them to be supporting, blindly, the wrong side as it were. Ms Dommisse saw, clearly, the moral value of Miss Hobhouse's life's work. And so do I. And so did the SABC. In those concentration camps approximately 26,000 victims of British greed for gold died; and that out of a very small total Boer population. Eventually, when the Afrikaners were able to, they built a memorial in Bloemfontein. They call it the Women's Memorial. And when Miss Emily died, Afrikaner women arranged for her ashes to be carried from England to be interred in that Women's Memorial. Field Marshal Jan Smuts spoke the oration: 'We stood alone in the world, friendless among the people, the smallest nations ranged against the mightiest Empire on the earth. Then one small hand, the hand of a woman, was stretched out to us. At that darkest hour, when our race appeared almost doomed to extinction, she appeared as an angel, as a heaven-sent messenger. Strangest of all, she was an Englishwoman.'

Well, having written the story for Ms Dommisse to film, both she and South Africa's best known film director, Mr

William Faure, asked me if I would 'perform' the British side of the story while Hermien spoke for the Boers. Bill Faure is a fearless and imaginative director and so I happily accepted my responsibilities. As with all of my films, we would shoot on the historical locations. And what an exciting (if you know your history) and beautiful country South Africa is!

Only once before have I tried this film duet: with the late Lee J. Cobb in *Suddenly an Eagle*. Of course, my style of committed storytelling is – like it or not – unique and only two directors, Antony Thomas and Michel Pearce, have had any chance to develop it. And for the new storyteller also it is inexperienced ground. I, with many years of practice, hold a big advantage. Michel once made such a film without me; he made it with a fine American actress. Michel explained to me the problem: the actress was skilful in the acting pieces – becoming the different people – but it was when she had to speak authoritatively, as herself, that she faltered. As I wrote above, you have to have total conviction, total belief, total faith in what you are saying. Chutzpah! That in the first place. Even with me, the acted characters and the subjective personal sequences (though both are written) are *different* skills. Nevertheless, Hermien did well; I was particularly impressed with her President Paul Kruger; we used no make-up nor historical costumes.

We were filming in the great docks of Cape Town, doing Emily Hobhouse's exit from South Africa. She was virtually manhandled out by the British authorities because she was exposing – internationally – our imperial crimes.

I meandered amongst the ships, exercising my imagination about the great sagas of history that had happened around me.

Hermien and I told this noble (on the part of Emily) and horrific (on the part of the infamous British Government) story where it had taken place. Twenty-six thousand – mainly women and children – dead! How can one make a Saxon, an Englishperson, digest any truth about British atrocities? No matter how awful, the first and unshiftable instinct is to deny the crime's very existence. Uninformed defence is immediately and thickly invented and usually nothing is allowed to be said; no simple and shocking acts can be presented that can shift an

Englishperson's faith that he or she is doing the right moral thing. The Six Counties of Ireland is the present terrible example. Our partially baked Prime Minister, John Major, admonishes the Irish Irish Republicans and even (a recent innovation) carefully regrets the indiscriminate murder of Catholics by the Scottish–Irish Unionists (unionists with us on John Bull's Island – God help us!) and never, never – not even with a nervous twitch – acknowledges that we British carefully and deliberately contrived the whole bloody arrangement and for our own material benefit. Decent John Major, I have serious difficulties in comprehending unadulterated evil; I believe that like most of us he is insensitively thick. As for our current Northern Ireland Secretary – Mayhew – well, there is something else there: tight lips and a glint. But insensitive ignorance rules. As for the political Left and Centre of our country: much the same, but softer.

However, there has always been, thank God, the odd renegade Englishperson who has stepped out of line and who has uttered the shocking truth: Pitt the Elder; William Gladstone, continuously, on many Tory misdemeanors, often on behalf of the massacred Irish Irish people; Emily Hobhouse; and today, Anthony Wedgwood Benn. They did not believe in 'My country, right or wrong'. The Liberal Party leader at the time of the Anglo-Boer War, Henry Campbell-Bannerman, heard Emily's loud, strident objections to British brutality in South Africa and he stood up before the National Reform Union and asked: 'When is a war not a war?' And he gave his own reply: 'When it is carried out by methods of barbarism in South Africa.' But Mr Bannerman was not able to stop the slaughter of the innocents by the British Army. However, above all others, Emily Hobhouse eased the situation, and for her moral perception, was pilloried and persecuted by, primarily, the English. How many of those who have spoken out against British national criminality were of identifiable Saxon stock? I don't know; but I am interested. Is the problem an ancient German root? I don't know. About herself Emily Hobhouse claimed to be Celtic. We (her ancestors) were driven Westward by the Anglo-Saxons . . .

*

My life to some extent has become fused into one lump, extending now to seventy-two years. I have been alive for a long while and I do not find it easy to divide the events, the chapters, so please do not expect any strict chronological order in this book; I am doing my best, but it isn't very important. I haven't kept a diary; there have always been other priorities; not least, frantic survival. However, I remember so much of my personal saga, vividly. And I am still puzzling what exactly has driven me in this life.

I think of the image that crossed my dazzled mind when I stumbled through an ancient arch in what was passing for St Petersburg, when I was portraying Raskolnikov in Dostoevsky's *Crime and Punishment*. It was that live production so long ago for BBC television. Ahead of me lay over two hours of intensive dramatic meaning. I couldn't recall the first words that I was expected to speak and a camera was peering at me very close. The image that came into my poor youngish head was that I was alone in a small sailing boat on a vast windswept ocean – at the mercy of what? I am not convinced that the Creator has plans for me. I am an agnostic; but then, I sometimes wonder: I have been the recipient of so many incalculable coincidences that seem to have nudged me along. My pleading conversation with calm Rabbi Jacob Bulka on the Lower East Side of Manhattan: 'Sometimes, Rabbi, I feel that Something is trying to tell me something.'

'Mr Griffith, I *know* that Something is trying to tell you something.'

Since I was nine years old I have been listening to cries of pain from Ireland. Gradually I have garnered the facts, even more gradually it has dawned on me that those oppressed Irish people are *my* people and I have felt compelled to speak up for them to their British oppressors. And then Huw Wheldon gave me the biggest of all pulpits: BBC television. The establishment centre of Britain suppressed our efforts on behalf of the Irish Irish, but the story of what we were trying to say is fairly widely known. The Mayhews of our British world will not win in the end. All of this I had to do for myself. It was my isolated effort. I had no choice. Now, and after receiving a farcical death threat (via the BBC) from my sometime fellow Protestants in the Harland and Wolff shipyard in Belfast, I find that thousands and thousands of Irish Irish Republicans have been watching me from a silent distance for many years. It had never occurred to me that I was in no way alone. This realization has been the most moving experience of my life – and a revelation. And on top of that so are many of my fellow Welshpeople rallying round. There is something of Celtic solidarity happening. But I am just left wondering what exactly were those winds that drove my little sailing boat?

All of this is a preamble to what happened to me next. Yes, it's a bit hazy. Certainly I was drawn back to South Africa and there I was employed to write a number of scripts and to do so in one of the most beautiful places on this earth: a small town on the most southern coast of Africa, named Knysna. It was the first period of my life when I came close to dalliance; I sat at a window which looked down on a great lagoon, bounded by trees. The house Chiara and I lived in was on a hill which is called Paradise and that was an essential part of the postal address. My sometime wife, Carole, wrote to me and unerringly remarked: 'I'm glad you've found it at last!' Yes, touché, but the truth is I have never consciously searched for Paradise; I have always battled to survive: materially and – dare I write it? – spiritually, and both of those roads have been generally very rough. And then, unexpectedly, I would run into a patch like Knysna and the lagoon and the vast unspoilt territory and ocean that embraces the place.

One of the jobs I did was to write a script about the founder of Knysna, George Rex. There has been a small industrial development to the east of the town and in the middle of it is a quiet stone-walled oasis and within it is the grave of this man. The astounding legend is that he was the eldest *legitimate* son of the British King, George III. The question is still very much alive in certain interested quarters; as far as South Africa is concerned some advocate the belief and some denounce it. After long and careful research I am of the opinion that the story is possibly true. What am I sitting here writing? That Her Majesty is not the legitimate sovereign of

Great Britain!? Possibly not. Here is the gist of the argument. George Rex was born in England; his parents were the young Prince of Wales and a Quaker woman. They were secretly married in Mayfair. When the father became king and married – for a second time – a royal and therefore more acceptable woman, he interviewed young George Rex and gave him his tragic sentence: 'You must leave England never to return and you must *never* speak of this conversation. You will be taken to Cape Town in South Africa and you will be well looked after for the rest of your life.' And at this point very firm history takes over.

The Rex family still survive. There is an uncomfortable dichotomy about their ancestor amongst them. Georgian relics still survive and are proudly held, but while I was living there, a man who runs pleasure boats on the lagoon was about to launch a new vessel which he proposed to call *The George Rex*. I was told that the Rex family intervened and I believe another name was selected. You see, George Rex lived with two black women (strangely enough mother and daughter), but not concurrently, and therefore, with the whiff of apartheid still in the air, they were reluctant to publicize the old African connection. Their whole status might become changed. I presume, but not with any conviction, that the potential racial stigma is now less . . .

While I was working on the Emily Hobhouse film, which I titled *The Englishwoman*, I had to do some research in the unforgettable museum housed in Cape Town's castle. Basically the contents are one man's collection of items that interested him; therefore it is unusually eclectic but bound together by the collector's lively mind. I was hurrying through the enormous rooms with the lady curator; she was setting the pace. Out of the corner of my right eye I fleetingly registered a Welsh object; it was a pair (I think) of ebony (they looked like it) chairs: on the back rest of each one was the Prince of Wales' feathers.

'Excuse me,' as I managed to halt my speeding hostess, 'that is a Welsh emblem; what is their significance?'

'Oh! They came from the estate of George Rex.' And onward she hurried. Now, none of those who decry the astonishing 'legend' know about these matters that I researched and stumbled on.

And one last curious discovery: when I returned to Britain I learnt that Knysna in South Africa is very famous in medical circles; that there is a very rare disease called Porphyria, and that every case south of the Limpopo River could be traced to the Knysna area. King George the Third is considered to be the most famous victim of Porphyria!

It was a good mixed year in that mysteriously beautiful territory known as the Republic of South Africa. My friend, William Faure, took on the gigantic task of making a series of films on the life of the astounding King of the Zulus: Shaka. And William approached them burdened with weighty shackles: he was provided with little money to make an essential blockbuster. But somehow this did not deter him for one second as far as I could observe. And I did observe it because he wanted me to be around. William Faure explained to me that he wanted more European characters in the films than the American script provided and would I invent them and weave them into the story. But I believe he really wanted my company. Suddenly my toiling life was becoming a comfortably packed holiday; it had never happened before. I sat at the bay window on the top of Paradise Hill in Knysna, studying the history of Shaka Zulu and in particular his mixed bag of startling associates and jotting away like the happy adventurer I was. Oh yes! When I heard the distant steam train approach the great lagoon I would walk to the stoep and watch the gently spectacular progress of the engine and carriages across the delicate long, long, viaduct, moving diagonally from George Rex's Belvedere almost to my feet; though far below me. And then back to quiet work on Shaka.

When I arrived at the George Hotel, Zululand, in which was the production office, I realized what a thin shoe-stringed organization William Faure had as his immediate base; in military terms one could call it the advance base. He took me to an outhouse – nothing more – where the editor was working. I remember three stages of watching: I leant back on my chair;

then I sat bolt upright and finally cupped my eyes as I peered closely. I said: 'William, it's wonderful I have never seen Africa on a screen like that – ever!'

My friend said: 'Do you really mean it? The South African Broadcasting people looked at it yesterday and said nothing before returning to Johannesburg.'

I have often wondered whether ignorance is really bliss. I am reminded of words which that splendid Pole, Joseph Conrad, once wrote to a woman cousin: 'One must drag the ball and chain of one's selfhood to the end. It is the price one pays for the devilish and divine privilege of thought, so that in this life it is only the elect who are convicts; a glorious band who groan and comprehend but which treads the earth amidst a multitude of phantoms, with maniacal gestures, with idiotic grimaces. Which would you be, idiot or convict?' Yes, this does apply to the office-dwellers of the SABC in South Africa, but it also applies to a large part of the people who are running British television today. People who can't see beyond their mean statistics and the very few who can, between the masses who have no ability to care and the very few who do. I would like Mr Conrad's thoughts to permeate this book. It is really the story of how I have stumblingly tried to be a convict and not a lunatic.

Henry Cele was given the role of Shaka. The Americans, idiotically, wanted some Black star from Hollywood. But William Faure stuck his obstinate heels in; he wanted Mr Cele. Henry is enormous in size; formidable to look at. He had been a professional footballer in one of the Black townships and then a chauffeur. William, through sheer stubborness, got his way and Henry was a great success. Now I am set against directors telling actors what to do, but this was different; Henry had never been an actor before and endlessly little William (about my height) talked into the ear of this giant, who listened intently. Of course, Henry himself carried the fundamental secret. He understood his big responsibility: he was representing his Zulu people on a vast international platform. Henry Cele is a formidable chap and William Faure pushed a clear vision beyond the scripts; he explained to

Henry that he must create a Black Napoleon – nothing less. What a struggle to make something worthwhile . . . And they succeeded movingly.

William had told me: 'Write a part for yourself,' and I included amongst my inventions an elderly wise Jew. Like many other instances in this filmed story, there was no such person in history. There *was* a young Jew involved with Shaka, but I am well past youth. I thought that it could be an interesting element since Shaka, in our epic, became interested in Jesus Christ. A while ago, William Faure was reminiscing about various adventures in Zululand and he said that the scene between Henry and Robert Powell and myself, where the enigma of Jesus being a Jew is discussed, was his favourite scene. I did not resist reminding him that I had written it; one of my few contributions.

There were many unforgettable experiences. Because of the raw country and the strong emphasis on traditional culture in Zululand, no dramatized history had got nearer to historical reality. Shaka's vast royal kraal was reconstructed amongst the magnificent hills and thousands of Zulus were assembled and sang their chilling music and performed their terrifying wardances. Sometimes I could not believe my good fortune: in the middle of the night (filming never stopped it seemed) groups of near-naked Zulus would break away, form a tight circle and sing in the most beautiful harmony, creating vocal music the like of which I had never heard before. And this for their own pleasure and illuminated by masses of firelight.

William Faure had to tour America to help publicize the film. On one television chat-show he was confronted by crass representatives of the African National Congress – and in my alarmed experience human beings don't come any crasser – who demanded why he had shown naked black female breasts but not white. I baulk at what could happen to South Africa if such ignorance takes power and that is the weighty question. The world may soon have to examine what is the truth about universal democracy.

THIRTY-FOUR

In the middle of all this good-time adventuring I received a letter from the new Prime Minister of India, Rajiv Gandhi. My friend, his mother, had been murdered by a guard who had taken a solemn oath to protect her; indeed, his Sikh name should be recorded as the ultimate definition of treachery. Rajiv Gandhi, whose quiet self-effacement had reassured and impressed me, was asking me if I would now go to India and make a life of his grandfather, Mrs Gandhi's father, Jawaharlal Nehru. He wrote: 'My mother for a long time wanted you to do this.' Chiara was with me there in Zululand and I showed her the letter. I knew that now I had to go and make that film.

I have written a book about this adventure; it is called *The Discovery of Nehru* and that is precisely what it was for me as well as discovering much else besides. As I have written, I could not see the well-shaped story essential for one of my films when Mrs Gandhi had originally asked me; I still couldn't, but now I instinctively felt I *had* to do it. I buried myself in Jawaharlal's Nehru's writings and I plunged into a welter of very varied biographies. The first and essential element to achieve is to understand exactly *why* you are telling the story. I don't mean the emotional response to a murdered friend, but what the subject's life can say to universal humanity. I believe that every human being who has ever lived carries such a message. Of course, in this case, Nehru's, he was moving in the shadow, or perhaps I should write 'the light' of Mahatma Gandhi. But if one looks hard enough, the story is always there to see; my original reservation was superficial. Nehru's journey through life was a subtle, ever complicated matter; an unexpected fate. A person's character is acquired through a multitude of chances from genes to environment and then that human result is subject to innumerable opportunities to do one thing or another. I have long seen them as doors which are presented. The individual can decide whether or not to pass through the door into what lies beyond. I, personally, have tended to go through more doors than most people; they are the routes to adventures and knowledge and a way of educating oneself. But I have been wary of any hint of an easy way out – cigarettes, booze, drugs, etc. I am back at the definition of unnecessary risks. Nehru's route to his final destiny was very finely balanced.

He came from a privileged background: he was a Brahmin – high caste, or as we Europeans used to say, high class (now, it seems, we are all becoming low class). Nehru's father, Motilal, was a wealthy, extrovert lawyer, who was so seduced by the blandishments of the British Raj that it could appear that his highest hope for his only son was to make him into an English gentleman – and a lawyer to boot. He sent him to Harrow Public School in England and then to Cambridge and finally to the Inner Temple, a legal institution.

However, Motilal's plans for his son were not going too smoothly. Jawaharlal was steadily becoming a radical. He began to take an emotional interest in Britain's persecution of Ireland; he wrote about the Irish patriots: Roger Casement and Michael Collins – two men that I have now made films about – and he wrote about the Italian liberator: Guiseppe Garibaldi, and though I have not had the honour to make a film about him, I can look up from this seat and there is a large portrait of the man, hanging on a wall of this room in my house in Islington. So I quickly realized that my pending subject and I thought and felt in the same direction.

Jawaharlal Nehru returned to India and began to perform somewhat aimlessly and unhappily as a lawyer. And then the most significant door of his life confronted him; he was in the fabulous city of Lucknow and there he saw and heard Mahatma Gandhi speak for the first time. Nehru then knew exactly what his purpose in life was.

Lucknow *is* a fabulous city and there are, overwhelmingly,

more ghosts there than anywhere else that I have visited. It was once an extravagant, degenerate place; that is, from a West European perspective, and the sometime opulent, now-decaying architecture remains there and is the natural home for these threatening Asian phantoms. The astonishing extravagances of these ancient buildings is achieved by massive use of plaster-work, which also accounts for the crumbling. When we were communicating this first encounter between the two leaders, our film director, Mr Alan Birkenshaw, had selected a very high elevation of one of these buildings from which to tell the tale. However, by the time that we had come to film it, the sun had inexorably moved. I observed Alan clamber over a balustrade and heave his weight onto an outside ledge. Then, climbing back, he said: 'Ken, it's a marvellous shot and the ledge is solid.' (It was indeed a startling image of Lucknow but he had tested only a bit of it.) 'Would you do the piece walking along the outside?'

I replied ungraciously, 'Get it right *first* time.'

Whenever I have viewed this sequence I have always peered closely at my face, to see if there is any sign of the terror of an unpleasant death which is what I had every right to feel. I appear to be totally calm and in command of myself. It is a fact, amongst serious film makers, that they will take alarming risks if they believe a shot is valuable. A necessary risk I suppose.

But long before all of this happened I had to experience the agony of being placed in the hands of a totally different culture and for much of the time it became hell in India. I have always tended – and inevitably still do – to behave on trust. When I arrived in India, Rajiv Gandhi addressed me: 'Whenever you are stuck, Mr Griffith, please come to me.'

I wondered: 'Why should I get stuck?' My commission was clear: I simply had to make a life of Nehru; it could be completed from beginning to end in, say, seven months. It never occurred to me that Indian politicians and their wretched bureaucrats would work against me – or some of them.

The short of it is that *nothing* happened for six to seven months. Mark you, it wasn't all bad news. I was placed in the best of the Government hotels, the Kanishka, and I had a car and a driver; and the head of public relations for their State Television monopoly (Doordarshan), a Mr Malhotra, called on me almost every day.

I wore Indian clothes the entire time; that time eventually took over two years! I had reasoned that since I was working for India and in India, it would be fundamentally correct for me to dress thus. Soon after my arrival I was invited, formally, to meet the Minister of Information and Broadcasting, Shri (Mister) Gadgil. I arrived in a well-cut Jaipur suit (buttoned up to the neck). Ranged around the Minister were all of his heads of departments, seated in a wide semi-circle; they were all wearing European suits, but fortunately for me Shri Gadgil was wearing Indian clothes. He was always a kindly man and as I approached the formidable gathering he quietly referred to my suit: 'It sits very well upon you, Mr Griffith.' But I sensed at that meeting that there were very varied alien attitudes towards me. Most of them did not recognize the simple truth: that I had come to India, at the invitation of their last two Prime Ministers, to serve India. Perhaps they resented my suit. I couldn't help being a Brit. Perhaps at that meeting I felt that because the Minister, Mr Gadgil, was on my side (he told me that he was deeply impressed by my work), I was safe; I was soon to learn that these bureaucrats and politicians of India are generally an incorrigible and treacherous bunch; they all grasp metaphorical knives. Mr Gadgil was himself in no way immune and, as for me, they were fingering their blades before I had even opened my mouth.

On the other hand I had a few steadfast friends: my old ally Admiral Satyindra Singh, Admiral Rustam Ghandhi and the Sharman family. The latter are a creative oasis in the middle of Delhi: Jalabala and Gopal and their daughter Anasuya. They live above their own beautiful theatre. Jalabala is a celebrated actress and home-provider; Gopal is a writer, a director of plays and films and a true mystic. Their home became my home in Delhi; without that human safety-net I cannot imagine how I could have survived the combined hells of Doordashan and India's bureaucrats. Of course, one only grows up out of travail.

I cannot bear a vacuum so after a few months of trying to cope with the Indian obtuseness that enveloped me, I took decisive action: I moved out of the tourist-ridden Kanishka (full of closely guarded Soviet Union visitors) and moved to the long-ago Maidens Hotel in Old Delhi and from that base I began to contemplate the Indian Mutiny of 1857, which Indian Nationalists very understandably call The First War of Independence. I had stayed at the Maidens on previous visits to India; all around me now were the remnants of that horrendous conflict. And always the ghosts. Ghosts thrive in India; sometimes I seem to hear screams of terror.

During my long sojourn in India I had only two drivers; the first was Umrau Singh and then Yatendera Singh; they both became good friends of mine. Why can't I truly say that about any of the multiplicity of bureaucrats that I daily met? Was it because Umrau and Yatendera came from a traditional countryside? I visited and stayed in Yatendera's Rajput village. Oh, yes! I saw India all right. Jonathan, my middle son, had joined me and we both slept on beds with mosquito netting in what we Europeans would call the village square; we were constantly guarded by the village elders.

Finally the Indian Government and I came to an agreement that enabled me to begin producing the film. I had already done all the research I would need to write the script; now I needed peace to write it. By this time my distinguished friend, Admiral Rustam Ghandhi, was the Governor of Himachal Pradesh in Northern India, with its famed capital, Simla, perched in the foothills of the Himalayan mountains, and Rustam arranged for me to stay in a high wing of the State's University. I lived and wrote the script in rooms which jutted into the forest; being up high, monkeys chattered and stared at me from their wild tree-tops.

The Indian who anxiously cooked for me would sit crosslegged on the floor after serving my food and play his flute. We also became friends and he invited me to an evening meal in his house, deep in the forest. I insisted that I knew the way and while making this journey I came across a strange sight. Above the great trees a full moon was shining, and coming to a small clearing, I found a man staring at this moon with his arms outstretched. I froze and watched. The man articulated nothing. I don't think that he heard me. I watched him in this strange static pose for perhaps five minutes and then I quietly bypassed him through the trees. My friend's house was very simple. He was a typical mountain man who wore traditional Himachal Pradesh clothes. On such an occasion I would wear a simple kurta: cotton collarless shirt and trousers with a patterned Indian waistcoat and Indian sandals – chappals. My friend's wife very quietly served the food and I told them about this near-apparition in the forest. 'Oh, he was praying to the moon.' Well, I like the idea of anyone praying in privacy, even more than in congregation.

'Would you like to meet him?'

'Yes, please.'

On my way back to my home up there with the monkeys, my host accompanied me through the forest and he led me to an isolated, totally darkened house. He instructed me to wait as he went inside and suddenly the praying-man was in front of me. I didn't see his face; it was too dark. He was tall and again with a sudden movement he was down on his knees, touching my feet with his hands. It seems to be a universal custom all over India to perform this act as an expression of respect. It is usually done to honour old people. And then the man was gone again. I like to think that he knew what was in my mind. Telepathy. We Celts are part of the great Indo-European mystery after all.

Governor (as he then was) Rustam Ghandhi is a born actor. He loves the drama and pageantry that life sometimes offers. Inside the Residency he described to me the formal occasions when he and his wife Bubbles would descend the great staircase, amidst pomp and ceremony. Of course, active service admirals should be good actors; Horatio Nelson understood that.

The Jimba Lama, a refugee from the crudities of Marxist Chinese depredations in precious Tibet, invited me to visit him in his monastery at Sanjouli. I watched the monks at prayer for a long while and tried to grasp some understanding, but Buddhism requires longer than that I suspect. However, the Jimba Lama jollily took me to his living quarters and there I was served lunch. In his main living-room there was a high dais on which was a throne. His Holiness told me to sit there and though servants carried the food into the room, the renowned gentleman served me himself and so I learnt more about the ancient philosophy (one has to be careful of our Western terminology when describing the East) with him than I did watching the prayer wheels spin while the monks chanted. We talked about the tragedy inflicted on his country, Tibet, and in contrast the warm welcome offered to Tibetan refugees by India. I confessed to some minor physical complaint (I even forget what it was) and the Jimba Lama asked for the presence of his senior medical adviser. He was an old, tall lean man who had recently escaped from Tibet, and at my request he showed me his vicious torture wounds that had been inflicted on him by the Chinese. What a mystery those Orientals are! They have produced great cultures, but now they seem to have metamorphosed themselves into degenerate bureaucrats served by a dehumanized military machine. The Buddhist physician examined me and produced some large black pills, which, to write the truth, I funked devouring. When I left, the Jimba Lama presented me with a traditional white scarf and a Tibetan prayer carpet which is now one of the memorable treasures that fill my house.

Chiara Peretti arrived in Simla. We had a stylish meeting. She travelled up the mountains in the small entertaining steam train that puffs from the plains far below. I waited for her arrival wearing my extremely well-cut black Jaipur suit which always encourages me to stand upright and to bear myself elegantly. Yatendera was with me and, of course, so was our car. Chiara always arrives when she says she will, even if she has to cross continents. Perhaps one wouldn't guess that this is likely, but she is full of all sorts of surprises.

While making *Clive of India* Chiara and I had visited the famous Kulu Valley which again lies in the foothills of the Himalayan Mountains beyond the princely state of Mandi, but this time Governor Ghandhi arranged for us to stay in the guesthouse of the Tibetan Border Police. It was a big stone edifice which had once been occupied by British adventurers during the nineteenth century. The truth is, the house had a sinister history and I was informed locally that it still had its uneasy problems. But enough of that. Take my word for it, Alfred Hitchcock would have required no additional embellishments.

During our stay we visited the annual Kulu Festival when all of the village gods are carried great distances on palanquins to the King of Kulu's Palace. Each converging procession was accompanied by a man dressed in a skirt who was clearly in a trance and whose voice – so I was assured – was not his but was the voice of the village god. As we entered the city of Kulu itself, the great cavalcade was headed by the King of Kulu in person and somehow I managed to inveigle myself in a position immediately behind His Majesty. Suffice it to write that the fly whisks that were wielded to protect the King also protected me. It was a unique experience for me to be overlooked by cheering and waving people who leaned out from their houses in the city's narrow lanes. Finally the King and I were separated by many thousands of people when we arrived at a vast parade-ground where His Majesty and his court mounted a great chariot and there I witnessed them being pulled by literally hundreds of men across the arena. I thought of Tamburlaine: 'To ride in triumph through Persepolis', and probably I wasn't far off the mark.

Chiara and I followed the gods to the Palace Temple where they were imperiously rejected by the Palace Guards. The entranced men in skirts beseeched for permission to be allowed to enter the royal area. I, as an actor, was disturbed and impressed to see genuine tears stream down their faces. Eventually, many were allowed into the courtyard, some were permitted to rest on the royal veranda, but only one entered the Palace itself. This much-decorated effigy, on its palanquin, rested in the centre of a royal reception room. Apparently, the selected god of all the gods. Somehow Chiara and I were there, now resting amidst royal shade in big armchairs. We seemed to be accepted as members of the royal family. Of course, one needs plenty of Italian and Welsh chutzpah.

That evening, in Kulu, there was a festival market. It covered acres. Wonderful. Hundreds of village vendors with their wondrous village offerings: sweetmeats, simple toys and copious colours. And, suddenly, I met the King. No one except me seemed to recognize him. He was walking amongst the stalls, holding the hand of a small boy, whom I took to be his son or small grandson. I bowed my head and placed my hands together and he reciprocated in like manner. For me, it was a very satisfactory meeting.

We filmed all over India: north, south, east, west and in the middle. It was a rare opportunity; it was inevitable because of the style of my films: we had to relate the significant episodes of Nehru's life wherever they had happened and there were few areas of India that he hadn't visited. But these continuous astonishing adventures were tempered by burdens: primarily the often great heat and, of course, Doordarshan itself, which, little doubt, was being pushed into dishonourable behaviour by the government bureaucrats. They inflicted upon us a stream of lunatic, financially wasteful (their money) inhibitions. It was all incomprehensible to a European mind unless one calculated naked vindictiveness. But why? Ah! East is East and West is West and never the twain shall meet except for a handful of unfortunate-fortunates like myself. During that initial seven-month time-warp when I took to researching the *Indian Mutiny*, I spoke of my tribulations to a significant official at the British High Commission and he indiscreetly replied: 'Exactly the same over the helicopters; one week they're going to buy them, the next they're not!' I derived some reassurance that I was comparable to British helicopter sales.

My book *The Discovery of Nehru* is packed with horror stories about the Indian bureaucracy and the smell of miasmic corruption. I began to learn the dreadful reality early in my visit. I explained that I would require a film crew of no more than nine or ten people including myself and Admiral Satyindra Singh – who would guide us through the Indian pitfalls as he had subtly done on the *Clive of India* film. But soon I realized there was a sneaky war going on between Doordarshan and the Indian Film Division in Bombay. No such thought as the good of India existed in those respective quarters. Sometimes I felt that I was the only person involved who carried such sentiments. I quickly found myself landed with a crew of thirty-five souls and that there was nothing that I could do about it! Out of this mainly unnecessary concourse of people I recognized one soul-mate, a certain Shri Chiplunkar, who was a light boy; he carried lamps. He was quietly concerned about my welfare. I have wondered – now knowing something about that particular vindictive Indian world – whether these words of gratitude will do him any harm if they are read by his masters.

But then there were the wonderful compensations. To travel around that subcontinent and to meet so many spiritually uplifting uncorrupted souls; the people that Mahatma Gandhi was primarily concerned about and whom Jawaharlal Nehru learnt – through Gandhi – to be concerned about, was a great, fortunate privilege. Do the meek inherit the earth? Perhaps, after all else, they do.

The actual filming of Nehru's life was completed and the editing had been in progress for a long while when Alan Birkinshaw and our editor, Reena Mohan, took the film to England for the various laboratory processes. My contract with the Indian Government was not completed until I handed over the finished acceptable print. I was now confronted with what to do while I waited for the film's rearrival from London. The problem was always the fact that there was no one, with any authority, to discuss immediate problems with. It was always an awkward prickly mess. And so Chiara and I withdrew from the spiritual discomfort of Delhi to the village of Dona Paula in Goa, where we had met all of those years before, when I was acting in *The Sea Wolves* and where I had written the script for *The Most Valuable Englishman Ever*. To justify my time there I studied Indian history and in particular – once again – the so-called Indian Mutiny. And I also worked to understand the history of Goa.

I used to eat my breakfast in a small restaurant on the edge of that Arabian Sea and each morning I would be given a local (Goan) newspaper, *The Herald*, which during Portuguese times had been called *The °Herald°*. I was astonished at the quality of its democratic and aggressive journalism; morning after morning the six sides of print openly attacked the varied corruption that was being perpetrated from one end of Goa to the other. No one was spared: neither the police, the politicians nor unscrupulous capitalists. I asked various people: 'Who writes this?' The answer was always: 'Rajan Narayan.'

One evening I was in the same restaurant while the monsoon howled all around, when, out of the rain and wind appeared a man who had managed miraculously to keep his cigarette going and who whispered briefly into the waiter's ear and was gone. The waiter came over to me: 'That is the man you ask about; that is Rajan Narayan.' I dashed out into the drenching rain and caught up with him: 'Mr Narayan, I'm a keen admirer of your writing.' Today he is one of my best friends. People informed me that it was this Indian who had achieved statehood for Goa, more than any other person. The enormous state of Maharashtra, to the north, had wanted to swallow it up greedily. And that the local language, Konkani, was now the first official language – and against formidable opposition – because of his fighting efforts which rallied the easy-going people of Goa. Rajan Narayan is not from Goa; he is from Bombay. He once confessed to me that his titanic efforts weren't because of his love for Goa; he explained that as the editor of a newspaper he had a professional obligation to represent the rights of his readers. He implied that he would do the same for the citizens of Timbuctoo – that is if he were the editor of the *Timbuctoo Herald*.

Rajan Narayan, in my opinion, is up there with W. T. Stead the great editor of the *Manchester Guardian*. Of course it was a revealing boon for me to be taken under his influential wing. While I was in Goa during this visit I saw and heard everything of consequence that was going on: the machinations of political intrigues, which always made me feel that I was in a great Mogul's Court; the oblique language of gangsters and not least, the near universal love and respect for a dedicated hero. Hero? Yes; after I left Goa his enemies tried to assassinate him. At night, while approaching his simple home, they clubbed him with crow-bars, but they failed to kill him. Now he is severely maimed, but he painfully, and not without humour, goes back to his desk to continue his revelations about the villains of Goa.

Eventually the Nehru film was delivered and Chiara and I left India. The lack of grace from Indian officialdom was constant to the end, with the exception of one or two members of middle-management: Surendra Dhir and Jawaharlal Malhotra come to my mind. Their reward is my respectful remembrance; the penalty is the probability that they will not be advanced in their Indian lives if any of the bigwigs of Doordarshan read this.

Before leaving India I said my farewells to beloved friends and finally to Doctor Bal Ram Nanda and his memorable wife Shrimarti Nanda. After I had completed writing the film-script, and before we had started filming, I had had a series of meetings with this distinguished historian. As I was saying farewell, they expressed the hope that we would meet again soon. I replied that I would return to India within a year.

'Good! Will you come on holiday?'

'No, I want to make a film about Doctor Ambedkar [the significant leader of India's Untouchables].' This remark by me instantaneously created an extraordinary atmosphere in the room. I was even startled. After a prolonged silence the doctor spoke: 'Be very careful, Kenneth; you could easily make Ambedkar look like a hero.'

Now the thought that hit my brain was that it would be very difficult in telling the facts of Ambedkar's life to avoid making him the extraordinary hero that he was. I am not given to keeping my mouth shut, but on this occasion I did; I was so astonished at Doctor Nanda's words and I *was* saying goodbye to my friends that the truth is I said nothing. I presume that Doctor Nanda was speaking as a Brahmin and I began to digest the stark reality of India's caste system.

What had happened was this. Previous to my meeting with

Doctor Nanda I had nipped back to Britain for some business or other and I was invited to call on David Elstein, then the programme controller of Thames Television, and David had asked me if I would return to the subcontinent and make a film for Thames about the Untouchables. I replied that this was impossible, explaining that it was not a simple matter of bad Brahmins (highest caste) and good Untouchables (beneath caste); that the origins of the Hindu caste system were lost in the labyrinths of even Indian pre-history and that it was inextricably enmeshed in Hindu religious matters and that 'even if you gave me twelve hours' screen time I could not unravel it *fairly* – and neither could anyone else'. But David Elstein persisted and I finally replied: 'Well, what I could do would be a life of Doctor Ambedkar.'

'Who's Doctor Ambedkar?"

And I told him about this Universal Man who was an Untouchable and who inspired many millions of Untouchables to stand up and be decently counted. David Elstein said: 'Go ahead,' which should remind every reader who cares about the prospective well-being of Britain how Tory thinking and Mrs Margaret Thatcher's thinking in particular has seriously degenerated the quality of British Television, and in so short a time. With the coming of the most irresponsible policy of money-at-all-costs, the moral uplift of which Lord Reith, Sir Huw Wheldon, Lord Sidney Bernstein, Jeremy Isaacs and, then, David Elstein stood for has been wiped out by bloody awful Tory thinking. However, they can redeem themselves and they must.

I must confess that the prospect of returning to India did not enthral me. The truth is that I had finally returned from the Nehru expedition in a state of serious shock. For two weeks I avoided leaving my house in Islington and then I was impelled to visit my bank in the Haymarket, central London. I happened to pass a travel agent and out of the corner of my right eye I saw a large advertisement: 'You are only nine hours from India.' Did I jump twelve inches in the air? Well, I almost turned round to run home.

But I researched the subject and wrote the script and the

investigation of that noble man Ambedkar was vastly reward-
ing to me. And then I had to travel to India to reconnoitre the
locations and meet representatives of Ambedkar's millions of
followers. As a preamble to this preliminary expedition I
attended at India's High Commission House in London. I was
known there and was received with apparent courtesy and
well up the pecking order: 'Of course, Mr Griffith, go to India
and complete your preliminary work.'

But I sensed the old bureaucratic poisonous cunning.
However, off I went and observed reassuring facts. I was in
Bombay for the annual celebration of Ambedkar; on that day
hundreds of thousands of Untouchables patiently and quietly
queued through the streets. They stretched for many many
miles; they kept careful good order, quietly talking to each
other. It was one of those unforgettable experiences. When
they arrived at Dr Ambedkar's shrine (a simple affair which is
on the edge of the sea) they simply placed their hands together
in unostentatious obeisance. It was all a massive, simple thank
you for help given to the downtrodden – by the downtrodden.
Shortly afterwards I visited my old friends the Sharmans, at
their Akshara Theatre in Delhi, and I told Gopal about this
extraordinary experience.

I asked the innocent question: 'Do Indians celebrate even
Mahatma Gandhi on such a scale?' (They don't.)

My old friend hit the roof in anger: 'Are you suggesting that
Ambedkar was greater than Gandhi?'

Well, I wasn't asking that . . . but now, knowing both of
their great lives, I would have to ponder seriously which man
I prefer.

The British Raj recognized Ambedkar and he was invited to
participate at an Indian Round Table Conference in St James'
Palace in London. He fought for two political advancements
for his people: Separate Electorates and Reserved Seats; without these, he argued, the Untouchables would always be in the
pockets of Caste Hindus (they were part of this religious structure – though well beyond the pale, in Irish parlance). And
again to Britain's credit this great social advance was granted
and under Ramsay MacDonald's leadership. Perhaps the last

progressive flash-in-the-pan from this falling British leader.

But Mahatma Gandhi was also present at the Round Table Conference. It is a novel experience to cast Gandhi as the villain of a piece, but that is what he was from an Untouchable point of view and, after all, I am an Untouchable, so my sympathies are with them and not with the Brahmins of this world. What troubled Gandhi was that in his struggles to emancipate India from Britain, he wanted no break in the Hindu ranks, and as I keep reiterating: Untouchables were an unfortunate appendage of that Hindu arrangement. On his return to India, Gandhi was incarcerated in Yerawade Prison and there he announced that if Ambedkar accepted the separate electorates and the reserved seats concessions, given by the British, he, Gandhi, would starve himself to death; he meant it and indeed he proceeded to do so. Doctor Ambedkar was being held responsible for this lethal situation by the near-countless millions of Hindus; he was being called 'the murderer of Gandhi'. A few days before the Mahatma was expected to die, leading members of the Congress Party escorted Ambedkar to Yerawade Prison and Gandhi was carried out of his cell and placed in the shade of a tree to meet the Untouchable.

Gandhi said: 'I believe, Doctor, that you are interested in saving my life.'

'Yes. Mahatma.'

'Then it is entirely in your hands.' The demand was simple: reject the social advances that the British had already granted to the Untouchables – or else.

Ambedkar said: 'You are blackmailing me, Mahatma. How can you accuse the British of enslaving India while you Caste Hindus enslave us?'

But the pressure was too great and Ambedkar did not accept the British offer. Two weeks later he confessed: 'It was a sentimental blunder.' As far as I know this was the only step backwards that Ambedkar ever made.

When India achieved its independence from Britain, a troubled Nehru said to Gandhi: 'I cannot find an Indian with the training and experience to supervise our pending Constitution'.

Gandhi replied: 'I know of one.'

'Who?'

'Doctor Ambedkar.'

And if you visit the Indian Parliament, the Lok Sabha in Delhi, you will be confronted with an enormous bronze statue of the hero: horn-rimmed glasses, a pile of books under one arm and with the other a finger pointing warningly. As far as I can recall the legend underneath reads: 'Doctor Ambedkar, the Father of Our Constitution'.

When I returned to London from this investigative research expedition it began to emerge from the Indian High Commission in London that a conspiracy against my *filming* in India was well advanced. How to share the reason for this covert action between my miserable enemies at Doordarshan in Delhi and a Brahmin determination to bury any truths about their own depredations, it is difficult to know . . . It could be either, but probably both. The officials in London were identical to those in Delhi: smarmy, treacherous, cowardly liars. Such Asians, I have presumed, cannot comprehend a simple truth. All men (and women) are *not* created equal and it is a dangerous assumption to believe so. Even amongst fellow-Europeans; well it will be the rock on which European unity will founder, no matter how greedy for profits our businessmen are. I am now back in the Biblioteca Comunale di Faenza, Italy, and I can assure you that it isn't remotely like Munich, Germany. Quite incidentally, do I offend our British racial laws if I write that I *prefer* Faenza? Or do these mendacious laws in Britain only apply to Nigeria or Jamaica? What sort of soft-centred lying mess are we British getting into!?

While I was wasting time with dishonest officials at the Indian High Commission in London, I received a request from other Indians, living in Britain, asking if they could call on me. I presumed that they were interested in perhaps seeing the Nehru film. When the six gentlemen arrived I talked to them about Nehru.

'Oh no, Mr Griffith, we want to discuss Doctor Ambedkar with you; we are all ex-Untouchables, now Buddhists and followers of the Doctor.'

They asked me if they could read my script and they departed with a copy. Thirty-six hours later their spokesman, Shri Gautam, called again and stated that they wanted nothing changed in the script and he confessed that he had been moved to tears while reading it. He offered to give me all of the support British Untouchables could give. I reciprocated and the result of this has been that I have spoken at Ambedkar–Buddhist meetings from Southall (London) to the British Midlands; I have marched with them through London and I have sat with them on various committees. After a while they quite formally made me one of their own: I became an Untouchable. It is, no doubt, revealing about my curious character (which sometimes mystifies *me*) because this acceptance of me by them gave me a feeling of contentment. Shortly afterwards, while speaking in Birmingham, I told the assembled Ambedkarites: 'I now realize that I have always *wanted* to be an Untouchable.' This statement was met with a roar of delighted laughter. But I meant it – deeply. Or let me put it this way: I would dread being associated with the Establishment in any form. For me it would be surrender; the death of my poor spirit.

Finally it became creepily clear that I would not be allowed into India to film; I was a prohibited person. And it also began to emerge that the Indians were going to bury the Nehru film. Why? Well I would submit that Napoleon was right (he usually was) when he stated: 'It is only the truth that hurts.' I had, in the Nehru film, exposed a few home truths about Kashmir which made the more politically minded Indians, who knew what I had said, clearly uncomfortable. I remember replying to them: 'I am now weary of you all; my resistance is low; cut the offending sequence if you want to, but should Muslims ask me – and they will! – why I have not told the whole truth, I will inform them, very loudly, that you prevented me.'

The sequence remained in the film but perhaps the issue was resurrected later. Anyway it doesn't matter much; I have come to the conclusion that in our astounding journeys through life, all we should try to do is our humble best. If other human elements choose to mess it up, well, that is all part of the whole. But a clearish personal conscience is important.

Thames Television did a generous act: they paid my salary in full; just as if I had been allowed to make the film. Mark you, I had worked hard. I had become a master of Ambedkar's life and I had written the script. But the failure to film was not an act of God; it was an act of sneaky Indians in Delhi and of their distant creatures in the Indian High Commission in London. The Nehru film, *But I Have Promises to Keep*, having initially been suppressed by the Indian government, *was* transmitted throughout India, in 1993, on Jawaharlal Nehru's birthday. Not so much as a postcard from the Asian authorities, but several Indian friends telephoned me and wrote to me and they assured me that nothing had been cut from the film.

All of these miserable Indian events had taken place under the premiership of my friend, Rajiv Gandhi, but I suspect that he didn't know much about it and I always rejected the idea of bothering him – though he had told me: 'Come to me when you are stuck.' I felt that I should cope with my own problems and thereby give him more time to worry about China and Pakistan and other affairs. When V. P. Singh became Prime Minister, he promptly lifted the ban on me; but irony upon irony, by this time Thames Television itself was in jeopardy. The company had dared to make a film honestly investigating the shooting of unarmed Irish Republican Army personnel by British agents on Gibraltar, and Margaret Thatcher was after them; she and her questionable Government tried to get rid of David Elstein and his head of documentary films, Mr Roger Bolton, but the Tory instinct was too overt and embarrassing and therefore they failed.

The last words, so far, on Doctor Ambedkar and myself occurred last year. It was the centenary of the man's birth and I was informed that I was to receive the Ambedkar Centenary Award and that it was to be presented to me in the House of Commons, in London, by the sometime Prime Minister of India: Shri V.P. Singh. The hall was packed with us Untouchables and up on the high table was the Indian High Commissioner and an array of Britishers who had, in the past, done the subcontinent some service. I was most conscious of my fine friend, Michael Foot. For me it was a moving, disturbing, occasion. I was asked to speak and after explaining to the distinguished and famous guests exactly what my relationship with the Untouchables was – indeed that I was one of them – I rounded on His Excellency, the High Commissioner, and told him that it was *his* Government and *his* system that had prevented the film on the life of Ambedkar being made. What goes on? Is it simple hypocrisy or casual ignorance? I ponder this question very often; these days primarily about Ireland.

THIRTY-FIVE

Sitting innocently in my home in Islington I received a telephone call from my friend William Faure in Johannesburg. It was the eve of one of those Mandela pop concerts. The pop world was clamouring to get onto this lucrative bandwagon; not only was there money to be made, but also vast publicity and a good whack of that easy do-gooder feeling which is so shallowly raised in such a climate. Well, William, who is probably more sympathetic towards the African National Congress than I am (I have chanced my arm more than once, asking questions and observing around Soweto and such torrid places), therefore happened to be speaking to the right man for his purpose. He explained that he and some other media people in South Africa were a bit fed up with the half-baked (not his words, I think, but that was the gist) liberal world who easily attacked all Whites in South Africa and who rarely criticized the non-stop atrocities committed by the ANC and other Black groups. He certainly didn't say all of that, but it was my thoughtful response to his words. He and his colleagues had formed a small group with the slogan: 'An Appeal to Moderation', and they wanted this reasonable request to be put before the pop groups: that the pop groups should consider exactly where the money would go from such events. It was a time when Winnie Mandela was thought of as a decent woman and I was getting some flak for expressing a different opinion of her.

What a slow, painful process it all is. William wanted to know how much it would cost to put such an appeal to moderation in a British national newspaper, which newspaper would be preferable, and so on. I sensed that my friend needed my practical help. Well, first I told him that I thought that this appeal was a lunatic idea. I went on: 'Can you think of one pop star who is capable of considering such a serious concept?' None of them that I could think of has the mental substance to grasp anything that was not facile. It is the nature of their business. Incidentally, my middle son, Jonathan Griffith – to whom I listen very carefully – assures me that some Americans (I presume) who please to call themselves The Grateful Dead are serious, worthy men; but I haven't had the privilege of knowing them personally. Anyway, William persisted and I offered to attend to the matter, 'if I agree with the wording'.

'How much will it cost?'

'I don't know.'

'Where shall I send some money?'

'To my account at the National Westminster Bank in the Haymarket, London.'

And then the South African miracles began to happen. The very *next morning* the statement was delivered to my door in Islington. I had no objection to the wording. Things were happening! I quickly phoned my friend and bank manager (few can write that!) and told him the unlikely story.

'So, Kenneth, if money is paid into your account you want me to inform you immediately?'

'Yes, please.'

A short while afterwards John phoned me: 'A young man has just walked into the bank and has deposited £10,000 – in cash – into your current account.'

Wow! I puzzled my head and remembered that formidable young editor of the *Telegraph*, Mr Macdonald Hastings, who had once approached me on a railway station to tell me that he thought well of my work.

'I see no reason why we should not place it, Mr Griffith.'

I was invited to lunch and whizzed round. There I saw, in passing, Lord Deedes, who had once argued with me (in my film *The Public's Right to Know*) about the wisdom (or from his English point of view the unwisdom) of telling the truth about Ireland; he smiled wryly and spoke a few friendly words. Over lunch, I negotiated a space, for the following day, which was the eve of the concert, for £7,000. Yes! I did return the balance to South Africa. At about 11 pm that night Mr Hastings himself telephoned me: 'Mr Griffith, every political statement published in a newspaper – and this *is* a political statement – must have a name after it.'

I quickly considered the question and realizing that the sponsors of 'Appeal to Moderation' all had Afrikaner names and considering the blind prejudice that usually enshrouds the do-gooders, I replied: 'Mr Hastings, put my name.'

To which he replied: 'I thought you'd say that.'

I never saw the printed appeal; I didn't buy a newspaper, but on the Monday morning as I entered a meeting, a business friend said to me: 'Kenneth, I didn't know that you were involved in advertising . . .'

'What advertising?'

'The *Telegraph*.' And I knew that the task had been achieved.

During that telephone chat with Mr Faure, I had remonstrated loudly and had demanded: 'Why don't you *think*!'

'Think about what?'

'About the true character of the ANC – to counter all of this Noble Black bit.'

'How?'

And off the top of my head and without any preparatory warning, I said: 'I can think of *one* Afrikaner who is not universally looked down upon by the Western world, in spite of the ANC's hardest efforts.'

'Who?'

'Zola Budd. Why don't you make a film in which you ask a wide section of interested people, "Why do the massed ranks of the ANC continuously hit this innocent teenage girl?" You will at least expose that there are no bigger racists than the Blacks and I am sure that you will begin to expose their true nature.'

And so the seed was sown. I couldn't make the film. I had not thought of making the film myself; I was due, very shortly, to leave Britain to work on some other project. But then my departure was postponed and William Faure heard about it: 'Come to South Africa and make the Zola Budd film yourself.'

'I've only got six weeks.'

'You can do it.'

And off I went. I made a list of people, from different experiences, whose opinions about the persecution of Zola Budd should be interesting: the chief operator (for whom? I wonder) in London, Mr Sam Ramsamy, who had attended to the nitty-gritty of embarrassing her while she was in Britain; Mr Albie Sachs, the South African Marxist, who was a member of the ANC and who was also an exile in London; Mr Peter Hain (now a Member of the British Parliament); Mrs Helen Suzman, the charming and famed Liberal South African; Doctor Christian Barnard; Chief Minister Buthelezi of Kwa Zulu, whose distaste for the ANC is understandable – that is if you know anything about the subject; Mr Errol Tobias, the distinguished Coloured (mixed blood) rugby player; Mr Gary Player, the renowned golfer; Mr Graeme Pollock, the Springbok cricketer; Bishop Desmond Tutu; Mrs Winnie Mandela; the Coloured man in Cape Town whose job it was to disrupt sport for political ends (and whose name I have understandably erased from my memory); and finally Mr Oliver Tambo, the ostensible head of the ANC, whose headquarters were in Lusaka, Zambia.

Mr Sam Ramsamy, whom I thought was of Indian extraction, lived in a high-security apartment up Hampstead way. His exposition was well-rehearsed political jargon and therefore one wasn't going to probe truthfully. Mr Albie Sachs was a different matter; he was Jewish and his late father 'Solly' Sachs had been an old friend of mine since my first visit to South Africa in 1952, when I was there with the Old Vic Theatre Company. At that time Solly – a hard-working Marxist, like his son – was the head of the Garment Workers' Union of South Africa, and he was on trial for some political offence. He was expected to get a very long sentence and he looked forward to this politically useful martyrdom. I remember him being angrily frustrated when the clever authorities gave him a mere twelve months and – I think – suspended it.

When Solly finally escaped to England he came to me and indeed I was able to give him a little financial help. He was anxious to give me some valuable letters written by the famous South African writer and feminist, Olive Schreiner, as collateral and it is to my credit (to set against my sins) that I refused them.

I was now with his son Albie, whom I had known since he, like his father, had escaped from the South African Republic, after a long period in prison. It is a curious fact that in those days, such South African activist refugees visited me for support. But I have never, yet, joined any ideology or political party and therefore my mind was free to move wherever new information led me and so these old connections began to fray away. I had, long ago, begun to dread what would happen south of the Limpopo River if Black Africans took power. I wasn't blind to what was happening elsewhere – everywhere – on that vast continent and as I have already written I had no political ideology to inhibit me in the direction of reality.

There had been an attempt to kill Albie Sachs while he was operating from Lourenzo Marques, the old capital of the sometime Portuguese colony of Mozambique in South East Africa. He was blown-up in his car and I had acquired some extraordinary and terrible film material of the event. There was Albie, presumably dead, burnt and maimed, being carried away from his fiery vehicle. I have never seen anything more shocking on film. But young Sachs unbelievably survived and I hadn't seen him since the assassination attempt and I was nervous at the prospect. Also I knew that I would have reservations about this brave man's point of view. Albie was badly scarred and maimed, but I have never talked to any person in my whole life who was in better command of thought and word. It became an unforgettable filmed interview and there was no bigotry. About Zola Budd he said that he was initially opposed to any persecution of her; he emphasized that she was simply a young woman who was exercising her talent, but that when people began to use her for their political ends he veered to a different view. I thought and said to Albie that even if his political conspiracy theory was true – and it could only be slightly true – this, in my opinion was no reason to injure her; she, I suspected, was innocent. This argument, I knew, disturbed Albie Sachs; he is a brave, intelligent humanist.

Mr Peter Hain was also, as we know, committed to the Left in politics and we visited him in West London. He gave me the impression that he was fundamentally an Englishman: polite, reasonable, and the nearest he and I came to a conflict was when I raised some arguable point about conditions in Soweto and other African townships (many Britishers would value comparable facilities – except that the Africans tend to destroy them themselves and perhaps I mentioned that the conditions in South Africa are noticeably superior to those in 'free' Africa). At this statement, Mr Hain admonished me with a quiet but serious: 'Now, Kenneth, if you go on speaking like that, I will get cross with you.' Again it was the problem of the interviewee having given difficult years to a cause and therefore being unable to consider any alternative prospect.

I met Mrs Helen Suzman in her elegant home in Johannesburg. She was definitely sorry that any harm had been done to Zola Budd. She could see no excuse, whatsoever, with interfering in her personal innocence. But, of course, having gained admittance to such interesting people and with two cameras running, I could not resist moving questions beyond Zola in particular. I had the temerity to ask Mrs Suzman – who is Jewish – what she felt about the similar situation to South Africa in Israel: a disciplined, essentially democratic people being surrounded by an unpredictable and often treacherous alien culture (I mean the Arabs). One of the reasons why the Israelis would *not* annex the West Bank is that their democratic mentality would make it inevitable that they would have to give the Palestinian Arabs the vote and that that would threaten the balance of voting power within Israel which would inevitably corrupt the Israeli way of life. This, the main reason for South Africa's apartheid policy, is basically the same: to protect the old European concepts of democracy, give the various tribal groups their respective homelands where they can each evolve their separate way of doing things, which has never been, in any part of African Africa, truly democratic. In post-colonial Africa, potential Black leaders have apparently adhered to the machinery of democracy, but having achieved power through the vote, have dismissed the democratic process as speedily as possible. Zimbabwe, under Mugabwe, is a relevant example. I see no remote reason why the Republic of South Africa would be different; that is if the April election happens and when eventually good Mandela loses control of his Black people. Unless, that is, the remaining European concepts and Western big business can master the situation.

To the question about Israel's predicament in relation to Mrs Suzman's political achievements in South Africa, she winningly parried the matter: 'Oh, Mr Griffith, please spare me the Israeli problem. I have enough to worry about here!'

She also said to me: 'You are a very clever devil's advocate.' But I did not think that this was the role that I was playing.

Doctor Christian Barnard, the first person to achieve a heart transplant, was on his farm in the Karoo (the thinly populated area in the Northern Cape which extends into the Orange Free State). He was working furiously and manually in that clean open-air, but we conducted the filmed chat inside his fine farmhouse. Again, he was sorry that Zola had been misused and, as a scientist, clearly dissected the facts of the matter. Of Africa, generally, he said that there was one unalterable rule throughout the continent: that the most powerful tribe ruled. It was a fact of African life.

'But the problem here in South Africa is that the most powerful tribe happens to be white.'

Very true; but on top of that a guilty White world (slavery and colonialism) has decided to support Blacks at almost any cost. When will some sense begin to dawn? We don't live in Paradise and shallow hypocritical delusion doesn't cover the holes.

Chief Minister Buthelezi, as readers of this book will know, is a long-time friend. I telephoned him in his Zulu capital, Ulundi, and I was asked: 'Can you get here by tomorrow?'

'Yes, sir.'

And then my colleagues threw our equipment and ourselves into vehicles and sped, through Africa eastward; it is a long journey. En route, in Johannesburg, I had bought the finest edition of William Shakespeare's collected works that exists to give to this African leader. Not only was I glad of his friendship, but when the British Army disgracefully invaded his country in 1879, fellow Welshmen – the South Wales Borderers – had been pushed to the fore and I significantly inscribed in the heavy volume, words to the effect that Shakespeare's written wisdom was the only intrusion that was proper. He showered me with gifts in return. Like the efficient man he is, he had familiarized himself with the facts of Miss Budd's (now Mrs Pieterse) life, and he reasoned that this was no way to treat a young lady. Of course there are many other sound Zulu reasons why he opposes African National Congress methods.

The two distinguished athletes, Mr Graeme Pollock and Mr Errol Tobias, both naturally sympathized with Zola Budd. Keep sport – particularly when it is innocent – out of politics.

Our confirmed appointment with Mr Oliver Tambo was at hand, so off to Zambia I flew. I joined up with my new cameraman, Mr Tim Leach, who normally worked for Independent Television News and who was based in Harare, Zimbabwe, and other members of the film crew. They were experienced in African methods so that gave me comforting support. Our appointment was fixed to join Oliver Tambo, but was soon postponed, and then day after day it was remade and postponed again and again. Finally I said that we should simply plant ourselves at the headquarters of the ANC's Government in Exile and have some sort of a showdown with these backward, discourteous people. I feared that we might have some difficulty in getting inside, but not a bit of it. We drove through big ramshackle metal gates and were shown to an empty room to wait. We waited and nothing happened. I remember telephones ringing and that no one bothered to answer. I thought to myself: 'God help South Africa if men like these have any responsible part of it.' And then, out in the yard appeared the mastermind behind it all: Oliver Tambo. He was dressed in a white tropical suit. He did nothing; just stood there, looking like a vague, ridiculous figure. The phones continued to ring and still no one answered them. To me it was a nightmare. I wondered why there was no security; no one had asked us or searched us for guns. It was a picture of African uselessness.

I then announced that I was going to leave the wretched place. That I would return to civilization in Johannesburg on the first aircraft that would take me. Indeed I stated that I had an appointment with the golfer, Mr Garry Player, and that *I* kept *my* meetings and off I hoofed. No, I never interviewed the late Oliver Tambo and I sense that my life is a little cleaner for that fact.

But, the mysteries and setbacks piled up; I and my original crew arrived, in due course, at Gary Player's enormous country estate. I felt uneasy from the beginning. First we came to very tall electronically controlled wrought-iron gates, which were guarded by a Black man wearing a smart uniform. Having entered and driven through the lush gardens, we stopped short of the grand mansion. There we were met by Mr Player's son, who was clearly agitated as he explained to us that his father 'regretfully' couldn't give the interview that he himself had arranged and promised.

'Why?' I asked. 'I've travelled a long way.'

Mr Player Junior was hesitant to reply, but finally: 'Well, my father's business advisers telephoned from Cleveland, Ohio last night and told him that you had had some disagreement with Oliver Tambo and therefore it was in my father's interest not to give the interview.'

Wow! In so short a time. What! Thirty-six hours? The venomous words had passed from those black nincompoops in Zambia to somewhere in the middle of the United States of America and back to Gary Player in South Africa, not to cooperate with me. So the Lusakan ANC telephone could be used to effect. I was now on the ANC poison list, like Zola Budd. I then said to young Mr Player – who was shortly to get married, I recall – that I thought his father should come outside and confront me himself. Player Junior said: 'He's very upset.'

Gary Player *did* eventually come out and I wish I could have run a camera on him. He was *very* agitated; he shook my hand and said: 'You are a brave man! (I didn't feel brave.) But what can I do? I pay these people (in Cleveland presumably) a lot of money to advise me; I must listen to them!'

He said some uncomplimentary things about the South African Government: 'I've just lost a contract to build a great golf course in Japan because of them!'

Standing amidst his obvious wealth, I couldn't help but wonder what he needed a few more millions for.

He then spoke with sympathy for Zola Budd: 'She's a good athlete, just like me . . .'

But he wouldn't give the interview for fear of the ANC. However, I had promised a friend in London, Mr Roger Miran, a keen golfer and who thought of Gary Player as only a little less than God, to ask for a photograph dedicated to himself by name and stating that he, my friend, was 'The best golfer in the world!' and signed by Gary Player. Mr Player invited me into his house but couldn't write an untruth. He inscribed: 'To Roger Miran – who is *not* the best golfer in the world. Gary Player'.

And then we went after the old man-of-God himself: Bishop Desmond Tutu down at Bishop's Palace, Cape Town. No audience was granted. The Bishop 'is away' and no further information was forthcoming; but there was an unenthusiastic agreement that I could call and have a word or two with his Reverend's Secretary. On this occasion we took the precaution of keeping a camera running even as we approached the Palace. We kept it going as we entered. The clerical secretary, who was White, ushered me into an inner sanctum, but firmly shutting my crew, with the camera, out. I suggested to the Holy Anglican that what I would really want to ask the Bishop was – with his lengthy experience of the New Testament – 'What would Jesus Christ feel about the persecution of young Zola?' But I very much suspect that the Christians had a pretty fair idea what I was intending to ask and that is the reason why I didn't have a hope in hell of speaking to Tutu himself. 'It is only the truth that hurts.'

The man in South Africa who was responsible for disrupting mixed sport – any event that could be construed as denying the racial barriers – was, I presume, an ANC man. He lived in a fine house, facing the sea in Cape Town. He was Coloured. These people are, understandably, the most bitter section of the racially varied society; they are not easily accepted by either the Blacks or the Whites. I have met a dangerous bitterness in them and this gentleman was no exception. Soon our interview degenerated into a slanging match, with the two cameras turning. His hatred of Zola Budd – an Afrikaner – was expressed very clearly and I spat back: 'You only speak of her like that because she is White!'

That did it; the truth was hurting all over the place. Some people have thought that I shouldn't have included any spasm of that row in the finished film, but it happened and I had no intention of censoring what actually took place, even though one of my weaknesses was exposed.

And then we confronted the most dangerous of our tasks: to pursue Mrs Winnie Mandela into her stronghold of central Soweto. On the edge of this enormous Black township is the formidable paramilitary police headquarters. We were received by the senior officer and given copious coffee and biscuits. He said to me: 'Mr Griffith, you are a foreigner and may not understand our problems here and I don't want you misunderstanding or misinterpreting anything. My first concern is that you will observe that Soweto is filthy; you will see rubbish everywhere. That is not our wish. But if any Black attempts to clean up, he or she is marked by the ANC for a painful death. Tidying up would be interpreted by the ANC as co-operating with the authorities. I asked: 'How many have been killed for such reasons?'

'No one will ever know. We can account for some seven hundred odd. The most popular method with the Blacks is to burn the victim to death by lighting a petrol filled tyre which has been put around his or her neck. They call it "the necklace".'

Some days later I was shown some filmed sequences of the custom; it was the most obscene film material I have ever witnessed. It was being carried out by people while they laughed.

Our police officer and I then haggled over our film crew's protection. He emphasized that we would be in serious hazard if we approached Mrs Mandela. That she was surrounded by a collection of ANC thugs who were known as her 'football team'. I argued that my task – to gain an interview – would be virtually impossible if I was accompanied by police.

'I cannot allow you to go in there, Mr Griffith, without some armed protection. The truth is, they would have only one wish for you and your colleagues and that is to see you all dead.'

Finally we arrived at a deal: there would be only two policemen and they would wear civilian clothes and keep two hundred yards up the road. I had myself fitted with a concealed radio microphone to pick up any conversations that I might have. First we visited a newly built, ostentatious mansion which the Mandelas owned; it was unoccupied. Then we visited a second home and that was deserted and finally we went to the third house and we found the notorious football team in intimidating force. We parked our camera van a short distance away and began to film with a concealed camera which had an appropriate lens. I then began to walk towards Mrs Mandela's men, giving peaceful greetings as I had observed in American Western films when the White guys had to parley with the Sioux. Immediately the Black women present – led by a particularly vicious woman, Xholilwe Falati, who is ironically at this time threatening to expose Winnie Mandela further – began to gabble loud abuse at me, but the men stared stonily.

I explained to these hostile Blacks that I merely wanted to ask Mrs Mandela what was her attitude to the whole Zola Budd affair; after all it would give her an open invitation to express her general hatred of White people. The men replied that I had police with me. I turned round and noted the two officers, both in civilian clothes, and far up the roadway, busy around the boot of their car. I replied to the Blacks that I had argued forcibly with the chief police officer to be excused this escort. I said that I was a foreigner and that 'you know better than I that the police would not allow me to come this far without their presence'.

'Tell them to go away and we might talk to you.'

The Black women were getting hysterical with their abuse and I began to feel certain that Winnie Mandela was not going to appear, so I withdrew and returned to my colleagues. Of course all of this had been recorded on film and sound – from a distance. We used a bit of it in our compilation.

The interview with Zola Budd was conducted in her neat, small house in Bloemfontein, which is the capital of the Orange Free State. Personal communication between us had been arranged by a lawyer friend of mine, Mr Andre Bezuidenhout. Zola is a shy, sensitive young woman, yet courageous and determined. I looked at her books and noted various histories of her people: the Afrikaners. I suggested that she and I should have a private talk in which I would tell her everything that was in my head about the reason for making the film. We repaired to her small bedroom while my colleagues set up their equipment. I told Zola that in my opinion the world outside of South Africa was being sold a false picture of her Afrikaner people and was also being sold a false picture about the Black people. And that although it seemed to be virtually disallowed on British television – particularly on our British Channel Four – to put a White point of view, I thought that with such world interest in her dramatic, if not tragic life, we might be able to break this prejudiced taboo, even with Channel Four. She fully understood what I way saying and trusted me that I was unreservedly sympathetic towards her. Quickly she responded to me as a friend; I felt protective towards her – and small wonder.

The interview went searchingly and when it was finished I told her that we had a video of the Olympic race which the ANC had prevented her from competing in. Up until that time she had resolutely refused to watch it; the whole cruel circumstances were too painful for her. This rural girl had trained herself for what she suspected was the greatest event of her life. I told her that what I would like to do would be to visually record her while she watched the race; that this would be the end of the proposed film. She agreed to allow this, with a mixture of interest and dread. The result was unforgettable. I have never, before or since, observed eyes tell such a detailed, painfully felt story. She may, initially, have felt unease that a camera would be scrutinizing her, but once the race was underway, she was oblivious to all else. The truth is, she ran it herself, sitting on a settee in Bloemfontein.

Later she wrote to me about a national election in South Africa. She informed me that it was a great relief for herself that she wasn't eligible to vote (presumably because she had accepted British citizenship); that even in a secret ballot she wouldn't have to put a cross against any party. The ANC and their questionable do-gooder supporters had bullied her for so long, baiting her to express open support of her people – the Afrikaner people (and in my opinion, a noble people, as human beings go) – that she was grateful that she could now rest in some degree of peace.

The distinguished television commentator for Independent Television News, Mr Michael Nicholson, who has long been a supporter of what I try to achieve on television, looked at the completed film which I titled *Zola Budd: The Girl Who Didn't Run* and offered to take it personally to a Mr John Willis, who was then the head of Channel Four's documentary film department. Mr Nicholson was taken aback; after viewing it Mr Willis was direct enough to say: 'I cannot bear to look at him [me].' Now as far as I know, we have never met, so I must deduce from this reported remark that it was simply watching the Zola Budd film that had erupted such antipathy. But, fortunately, even as I was digesting this statement, Mr Paul Hamman of the BBC contacted me and asked if the film was available. After viewing it, he promptly bought it and it was duly transmitted by BBC2.

After it went out I received about three hundred letters addressed to me personally; they were overwhelmingly and even disconcertingly supportive. Why do I always receive about three hundred letters? What are the calculations behind this curious number? Out of one bundle of ninety-seven letters, tied up with string, only two were opposed to my point of view. Of these two, one was a postcard which simply stated: 'Until last night I regarded you as the greatest living Welshman (the card came from Wales). Never again!' An uneasy mixed compliment . . . As for the rest – the supporters of the film – they were summed up by: 'Thank God! Someone's said it at last!' And I felt a little ill at ease; they certainly expressed widespread insecurity by White Britishers about Black Britishers. Not precisely my purpose; that's another matter. But I have no regrets, whatsoever, that I spoke up for Miss Budd, now Mrs Pieterse, and for the Afrikaner people. Perhaps it was the first time that anyone had wholeheartedly done so on British television. It seems to be my lot in life to be the advocate for the generally perceived pariahs, whether they are Afrikaners, Israelis, Indian Untouchables or, now: Sinn Feiners. Of course, in speaking up for the Untouchables of India, I might uneasily stray into the company of those very do-gooders; I wouldn't relish that company at all! Recently a youngish lawyer came to my door in Islington, appealing for support of Amnesty International. I asked him why British Amnesty did not complain about the political and armed-force injustices that are currently going on in the Six Counties of Ulster – I meant by our British side. He gave me the stock Amnesty reply. Oh, I've heard it before: 'There is an international agreement by Amnesty not to criticize the respective *home* governments.' What open weak-kneed hypocrisy! How comfortable to be an Amnesty do-gooder! Mark you, I don't dismiss them entirely; they achieve much good and I congratulated my caller, indeed thanked him, for the time he was giving on a pleasant day. I went even further: I offered him 'fifty quid, which I can ill afford, if you can give me proof that you have officially raised my argument with Amnesty that we should also attend to our *own* crimes against humanity'.

Not a peep from him and I'm that fifty quid better off.

THIRTY-SIX

Time meanders onward ever more swiftly for me. In this book I am merely picking up the occasional unusual memories. My first line of business for many years has been these storytelling epics that I hope will startle new lines of thought; but the structure for access to this mode of communication, as I have already written, has fundamentally changed; the great impresarios who saw a golden orb of responsible enlightenment through television have either died or been dismissed and so our national hope of resurrection is diminishing. I believe it is as serious as that; if you observe internationally, and at first hand, you will begin to discover that what a nation's television is so that nation will become. Of course there is also the fact that in a rubbishy nation they will *initiate* rubbishy programmes. But now, primarily, the quality of television *precedes* the quality of the nation. Television has become a lethally dangerous commodity in our national lives. Not because, I submit, of the likes of me, an outsider radical voice, but because of the murdering of Lord Reith's (and then his more liberal inheritors') concepts. Today the system has become a large group of salesmen carpet-bagging their proposals to commissioning key men, and women, who may not have the nous to understand a decent letter, leave alone write one. These people can be often envious and malicious. The old impresarios – I have spelt their names out earlier – followed a highly honourable profession, even while they became millionaires. Would to God they were back in the driving seats. But, ironically, it was Tory policy that stipulated the bigger the capital sum gained, the better the product; but perhaps to consider the *quality* of the product was beyond the capacity of their minds. However, I have recently discovered – what is it – University of the Air? And though they make films on an apparent shoestring, they can be first-class. In history programmes, which is my forte, they are not ignorant of the great *drama* of events; I have dared to believe in the privacy of my solitude that they have learnt something from me. Anyway, I like to think so . . .

When I wake up, I perform my ablutions, get dressed, make my breakfast, wash up, attend to urgent letters and do a whack of whatever creative work is to hand. Lunch and a short rest. Then I might go shopping and back to a little more study or composition. After supper, the delight of my life: I climb to the fourth floor, to my library, and there work on writing an encyclopaedia of the entire postal history of the Second Anglo-Boer War of 1899 to 1902. Pretty esoteric! But I believe I know more about that subject than anyone else on the face of this earth. Of course, the work has much to say about imperialism and courage and principle and history itself. I confess that I *enjoy* the endless research and discovery; strangely it relaxes me; it frees me from the traumas of everyday life. If the research is not too complicated I play music on compact discs; above all, great wonderful Mozart. Today, here in Faenza, I said to Chiara, over lunch: 'And to think that Amadeus Mozart was sometimes short of a bob or two. What this civilized world owes to him! He could have counted on me for – not a loan but what I owe him.' Recently, on a train in England, I almost had a row with a new acquaintance because he remarked that Mozart was old-fashioned. I found myself barking: 'Mozart is a much-admired friend of mine.'

I don't go out much socially, unless I am invited. My house is structured to meet all of my needs that I can contrive; it is packed with objects which are all meaningful to me. For me it is aesthetically pleasing, sometimes, as now, when Mrs Mary Docherty, who helps to keep the place – and me – tidy, is away (she is currently attending her sick mother in Ireland) my house looks a bit run-down; but the quiet acceptance of such a state is not unpleasant. 'I have only one pair of hands,' as my grandmother used to say. I have some outstanding friends who call on me regularly: David Reid, Dedwydd Jones, Gordon Kells, Lawrence Corry, John Young, Philip Stogdon and my children: Huw Griffith, Eva Griffith, Jonathan Griffith and his wife, Julie and their two daughters: Kate and Lilly. My eldest son, David Griffith, called on me with my grandson, Oliver, every Sunday morning that I was in London, until recently. He objects to my adherence to the Irish liberation political party, Sinn Fein. For me it is a sad loss, but so be it. Polly Griffith is a committed wanderer, usually around West London, but now in Thailand. Most of those friends are liable to call on me at least once a week! Others, I believe, would if they could but can't. I receive powerful support and thereby comfort from many more: my old employer, Roy Boulting, Jim Bowen, Michael Morgan (the latter two as if I were their son; though they are young enough to be mine). Dennis Selinger is unshiftingly loyal to me. And my one long-standing actor friend: Peter O'Toole. Evelyn Ward, my teacher of English at Tenby Grammar School and still my patient tutor. My second wife, Doria Griffith, will remain my committed friend to the grave. There are a few friends who telephone me very regularly from distant parts where they live; first and foremost, David Phillips from Israel. This list now becomes dangerous. It could be extended greatly.

The author of international repute, Mr Anthony Holden, is ever interested in my work and thereby is concerned that I keep afloat. And this comforting asset also applies to the distinguished journalist and photographer, Ms Ros Drinkwater. Such people ensure that my life is worth living; they are not less than that.

My extraordinary and special friend, Chiara Peretti, is of great significance in my life. Neither of us is placid. The storms between us have been regular and startling, but somehow we are inseparable till death do us part. Shortly she will appear here at the Biblioteca Comunale, Faenza, to walk me home after a formidable afternoon of this scribbling. If this isn't love I don't know what it is.

Without any of these people and many others not mentioned, my life would be lonelier; fortunately for me, they are all younger than I am. Even as I write, my mind is filled with other caring friends; I am indeed blessed.

I am desperately dependent upon patronage. I am not a hustler; this may be a weakness in me. Yes, long ago, when I was barely sixteen, I asked Mr Peter Hoare if he would give me a job as an actor and having watched me audition, he gave me one. From then on I have hoped and nearly prayed that I would survive and advance on simple merit. Lunatic concept! But I have had some grand patrons; without them I cannot imagine how I could have survived. No wonder I am even obsessed with them.

These days in British television it has become, within a whisker, impossible to survive on merit. If you can produce large viewing numbers, yes! Shakespeare put his finger on minority viewing: 'caviar to the general'. But miraculously I *am* surviving. Mr Roy Davies, who until recently was the head of the BBC's history series *Time Watch*, wanted me to work for him. He simply asked me – as television executives used to: 'What do you want to do?'

'A life of Horatio Nelson,' I replied. 'A film in praise of the Englishman, to prove that I am not anti-English.'

'Fine,' replied Mr Davies, but shortly afterwards astounded me with: 'Have you ever considered making a film on the life of Roger Casement?'

I don't know whether Mr Davies noted my long pause before I answered him. After all, I had made two films about Ireland (*Hang Up Your Brightest Colours* and *Curious Journey*) which had both been suppressed, and Mr Davies must have known what my feelings for Roger Casement would be and that I would be unlikely to pull any punches in order to appease English Establishment thinking towards Ireland. I suspect that he did note the pause.

I replied obliquely: 'In this house – I think – I have every book published about Casement. I have copies of all of the so-called "Black Diaries" that have escaped from British security.'

Roy added: 'I think that you should do Casement.'

'Thank you.' And I proceeded to write the script.

So, what could Roger Casement do to encourage British people to look at the carefully hidden truth about our British role in Ireland? A very great deal; that is as long as the British way of governing did not suppress this third film – having suppressed the first two. I am deeply grateful to Mr Roy Davies and to anyone else who may have backed him, for the opportunity to make it.

Roger Casement was brought up as a Protestant and his teenage years were spent in a grand house belonging to his distinguished family in County Antrim, which is one of the notorious Six Counties. The first half of his professional life was initially spent in Africa, primarily as an agent of the British Crown; he became a valued British Consul. During this period, that master of the English language, the Pole, known as Joseph Conrad, met Casement in the Belgian Congo. This vast area of Africa was virtually owned by King Leopold of the Belgians, who kept himself royally above the monstrous obscenities that were being perpetrated on the Black people, in order to increase production of mainly rubber for His Royal Highness's increased profits. Roger Casement, as it were, declared war on the King. That situation is what Joseph Conrad observed and he quickly came to admire and to be intrigued by the Irishman. Conrad wrote a story called *Heart of Darkness* which was inspired by the African presence of Casement. I titled our film: *Roger Casement: The Heart of Darkness*.

Whenever it is possible we film our histories in the precise location where the events took place, but speedily and firmly I was informed that under no circumstances could we film in the Congo – today's Zaire. It was spelt out to me that our only hope of survival in the State were two thousand Belgian troops who were holding a thin jungle-green line. And so I peered at my maps of West Africa and eventually I decided we could make the film in Ghana.

The haunting coast was punctuated by great castles from even Portuguese times. We actually filmed in one of them: Elmina Castle. All of the terrible arrangements were there: the reception tunnels, the cavernous underground storage chambers for human beings; the passages to the heaving seas for transportation to the West Indies and the Americas. The castle was well-kept. There were occasional offices and a few men ran a small, pleasant restaurant, where I was served well-cooked fish. The impressions that bombarded me were multifarious. There was a large parade ground and the colonel's quarters, perched high like the bridge of a ship. And graffiti, written by British soldiers not so long ago, were still on whitewashed walls.

Finally we reached our great rain forest. We were fortunate in being given shelter in a vast logging camp; I believe that before the Ghanaians took over, a British company had ruthlessly and greedily raped that forest area.

Michel Pearce and the rest of us reconnoitred up the river, between towering jungle. Quick mental adjustments were required; our transport was local, native-made canoes, paddled by confident young men. We also trekked inland, away from the river, and met Africa as it had once commonly been. Children shouted and scuttled to safety at the no doubt unattractive sight of pale faces; women withdrew into straw huts, but when the head-man appeared, he calmly made us welcome: Ashanti stools were produced and fruit. Through our interpreter he confessed that he had seen a White man before, but had never spoken to one.

Working on the river was an experience full of wonder. It was so beautiful and yet, at times, dangerous. I witnessed inexplicable sights: an object whizzing over the surface of the water at such a steady pace and too small for a bird and then I realized that it was a snake's head. When the naked African boys saw these swimming serpents they hurled pebbles at them, across long distances and with remarkable accuracy, but I never saw the fast moving reptiles hit. I think that this instinct and universal fear of snakes is even a prenatal matter.

But our greatest danger was on the river at night. For some of these scenes we had lashed two of the primitive canoes together. In the larger craft were Michel Pearce, Peter Ditch, Michael Shoring, Nigel Morgan, plus the camera and sound equipment. I was in the smaller canoe with my Ashanti paddler. Peter Ditch was anxious to film some moonlight through the trees, but God has ordained that the moon must move and Peter was getting a little upset over the loss of this effect. Soon, apart from our portable lights, which were used to illuminate, primarily, my ever-talking face, it was African-river dark and, believe me, it doesn't come any blacker. Suddenly, Peter Ditch stopped complaining about the moon and starkly said, 'We're sinking,' and in the middle of this wide, almost undiscovered river! I peered past the glaring spotlight which was trying to eat my eyes, into the darkness beyond, towards where Michel Pearce presumably was. After all, he, I silently decided, was the person to order: 'Abandon canoes!' Yes, the normal level of water inside their bigger craft was rising! Michel Pearce (from out of the night): 'What do you think, Ken?'

'Let's get the bloody shot!' I replied. This was undoubtedly brave of me because, being rope-lashed to them, if they foundered, so did I – together with my Ashanti mate. I knew that everyone, except me, could swim like a fish. They were all, Whites and Blacks, a pretty athletic lot, so I made a very clearly enunciated statement which sounded most effective across the water and into the jungle: 'Listen to me clearly, lads: in my hip pocket is my wallet which is stuffed with bank-notes. As you all know I *can't* swim a fucking inch. The man who gets me to the bank – should we go under – gets the lot, no argument.'

Michel said: 'Roll camera,' and so we filmed the scene while the boats tilted threateningly.

But this was not the end of my tribulations; the spotlight on my face had attracted an unbelievable number of near-deadly African insects. It was an entomological paradise and I was the only one who *had* to open his mouth – in order to tell my tale about Roger Casement. I am sitting here, in Faenza, writ-ing the bare truth: my mouth was crammed with these unidentified specimens and I masticated many of them. We got the shot and with me choking, we limped to a sand-bank. To this day I am ashamed of the language I used. What motivated us was this near-uncontrollable compulsion to get the shot. If medals are handed out to soldiers, certain film makers should get them as well.

Some people were surprised that I put such an emphasis on Roger Casement's humanitarian work in Africa. The Irishman is generally famous – or, to the enemies of Ireland, infamous – for his work for Irish freedom, but the *context* of all human activities is vitally important, if one truly wants to understand them. Britain has worked diligently and ruthlessly to denigrate Casement as an Irish patriot, but this chicanery becomes gapingly exposed if one presents his towering humanitarian work before he turned to the suffering of his own people – the Irish. Casement virtually broke King Leopold and his murderous style in the Congo. The British Government honoured Casement with this and that and finally knighted him, which honour he tried to decline, but as an employee of the British Crown, failed. He became Sir Roger Casement. Perhaps the most extraordinary tribute paid to him was when a sermon was preached in Westminster Abbey which extolled his great humanitarian work; he was dubbed as being 'One of the greatest heroes of the British Empire'. But then he made a devastatingly embarrassing statement – as far as British imperialism went. He said that as deeply as he felt for the natives of the Congo and elsewhere, he felt even more deeply for the plight of his own Irish people under Britain and with that pronouncement he shifted his whole will and strength towards emancipating them.

Casement's work for Sinn Fein and the Irish Republican Army was relentless; he did all he could and perhaps some things that he shouldn't have done. Initially the British Government were comically disconcerted. How do you talk your way out of this one? It is almost lovable how the English try so hard to convince – even themselves – that they could not be guilty of anything that was not quite cricket. But the blood at their feet has sometimes proved embarrassing. And then the English will call in the not-always-intelligent brigade, who are sometimes incapable of hiding the gritty glint at the back of their eyes. Currently it is one Sir Patrick Mayhew; for Casement it was a very intelligent enemy: F. E. Smith, soon to be rewarded, if you value that sort of indignity, by becoming Lord Birkenhead. This classic Anglo-Saxon first contrived to destroy Casement's conventional reputation as a humanitarian by broadcasting as widely as to the Pope in Rome, the King (George the Fifth) in England and finally the President in Washington, that he was a homosexual. Of course whether Casement was or he wasn't is entirely irrelevant; some of the best quality people that I have met in my life were homosexuals. Wretched F. E. Smith used some personal diaries which he claimed had come, untouched, from Casement's home in London. Certain distinguished historians have believed that the lurid sexual allusions in these diaries were forged by the British Government's dirty tricks department. Today I suspect they were but I have no proof. However, the British Home Office refused to allow me to view the Casement police-file; that is seventy-eight years after his death! It was the BBC they rejected; I took the precaution of applying through that still nearly august Corporation.

Well, F. E. Smith and the British Government contrived to hang Roger Casement during 1916, in Pentonville Prison, London.

As I wrote earlier, I am in no mood to pull punches over Britain in Ireland. I have scant respect for our Government's policy. To the very last day I half expected to hear that the British authorities had intervened at the BBC and that the third true story about Ireland that I had been responsible for was being withdrawn, but nothing happened and it was transmitted a year ago on BBC2. I received that mythical-like three hundred-plus letters. Again they were overwhelmingly supportive and (Hallelujah!) a large percentage were from English people. I do believe that the English, if they were told the truth in depth about our doings in Ireland, would want us to remove ourselves from, let us call it, St Patrick's Island.

Oh! Amongst those letters addressed to me was one from the head of the Casement family in London. For me it is a precious document; indeed I have it framed. And there was one other communication amongst those letters which I have also hung on the wall of my house; it is a death-threat from my fellow-Protestants, at the Harland and Wolff shipyard in Belfast. What a merry-go-round!

THIRTY-SEVEN

The British Broadcasting Corporation in Cardiff (or was it the Film Foundation of Wales under Mr John Hefin, or was it Channel Four Wales under Mr Geraint Stanley Jones? – I have never been clear) decided to make a film about me! I had been responsible for, up to last year, about twenty-four films about other people, but I almost freeze at the realization that others had decided to focus on my straggly, struggling life. Not that I objected; no! In fact, like this book, I felt that the idea was unexpectedly rounding off my life. It might be nice for my children, I thought; much as I sometimes think about this book, when I ask myself: 'Will people that I have never met be interested in all of these travails or even be interested in my happy times?'

The two men who were the actual executives of this venture were my old friend and producer, John Hefin, and my new friend, Ken Griffiths. Already, dear Reader, I can sense you boggling over these words: 'He had the big-headedness to produce a film about himself!!' No, no! This is *another* Ken Griffiths and you may note that he likes to shorten his Christian name to 'Ken' and that there is an 's' on the end of his surname. Nevertheless, there must still be many astounded viewers, who, having read those screen credits, think the worst of me. We two K.G.s thought and spoke of ourselves as 'K.G. Llandeilo and K.G. Tenby'.

Many years before, indeed many many years ago, I was acting in a television play written by the distinguished Welsh writer, Mr Alun Richards, and also in the cast with me was that fine actor Mr Clifford Evans. Well the short of it is that Clifford got it into his head that Alun, who happened to be staying with me in London, was editing his drama in my favour. Of course, as everyone of any consequence knows – unless one was emotionally involved like Clifford – Mr Alun Richards is the personification of gentlemanly ethics and that any such favouritism was out of the question! But Clifford's groundless suspicions persisted and I suppose that I might have retaliated (we're all human) and the resultant explosion caused Alun Richards to call me: 'The Tenby Poisoner'. When John Hefin heard this story, he exercised his director's authority and there was no point in arguing; my filmed calvary through life *had* to be titled *The Tenby Poisoner*. With little doubt, Mr John Willis, of Channel Four, London, and a number of my fellow Protestants from the Welders Department of the Harland and Wolff shipyard in Belfast consider *The Tenby Poisoner* to be an acutely observed title.

It was Geraint Stanley Jones himself who interviewed me for the film, with a series of apt questions which were now and again hair-raising and Geraint had a good idea that I wouldn't duck them. I am still waiting for the day when I may have to reply: 'No comment!' But those words, so popular amongst the Saxons, do not exist in any version of the Celtic language. Suffice it for me to wish that some of my replies could not possibly have been used in the finished film – and I am sorry about that.

And then Hefin and Griffiths (Llandeilo) turned to a selection of people who have had very varied experiences of me over the long years: Evelyn Ward (my teacher); Peter O'Toole (my great actor friend for thirty years); Roy Boulting (my friend and often employer); Alun Richards (the proud author of the film's title); Jeremy Isaacs, one of the best influences in British television; Eva Griffith (my eldest daughter); David Griffith (my eldest son); and an Israeli opinion from Magen Broshi, the 'Keeper of the Dead Sea Scrolls' (who is, in my opinion, Israel personified); and finally Mr Martin McGuinness, who did me the honour of making a statement on behalf of Republican Ireland. Of course Mrs Thatcher's farcical law prevented us hearing Martin's actual voice, but I take this opportunity of congratulating the distinguished Irish actor who so-skilfully dubbed his voice; you cannot tell that it isn't the real man! Unfortunately I cannot mention my fellow Thespian's famous name; they would try to victimize him to the point of ruin if I did. That is the reality under our putrid system towards Ireland.

As usual, when making such films, there were one or two contributors who couldn't be fitted into the producer's concept of the story that they wanted; I still cringe at their omission, but it was correct that I had no say in the matter.

Also the producers wanted two other contributions: from Chief Minister Buthelezi from Africa, and from that great newspaper editor, Rajan Narayan in India; but a camera and crew failed to reach these two very distant men, though I am told, they were poised to speak their piece.

However, the film, in my professional opinion, was excellent. The astonishingly experienced film maker, and therefore merciless critic, Mr Roy Boulting, told the producers that it was the best biographical film that he had ever seen. Certainly it was neither sentimental (not with a title like that) nor sycophantic – which are the two most common disasters in such films.

But my people, the Welsh, had further plans for me. Mr Roy Davies, who had moved from being head of London's *Timewatch* to running BBC Wales' documentary department and much else besides, it seems to me, began operations to release my life of Michael Collins (*Hang Up Your Brightest Colours*), which had been suppressed for some twenty-one years. He called me in to help in the process. Its release was as simple as its suppression was absolute. Again I find myself reluctant to probe such mysteries; my instinct is to put my head down and keep those fingers crossed. I believe that Mr Davies took the news of the freeing of the film to the BBC in London, for, presumably, networking. I don't know what happened; such activities within the BBC are always under heavy wraps for the likes of me (except in the good old days of Huw Wheldon, when he would tell me, his chum, how some of the machinery worked). The next I knew was that BBC Wales were going to transmit a season of my documentary films, over a week's period. They announced that they would kick off with *The Tenby Poisoner* on March the 1st (Saint David's Day) 1993, followed by *Hang Up Your Brightest Colours* (Michael Collins), *Black as Hell; Thick as Grass* (British–Zulu War) and *Bus to Bosworth* – a meaningful but fictional tale.

It is difficult for me to communicate what effect this had on my psyche. Remember, I had travelled across to London from rural South West Wales when I was sixteen years old to become an actor. I was nigh totally inexperienced and unsophisticated. And I came from an area hurtfully called 'Little England Beyond Wales' (because of ancient historical reasons and because of Tenby's great natural beauty, which brought many better-off English people to settle there). It was a seemingly impossible expedition which had suddenly culminated after fifty-five years in this best of honours. And because I came from Little England, where the Welsh language is sadly not spoken, most of the Welsh-speaking actors in London were tempted to look at me askance; therefore this wholehearted embracing in Wales was all the more poignant for me. My filmed biography being transmitted by BBC Wales on Saint David's Day!

Over the past two or three years several events have been quietly placed in my lap which have been beyond fantasy for me. The BBC in Cardiff asked me if I would agree to a reception at their headquarters at the ancient Celtic centre of Llandaff and if there were any friends I would like to invite . . . Well, I asked very few; after all, it is a long way to travel from London to Cardiff, for perhaps – so I imagined – a bun and a glass of wine. But it wasn't like that at all: it was warmly Welsh, but semi-formal and very generous. I can afford, and at long last am wise enough, not to want anything from anybody unless they are anxious to give it. Expectancy is now the all-destructive element in Britain; for many years, indeed since I was a child, I have expected no boons, no handouts; but now, on this last lap of my life, I am being inundated with disturbing rewards. Chiara was with me in Cardiff on that day; my dear teacher, Evelyn Ward; my daughter, Eva and other friends. In contrast to my reluctance to invite friends to make the journey from London, I happened to mention, over the telephone to David Phillips, that the event was happening and he promptly left his business and flew from Israel to be there. Speeches were made and I replied. I was in a state of shock; not less. I learnt, finally, on that day, that praise is more difficult to bear than blame. Of course the two poles are very different. The words of John Willis sting and disappoint but uninhibited praise makes me face up to the fact of how inadequate I essentially am. I almost bend double when confronted with the latter; when the former occurs, I am bolt upright, spoiling for a fight, as readers of this book will have realized.

Geraint Stanley Jones gave a dinner-party at – I think – Channel Four, Wales. I sat on his right-hand side. There were some distinguished and interesting (far from being the same thing) guests. My friend spoke and he referred to me as a great Welsh Nonconformist. I am uneasy about 'great' but 'Nonconformist' has a very special connotation in Wales; I have difficulty in disassociating its implication from the Chapel. I sat there listening and wondering and then I suffered a glow of delight. Yes! I am a Welsh Nonconformist; that is exactly what I am – born out of my Celtic nature! Of course this individuality, this tendency to revolt against what we consider to be wrong, has also weakened our enormous Celtic potential. One Celtic family could rarely agree with the next Celtic family, so how could we successfully oppose the highly drilled and disciplined Roman armies? Or the German – I mean the English, the Saxon – invasions? Finally the Saxons pushed us British (the Welsh) westward and eventually we became darkly subdued under the heavy blanket of Christian Puritanism. But we Welsh are not dead; indeed I sense that we are raring to go! No more *orders* from London, proper cooperation yes, but no more begging bowls. And that applies to the BBC arrangement too; television is an all-powerful influence that we cannot delegate to a different culture.

The Irish Irish people are the unadulterated Celts. Their country (which includes the Six Counties) is Ultima Thule, the edge of the world. There you can see the strength and weakness of us Celts. For 800 years they have hit the overwhelming

English presence, but they still refer very sturdily to 'the Kerry Man', 'the Cork Man' and, as I hear at least once a week from my friend – Lawrence Corry: 'the Armagh Man'. And the Irish still hark back to the Welsh-led (Lloyd George) English-created Irish Civil War: 'Are you a Republican or a Free-Stater?' Forget the latter catastrophe totally; it was a blessing for England and an aberration for Ireland. Until the English have finally departed from all of Ireland think less of your specific Irish tribe and call yourselves simply 'Irishmen' and 'Irishwomen'. And what can we Welsh Celts do to help? I myself am going to start concentrated work for *Celtic solidarity*. I want us new-positive Welsh to address England openly and firmly: 'Stop messing our fellow Celts [the Irish] about, or you will have to contend with *us* also. I am not against the Saxons – the Germans – the English. As I have written already: 'Some of my best friends are English' – but they *must* stop, at long last, injuring our very own Celtic people, in Ireland. I am not even against a United Kingdom; there *are* clear advantages. But perhaps we should rotate our monarchy: five years for the English (even though their present arrangement seems to be a mixture of Greece and Germany); five years for the Scots (I wouldn't mind the Stuarts having another go); five years for the Welsh (I would delight if that saint-like man, Richard Rhys, the Lord Dinefwr, not only ran my part of Wales, as his ancestors did in all of those centuries ago, but the whole hotch-potch island); and perhaps, finally, Ireland itself might happily volunteer to join Britain if there were a royal Irish stint (I very much like the idea of King Gerry Adams with Martin McGuinness as the Lord Protector of All).

I felt that there should be a viewing of the newly freed Michael Collins film in London; it is needed most in England. To suppress a political film for twenty-one years and then very quietly release it is no everyday event. Anywhere else in the world, that was not a totalitarian tyranny, would have had some sort of national fiesta – as was about to be held in Wales. But not only is Britain going down hill at a crashing rate, but Mrs Thatcher's chickens (and I don't mean her well-known children) have proliferated alarmingly and are aware of little apart from profits. (Isn't this Thatcher phenomenon interesting as we move into naked bankruptcy?)

Well, I got the nervous idea of approaching the British Academy of Film and Television Arts, in Piccadilly, London. I, with my openly expressed unease towards the Establishment, felt that I was asking for help from the top brass of our society, whom I had even assailed. I telephoned the august body and cheekily (though not inwardly confident, I am not an actor for nothing) asked for the boss. Immediately Mr Anthony Byrne spoke to me: 'Mr Griffith, what a pleasure to speak to you!' I *am* paranoid at times and this occasion was, little doubt, one of them. Mr Byrne urged me to call on him personally and as speedily as possible. We would share coffee (and there were top-class biscuits as well; a poor old actor registers such things). There is no greater put-down than warm graciousness in the teeth of ungraciousness. I quickly felt humbled. I explained to Mr Byrne the freeing of the Michael Collins film.

'This is splendid news, Mr Griffith!' and I mumbled on about my hope for a viewing in England: 'Would it be possible at BAFTA? What would the cost be?'

'Mr Griffith, this is an important event: the release of this film! There would be no charge; BAFTA would be proud to present it themselves.' And a date for the event was quickly arranged. As I contentedly nibbled my fourth biscuit (they were *very* good) kindly Mr Byrne happened to mention that two of his great-aunts had attended the funeral of Michael Collins at Glasnevin Cemetery in Dublin. I confided the historical information that *many* women – and not only in Ireland – were in love with the Big Fellow. Of course I had hopefully wondered about the name Byrne before I met him; it had a warm Irish ring about it.

The British Academy of Film and Television Arts organized a first-class evening for *Hang Up Your Brightest Colours*. They invited that formidable young man, David Elstein, to chair the evening, which he accepted. This choice impressed and pleased me very much because he or Jeremy Isaacs would have been my wish. There was a substantial gathering of people whom I knew, but the majority were members of the Academy whom I didn't know. Again – as in Cardiff – I was in pain with emotion. It wasn't fear of speaking; I have no problems with that duty. It was this support and expression of approbation.

David Elstein spoke his mind, as is his wont; he praised some of my work, but also mentioned that on other occasions (one or more, David?) he has wanted to put his boot through the television screen. I suspect that this impulse was chiefly provoked by my film on the life of David Ben-Gurion. Though not blessed sufficiently to be Jewish myself, I have good reason, through the experiences of my life, to be aggressively pro-Semitic; indeed I am a committed Zionist. My film on Ben-Gurion was meant to be *Israel's* case through the great man's life. I have a number of Israeli friends who are amused but shocked at my defence of, say, Ariel Sharon, the burly man of fierce action, or of Avram Stern. You see, the trouble is, Jesus Christ was a hard-working Rabbi and that bit about tending to the mote in one's *own* eye before attending to the what-was-it in someone else's is a very strict Jewish instinct. I have presumed that David got worked up about this Welsh Goy blabbing on about the seamless virtues of Israel; it was more than he could bear with equanimity. But if my guess is near the mark, I must remind him that I did raise – strongly – the one atrocity of which Israeli guerilla fighters might have been guilty, at Dir Yassin; though whether there was conscious evil in that, I have my doubts. Immediately after the event, Ben-Gurion sent an urgent apology to King Abdullah of Jordan – while they were still at war. What more do you want, David? But like all *good* Jewish people, he wants his people's failings stated clearly.

The film itself was watched and listened to with wrapt attention. It was beautifully and imaginatively directed by Antony Thomas, finely photographed by Grenville 'Rabbit, Rabbit' Middleton and sensitively edited by Roger James. At the end the audience gave it a remarkable reception; they stood up and made a lot of noise. Michel Pearce, who was present, afterwards reported to me darkly: 'Only three people remained seated and I've got their names for you, Ken – and their addresses . . .' I then spoke and answered questions and a few of them were challenging. I have been congratulated by two Irish Republicans who were politically present assuring me that I answered them with clarity and historical accuracy. To tell you the truth I was once again in a painful state; I recall that three times I told the audience that I felt ill because of the occasion, which somehow they thought was funny. Well a few laughs do no harm.

To some people present I must have appeared to be ungracious. I couldn't fully cope with it all. I talked with my old colleagues stretching back over many years: Antony Thomas, Roger Jenkins (no longer a film editor but now an executive with Central Television) and with Michel Pearce. I did not speak to everyone that I should have. I had been knocked off balance; I was like a boxer who had barely survived to the end of the fight. I received two valuable messages of goodwill from distant parts: Christopher Dunkley in Italy and Michael Nicholson in Moscow. I sloped off with my two rugby football mates (oh yes, they were represented): Jim Bowen and 'Micky' Morgan, who, as they ever have, stood me a good meal.

I received a message the next day from a journalist connected with the *Sunday Times*: 'I was so moved and disturbed by the occasion that I hurried out of the theatre; only two people were ahead of me going down the stairs. They were a middle-aged, middle-class English couple. The woman said: "I've learnt a great deal tonight." The man didn't reply immediately, but suddenly stopped and said: "Makes you think, doesn't it?" ' What a sense of achievement I enjoyed from those words and still do! When the British people generally feel that, the light will truly begin to shine in Ireland and the warfare will stop.

THIRTY-EIGHT

About this time I began to realize that I had even more unexpected support. Irish Republicans in London contacted me, more than they had done before, and were anxious to give me any help that they could. They were especially concerned about the death-threat which I had received from the Protestant–Unionists in Belfast, though, as I have already written, it does not disturb me at all. This is not bravery on my part; I simply know that there are far more urgent targets than me who are far more conveniently located for assassination than I am. However, my sentiments did not deter them and I am carefully supervised. But the result of this is that I have made some new and invaluable spiritual friends. We are a social cell of Celtic brothers – and sisters – in the middle of London. Earlier this year I was invited to the Irish Centre in Camden Town where the Irish actress, Ms Kate Sommerville, skilfully and bravely read out a lengthy citation directed at me and then I was presented with a large framed picture which was wrapped. Again I found it difficult to digest what was happening to me; in no way had it been dreamt of. I unwrapped the paper in front of the London Irish; I expected to see a view of Ireland. It was nothing of the sort: it was a splendid print of British soldiers making a last stand during the Second Anglo-Boer War. It was by the famous Victorian artist Caton Woodville and was an item that I had long wanted to hang on a wall of my weird house in Islington. Someone had done some diligent research.

Soon after this event I received an invitation from the Republican ghettos of Belfast to be their guest for the week commencing 2 August 1993. The annual occasion is called

The West Belfast Community Festival which truly is a euphemism for the Sinn Fein Festival; there is, strangely, a tendency by Irish Republicans not to be unnecessarily provocative in that war situation which exists. This is a strain of behaviour that I have observed throughout my relationship with the Irish Republican Movement. Yes, a bloody war exists but we are deeply sorry that it *has* to be fought. But no one must mistake this for weakness; indeed this serious general concern by the leadership for suffering is a sign of their strength. To feel compassion for *all* sides in the conflict and yet with no prospect whatsoever of becoming bent is an impressive demonstration of moral strength.

Mine is an outstanding method for trying to persuade people to think differently. National interests are Establishment interests and soon, through the media, they are converted into popular consensus. Recently a television programme called *The Cook Report* mendaciously attacked Mr Martin McGuinness as, virtually, the murderer of the two boys in Warrington; I happen to *know* that when Mr McGuinness heard of their deaths, he put his head in his hands. But he painfully knows that there is a war going on which, by and large, has extended over 800 years and was caused by England's brutal conquest of Ireland. Mr McGuinness did not want the boys killed, that I can assure you, but he does want such people as Mr Cook to be aware of how many millions of Irish people have been erased by, primarily, the English and that, at long last, the Irish people, Protestant and Catholic, must live together, united, on their small island. The Union Jack, in historical truth, is nothing less than a bloody symbol of oppression over Ireland; it must be removed.

And, when two young members of the Irish Republican Army carried a bomb into a shop, in Protestant Belfast, above which was the headquarters of the leading 'Protestant' assassination organization, and when that bomb exploded prematurely, killing one of the young men, Mr Gerry Adams did not consider political expediency and he openly carried the young man's body to his grave. Mr Adams knew well enough what a large range of British newspapers would make of his action and unlike any British politician that I can think of (with the exception of Mr Wedgwood Benn and Mr Kenneth Livingstone) he demonstrated the proper truth. This led one shallow popular British newspaper to concoct a commercial headline which claimed that 'Gerry Adams' were the two dirtiest words in the English language. In actual fact he is a mature, intelligent and kindly man who has offered his life for the final emancipation of his country.

What do I feel about bombs, readers of this book will properly ask? If Winston Churchill and 'Bomber' Harris had consulted with me on the eve of attacking Dresden where, I am assured, there was no comprehensible military target, I suspect that I would have said: 'I don't think so.' And if the IRA had consulted with me on the eve of Warrington, I would have probably said: 'No, don't do it.' But in both cases a war is being waged. In the case of Britain, our Second World War could logically be called a war of defence; in the case of the IRA it can logically be described as a war of final liberation from the British. I had a few old chums – brave innocent lads who were on the Dresden trip. I am told that they managed to kill about 40,000 women, old men and children. But neither Dresden nor Warrington, thank Providence, was my direct responsibility. Irish Republican soldiers had to decide and weigh the risk.

And another friendly warning, Mr Major and company: the world is looking at the behaviour of us British in Ireland in a mood that is more than suspicious of our moral integrity. World leaders, Mr Major, may be too polite or diplomatic to tell you what the world knows about our presence in Ireland, but they do *know*. Of course, most of these world powers have a great deal to hide themselves. That is another reason for their discretion in your hearing. But they know the truth, Mr Major and company; make no mistake.

Before I left London for Belfast I reiterated to my Irish Republican friends that they must not spoil me in this fashion; that it was not good for me to be cosseted. To which they replied: 'You wait till you get to the Falls Road . . .' What did this mean? In no way was I remotely prepared for the reality of what lay ahead of me. While still in London I was asked if I would be prepared to visit three young – undoubtedly Republican – men, held on remand in the Crumlin Road Gaol. They were Liam and Patrick Gallen and Sean Corry.

'Certainly I will, but won't they wonder who this old Welshman is?'

'You don't understand, Kenneth; you are about to find out.'

Three Irish Republicans insisted upon driving me to London Airport. I boringly nagged that I always (these latter years) like to be early for every appointment and so we four Celts set off with hours in hand. Unfortunately, our driver was accustomed to taking a route through the City of London; he had overlooked that it was prohibited by a 'ring of steel'. The deviation we took caused us to cut it fine for the airport. As far as I can remember, none of us said anything about the cause of our delay.

The three young men that I had promised to meet in Crumlin Road Gaol had been on remand for some two years each. This information shocked me! One hears things and they can pass with only slight thought. Two years each without trial! Is this legal? I announced while still in London that I wanted to know everything about each of their cases: 'When I return to London I want to be carrying facts that I can put to influential and concerned people like Neil Kinnock and Wedgwood Benn!'

The flight to Belfast takes less than an hour and I found that during the short journey a profound metamorphosis came over me. First, I didn't want to ask anything about the Gallens and young Corry more than I knew already: that they came from a prosperous background and that they were being held on suspicion of actions prompted solely by their Republican Nationalist convictions. That is all, I decided on the aircraft, I needed to know. I found it very curious that, simply being on the flight to reality – as against my intellectual reasonings – was radically shifting my vision of things. Yes, I had been to Ireland before; I had been in the Six Counties before; I had been to Belfast before; I had been to Derry City and I had immersed myself in the appalling history of England in

Ireland; but I was now going to visit the people in the front line of the conflict and that reality shifts a few thoughts, which had been generated from a considerable distance. I was already doing some adjusting.

At Belfast Airport I was greeted by two uniformed security officers: 'It is Mr Griffith, isn't it? Welcome to Belfast.' They were smiling and friendly. And then I was approached by two young men: 'Mr Griffith, we've come to drive you to West Belfast.' I was told that 'Gerry and Martin would like to welcome you,' and the car drove into a factory area. I got out and after a few minutes I was told that they were 'round the corner, waiting to meet you'. The two leaders of Sinn Fein were standing together unaccompanied. They both were smiling and I have received the impression that they regard me as a bit of a card; which is a role that suits me well enough. Mr Adams spoke about the Roger Casement film; he said that he had missed a fair piece of it because he was on the telephone urging friends to watch. He couldn't believe that the BBC were allowing incisive historical truths about Irish history to be broadcast. Of course the film was everything that Mrs Thatcher had viciously opposed. She had called for 'prohibiting the oxygen of publicity'; what this really meant was the prohibition of certain truths. And I, at least as far as my films go, do not stray from the terrible facts of history.

And I *am* a bit of a card; but I was about to learn that my relationship with my fellow Celts within the Republican Movement goes much deeper and that the rate of acceleration of this discovery for me was to continue increasing throughout my visit. I was beginning to experience the most vivid week of my life.

Mr Jim Gibney was allotted to look after me. I presume that this started off as a simple duty for him; before I departed from Belfast he had become one of my dearest and, I am sure, enduring friends. Never before in so short a time have I become so devoted to a human being. Jim, it seems to me, is my alter-ego; he seems to be the brother I never had. I cannot truthfully write that he is the man I would have become if I had been born into his Catholic–Republican situation, because

I very much doubt whether I have his grit and courage. He is a highly sensitive man and the daily physical threat that he is subject to has gone on for many years. As I have already explained I had quickly suffered the instinct *not* to ask painful questions. However, I soon learnt about Jim Gibney's time in British prisons; but I was also realizing that virtually everybody around me had spent years in our penal institutions and *always* because of their love of their people and their country. I would like to inform you about everything I know about Jim Gibney, but that would be indiscreet of me; let it suffice that he has clearly lost all of the normal joys of this life for what he *has* to do to help to achieve a United Ireland.

A very full schedule had been worked out for me, and Jim Gibney supervised it. There were showings of my suppressed Irish films and I spoke and answered questions to packed gatherings of Irish Republicans. They were warm, humorous and happy occasions. I had not experienced anything remotely like it since I was a child before the Second World War, when, ironically, my life revolved around our Protestant, Wesleyan Chapel. I was being embraced by an enormous family; many thousands of them. In London I had been told: 'Irish Republicans trust you.' To some extent I wondered what that meant. What was the strange implication of that statement? In West Belfast I understood with little time to ruminate; I was simply and wholeheartedly accepted as part of the fighting family. I then wondered how it was possible for them to trust me so completely? After all the British Intelligence Organization in the Six Counties has gone to astounding and grim lengths to falsely ingratiate themselves with the Irish Republican Movement in order to infiltrate into their ideas and plans. How could they be so sure of me? But steadily I realized the fact that they had been totally thorough; you might say that they knew more about me than I know about myself. Very thorough homework had been done. Yes, I *am* to be trusted because they are my Celtic people and I feel, profoundly, for my Celtic people. I hope that that is not in any way an arrogant boast. And it is not in the nature of the people of the Falls Road or of the Ardoyne to boast. They simply have a quiet determination to remove the British presence in Ireland once and for all. And around these traumatic discoveries of mine was one week of music and dancing and serious lecturing on a number of wise but surprising subjects like the prevention of drug taking and alcoholism. Through all of those old-fashioned simple pleasures there ran a strong line of social responsibility and all during a wartime.

There was a joke about me in the Falls Road during that week: 'Ken has not yet finished *one* cup of coffee.' Having consumed half the coffee – of course there was a great deal of talking going on in which predictably I would have my share – I would see Jim glance at his watch and then give me a hard stare and off we would go to the next astonishing event. And this is the point that I want to make clear to you, dear Reader: wherever I went, from the old people to the young people, I was received with such generous homely affection. And why was this? The answer is now very clear to me: I am not an Irishman, I am a Welshman; I am not a Roman Catholic, I was brought up a Protestant. And yet, they recognized that I understood the wrongs done to them and as a fellow Celt that I totally identified with them. It is normal and understandable for human beings to find any excuse to keep out of other people's fights. But I have seen that this is *not* someone else's fight; this is – or should be – our own Welsh Celtic fight. Sometimes, when Wales has played rugby football in Ireland, Dubliners have put messages of welcome, in the Welsh language, in their windows. I want to hear more of this and vice versa when the Irish visit us in Cardiff. And England has dragged us Welsh into their exploitation of Ireland and we Welsh should resist. This should not be our Welsh game. Well it so happens that I, without realizing it as I ploughed my own ideological furrow, had become a pretty lone pioneer in this Celtic instinct and now I call upon every Welshperson with any national pride, to join me and to share with me the heartfelt welcome that is waiting for you amongst the Irish Irish. And, strangely, I believe that Scottish Nationalists can bypass their churlish cousin, the Reverend Ian Paisley, and help to remove the Union Jack from someone else's soil. And finally the cockneys and the North of England people, and the West Englanders (mainly Celts) will be prepared to apologize for past English misdemeanours and will help the withdrawal from Ireland process. It is the proper and best solution and we will all be the stronger for it.

Tom Hartley, the chairman of Sinn Fein, took me on a comprehensive tour of the Republican areas in Belfast. He is a humorous man and it was a curious experience for me to have to thread our way through the ubiquitous patrols of Royal Ulster Constabulary paramilitaries and my own young fellow-countrymen, armed with very advanced weapons, being British soldiers. No one – and certainly not me – could begin to comprehend the intensity of these non-stop operations unless they witness them with their own eyes. Winding, domestic streets, with rows of neat, very simple houses, with children playing in their tidy gardens. And there, ritualizing up the roadways like a murderous animal, is the British military column. The Royal Ulster Constabulary are less formal than our own 'homeland' soldiers; they look older in their black uniforms and appear to be sturdier because of their thick flak-jackets and carrying their formidable guns ever at the ready. My true fellow-countrymen appear to be very young and wear a thorough camouflaged outfit and they follow a strictly drilled routine, like stiff dancers. Guns are poised as they walk up the homely pavements while behind them one of their comrades has dropped to one knee and is scanning the rear of the operation. On it goes, continuously, from the beginning of the allotted area to the end of it.

The Irish Irish people totally ignore them; not only has the hideous charade been going on for so many years, but it is the Republican rule of behaviour. These armed 'British' intruders are the last awful twitch of our occupation of Celtic Irish territory; it is the final English insult, and the least you can do while they intrude onto your front garden is to ignore them. That is what Tom Hartley and the Irish children around us did. Tom chatted on to me about this interesting matter and that. But this busy threat of guns was not so easy for me to ignore. I have never observed such an open threat during any of my adventurous perigrinations: not in dictatorial West Africa, in Kashmir, in the West Bank adjacent to Israel, nor in Iran shortly after their murder-happy revolution. And not only was the experience threatening and novel, but the armed soldiers were our British youth. Their expression generally seemed to me to be a mixture of how a soldier should look and suppressed insecurity. I was amongst them and resented the wretched job that they had been given to do. I was not without sympathy and since I have a compulsion to always express what I feel, I said 'Hello' and 'Good morning' to the lads. And the result was memorable: they were startled; I got half-smiles and uncertain lip movements as if they were wishing me the same. Get it into your apparently limited sensitivity, Mr Major, that these young men *must* be taken back to London, Cardiff and Glasgow without more ado. And incidentally, don't send them on to Germany; the Germans can look after themselves. Please don't keep our young men in Ireland, not even for the questionable political support of Ian Paisley and company. Make a decent historical name for yourself: you've got the chance of a Prime Minister's lifetime. Otherwise you'll fade away like Mr Baldwin. I explained my not unfriendly greetings to Tom Hartley and though the soldiers were the paid enemy of his people, he understood my feelings; Tom is a singularly reasonable man.

During one meeting which I had been invited to address (sharing the platform with Tim Pat Coogan, the distinguished sometime newspaper editor and now successful biographer – most recently a life of Michael Collins and then Eamon de Valera – and a formidable young man, who had written a highly thought-of book while imprisoned by the British for his political convictions) I ran into unexpected opposition. In explaining that I had never joined *any* political party during my life (no, I have not joined Sinn Fein), I confessed that I had once thought of applying for membership of Kwa Zulu's Inkhatha, because my friend, Chief Minister Buthelezi, had told me that all he now wanted to do with his life was to simply advance his own people, the Zulus; separate development of a culture: in fact, apartheid. I told the audience that I hadn't joined Inkhatha; it was merely a passing fantasy. But a sturdy group of young men at the back of the chamber, loudly picked me up on the point; they were, I quickly presumed, very lively activists and inevitably ideologists and predictably were committed to the African National Congress and, as I was to discover later, to the Palestine Liberation Organization; a movement which again does not warm my heart. I, inevitably, squared up to my Republican activist critics, saying that I was concerned about the preservation and development of *all* decent cultures. I may even have said that I would be prepared to fight for the decent advancement of the English culture, if it was improperly threatened. Anyway, the short of it was that Jim Gibney jumped to his feet and stopped the heated altercation. I remember Jim saying that though this South African debate was very interesting he thought that it should be held separately on another occasion. But, as always during my visit, I was so generously and warmly embraced by these noble and unpretentious people. I was bought many many glasses of Guinness and they even sympathetically accepted the astonishing fact that I only wanted half pints.

My visit to the three young Republicans: Liam Gallen, Patrick Gallen and Sean Corry, in the Crumlin Road Gaol was another episode in my rapid, compressed education. I had been given my prison pass in London and it had been arranged for another young man, a relative of the prisoners, to escort me through the security organization. It was an early afternoon and I carried with me several books that I had been responsible for, as presents for the young men. Yes, I was nervous. I had little idea of how I would be received by either the prison officials or the prisoners. The Crumlin Gaol is your hard Victorian edifice; I believe that it is now only used for remand prisoners – those awaiting trial. But, as I have written earlier, the three men that I was visiting had already been awaiting trial for some two years and they are waiting still . . .

Access to the prisoners is quite a complicated process. I and my new young friend, having been searched, presented our intended gifts. The warders, from first to last, were affable towards me. After quite a lengthy routine we were escorted

to the meeting area. I had expected an awkward, unfriendly
arrangement; not a bit of it. We entered a large white painted
room with perhaps twenty white tables with chairs and only
one warder casually supervising. I was escorted to a table
where my young men sat. They got to their feet with smiling,
openly excited faces: 'Pleased to meet you, Mr Griffith.'

I don't believe in hiding my feelings: 'I'm proud to meet
you.'

What a graphic discovery they were; they were intelligent,
enthusiastic young men in their twenties. My question back in
London: 'Won't they wonder who this old Welshman is?' was
fully answered. They knew a great deal about me and my
presence appeared to be a treat for them. It was not the first or
last time that I felt deeply humbled and perhaps unworthy of
their obvious esteem. I was filled with significant curiosity:
'Tell me, being in your present situation, how can you be so
obviously happy?'

The answer came tumbling out with a spontaneous una-
nimity: 'Oh, it's the comradeship, Mr Griffith. The
comradeship is wonderful! And thanks to Bobby (there is only
one 'Bobby' in the world and his surname is 'Sands') we can
study what we like and debate what we like and, as you can
see, we can wear our own clothes, not prison clothes.' . . .
Thanks to Bobby and the lads who followed him. And one of
them, who expected to go on trial soon (he hasn't yet,
December 1993) added: 'And when they put me into Long
Kesh [he seemed to have no doubt about his pending fate] I'll
be able to take a degree! Thanks to Bobby and the boys.' He
spoke with the unadulterated excitement of a keen young man
who was about to go to university.

I had to control my emotions. They were talking about the
young men who had deliberately and agonizingly starved
themselves to death in the hope that Mrs Thatcher's Anglo-
Saxon mind could begin to perceive by their sacrifice that the
cause of Irish emancipation was just. But the chilling truth is
that there appears to be in that female persona nothing of
that nature to reach. Yes, she can wipe away a sentimental tear
when she is – no doubt treacherously – sacked, or perhaps

when sentimentally laying a wreath on a Falkland Island. I took the liberty of physically embracing the young men when I left.

Jim Gibney asked me if I would like to meet Mrs Sands, Bobby's mother.

'Oh, no,' I replied, 'I wouldn't want to disturb her.'

'I think she might like to meet you, Ken.'

Jim drove me to a row of modest terraced houses on a modern open estate. We were taken into a pleasantly decorated sitting-room. Mrs Sands was a fine-looking, pale woman, whose face showed a disciplined suffering; she sat on a settee, prettily and conservatively dressed. Her daughter, Bobby's sister, a beautiful looking woman, was present, with her own daughter. Slightly behind me, with his back to a window, was an older man whom I took to be a friend or an uncle of Bobby Sands.

Again I felt inadequate at the honour that was being done to me. I now realize that I had truly won my spurs. Sinn Fein realize, better than me, that such a mother needs all the peace that is going, but somehow they had decided that the most sensitive accolade should come my way. From the bottom of my heart, I have my doubts about my worthiness. I felt a desperate need to justify my presence and to be taking tea with her and her family. I told Mrs Sands that I had sent postcards to her son while he was on hunger strike in Long Kesh prison. That I tended to select pictures of spring and summer flowers and how I had argued with postal officials at Islington's post office who told me that they couldn't register postcards. In the end they did and I told Mrs Sands that once when I was filming in West Berlin I even sent her son a postcard of the Berlin Wall which had 'Bobby Sands' painted on it and I wrote a message that Mrs Thatcher was a liar when she stated that no one was taking any notice of the hunger strikers. Mrs Sands stared at me incredulously: '*You* sent *that* postcard? How often have I asked: "What wall is that?"'

I had many times wondered if my small efforts had ever reached the indomitable suffering man. Well, it had reached the prison at least and it had been sent to his mother with the rest of his effects. Mrs Sands excused herself and went upstairs. She came down and gave me a Roman Catholic publication, commemorating his going.

I was saying my farewells and finally turned to the silent man who was slightly behind me: 'And tell me, sir, who exactly are you?'

'Oh, I am Bobby's father.'

He was quiet and found my whole focus on Mrs Sands as perfectly proper and normal. Amongst the Irish Celts, when dealing with family matters, the mother is paramount. Perhaps a combination of the importance of Kathleen N'Houlihan and Mary; certainly it is a matriarchal society.

As we drove away I stared at a vast mural of Bobby Sands, covering the whole side of a house, and as we progressed down the Falls Road I gazed at others. The young martyr lours over the Six Counties; in physical image over the Republican areas and as a spiritual reality elsewhere.

There was to be a viewing of the Michael Collins film in the alternative Republican ghetto, the Ardoyne. Again I urged my hosts to get me to the location in plenty of time. They got me there half an hour early; very good, I thought, and then we were informed that the proceedings did not commence at 7 pm as we had thought, but at 8 pm.

As far as I can recall I was accompanied by Jim Gibney, Tom Hartley and two other Republican friends. It was suggested that we could go for a walk and indeed that they would show me the Ardoyne area. As we began to stroll along a pavement we were joined by a fine looking young man – but he couldn't have been so young because someone informed me that he had recently completed (was it?) sixteen years in prison for his patriotic convictions. Somehow I lagged behind the others with this man. I was deeply curious about what he might have to say. He was serious but expressed no complaints about his fate except that part of his country was still occupied by the 'English'. And then, ahead of us, Jim and Tom and company were joined by a grinning young man on a bicycle. He looked little more than a teenager but again I was very wrong because I was informed that he had just been released on parole after having served five years. My miscalculations are due to my age I suspect: everyone now looks young and many very young. The man with his bicycle never stopped smiling; he laughed as he told us that there was something wrong with the chain on his machine. I was intrigued by this euphoria; I asked: 'Are you so happy because you are out of prison?'

Someone interjected: 'Oh, he's *always* like this.'

Laughing, he said: 'Well, I'm glad to be back with the wife and children . . .'

At that point, as we were all congregated on the pavement, the inevitable happened: around a bend in the road came an armoured car containing members of the Royal Ulster Constabulary. These formidable vehicles seem always to have darkened glass. By this time I was beginning to learn a few things and immediately behind that vehicle was a camouflaged fighting truck, stuffed with young British soldiers. On this occasion there was no foot patrol. Again, all of my Republican friends took no apparent notice of the armed demonstration and I tried to follow suit, but I was conscious enough to register that they were slowing down as they came parallel with us on the far side of the small roadway. Without interrupting our general conversation someone said: 'It's *you* they are interested in, Ken.'

I glanced up and looked at my compatriots, the British soldiers; whatever the present legal status of the personnel of the Ulster Constabulary may be, I do not accept them as fellow countrymen of mine. Any name that I wish to record from Ulster is entered on the blue pages of my address book for foreign countries. But the armed convoy did not stop; it accelerated on up the street and then took their first turning to the right. I announced to my Republican friends that 'those gun toting British soldiers are your average football supporter. They are no worse and no better than any other young men. It makes me so angry to see them in this improper role, and acting – so they are told – on my behalf!' The Republicans allowed my outburst to pass without any spoken comment. Our conversation continued as if nothing had interrupted it.

Perhaps my friends were not surprised, but after five minutes or so I was; the same armed convoy reappeared from the
same direction that it had travelled before. After viewing us
the first time, it had simply progressed around the block of
houses. I sensed that this was mildly ominous and when it
came to a halt, directly opposite to where we were still chatting on the pavement. I sensed that it was 'OK Corral' time.
The door of the leading conveyance opened and out came
three men in their black uniforms, looking barrel-chested with
their heavy flak-jackets and with their automatic guns held at
the stipulated angle. One of them drilled himself into a position close to the truck while the other two advanced towards
our happy group. The young British soldiers, high up in their
khaki-coloured vehicle, eyed the approaching encounter with
as much unconcern as they could muster – or so it seemed to
me. Again the warning was whispered at me: 'Ken, it's you
they're interested in.'

But the leading officer, and as it turned out, the spokesman,
didn't look at me immediately, though I was the nearest to
him; he swung to his right and addressed my new friend, the
man who had completed those sixteen years in prison: 'What's
your name?'

The formidable youngish man did not pause: 'Why do you
ask what my name is *every* day? You know *very well* what my
name is! And why do you make us take our shoes off in the
street?'

Well, the exchange wasn't gunfire, but it came hard and
fast. I sensed that the Republican's aggressive reply surprised
the police-officer. I suspect that my presence – the old Welsh
Protestant – was a silent factor in what was happening. There
was a silence and I was into it with alacrity: 'Officer, *my* name
is Griffith – Kenneth Griffith. I'm a Welsh Protestant. Would
you like my card?'

Now I had learnt an important lesson years before when I
had unthinkingly pounced my hand into my inside breast
pocket to extract an innocent letter, to hand to Ibrahim Yazdi,
Iran's then foreign minister in Teheran and when his bulging
guards had distinctly reached for their guns. So I did not

plunge for my wallet in my hip pocket until everyone, including the poised British soldiers, clearly heard and understood exactly what I was reaching for and *then* I duly presented the now-disconcerted paramilitary with my formal visiting-card. I continued sensing that the initiative was now mine: 'And, sir, I have to tell you that when your convoy disappeared around that corner, I turned to my Republican friends here and told them that my fellow countrymen up there (and I nodded towards the lads) are your average British football supporters; no better no worse than any other youngsters and that it sickens me to see them doing this disgraceful job!' I suspect that though I was addressing the policeman, I nevertheless knew that my soldier compatriots could hear what I was saying; after all – though I write it myself – I do enunciate the English language uncommonly clearly and therefore it could be proven that in speaking my truth, I might be committing some form of high treason. I do remember many things in my life, including Lord William Deedes' warning to me, years before, on this very subject. But I unhesitatingly ploughed on; I mean I had an unrepeatable audience: behind me was a group of most distinguished Irish Irish Republicans and in front of me were three Scottish Irish paramilitaries and beyond them were the chaps from Cardiff, London, Birmingham, Manchester, Liverpool, Glasgow, etc. I made sure that my voice could be heard at the back of the pit. 'And you know, sir, as well as I, that, in the past, many of the greatest leaders for Irish emancipation from Britain have been Protestants like ourselves.' And I reeled off the resounding names of Wolfe Tone, Parnell, Roger Casement, etc. And turning to my Irish Irish Roman Catholic mates, I said: 'Of course the Protestant leadership for freedom from the oppression of England is no reflection on the ancestors of my friends here; you know that my government in the past denied them an honest free education – and particularly in their own language. Sir, if you are wondering why I am so angry, I am simply appalled that my country, Britain, has deliberately divided decent Protestants from decent Catholics and I gestured at him and then behind me. 'And as always it has been done for England's material benefit.'

At this point the Royal Ulster Constabulary spokesman – though in all fairness he hadn't been given much opportunity to speak anything – did what he could to divide us Republicans and rule us: 'Mr Griffith, I can see that you are a very well educated man. *You* are clearly an intellectual —' I took this, rightly or wrongly, to be a play to separate me from my comrades and so I interrupted: 'Ah, sir, you are miscalculating me; I left school before I was sixteen years old, but, on the other hand, I suspect that my Republican friends here have a few university degrees between them.'

'Look, Mr Griffith, I am only doing my job.' At this RUC statement there came a jumble of *sotto voce* comment from behind me which, nevertheless, from their tone alone were uncomplimentary. The officer remonstrated: 'Do you think I like putting this flak-jacket on every morning?' And he punched on, gamely: 'And what *you* said' – turning to the sixteen-years-in-gaol man – 'is not true about me; *I* have never ever ordered anyone to take their shoes off in the street!'

For my part, incongruous as it seems, I felt some sympathy for the police-officer. I said: 'Sir, I believe what you say . . .' And at this, the vocal rumble behind me increased in volume, so I continued: 'Of course you can't expect my Republican friends to agree with me; they've lost too many beloved comrades.' This remark of mine was, of course, the RUC officer's cue to retaliate with the obvious reply: 'And we've lost too many of our beloved friends,' but he didn't. He stared at me. I suspect that he was aware of that obvious reply, but realized that he had already obtruded beyond orders. Their job is to intimidate and he had been tempted into debate. I then held my hand out but he didn't take it. True, my hand was low down and his flak-jacket jutted out. I like to think – and it is possible – that he just couldn't see my offer of friendship, so I reached further and grasped his free hand; he gave mine a little pressure and then said: 'Well, good day,' and back they went, behind the dark glass.

As the military presence moved off, we continued our conversation, but later it was remarked that never before, as far as anyone knew, had such a chat happened on the streets of Belfast.

A young Republican had given me a precious badge with Bobby Sands' portrait on it. It had been issued at the time of his death and I was now wearing it on the lapel of my jacket. After the viewing of the Michael Collins film, there in the Ardoyne, I was answering questions from the audience when a young man challenged me: 'How can you make such a film in praise of Michael Collins *and* wear a badge that is a tribute to Bobby Sands?' This, to me is indeed a terrible question to ask; as destructive a question for the future of Ireland as could be devised. And yet it is horribly common. The question was created out of the Irish Civil War. One of the greatest – perhaps the greatest – of all Irish Republicans, Michael Collins, had no rational choice except to lead the Free State forces that were eventually forced to face the undemocratically decided and doomed 'Republican' dissidents during 1922. The young man at our viewing in the Ardoyne was fanning alive that disgraceful and destructive conflict. I demanded of him: 'Are you daring to suggest that Michael Collins was not as devout a Republican as Bobby Sands!?' I suspect that Jim Gibney once again reached for his olive branch, but fortunately the young man subsided of his own accord.

THIRTY-NINE

On the Sunday before I left Belfast on this astounding visit, there was to be a march by the Republican people of the various ghettoes to the City Hall of Belfast and there, outside that centre of administration where Protestant Unionists freely hold their gatherings, Gerry Adams and Martin McGuinness and a few representatives from non-Irish Celtic areas of the world were planning to address us. It was explained to me that never before had the Republican, largely Roman Catholic, Irish Irish people, succeeded in reaching their goal. Always, before, the military presence had intervened and had, of course, broken up the march.

By this time I had learnt all of the basic realities of the dreadful city called Belfast. Earlier in the week there had been a request to Sinn Fein from a group of film makers in 'Northern Ireland', asking if I would meet them for lunch and a talk and I had readily agreed. This meeting entailed entering Belfast proper. 'So what?' I might have, then, asked. As always I was escorted by a Republican, but on this occasion not by my friend Jim Gibney. In retrospect I ask myself: Why not Jim? The man who did accompany me was formidable in several ways: intellectually and physically. We entered the city itself and we walked through the crowded streets. I chattered away about nothing of particular significance when my companion said: 'Kenneth, keep your voice down.'

'Why?'

'If they (the Protestant shoppers) knew who we are, we'd be in considerable danger.' It was all part of my rapid learning process.

Incidentally, the luncheon meeting itself was very interesting, but so was everything else connected with the beleaguered Republicans of Belfast. My minder (from Dublin) and I arrived at the modern spick and span film offices and soon about seven men and one woman – apart from us two Republicans – had assembled. My new friend and I sat on one side of a long table with our backs to some windows and our hosts arranged themselves on the other side. The meal was excellent and I immediately declared, as is my custom, the reasons for my support of a United Irish Republic. Our hosts' chief spokesman responded by saying that he didn't share my hopes and *that* basically stated disagreement I now believe created the whole, slightly awkward atmosphere. I had expected to be asked some film making questions. But from that cards-on-the-table point hardly anyone else uttered a syllable. However, it was a fascinating experience to be judging the moods of silent people who were simply staring at one. I could have given a written assessment of the degree that I was liked or disliked by each single speechless person. It was explained to me later that after I had spoken my opinion and after the leader had replied, it might have been unwise for anyone of the others to risk getting out of line. Those who showed a hint of liking me – I couldn't put it stronger – were the younger ones, which I like to think of as a pale ray of hope. My Republican escort only spoke once during our visit; he was sitting on my left side. As we departed and had reached a quiet street, he told me: 'Kenneth, I felt very uneasy there; I didn't know *one* of them.'

Now, in any city in the rest of the world, I could ask: 'But why should you know any of them? You're not even in the film business.' But Belfast is different. Guessing that my friend had suspected a possible set-up of sorts I replied: 'Well, when they cast a glance at *you*, it crossed my mind that they were a shade worried about *your* plans.' Yes, he did look very formidable and I have no doubt that he is – come to a pinch . . .

All of the above is a mere aside to give the uninitiated an idea of what it is like for a Roman Catholic Republican, if he or she contemplates entering the City of Belfast. And now, in the Falls Road, some ten thousand were preparing to do so. It was a happy, informal assembly, yet very thoroughly ordered. It had the innocent excited atmosphere of one of those old-time Sunday School Treats that occurred annually in Tenby before the war.

The grand march was led by Gerry Adams and Martin McGuinness; behind them was an enormous Republican flag, carried horizontally by perhaps a dozen young men and women and therefore could best be viewed from above where, incidentally, there was no shortage of police and military spotter aircraft. Jim Gibney guided me into the ranks immediately behind the big flag. The various bands struck up and off we went, towards the gateway into Belfast. It was a beautiful day and though we were many thousands, the Falls Road was lined with thousands more, clapping and cheering us on. Just behind me I saw my old colleague and friend from *Curious Journey* days, the Irish–American Timothy O'Grady, who had hastened over from the United States in order to be present. There were unobtrusive Sinn Fein marshals who smilingly kept control of everything.

The rumours about what the Royal Ulster Constabulary and the British Army might do or not do to us had been varying throughout the preceding days. This morning the air quivered with optimism. It was said that it could be a great historical occasion: that for the very first time, the Republicans of the Six Counties would reach the centre of their city. And this was not just two of us, but ten thousand of us.

I cannot recall seeing any British soldiers; this made me feel enormously relieved. However, the black uniformed paramilitary police were everywhere, particularly as we reached the city's perimeter. Of course it could be argued that they were not only there to intimidate us, but also to protect us from any Protestant Unionist attack. But I, and the ten thousand, had little doubt who the Royal Ulster Constabulary would favour if there were physical conflict. For what my subjective emotions are worth, I felt that their stony white faces and the way that they held their guns, boded not less than sinister threat. At one point we were brought to a standstill and I feared the worst; way ahead of us I could see a convoy of the RUC armoured vehicles crossing our path. But then we moved on again and it seemed to be clear that the British powers-that-be had decided to allow us through. Apart from our great march, the City of Belfast seemed to be deserted, except, of course, for the well-armed police; now they not only stood at every street junction but were watching from all possible rooftops. One curious and disturbing image for us was of very distant walled-off streets, over which permanent barricades, you could see heads bobbing and hear the distant howling of abuse and there with them, far away, were frantically waving Union Jacks.

As the leading marchers entered the city, a massed cheer went up which continued for perhaps an hour as the vast tail-end entered. We reached the City Hall and the cheering became tumultuous. Young men appeared high above us and quickly arranged Republican banners and slogans and steadily the RUC faded away from the roof-tops, including the City Hall. But we were all aware of their now hidden presence. It struck me that some wise British thinking had been going on; it seemed to me that their ordered withdrawal was to avoid giving any visual provocation.

A large wooden platform had been constructed and Gerry Adams spoke to us; the total silence that was given to him by such an enormous crowd was an astonishing expression of the high respect he receives from his people. I don't think that the British Government should have any doubts about his strength. As far as my memory serves me, his opening statement was: 'No one present should think of this occasion as a triumphal entry; we are here because we have a right to be here . . . And, please God, when *any* of us present hears of a death or an injury, whether the victims are Catholic or Protestant, Republican or Unionist, please God we *all* grieve. But there is a war in progress.'

I am sitting here in Northern Italy, writing this from memory – as every word in this book is from memory. I claim that it is an honest well-meaning memory. I have to paraphrase and of course I must have made mistakes and people inevitably see and hear events from their own subjective points of view. All I can write here is that the above is what I remember hearing. And I recall reading no decent British account of what took place on that day in Belfast. I am usually sceptical about conspiracy theories, but I am shocked at the endless ill-informed prejudice that we British are made to suffer via our diverse media.

Martin McGuinness followed Gerry Adams and they are both formidable, courageous and intelligent leaders. After it was all over we made our way, jollily, back to our indomitable ghettoes.

It was the last day of the West Belfast Festival, but the multiple events stretched on even into Monday morning. Next on my schedule was for that Sunday evening: a reunion of – did I hear right – ex-prisoners. As always, I didn't pester with questions and was simply guided by Jim Gibney from one function to another. If the evening was for ex-gaol-birds, Jim certainly was entitled to a ticket. The unusual get-together was held in a huge sometime linen mill. My imagination waffled around the picture of, say, twenty old political lags to – what – a hundred? We climbed a great stone stairway, up and up and into a high stone vestibule. There the stewards were busy checking everyone who entered; big, husky men: 'Hello, Jim! How's it going? Good evening, Mr Griffith! You're very welcome here among us.' Beyond, through a door, there was a human roar: it sounded like more than even a hundred men . . . Jim ushered me through and the sight was once again beyond my imagination: sitting and drinking and laughing and talking were, so I was told, about seven hundred ex-political prisoners, all of them having been incarcerated in a selection of Her Majesty's gaols. I was told that they had averaged eleven and a half years inside apiece. They had congregated here from all of the Thirty-Two Counties of a United Ireland. The energetic bonhomie was overwhelming. Some of them were meeting after many years of enforced separation. Unlike my young friends in the Crumlin Road Gaol, these men were generally older; even edging into middle-age. And they all had one heroic quality in common: they had volunteered to put their lives on the line for the love and dignity of their country. I began to realize that it was even probable that I was the only man present who had not been committed to prison. Later I spotted my friend, Timothy O'Grady, and with a little psychological relief, felt that I was not unique; at least I don't think that Tim has done any porridge.

I have already written about the unease that I have felt when people who have sacrificed so much more than I myself make a fuss of me; spoil me. On that score this evening was far and away the most painful time for me. It began to appear that I was known to virtually all of them: 'Mr Griffith, would you mind if we had a photograph taken with you?' I cringed at the thought of my position and, in my opinion, my relative unworthiness of such respect. I tried to explain what I felt through a joke; I told them that on the march, earlier in the day, I had planned that if there were trouble, I would have done my best to become involved and then, perhaps, I could say: 'Well, I have spent *one* night in a British gaol for my political beliefs.' Yes, I had fantasized about this possibility, but all had passed peaceably. The very-long-term men did find my story funny – coming from the old Welsh Protestant. And there again lies the kernel of the affection shown to me: I was someone who had been very much outside of their national tragedy, who had chosen to come inside of his own accord and who had done what he could to help. Usually they only have each other, which accounts for the intense comradeship which I was told about in the Crumlin Gaol; and which I had observed all around me. But for them, an outsider who walked inside was something else and they wanted to express their emotions.

A number of ex-prisoners asked me if they could tell me about deep personal traumas that they were suffering from, born out of the brutal war. I have decided that I cannot relate these personal tragedies here; they are too dangerously private. A very wise Republican friend explained to me what he thought was happening. The Vatican in its sometimes questionable wisdom has withdrawn much of its Christian service from members of the Irish Republican Army. And these men who had volunteered to transgress certain of the Ten Commandments, have been brought up, conditioned, to the ease of confession.

Again the old Welsh Protestant, who respected them, was a person to turn towards. Several times before any details were given to me, they told me: 'I know you . . .' They meant from watching my documentary films.

Incidentally, a few Roman Catholic priests in Republican areas have apparently refused to bow to Rome on this score and remain ensconced in Republican areas for all who need them. Perhaps Father Des Wilson is the best known and I bow to him. If he had the time to nudge me, I might convert.

After a while and after too many Guinnesses, I decided to explore the other floors of the linen mill. Up I climbed and found offices, and in one of them was Gerry Adams, talking to a group of friends and I was welcomed in. A young man hurried in and said: 'Gerry, half an hour ago they (the Protestant Unionist activists) tried to kill Councillor Bobby Lavery and his family; they missed him, but they've killed his eldest son.' I immediately began to withdraw from the office and as I made my exit I heard Gerry quietly say: 'Don't tell the men for two hours; let them enjoy their party.'

Two hours later, when I was back in the middle of the great get-together my friend Jim Gibney climbed onto a stage and called for silence: 'I'm sorry to tell you, but two and a half hours ago the eldest son of our friend, Councillor Bobby Lavery was shot dead in his house; everyone else is safe.' And at that piece of news I heard a sound which I had never heard before and I doubt that I will ever hear the like again: from the seven hundred men came a choked gasp and then they were back to the rough and tumble socializing. I should mention that though the gathering was overwhelmingly male, there were a few women present: widows of men who had died, women whose husbands were in prison and a few who had come along with their menfolk.

Jim Gibney had planned to take me to the final event of the Festival; a night-and-morning of music and dancing. I walked across the hall to where he was standing, after having made his shocking announcement, and he looked at me and said: 'Ken, I can't go anywhere else tonight; I'll get someone else to take you. I just want to go home.'

'Jim, I don't want to go either; let's just walk back to the house, quietly.' We were both staying at the same address that night and after saying a few farewells, off we went.

It was then about midnight and the weather was good and still. Our walk was up the Falls Road and would take us about three quarters of an hour. I knew that Jim was disturbed by the death; I suspected that he knew the young man and Jim hasn't got the temperament to get hardened by endless repetition. We walked in silence for some time and then he quietly said: 'This is a fucking awful country; what a fucking awful country!' Before this quiet outburst I had never heard a word of bad language from him; it was out of his normal character. He had momentarily dropped his guard in my presence and I was shocked to see his vulnerability exposed. Tomorrow I shall be sending him this last chapter of my autobiography for his approval or disapproval. If you read it, he will have replied, 'Go ahead.' It is the only piece in this, my entire life, that I ask someone else to judge on. The war is still in progress.

As we walked through the night-time, I reminded Jim of the words that the distinguished writer, Ulick O'Conner, had spoken to us a few evenings before: 'From this patch (the Six Counties) has come the greatest human self-sacrifice known in the history of humankind.' He was referring to the chosen deaths of Bobby Sands and company. Someone who was also present had unconfidently parried with: 'What about the Spartans?' But it doesn't bear comparison, does it? And Jim Gibney's momentary lapse was over; he had been inwardly grieving for the death of a young friend.

When we two, normally sober Celts, arrived at our lodgings, we had a glass more of Irish whisky and it was then and there that I exposed my still uninformed ignorance. I said: 'Jim, I suppose that some of our Republican friends are even now planning to hit back in return for this evening's death?'

Jim stared at me: 'What?' and I repeated my terrible words.

'Out of the question!'

'Do you mean that it was always out of the question?'

'Oh no,' replied Jim, 'but when Gerry (Adams) was released

in '77, he ordered that there were not to be any more tit-for-tats and there have been none.' And after sitting down, he added: 'Of course, no doubt the war will continue tomorrow.'

And that has been one of the many agonies for the Republican Roman Catholic activists recently. As the Unionist Protestant activists deliberately kill totally innocent Catholics with impunity – exemplified by the 'trick or treat' murders – they are left defenceless to reply in kind; forbidden by their own political advisers. And that can only be deduced as a humane decision. The appalling deaths on the Shankill road on 23 October 1993 were an attempt by the IRA to destroy the Unionist Protestant headquarters together with their high command, which operation went awry. The young man who attempted the operation had even planned to get the civilians out of the shop beneath before the building exploded. I *now* understand that the Irish Republican Army will only attack targets which they define as being legitimately strategic or military; the former apparently includes attacking the uninterrupted conduct of, particularly, English commercial life and, above all, Britain's big-finance prosperity. That is, until we British finally remove our administration, civil and military, from their island. That, of course, includes the Union Jack.

Mr Gerry Adams had asked if he and I could have a meeting before I left Belfast. On the morning of my departure I was driven just outside Greater Belfast where the car stopped on the perimeter of a large orchard. I got out and one of my escorts said: 'There's Gerry.' He was standing alone among the apple trees. He talked to me about the several times that I had spoken to Republican gatherings during the course of that week. He said that I had an unusual ability to speak about very serious matters and yet make the audience laugh when I chose. Yes, I think that this is true, but sometimes they laugh when I haven't precisely chosen . . . Mr Adams then asked me if I would consider doing the Irish Republican Movement a very big service. I have to confess that for a few lunatic seconds a ridiculous and fantastic thought zigzagged through my poor turmoiled brain. What 'very big service' – beyond my own job of communicating some historical truths through my work – could I do for my Irish Irish friends: carry a ticking box into the Bank of England? Was this cards-on-the-table time? Of course the whole string of moments was utterly demented on my part. In the first place such action was strictly not Gerry's job and secondly no member of the Irish Republican Army (and Mr Adams is not a member of that organization) would dream of asking the old Welsh Protestant. I replied (steadily): 'Yes, if I can.'

'Would you consider, Kenneth, touring the United States of America and speaking for our cause?'

'I can give you my reply now, Gerry: yes I would and what is more, I would consider such a job as a great privilege and indeed the culmination of my life.' And so we said farewell. As I walked back to my waiting car, I noted one or two men dotted around the edge of the apple orchard. My friend Jim Gibney saw me safely away to London Town.

I haven't performed that job in America yet. I hold myself in readiness should I be required. I suppose that the sudden movement between Mr John Hume and Mr Gerry Adams and between the British Prime Minister and the Irish Taoiseach have put the project on hold. I have asked the potential organizers of my proposed journey whether they can arrange for me to speak about my country (Britain) in Ireland to other groups besides Irish–Americans. In this request I have laid particular emphasis on American–Jewish people, who also know something about centuries of persecution.

FORTY

That's about it. This is pretty well up to date. For my future plans, now that this book is completed, I will hope and pray. I have been approached about making a number of films for television: a series of four programmes examining the Dark Ages in Britain – which were not so dark in fact, but, in truth, were very revealing; to make a film about Shakespeare's Shylock, demonstrating that our greatest genius was incapable of writing an anti-Semitic play; and a film about Decent Charles, the so-called Prince of Wales. Old potential employers in the United States of America are still urging me 'to work over here'. I have been approached to act once again in a cinema film. And my supervising editor at Little, Brown – Mr Alan Samson – and I are dickering with the idea of a book about my whole journey from that big armchair in Pembrokeshire aged nine years to the apple orchard in Belfast, aged seventy-two years. I mean my own journey of discovering the concealed truth about the terrible presence of the (mainly Saxon) English in Celtic Ireland. In short, the discoveries which have turned a Welsh Protestant into an Irish Republican. I already have the title: *Beyond the Pale*.

Oh! And while ensconced here in the Biblioteca Comunale in Faenza in Northern Italy, surrounded by many, mainly silent, students, my friend Chiara entered to tell me that there had just been two telephone calls for me from Wales, to enquire whether I would agree to be in Cardiff on January the 9th 1994, to receive a special award presented by the British Academy of Film and Television Arts, and that my friend and sometime employer, Roy Boulting, will give it to me. God willing . . .

INDEX

The Rise and Fall of the British Empire

Lawrence James

Spanning four centuries and six continents, James' magnificent survey examines the imperial experience and its legacy with tremendous verve. Informed, comprehensive and perceptive, it is the essential summary of the era.

'The range, sweep and sheer verve of the book are prodigious ... A masterpiece'
A.N. Wilson

'With this superb history of a mammoth subject [James'] writing career has reached its apogee'
Andrew Roberts, *Times*

'James never loses sight of his grand design, yet he still finds room for the telling detail which illuminates and enriches a narrative'
Philip Ziegler, *Daily Telegraph*

'His feeling for historical detail cannot be faulted and is made more engaging by his scholarship and infectious enthusiasm for the subject ... A thumping good read'
Trevor Royle, *Scotland on Sunday*

'James's epic is not only a first-rate narrative, but also a penetrating portrait of the British ... Having largely, if often inadvertently, selfishly or ham-fistedly, engineered the world we live in, we need the courage now to face up to our record as coolly and intelligently as Lawrence James has done'
John Spurling, *TLS*

'Outstanding ... An intelligible introduction to a grand subject'
M.R.D. Foot, *Spectator*'s Books of the Year